EVIDENCE CONSOLIDATION

W9-BKP-673

RE: *Pocket on next page*

DAVID BERKOWITZ

POSITIVE	.44 DEFORMED LEAD BULLET L/P	MORGUE
TOO DEFORMED	.44 DEFORMED LEAD BULLET RC	SCENE
TOO DEFORMED*	.44 DEFORMED LEAD BULLET RC	SCENE
TOO	DEFORMED LEAD BULLET BB	
	.44 DEFORMED LEAD BULLET MS	SCENE
DEFORMED*	.44 DEFORMED LEAD BULLET MS	
	TWO PIECES OF DEFORMED LEAD	
TOO	.44 DEFORMED LEAD BULLET CB	SCENE
	.44 DEFORMED LEAD BULLET BJ	HOSPITAL
DEFORMED*	PIECE OF LEAD BULLET BJ	
	.44 DEFORMED LEAD BULLET BJ	SCENE
POSITIVE	44 DEFORMED LEAD BULLET F / J1	MORGUE
POSITIVE	.44 DEFORMED LEAD BULLET F / J2	MORGUE
TOO DEFORMED*	.44 DEFORMED LEAD BULLET M / H	SCENE
POSITIVE	.44 DEFORMED LEAD BULLET V / D	MORGUE
TOO DEFORMED*	.44 DEFORMED LEAD BULLET L /D	SCENE
POSITIVE	. 44 DEFORMED LEAD BULLET V/P	MORGUE
POSITIVE	.44 DEFORMED LEAD BULLET A/ B 1	MORGUE
TOO DEFORMED*	.44 DEFORMED LEAD BULLET A/B2	MORGUE
TOO DEFORMED*	3 PIECES OF DEFORMED LEAD D	MORGUE
	ONE (1) PIECE OF DEFORMED LEAD	SCENE
POSITIVE	.44 DEFORMED LEAD BULLET S	HOSPITAL
TOO DEFORMED*	.44 DEFORMED LEAD BULLET S 1	HOSPITAL
POSITIVE	.44 DEFORMED LEAD BULLET M1	SCENE
POSITIVE	.44 DEFORMED LEAD BULLET M2	SCENE
POSITIVE	.44 DEFORMED LEAD BULLET JPC	HOSPITAL
TOO DEFORMED*	FOUR (4) PIECES OF DEFORMED LEAD	
TOO DEFORMED*	DEFORMED LEAD BULLET R1	SCENE
TOO DEFORMED*	PIECE OF DEFORMED LEAD R2	SCENE
TOO DEFORMED*	TWO (2) PIECES OF DEFORMED LEAD R3 & R4	SCENE

SON OF SAM

SON OF SAM

Based on the Authorized Transcription of the Tapes, Official Documents and Diaries of David Berkowitz

BY LAWRENCE D. KLAUSNER

McGRAW-HILL BOOK COMPANY

New York   St. Louis   San Francisco
Toronto   Hamburg   Mexico

2 3 4 5 6 7 8 9 D O D O 8 7 6 5 4 3 2 1

LIBRARY OF CONGRESS CATALOGING IN PUBLICATION DATA

Klausner, Lawrence D
Son of Sam.
1. Berkowitz, David Richard, 1953–   2. Crime and
criminals—New York (City)—Biography.   3. Murder—New
York (City)—Case studies.   I. Title.
HV6248.B483K55   364.1′523′0924 [B]   80-19921
ISBN 0-07-035027-2

Book design by ROBERTA REZK

Contents

Acknowledgments

During the past two and a half years, many people have contributed their time and knowledge to this book. Without their assistance and dedication the book, and the truth it contains, could not have been written.

Foremost among them, Nadine Novis gave of herself to a degree I can never repay, and Myron Arlen, M.D., who saved my life. Also, I'd like to thank Ira J. Jultak, who was instrumental in launching the project.

The following members of the New York City Police Department were especially helpful: Chief of Detectives James Sullivan; former Chief of Detectives John Keenan; former Deputy Commissioner for Public Information Ellen Fleysher; Inspector Joseph Borrelli; Captain Kenneth Bamrick, Commanding Officer Police Pension Section; Detective Sergeant Joseph Coffey; Detective Sergeant James Shea; Detectives John Falotico, James Gallagher, Marlin Hopkins, James Justus, Ronald Marsenison, Richard Paul, Joseph Strano; Police Officers Louis Marchini and Michael Speros.

A special thanks to the former Mayor of the City of New York Abraham D. Beame for the time he gave to me and his reading of the pulse of the city during the terrifying fourteen months when David Berkowitz was killing at random.

I would also like to thank the current Mayor of the City of New York, Edward Koch, and his staff for their assistance.

My thanks to former Chief William Polson of the Yonkers Police Department and to Detectives Thomas Chamberlain and Pete Intervallo. Also to former Chief of Detectives Frank Klecak of the Nassau County Police Department, Chief Carl Fulgenzi of the Westchester County Parkway Police, and to the Westchester County Sheriff's Department, Sheriff Thomas Delaney, Chief Salvatore D'Iorio, and to Craig Glassman. To the New Rochelle Police Department, the New York State Police, the New Jersey State Police, the Connecticut State Police, the Florida State Police, the Houston, Texas, Police Department, and the Port Authority of New York and New Jersey Police.

I would also like to acknowledge the assistance of the following agencies of the United States government: the Department of Defense, the Department of the Army, and the Treasury Department's Bureau of Alcohol, Tobacco and Firearms.

My thanks to the Office of the Governor of the State of New York and to the Office of the Governor of the State of New Jersey.

To the librarians of the following institutions: the Library of Congress, the New York Public Library, the Central Library System of Nassau County, the Hewlett-Woodmere Public Library, and the Peninsula Public Library.

A special thanks to members of the victims' families who gave of their time and emotions: Maurice and Catherine DeMasi, Nandor and Olga Freund and their daughter Eva Maria, Michael and Rose Lauria, Gerald and Neysa Moskowitz, Pasquale Violante, Yolanda Voskerichian and her daughter Alice, and to Charles and Elenore Lomino.

And of course to the surviving victims: Donna DeMasi, Carl Denaro, Judith Placido, Robert Violante, and Joanne Lomino.

To Valerie Scarpa and Thomas Zaino.

To David's natural mother Betty Falco and his half-sister Roslyn Rothenberg, and to his adoptive father Nathan Berkowitz.

To Attorneys Leon Stern, Robert Penn, Fred Scheinfeld and the offices of the Attorney General of the State of New York. A special thanks to the offices of the District Attorneys of Queens, Kings, and Bronx counties.

A note of thanks to Warden Harold Smith of New York State's Attica Correctional Facility.

My thanks also to Bruce Lee of McGraw-Hill for his patient guidance, and to Catherine Temerson for her most valuable work along with that of Rosemary Carrano, Kristina Lindbergh, David and Marcia Prager.

The Victims

December 25, 1975	BRONX	Michelle Forman, 15	stabbed
		Unknown	stabbed
July 29, 1976	BRONX	Donna Lauria, 18	dead
		Jody Valenti, 19	wounded
October 23, 1976	QUEENS	Carl Denaro, 20	wounded
		Rosemary Keenan, 18	not struck
November 27, 1976	QUEENS	Donna DeMasi, 16	wounded
		Joanne Lomino, 18	paralyzed
January 30, 1977	QUEENS	Christine Freund, 26	dead
		John Diel, 30	not struck
March 8, 1977	QUEENS	Virginia Voskerichian, 19	dead
April 17, 1977	BRONX	Valentina Suriani, 18	dead
		Alexander Esau, 20	dead
June 26, 1977	QUEENS	Judy Placido, 17	wounded
		Salvatore Lupo, 20	wounded
July 31, 1977	BROOKLYN	Stacy Moskowitz, 20	dead
		Robert Violante, 20	blinded

Police Officers Who Played Major Roles in the Investigation

NAME	AGE	1980 STATUS
Steven Bonansigna (P.O.)	34	Auto Theft Squad (P.O.)
Joseph R. Borrelli (Capt.)	50	Commanding Officer Manhattan D.A. Squad (Inspector)
John J. Cahill (Det 3rd)	57	Manhattan Homicide (Det 3rd)
Michael Cataneo, Jr. (P.O.)	40	62 Pct. (Det. Specialist 3rd)
James Chillis (P.O.)	51	Identification Section (Det 3rd)
Michael J. Codd (Police Commissioner)	65	Retired, 12-31-77
Joseph J. Coffey (Sgt)	43	Supervisor, Chief of Detective's Office (Sgt)
Richard V. Conlon (Sgt)	53	Supervisor Detective Squad (Sgt)
Robert Craft (P.O.)	38	Identification Section (P.O.)
Daniel L. Deighan (Capt)	50	Bronx Detectives (Capt)
Fred DeLuca (Sgt)	38	Bronx Sex Crimes (Sgt)
Joseph G. DeMartino (D.I.)	52	Manhattan Detectives (D.I.)
George Donovan (Det 3rd)	46	Brooklyn Homicide (Det 3rd)
Timothy J. Dowd (D.I.)	66	Retired, 7-21-78
John M. Falotico (Det 2nd)	58	Brooklyn Homicide (Det 1st)
Arthur Fasano (P.O.)	33	43 Pct. (P.O.)
William Fitzpatrick (Chief, Brooklyn Detectives)	56	Assistant Chief of Patrol, Queens
James Gallagher (Det 1st)	53	Queens Detectives (Det 1st)
William J. Gardella (Sgt)	39	Brooklyn Homicide, Supervisor Detective Squad (Sgt)
James Ghericich (Lt)	51	Identification Section (Lt)
Thomas J. Gleason (D.I.)	64	Manhattan Detectives (D.I.)
George C. Hambrecht (P.O.)	38	Bronx D.A. Squad (Det 3rd)
Charles Higgins (Det 2nd)	49	Brooklyn Homicide (Det 1st)
Marlin C. Hopkins (Det 3rd)	41	Queens Detectives (Det 2nd)
James L. Justus (Det 2nd)	40	Retired, 3-1-78
John L. Keenan (Chief of Detectives)	62	Retired, 7-17-78
Redmond Keenan (Det 2nd)	55	Queens Detectives (Det 2nd)
Charles Kelly (Inspector)	55	Commander Narcotics Division (Inspector)
Robert Kelly (Lt)	55	Retired, 1-5-77
George Lemburg (Det 3rd)	34	Fingerprint Section (Det 3rd)
Jeffrey Logan (P.O.)	39	111 Pct. (P.O.)
John M. Longo (Det 2nd)	53	Retired, 7-11-78

NAME	AGE	1980 STATUS
John J. Lugo (Det 3rd)	41	Bronx Detectives (Det 2nd)
Louis Marchini (P.O.)	37	43 Pct. (P.O.)
Ronald P. Marsenison (Det 2nd)	44	Bronx Homicide (Det 1st)
August Maurina (Det 2nd)	54	Brooklyn Robbery (Det 2nd)
William F. McCormack (P.O.)	43	Identification Section (P.O.)
Francis J. McLaughlin (Deputy Comm. for Public Info.)	42	Resigned, 10-7-77
Bernard J. McRann (D.I.)	62	Bronx Detectives (D.I.)
George L. Moscardini (Det 3rd)	51	Manhattan Detectives (Det 2nd)
Richard Nicastro (Inspector)	58	Manhattan Detectives (Deputy Chief)
John T. O'Connell (Det 3rd)	41	Queens D.A. Squad (Det 2nd)
Frank Pagiolla (Det 3rd)	31	44 Pct. Investigative Unit (Det 3rd)
Richard G. Paul (Det 3rd)	41	Bronx District Attorney Squad (Det 2nd)
Laurence Ponsi (Sgt)	56	Brooklyn Robbery (Sgt)
John J. Power (Lt)	55	Commander Bronx Detective Squad (Lt)
Richard Salvesen (Det 3rd)	48	Intelligence Division (Det 3rd)
James N. Shea (Sgt)	48	Brooklyn Homicide, Supervisor Detective Squad (Sgt)
John Sheridan (Det 1st)	55	Retired, 1-5-77
Gerald Shevlin (Det 3rd)	42	Brooklyn Sex Squad (Det 3rd)
Michael Shilenski (Det 2nd)	39	Legal Division (Det 2nd)
George W. Simmons (Det 2nd)	58	Lab Service Section (Det 1st)
Michael Speros (P.O.)	37	43 Pct. (P.O.)
Joseph A. Strano (Det 3rd)	39	Brooklyn Homicide (Det 2nd)
Francis M. Sullivan (D.I.)	52	Deputy Chief, Detective Bureau
William J. Sullivan (Det 3rd)	51	Bronx Detectives (Det 2nd)
Waldron G. Tidmarsh (Det 2nd)	55	Queens D.A. Squad (Det 1st)
Irwin Vale (Det 2nd)	53	Brooklyn Robbery (Det 2nd)
Edward Zigo (Det 2nd)	54	Brooklyn Homicide (Det 1st)

POLICE DEPARTMENT RANKS

D.I.—Deputy Inspector
Capt.—Captain
Lt.—Lieutenant
Sgt.—Sergeant
Det 1st—Detective 1st Grade
Det 2nd—Detective 2nd Grade
Det 3rd—Detective 3rd Grade
P.O.—Patrolman

Prologue

Quite simply, this is a story of a city clutched by terror. It was not terror brightened by heroism, as in Warsaw during the days of the Nazis, nor a terror played against revolution, as in Paris under the guillotine. The fright was primal. From July 1976, through July 1977, a murderer was abroad in the streets and alleys of New York.

The terror tore away certain illusions of civilization. More than three hundred New York police officers joined an increasingly hysterical search for the killer. Many of the cops were as solid as any you see in a television drama. Some were not. There was the promise of glory, promotion, and money for the policeman who broke the case. The intraforce rivalries became ferocious; that is not something the glorifying television shows display.

Two New York tabloids, the morning *Daily News* and the afternoon *New York Post,* were struggling for circulation among those people who did not choose to read *The New York Times*. The *News* had been losing readers for a decade. The *Post* was under the new stewardship of the Australian press adventurer Rupert Murdoch. If the terror did not lead both tabloids to practice yellow journalism (and there are those who say that it did) what they did practice was something less than Pulitzer-prize quality. A fire of fright was burning; they fanned it.

The public responded by buying newspapers and yielding to panic. According to police calculations, your chance of becoming a homicide victim in New York on any given night are about 600,000 to 1. Your chances of being murdered by a stranger—as opposed to a spouse, a rejected lover, or a disturbed child—approach two million to one. Your chances of being done in by any given killer, however maniacal, are so small as to be incalculable. But as the terror peaked in New York City, nearly 5000 people a day made frenzied telephone calls to their local precincts. The wall between civilization and anarchy is neither so high nor so sturdy as we comfortably assume.

THE KILLER himself was a drab, soft-faced man. He was not very good at studies or at friendships and, because of contradictory statements, some experts believe he is a virgin to this day. He was born out of wedlock on June 1, 1953, to a Long Island businessman named Joseph Kleinman and a waitress named Betty Broder Falco, during the course of a love affair that would last for twenty-nine years. Both Kleinman and Mrs. Falco were married, but not to each other.

The mother, a warm-hearted woman, named her son Richard David Falco and at once offered him for adoption. A childless Bronx couple, Nat and Pearl Berkowitz, took in the baby and changed his name to David Richard Berkowitz. David seems never to have felt sure of his identity. He was phobic as a child and suffered from overwhelming feelings of rejection.

His response, both to rejection and to a shaky sense of self, began with bravado. He boasted of achievements, strength, and sexual conquests that did not exist. To impress his peers with his toughness, there is history that he indeed could have set fires in empty lots. The pervading sense of the first twenty years of David Berkowitz's life is pathos. He wanted to be good-looking, popular, successful, romantic, and loved by young women. He was none of these, except in fantasies.

Then, in 1974, David's pathetic, passive fantasy life evolved into something that was not pathetic. Demons lurking in the abyss of his mind told him, he says, to kill. His victims were to be young women. If he could not conquer young women by seducing them, he could conquer them with the act of murder.

There is, of course, nothing rational about psychosis: psychotic behavior is the polar opposite of reason. When David first went forth to kill, on Christmas Eve, 1975, he armed himself with a knife. Then he prowled about a huge, dehumanizing apartment development in the Bronx known as Co-Op City. David was surprised and frightened that the women he stabbed screamed in pain and terror, and that they bled. Based on movies he had seen, David expected murder by knife to be tidy.

Six months later he drove to Houston, Texas, where you can purchase a handgun without a permit. There, with the help of a one-time Army buddy named Billy Dan Parker, David obtained a Charter Arms .44-caliber Bulldog. The .44 weighs only eighteen ounces, and it is not a highly regarded pistol but, like any .44, it is a devastating weapon at close range. Murder by gun, while hardly tidy, is surer and less personal than murder by knife. The killer is not stained with the victim's blood.

David shot his first victim at one o'clock in the morning of July 29, when he killed an attractive, dark-haired eighteen-year-old named Donna Lauria. Donna had worked as a technician in an emergency medical center before; ironically, her body was shattered beyond medical help. A bullet in the thigh wounded Donna's friend Jody Valenti, nineteen.

Within eight months, David had shot six more young people. He killed two of the victims, a secretary named Christine Freund and a college junior named Virginia Voskerichian. On March 10, 1977, two days after the death of Miss Voskerichian, Michael Codd, the New York police commissioner, reported that a warrant had been issued for an unnamed white male between twenty-five and thirty years old. The police were certain that the same unnamed white male had murdered Lauria, Freund, and Voskerichian. The link was the .44's unique ballistics, which left an unmistakable signature on each deadly projectile.

Without his psychosis (and his second-rate gun), David Berkowitz, born Richard Falco, was an ultimately anonymous man. Few knew he was alive. Fewer cared. But the pattern of his murders—his M.O., police jargon for modus operandi, method of operation—gave this twice-named psychotic a third name, which was the way that he first exploded, so to speak, into headlines. On the front page of the *News* and the *Post* (and later of *The New York Times*), Berkowitz became "The .44-Caliber Killer."

That is, to be sure, as much a label as a name, but it is a catchy label. In a bizarre way, it speaks of Madison Avenue. How do we package the product? We need a label. How do we get exposure? We make certain that the label pleases the writers of headlines.

Berkowitz's flair, aside from homicide, is for publicity. He makes news by murdering innocents, and then he milks the news he makes. He would not merely conquer women by destroying them; he would become famous as a conqueror. It is probably helpful at this point to remember that both Genghis Khan and Julius Caesar are euphonious names.

Berkowitz's spelling and grammar are shaky. (After graduating from high school, he attended a community college briefly.) But he possesses a doggerel skill at wordplay. During his thirteen months of murder he coined such phrases for himself as "The Wicked King Wicker," "The Chubby Monster," and "The Duke of Death." Certainly the last could be the title of a television movie. *We are sorry, ladies and gentlemen.* Charlie's Angels *will not be seen tonight. Instead we give you* The Duke of Death.

David Berkowitz's most famous name was created after his sixth attack, which took place on the northbound service road of the Hutchinson River Parkway in the Bronx. On that night, April 17, 1977, he killed both Valentina Suriani and Alexander Esau. He wrote a letter, on dime-store stationery, which he left in the street about ten feet from the victims' car. It was addressed to Joseph Borrelli, a 46-year-old police captain who had been appointed supervisor of a Queens task force assigned to capture The .44-Caliber Killer. In the aftermath of one of the blitzkriegs of press conferences the police unleashed, a CBS-TV reporter pigeonholed Captain Borrelli, asking what he thought of the killer's motive in attacking young women. Borrelli said, logically enough, that he believed "the killer must have something against women." Later, a television reporter interviewed Detective Harvey Schlossberg, a police psychologist assigned to the Hostage Negotiating Team, and asked the same question. Schlossberg stated that "the killer hates women," a statement mistakenly attributed by David to Borrelli.

"I am deeply hurt by your calling me a wemon [*sic*] hater," Berkowitz's note to Captain Borrelli began. "I am not. But I am a monster." (A confidential police profile had described Berkowitz as "shy, odd, schizophrenic and paranoid.")

Borrelli and Berkowitz both were responding to what they knew. Then Berkowitz composed the single sentence that would make him the centerpiece of thousands of headlines.

"I am the Son of Sam."

AFTER THAT, there were only two more attacks, one more murder. On the last day of July, Berkowitz drove his 1970 cream-colored Ford Galaxie to Bay 17th Street in the Bensonhurst section of Brooklyn. It is an area that occupies the southeastern edge of the borough and one that has remained quiet, middle class, and relatively safe. Berkowitz parked the Ford beside a hydrant and, wandering toward a lover's lane, accosted a fifty-year-old widow named Cacilia Davis. He meant to kill a *young* woman. After coming face to face with Mrs. Davis, he retreated toward his car.

He then regrouped, so to speak, and found his final victim,

a high-spirited blonde secretary named Stacy Moskowitz. Shooting into a car for the last time, Berkowitz struck the young woman in the brain and permanently blinded her date, Robert Violante. Miss Moskowitz died in a Brooklyn hospital thirty-eight hours later of what physicians called "swelling of the brain stem."

The press and television now beat the drums of chaos. Three newspapermen had been urging the killer to turn himself in to them rather than the police. This was a tactic devised years earlier by the late Walter Winchell, a columnist who believed that the pivot of all his stories was Walter Winchell. Television people cluttered the air with stories of victims and their families, with bad guesses about the Son of Sam's identity, and with speculation about where he would strike next.

He would not strike again. After days of frightened silence, Mrs. Davis told her version of all the events of the evening to the police, on August 3. On August 10, a Wednesday, two New York detectives visited Pine Street in Yonkers and found Berkowitz's car. Inside, one of them spotted what he believed to be a submachine gun and called for help. After a six-hour stakeout, a heavy figure approached the Ford.

A white-haired, chubby-faced New York detective named John Falotico said: "Freeze. I'm the police."

"Hello," David said calmly to John Falotico.

"Who are you?" Falotico said, from behind his gun.

"You know who I am," Berkowitz said.

"No. You tell me who you are."

"I'm Sam."

The date was August 10. In the old Ford, parked on a nondescript Yonkers street, police found notes suggesting that David planned to kill next among the finely shaped hedges and the $500,000 summer homes of Southampton, Long Island.

THE FOLLOWING PAGES address themselves not only to the facts of Berkowitz's solitary rampage but also to questions raised by society's response. Police will tell you that finding a single killer in the vast swarm of a metropolitan area is often impossible without the intervention of luck. Jack the Ripper, after all, is still unknown. But one can wonder—and find out —why the police moved so slowly once they had found the parking ticket that Mrs. Davis had reported, statements made by members of the Yonkers police department, and a statement by Sam Carr as to the possible identity of the Son of Sam.

The case also shows that the public has been misinformed about what police drawings and psychological profiles can do to help catch a killer. Making accurate conclusions from the modest input that a mass murderer provides by leaving bizarre notes at the scene of his crimes is problematic. It certainly is unlike what one reads about in a mystery novel.

One also wonders about the press. Berkowitz perked up television ratings. He sold newspapers. On the day after his capture, the *Daily News* sold 2.2 million copies, 350,000 more than usual. The *Post*, which headlined the word CAPTURED in red ink, surely finished in the black that day. Its circulation jumped from 609,000 to one million.

The three newspapermen who sought David's surrender —Jimmy Breslin, Pete Hamill, and Steve Dunleavy—later made self-serving statements about their roles. Dunleavy said "There are no rules when it comes to appealing to a killer." Hamill said he had spoken to psychiatrists who advised him to appeal to Berkowitz's "Dr. Jekyll side." Breslin protested that "the journalist's role in this situation was determined by the man with a finger on the trigger"—precisely the sort of statement that Breslin, in his own customary role as a street-smart, tough-guy columnist, would sneer into the oblivion it deserves. Certainly Breslin's actions in engaging Berkowitz in public correspondence created a furor amongst the columnists' brethren.

Our touchstones are violence and ineptitude, greed and ambition and David Berkowitz's erupting psychosis. The consequences do not advertise the glories of American society.

Finally, and incredibly, many jurists suggest that when the

drama reached its dénouement in court, there was not enough evidence to convict the killer. There is no reasonable doubt —no doubt of any kind—that Berkowitz was a homicidal maniac, but the legal case against him was so weak that if he had chosen to remain silent he probably would have been acquitted of homicide.

He chose, instead, to plead guilty.

THIS BOOK has been created from the most careful research of which the author is capable. I have interviewed and taped interviews with almost 300 people, including the families of victims and the surviving victims, policemen, politicians, attorneys, psychiatrists, and newspapermen.

I have proceeded with the sanction of the court, the Attorney General of the State of New York, and the Crime Victims Compensation Board. Half of my royalties—the money David Berkowitz would receive—will go to repay, as much as money can repay, survivors of Berkowitz's attacks and the families of those who did not. This arrangement is in the form of a court order, signed by Judge Carmine A. Ventiera of the New York State Supreme Court in Brooklyn. It was approved by the Conservator for David Berkowitz, and by attorneys for those victims whose families filed claims against David Berkowitz.

I feel I have known David Berkowitz for a very long time, and he is terrifying. So is the fact that his psychosis went undetected at schools, at the places he worked, and by the U.S. Army.

We like to armor ourselves against chaos by thinking of modern police techniques, of the vigilance of the press, and of the wonders of contemporary psychology. I am less comforted by such things than I was before I set out to encounter David Berkowitz.

As a child, he says, he liked to set harmless fires.

LAWRENCE DAVID KLAUSNER

1

A Night
Before Christmas

That Christmas Eve embraced New York in a clutch that was cold and dry. A three-quarter-size carousel spun in the windows of a midtown bank, and on Park Avenue the trees on the islands in the center of the avenue glistened with patterns of yellow bulbs. Bing Crosby's voice caroled on a host of loudspeakers, but it would not truly be a white Christmas, in the rich neighborhoods or in the poor ones. The cold wind might cut like a knife, but the sky was clear.

Executives from New York's seven largest department stores exuded Yuletide cheer. Retail sales were up almost eleven percent in the city that 1975, an inspiriting increase after the disappointing 1974 season. Most of the business people at the posh stores were commuting home to Westchester County, New Jersey, and Connecticut. A few even headed for the Hamptons, where Christmas among the dunes and mansions would have a chilly yet exotic appeal and a place that, twenty months later, a killer would fix as a target for mass murder.

According to popular commercials on television, New York is a series of small towns: Greenwich Village (a black plays a saxophone); the Upper West Side (elderly people move tentatively); Queens (school children play basketball); Grand Central Station (a dashing commuter offers a check, which is cashed in time for him to make his train). But to those who live there, New York is more complex than a TV commercial. It is fascinating and fragile. Too many people —a disproportionate number of them bright and beautiful and a disproportionate percentage depraved and poor—are crammed together in a city that is at once bountiful and brutal. New York is the grandest of all places in which to be successful. It is the most withering of cities for those who fail. But it is all one place, from the mean ghetto streets of the Bronx to the middle-class acres of Flatbush homes to towering Manhattan buildings fronting on Fifth Avenue or the East River where applicants for $1,000,000 cooperative apartments are turned away on the whim of screening committees that are as baronial as medieval courts.

No one really knows how many people live in New York City. The U.S. Census is notably inaccurate in poorer neighborhoods. Besides, illegal aliens avoid censustakers as surely as they avoid immigration inspectors. The estimated 1975 census figures set the New York population at 7,895,563. The true figure probably exceeds nine million. Whatever the precise number, successful New Yorkers regard their city and their populace as something set apart, not only from Iowa and Texas, but even from communities close by. They see the city as a place of unique tempo, style, and character. Some refer to it as The Fifty-first State.

THE CITY is organized into boroughs—counties, really— which sprawl from Richmond, an island close to industrial New Jersey, to the Bronx, which flows out of the southern tip of Westchester County. The Bronx was once a middle-class borough, distinguished as the home of the New York Yankees, a splendid zoo, and a handsome campus of New

York University that included the Hall of Fame for Great Americans. Its foundation, so to speak, was numberless six-story apartment buildings, neither lavish nor shabby, where families grew and loved and warred in five-room flats.

New York University has long since abandoned its Bronx campus. The Hall of Fame for Great Americans is now a windswept and deserted colonnade. The six-story apartments have lost their middle-class tenants to the lure of split-level houses on sixty-by-one-hundred-foot suburban plots. Landlords, unable to find new tenants who could afford rent, have walked away from buildings rather than pay real estate taxes. The result is literally miles of blight: buildings without heat or electricity where squatters live amid filth, rats, and vermin. That is one part of the Bronx, surely the sorriest of all American slums. But only five miles away—in the Bronx section called Riverdale—splendid mansions sit on knolls above the Hudson River. A ten-year-old middle-income high-rise community called Co-Op City falls between squalor and affluence. Sixty thousand people live in Co-Op City. All by itself, the community is more populous than Lancaster, Pennsylvania, or Galveston, Texas, or Charleston, South Carolina, or Danbury, Connecticut.

Driving north toward Westchester or Connecticut, the traveler passes the thirty-five buildings of Co-Op City that rise out of old marshy flats and landfills, twenty-three to thirty-two stories tall and oddly bleak. The development was built with assistance from various government agencies to create "a secure and attractive community," which even taxi drivers could afford. It is one of those pockets of urban development which seemed better in the planning than it has proved to be for those who live there. The significance of Co-Op City to this story is that Nat Berkowitz, now seventy years old, the adoptive father of David Richard Berkowitz, once lived in Co-Op City with David, and that these tall, bare buildings were the setting for David's first flawed attempts at murder, on the cold Christmas Eve of 1975.

NAT BERKOWITZ, who ran a hardware store on Melrose Avenue in the Bronx, abruptly closed his business after an armed robbery and retired to the Florida community of Boynton Beach in January 1975. The move ensured the older man's security and left David alone in New York. David found a drab one-bedroom apartment, in a five-story building at 2161 Barnes Avenue in the Bronx, two and a half miles west of Co-Op City.

David, twenty-one, spoke then of wanting to become a fireman, but he never took the qualifying tests. He liked uniforms and the sense of authority a uniform imparts. At length he found work as a security guard—a private cop—for a company called I.B.I., which operates out of the Jamaica section of Queens. David was assigned to guard the premises of the Universal Car Loading Company, a trucking jobber, located near Kennedy International Airport. He worked on the night shift, from midnight to 8:00 A.M. It was lonely work; it would be the loneliest time David had known.

Living by himself, working at a solitary job, his outlook darkened. In November he wrote a bleak letter to Nat:

> Dear Dad,
>
> It's cold and gloomy here in
> New York, but that's okay because
> the weather fits my mood—gloomy.
> Dad, the world is getting dark
> now. I can feel it more and more.
> The people, they are developing a
> hatred for me. You wouldn't
> believe how much some people
> hate me. Many of them want
> to kill me. I don't even know
> these people, but they still
> hate me. Most of them are young.
> I walk down the street and
> they spit and kick at me.
> The girls call me ugly and
> they bother me the most. The
> guys just laugh. Anyhow, things
> will soon change for the better.

This can be read on one level as a terrible cry of loneliness from someone who feels himself being overwhelmed by New York. It should also be read more pragmatically. It was a paranoid statement composed by a man who was no doubt already mad.

Immediately afterward, David Berkowitz took time off from his job at I.B.I. Security and sentenced himself to a term of solitary confinement in the small apartment at 2161 Barnes Avenue. For twenty-eight days he had almost no contact with other people.

He was upset that no one called to ask why he was taking time off. In the classic manner of those who live alone, he was troubled that no one worried lest he fall ill. If David was poorly equipped to live with others, he was not competent to live alone.

His bedroom was lit by a naked bulb that hung from a cord in the middle of a ceiling flaking paint. There were no shades. David nailed gray blankets over the windows to keep out daylight. The blankets made the bedroom air still and fetid. The mattress on which he slept and tossed was bare.

David left the apartment only to buy food: TV dinners, bottles of soda, containers of milk. His dining-room table, a gift from Nat, was littered with dirty dishes. The floor beneath it was covered with empty milk cartons and soda bottles. On walls in the living room, David scrawled messages in magic marker, which then stared back at him. The messages read:

"In this hole lives the Wicked King."
"Kill for my Master."
"I turn children into Killers!"

THE LIFE Berkowitz made for himself was not brightened by art or books or friendships. His principal occupation seems to have been brooding. His only source of pleasure was masturbation.

As David recalls Christmas Eve, 1975, he tucked a hunting knife with a four-and-a-half-inch blade inside the waistband of loose-fitting blue dungarees. He is not able precisely to recall his mood except that he had a sense that "the hunt was on."

It was about 6:45 P.M. He pulled tight a black leather belt that would hold the hickory-handled hunting knife in place, lifted a denim jacket from the back of a chrome-and-vinyl chair and threw it over his broad shoulders. It was a light jacket designed for late-spring wear, but David says "I never feel the cold." He buttoned the jacket carefully, making sure that it concealed the knife handle. He found his keys with one hand. His other hand hit a switch that turned off the light. Fumbling through darkness, he opened his apartment door and stepped into the building's shabby hallway. He took care to double-lock the door. David says the thought of intruders frightened him.

He looked into his mailbox in the lobby. There was no letter from his stepfather or anybody else. He shrugged and walked into the early winter night. Shuffling up Barnes Avenue, David passed an abandoned car. He stopped and looked inside. He felt angry at the unknown people who had let a functional vehicle deteriorate into a wreck.

His own cream-colored Ford Galaxie was half a block away. It started promptly. David let the cold engine idle for about a minute and then started driving north and west toward the familiar array of high brick rectangles that comprised Co-Op City. This puffy-faced young man, proceeding up familiar streets in an ordinary car, was seeking prey.

He followed Pelham Parkway South, where knots of people scurried about bus stops. He turned left onto Eastchester Avenue and six blocks later turned again into Allerton. No Christmas carousels spun here. Litter blew in the curbs. David felt distressed by the ambient filth.

From Allerton, Berkowitz turned into Baychester Avenue and then made a right onto Bartow Avenue, which crosses the six-lane New England Thruway by an overpass and leads into Co-Op City and its principal street—called, with a real estate hustler's grandiosity, Co-Op City Boulevard. It is hardly the Champs-Élysées.

Berkowitz drove slowly but with confidence. He knew these streets. Nat Berkowitz's old apartment at Co-Op City had been the final setting of the only semblance of adult family life that David would know.

He was looking for a woman alone. He could not later explain rationally why he was looking for a solitary woman. He believed, however, that he had been hearing voices, and that these voices were demons whose commands he had to obey or face the most awful retribution. David was raised as a Conservative Jew, but he changed his faith when he was twenty-one years old and announced that he had become a "born-again Baptist." He believed in God and Satan and Heaven and Hell. He had also seen the movie called *The Exorcist*. As David recaptures that bitter Christmas Eve, he says again and again that he was doing nothing more than what the demon voices commanded.

He saw a woman alone on Co-Op City Boulevard. She looked middle-aged. The demon voices had told him to kill a woman who was young. He slowed the Ford and stared at the woman and listened. The demon voices were silent. David drove on, slipping one hand to his waist to make certain the hunting knife was still secure. He now began driving in a looping pattern, following Co-Op City Boulevard, past the bright windows of the Co-Op City Supermarket, around to Baychester Avenue and back again. He was waiting to see "the right person" and hear the voices.

On David's third pass on the wide boulevard, he saw a woman leave the supermarket for the comparative darkness of the street. She wore a long, heavy navy-blue wool coat, its collar turned up against the cold. David could not see her features but suddenly he heard demon voices croaking "Get her." His excitement was overwhelmed by fright. He must obey or face the merciless anger of the demons.

He double-parked the Ford, cut the engine, and locked the door. Then, in an ambling shuffle, he hurried after the woman ahead of him. Close to her now, he reached for his knife. "She has to be sacrificed," the demon voices cried.

David heard the demons say they wanted ''to drink her blood.''

He lifted the hunting knife and arced it downward, striking the unknown woman in midback. He struck again, and he could feel the knife blade tear her heavy coat. ''I had a job to do,'' David said later, ''and I was doing it.''

A single street lamp glowed thirty feet from Berkowitz as he pounded the hunting knife at the woman's back. ''I stabbed her,'' he said, ''and she didn't do anything. She just turned and looked at me.''

In the dim Christmas-Eve light David saw that the woman was Hispanic. His fervid knife thrusts could not have hurt her very much. At first she did not scream in pain, or cry.

But after the woman had turned and saw a hulking figure with a raised knife, terror embraced her. She began to wail in fright. ''It was terrible,'' David said. ''She was screaming pitifully and I didn't know what the hell to do. It wasn't like the movies. In the movies you sneak up on someone and they fall down quietly. Dead. It wasn't like that. She was staring at my knife and screaming. She wasn't dying.''

The woman dropped her packages of groceries, which spilled onto the pavement. Trying to defend herself, she groped for David's large, soft body. Her screams were making David sick. He was not sure if the knife had penetrated the heavy coat. ''There was so much confusion,'' he said later, ''and the screams were getting me scared.''

Panicked, Berkowitz ran—away from the woman and away from his double-parked Ford. Later, he told a psychiatrist that he could not understand why the woman had screamed so. ''I wasn't going to rob her, or touch her, or rape her. I just wanted to kill her.''

No one knows who this woman was or what she did next, or even how badly she was injured. She never reported the assault to the police. She never checked herself into a hospital. Probably she never even had knife wounds treated by a private physician. Most doctors—any responsible doctor— would inform the police that there was evidence of a stabbing.

Police legends are bare of any such report for the night of December 24, 1975. Presumably, the woman returned to her home and survived. Nobody knows with certainty. Nobody knows her name. In the first pattern of what would become his ghastly modus operandi, Berkowitz had attacked a total stranger.

DAVID FOUND himself panting at a steel chain-link fence that divides Co-Op City from the New York State Thruway on the west. He braced himself and tried to catch his breath. Tossing his head, he saw a familiar building a block away: 170 Dreiser Loop. He and his fosterfather Nat Berkowitz had moved into that building in June 1967, after the fostermother, Pearl Berkowitz, died of cancer. From the ground, David tried to find the windows of the old apartment, number 17B. In the dark it was hard to count the lights, to count the floors. He wanted to find the apartment but he could not. Cars growled a block away along the Thruway. It was inconsolably lonely, David thought. And the demons. They had demanded a victim's blood, and he had failed them. They would seek him out now, in this life or the next. They would find him. They would be unforgiving. *Damnation!* David ran around the block toward the Thruway.

He saw another woman approaching from out of the darkness. She was younger, and attractive. The knife was still in David's hand. He concealed it within the denim jacket and stared after the second woman as she approached a pedestrian bridge that crossed the roadway. In the coldness of the bitter night, sweat streamed down David's face.

He resumed his lumbering murderous shuffle. He would attack her from behind. Michelle Forman, a fifteen-year-old sophomore at Truman High School, had reached the very center of the bridge when Berkowitz caught her.

Michelle first felt a stabbing pain in her head. The knife then struck her upper body three times. She grabbed the bridge railing to keep her balance and turned to look at her attacker. Blood spurted from her head.

David struck twice at Michelle Forman's face. She was a "pretty girl," David would say. He looked at her, thinking "Why aren't you dead?"

Fighting for life, Michelle Forman lashed at David's face. Then she lost her footing and fell to the concrete walkway. In agony and terror, Michelle writhed and rolled and shrieked. Traffic continued to growl from the Thruway below. "I never heard anyone scream like that," David said. "The way she screamed constantly. I kept stabbing and nothing would happen. She kept fighting harder and screaming more. I didn't know. . . . I just ran off."

Badly wounded, Michelle Forman still tried to clutch her attacker's legs. She wanted to see his face, to know who he was. But David ran off. Michelle struggled to her feet and was able to note that Berkowitz "ran with a sluggish gait."

She could not catch him. She had lost so much blood that the high buildings of Co-Op City appeared to spin. She stumbled and lurched toward the closest building, where she lived with her parents. Michelle reached for the lobby buzzer that would alert her family. Before she could press it, she fainted.

A neighbor found Michelle, whimpering, as she lay in a puddle of her own blood. She was hospitalized for seven days with six stab wounds about the head and body. One of Berkowitz's knife thrusts had gone deep enough to collapse a lung. Like the Hispanic woman, Michelle Forman did not know Berkowitz. Her description of a dark-haired, hulking man with an awkward gait could not isolate a killer among the 8.5 million people of New York.

DAVID HURRIED back to his Ford. He started the engine and drove off. He remembers feeling more relaxed. He had spilled blood. The demons would be satisfied.

Suddenly he felt hungry and stopped at an all-night diner on Eastchester Avenue. As he ordered his Christmas-Eve dinner—a hamburger, French fries, and milk—David heard the sirens of police cars speeding to Darrow Place, only a hundred yards from the footbridge.

The noise did not disturb his solitary dinner. It did not appear likely that the police would catch him.

THE CITY OF YONKERS, on the northern border of the Bronx, numbers 204,297 people, but it has never been a suburb of distinction. To the north and west lie such affluent bedroom communities as Bronxville and Scarsdale; to the south lies the vitality of New York City. Industrial, blue-collar Yonkers is noted for neither affluence nor vitality.

Once it was the butt of elitist jokes. In the days when New York University's Bronx campus flourished as the home of the University College of Arts and Pure Science, one distinguished history professor would pick out a student from Yonkers, much as the old radio comedians picked out people who lived in Brooklyn. "Would you kindly contrast," Dr. Theodore Francis Jones liked to say, "the relative intellectual achievements of ancient Athens and contemporary Yonkers?" The question provided an easy academic laugh.

But Yonkers is hardly a joke to the people who live there. The city has had to struggle to remain solvent without dangerously curtailing such basic services as police protection. As much as he would ever settle anywhere, David Berkowitz at length moved into a small studio apartment in Yonkers, 7E at 35 Pine Street.

Late on Christmas Eve, 1975, Officers Thomas Chamberlain, then thirty-one, and Peter Intervallo, twenty-eight, of the Yonkers Police Department responded to a disquieting call from a two-story house at number 42 Pine. Their car radio announced "Family dispute."

Police approach family disputes with apprehension and distaste. Family arguments serious enough to require police intervention are volatile. Indeed, the bedroom is the most common setting for murders. Even if the warring parties turn out to be harmless, the appearance of police officers may unite them. Then two people who had been fighting with one another abruptly make up and together abuse the cops.

It was 11:34 P.M. "I think we've been to 42 Pine before," Chamberlain said.

"And we'll be there again," said Intervallo.

The officers parked their prowl car between 42 Pine on one side and the new seven-story apartment house, 35 Pine, on the other. They proceeded to the noisy private house and rang the bell. The noise stopped as the police entered; two people began babbling at the same time.

The husband had disappeared for two days. Now, on Christmas Eve, he had returned, staggering drunk. Perhaps he was expecting an embrace. Instead, his wife began to beat him. The husband was too drunk to defend himself.

Although the couple was middle-aged, Chamberlain and Intervallo talked to them as though they were children. The young policemen spoke slowly and gently. The woman admitted that she had been striking her husband. She said she would not hit him again. The man began to cry. Through tears, he promised to stop drinking.

Tom Chamberlain and Pete Intervallo doubted that either promise would be kept, but the family dispute was solved for the time being.

The officers returned to their car, a four-door Plymouth, anxious to conclude their work shift and get home. Intervallo, the driver, remembers noticing the entrance of Pineview Towers, the apartment house at 35 Pine. Neither policeman anticipated, because there was no way of anticipating, the role that building and Pine Street would play in their careers across the next two years.

DONNA LAURIA and her family watched a televised Christmas Mass on WPIX-TV, Channel 11. Terence Cardinal Cooke, Archbishop of New York, was presiding over the sacred service in St. Patrick's Cathedral and the Lauria family, gathered in their comfortable living room with its beautifully trimmed fir tree, felt warm and relaxed and together.

The Laurias lived in a six-story brick apartment building at 2860 Buhre Avenue in the Bronx. The father, Michael Lauria, worked as a mechanic for the Manhattan and Bronx Surface Transit Operating Authority (MABSTOA), a bus company. He had taken only one vacation since Donna was born eighteen years before. Like his wife Rose, Lauria's first devotion was to his family.

Donna, a dark-haired and serious young woman, sat on the couch beside her poodle, Beau. Her former boyfriend, Vinny, had given her the dog as a present on her sixteenth birthday. Her brothers, Michael, nineteen, and Louis, thirteen, also watched the Mass, but Donna was the centerpiece of the Christmas scene. As a girl, she had suffered from deafness and a series of illnesses that incapacitated her for years. Surgery cured the problems, but during that time, her parents feared for her life. Now Donna was blossoming. She had become a medical technician with the Empire State Ambulance Service and was preparing for examinations that would qualify her as a New York State–certified paramedic.

More than that, Donna had developed a special gentleness and warmth. She patted the poodle in her lap and soon the dog fell asleep. The Lauria family says that Donna's touch was infused with a kind of magic.

She watched the televised Mass and gazed at the tree and at her family. She was still young enough to look toward Christmas morning with high delight.

It would be the last Christmas Donna was to know.

VETERAN POLICE speak of Christmas Eve with muted irony. "I've been on the force for about thirty years," a five-foot-ten-inch white-haired detective named John Falotico said, "and I can count my Christmas Eves at home on less than ten fingers." He shrugged. "That goes with the job. That's the nature of the beast." And that Christmas Eve, Falotico was working in an old white brick building set high on a grassy terrace—the new home of the Sixty-first Precinct, at Coney Island Avenue and 14th Street, in the Sheepshead Bay section of Brooklyn—as a member of the precinct's investigating team.

At the turn of the century, Sheepshead Bay was the site of a racetrack, which carried a certain social glamor. Even after the racetrack closed, the neighborhood held up well. Charter fishing boats left the wooden piers of Sheepshead Bay crowded with anglers on days the bass or weakfish or blues were running. On shore, seafood restaurants prospered. Behind the waterfront, you found the miles of private homes and middle-class apartments that make up Flatbush.

Falotico was working midnight to eight. As he sat in a worn wooden swivel chair on the second floor of the new precinct house, Christmas Eve gave way to Christmas morning. His phone rang. A patrolman was calling in "an apparent homicide."

"Apparent?" Detective Falotico said.

"I'm just doing what my sergeant told me to do," the patrolman said.

"Which is what?" Falotico said.

"He told me to turn the mess over to the detectives."

"He told you the right thing," Falotico said.

The detective took details from the patrolman. "Leave everything intact," Falotico said. "We'll be right over." If it was a homicide, Falotico would turn it over to the homicide zone detectives.

Detectives usually work in pairs, both for safety and for legal reasons. Two of them hear what suspects say. Then in court, if a case gets to court, it will not be the version of one man against the version of another. The suspect will have to go against the version of *two* detectives.

Falotico, who was fifty-two, called over his younger partner, Detective George Donovan. The two men hurried from the precinct building to their unmarked car. A wet ocean breeze made the night seem even chillier than it was. Clouds were beginning to shroud the moon.

"It's gonna be a long, cold night," said George.

"When you've been on the force a long time, every damn night seems long," said the silver-haired John Falotico.

SERGEANT JOSEPH COFFEY pulled his collar up against the bitter cold as he stepped out of the warmth of the Twenty-fifth Precinct house onto Harlem's East 119th Street at midnight, Christmas Eve, 1975. He was simply "going through the motions" until his reassignment on the first of January to the Arson and Explosion Division. Ever since his promotion to sergeant and reassignment to the Twenty-fifth, he'd wanted out. Coordinating the Neighborhood Police Team Project wasn't his cup of tea. Coffey was a detective, not a patrolman. He felt misused. But in another week, that would all change. His assignment to Arson and Explosion would place him in the middle of investigations into terrorist and subversive groups. It was what he'd been trained to do, and what he enjoyed doing. The only saving grace of the past two years he'd spent in the Twenty-fifth was that sometimes he'd be called on to administer the organized crime intelligence operation within the precinct. But now the drudgery was drawing to an end.

The sergeant walked briskly to his parked 1972 Chevrolet and climbed in. As usual, the cold engine was hard to start. In a few minutes he pulled away from the curb. His usual route home was the Triborough Bridge and Grand Central Parkway to get from Manhattan to Queens, then the Northern State Parkway to the Meadowbrook Parkway in Nassau until he would reach his home in Levittown, a community filled with cops, firemen, and blue-collar workers in mid-Nassau County. He knew that his wife Pat would have put the children to bed long before. It was something he'd learned to live with through the years ever since he became a cop in 1964. Not seeing your family is something all cops learn to live with. It came with the territory.

Three-quarters of an hour after leaving East 119th Street, Coffey made the final turn onto Periwinkle Road. The car seemed to know the way itself. It came to rest in front of a nondescript "Levitt ranch" almost identical to all the other homes on the street. The section of Levittown he lived in had been developed by the Levitt organization to house returning

Korean War veterans in the early 1950s. Mr. Levitt never envisioned that twenty-three years later his community would sink into deep financial trouble because of an inadequate tax base (no industry) and an overabundance of children. Most wives were forced to seek employment, and their husbands took second and third jobs in an effort to keep themselves solvent.

As he walked through the kitchen entrance, Joseph Coffey spotted his wife asleep on the couch. She had been waiting for him. He sat down next to her and placed his hand on her arm. She stirred, then continued her dream. Joe let her sleep; she deserved it. A year and a half later, Sergeant Coffey would miss many nights at home. But for now, he'd enjoy the prospect of a quiet Christmas Day with his children.

AT 11:00 P.M. on December 24, Detective James Justus, who would reach the age of thirty-four three days later, was driving from his home in Massapequa on the South Shore of Long Island to work at the Borough Robbery Squad at 2820 Snyder Avenue in the Flatbush section of Brooklyn. At one time New York police were required, as a condition of employment, to reside within the city. After lobbying by municipal-employee unions, the law was rewritten. New York cops, and New York teachers and New York firemen, were free to raise their families outside the threatening, challenging city where they worked.

It is, cops say, a sensible deal. They see the darkest side of New York; it frightens them. They say "I wouldn't raise my family in that jungle." New Yorkers themselves are less pleased. Every police officer, on duty or off duty, is required to carry his gun at all times and keep the peace. If every cop still lived within the five boroughs, New York would be that much richer in full-time police protection. "The cops work hard," says one long-time resident of Manhattan, "but it would be better for all of us if they lived in the town where they worked. The way things are, most cops are visiting firemen."

Such ironies were lost on Justus, a big man, six-foot-three and 225 pounds. Proceeding west this Christmas Eve, he was wondering whether to follow Southern State Parkway and pay a toll or drive the back streets of Valley Stream, Long Island, and save twenty-five cents. He chose the toll.

As Southern State enters the New York City limits, its name changes to Belt Parkway and it follows the shoreline, past John F. Kennedy Airport and Plum Beach, into Brooklyn. Follow Belt Parkway long enough and you drive through Coney Island and pass the Parachute Jump, the amusement sensation of the 1939 World's Fair. The skeleton of the jump still stands in Coney Island, but the white and orange chutes are gone. The ride seems closed for good. At the entrance signs announce WARNING: PROTECTED BY ATTACK DOGS.

Justus couldn't have cared less. He was annoyed at having to work on Christmas Eve. You had to get used to it, but you never really did. He had been a cop since 1962, and once they pinned the silver badge to your blue coat at the Police Academy, your life was no longer yours to command. You took the police oath and tried to accept what followed. Still, Christmas Eve. . . .

Justus was proud to be a cop and prouder still that he had become a detective. Unlike plainclothesmen, who carry silver badges and monitor pushers, prostitutes, and pimps, detectives are given gold badges and imbued with an elitist sense of mission. In a way, detectives are the aristocracy of the force.

Pleased with his advancements, Jim Justus eyed a further goal. He wanted to move up from Robbery to Homicide. The most famous detectives, the glory boys of mystery stories and real life, solved murders. Still, for the time being, Justus thought, driving beside a chilly late-night beach, the Robbery Squad was a good holding point. In time, he would advance.

He reached the squadroom fifteen minutes early. A backlog of paperwork—the debris of unsolved robberies—was waiting. From Justus' desk all Brooklyn seemed like a wasteland, where everybody stole everything that hadn't been nailed down.

The phone rang. Justus remembers thinking "They even rob on Christmas Eve. Business as usual."

At least it was cold. That was a plus for the Robbery Squad. Cold weather, Justus said, "keeps most of the animals inside."

CHRISTINE FREUND, a dark-haired, intense young woman, had left Salzburg, Austria, when she was five years old. Her parents, Nandor and Olga, had sought a better life in America. They settled in the Ridgewood section of Queens, and Nandor Freund found employment as a butcher at a packing plant called Trunz Meat Processing.

The pillars of the Freunds' life were their church and their daughters, Christine, who was twenty-five this Christmas, and Eva, who was eighteen. At 10:30 P.M. they walked five blocks through the cold to worship at Miraculous Medal Roman Catholic Church on Bleeker Street in Ridgewood.

Christine let her parents walk ahead up the wide steps of the church. Entering, she was startled by the sudden warmth and slipped off a multicolored kerchief, letting her long dark hair fall upon her shoulders. She stopped momentarily to look at statues of her favorite saints. Then she and Eva hurried to join their parents.

Olga Freund beamed as the two young women settled beside her in the pew. Christine, Olga felt, was as close to a perfect child as she could imagine. Her daughter had a good job as a secretary in Manhattan's financial district but more than that, Olga thought, Christine had a Christlike gift of kindness. "She had an inside feeling, I mean a feeling from inside, for the happiness of others. That I was happy made Christine happy. She was that kind of person."

The Christmas service made its solemn, joyous sound. It was almost one o'clock before the Freunds returned to their home. Christine and Eva took off their coats and fetched presents for their parents. They placed the gifts under the Christmas tree. As they did, both their parents fell asleep in the living room. The room was painted white and had a single large window on the south wall. There was an overstuffed couch, two armchairs, a glass coffee table sitting on green wall-to-wall carpeting. The girls woke their parents and guided them toward bed.

This was a world away from David Richard Berkowitz and his squalor. Yet long afterward, on January 30, 1977, Christine and David would have a brief murderous encounter.

Olga says of her older daughter "She was really the inside, from the inside, from here." The Austrian woman sadly touches her heart.

"She was always thinking for the family."

DONNA DEMASI, pert, popular, and nearly sixteen years old, was worrying about her final exams at Martin Van Buren High School in the Floral Park neighborhood of Queens. Not too many American high schools are named for Van Buren, protégé of Andrew Jackson, whose political enemies described him as a fox. Donna was no history scholar. She was concerned not about scholastic genealogy but about getting her homework done.

Her Christmas Eve was interlaced with minor problems. Donna's nose and throat felt dry. She was afraid she was getting a cold. She placed books and notebooks on the bed of her room in the neat single-family ranch home. Donna preferred to spend the evening on her holiday school assignments in order to get them out of the way. This would leave the remainder of the vacation free for fun. In the small living room, brightly wrapped packages lay on the floor beneath a Norway pine her father had purchased the week before. Her friend Joanne Lomino had just called and the girls agreed they would go to see the movie *Rocky,* playing in Manhattan, later during the Christmas week.

Catherine and Maurice DeMasi had gone out to attend a midnight Mass at St. Hedwig. As always, Catherine told her daughter: "Don't open the apartment door to strangers." The DeMasis had raised two sons—Daniel, thirty, and Michael, twenty-seven—but the boys were gone now, embarked on lives of their own. The parents were concerned about their daughter. They were worried, too, that such concern was overprotective.

Donna, a tall, slim, attractive girl, looked at the schoolbooks in front of her. She did not like being alone. Her parents' concern had made her particularly fearful of strange sounds. Unexpected noises gave her a chill. Homework was giving her a headache.

Donna meant to study, but the phone rang. It was Joanne Lomino again. She wanted to continue discussing their plans about seeing *Rocky*. It's too late to work anyway, Donna thought, and the girls talked at length.

On another night in Queens, Donna would hear a strange noise and find herself confronting David Berkowitz.

But Donna DeMasi would survive.

GRACIE MANSION, the official residence of the Mayor of New York, is a handsome, sprawling white structure built in 1646, which commands a view of parkland, the East River, and the vaulting spans of the Triborough Bridge. It stands on the Upper East Side, in one of the highest-rent districts on earth.

But even those living in secure buildings near the mansion are sensitive about violent crime. Housing projects and Spanish Harlem lie only ten blocks north. Some Upper East Siders take delight in strolling late at night through the park that surrounds Gracie Mansion, comforted by the two policemen in a tiny gatehouse who are assigned to watch through the night and guard the Mayor.

But the citizens' confidence in their police dropped notably a few years ago. The Mayor was away and the two policemen on this particular evening entered Gracie Mansion and poked about. Presently they found the mayoral hoard of wine and beer. Several bottles later, the two cops were no longer thinking about security. Instead, they began telephoning their precinct house and abusing the desk sergeant.

After that story broke, both policemen were reprimanded and East Siders felt a shade less comfortable. It is not clear whether the cops were required to pay for the wine and beer they had drunk or what vintage year they had chosen.

But on that Christmas Eve, 1975, the Mayor of New York was a short, white-haired accountant from Brooklyn named Abraham Beame. As he recalls it, Abe Beame was not especially concerned about crime that night, nor, of course, did he anticipate the terror that David Berkowitz would let loose on the city.

Instead, Mayor Beame, then seventy-one years old, was suffering from an accountant's woes. The City of New York seemed broke. There was no way it could repay the principal of $1.6 billion in short-term notes that would fall due on January first. So Beame had declared a moratorium. Bondholders sued but, on the morning of December 24, 1975, a state supreme court justice ruled that the moratorium was legal. Beame had felt a measure of relief. A city bailout was now possible.

Abe Beame had worked his way up through the Democratic Party, achieving some prominence when he was elected City Comptroller under dashing, charismatic Mayor John V. Lindsay. As Beame saw it, there was more dash to Lindsay than solidity, and he ran against John Lindsay in 1965. Lindsay won, but Beame persisted. In 1973, Abe Beame was elected as the first Jewish mayor in New York City history. He assumed office just in time to catch the full brunt of a fiscal deluge, a deluge for which Beame, as former Comptroller, had some measure of responsibility.

Still, the past was the past. Now Beame was trying to keep the city out of the poorhouse. The work was rewarding but grueling. The Mayor intended to spend Christmas Eve regathering his energies in the privacy of Gracie Mansion with his wife, Mary.

Christmas Day would be relatively easy, he thought. He had to meet with his press secretary and then lunch with the police commissioner, Michael Codd. The afternoon was free. "A mayor has to learn to relax any chance he gets," Beame says, "otherwise you'll be too tired to be efficient."

Beame drew the curtains of his bedroom. The digital

clock-radio on his nightstand read 10:56. He turned out the lights, climbed into bed, and found that he was wide awake. The financial crisis was palliated but not cured. Without help from Washington, without a more equitable return on the huge share of U.S. income taxes paid by New Yorkers, there didn't seem to be any solution. But the President, Gerald Ford, had a provincial Midwestern distrust of New York City. Besides, Beame was a Democrat, and Ford was a conservative Republican.

Not that everything was smooth within the Democratic Party. Some would surely want Beame dropped as candidate in the next election, two years off. The Governor of New York State, Hugh Carey, might turn out to be the dumper. A big issue dividing Mayor and Governor was capital punishment, which Hugh Carey opposed.

"I was once opposed to it," Beame says, "but society operated without it and look what happened. I mean crime. So I thought that night, 'Let's put a death penalty law back in the books, and see whether it has any value.' "

The Mayor wondered whether his position on capital punishment was consistent with his Jewish religious and ethical beliefs. Still, everywhere in the greatest city on earth, killers were loose.

Oh, Holy Night.

2

The Making
of a Killer

Afterward, when he was murdering wantonly and when he was caught, David Berkowitz emerged as a "classic paranoid schizophrenic." Some journalists, like some therapists, enjoy issuing instant analyses. "He was a nobody who became somebody by killing people," wrote Pete Hamill, a columnist for the *Daily News*. Another *News* headline that ran above a column by Jimmy Breslin said: SAM STRUCK OUT WITH GIRLS . . . SO HE STRUCK OUT. Steve Dunleavy, writing for the *New York Post,* told of David's receiving great numbers of letters and money from his admirers under the headline BERKOWITZ FANS SEND LOVE, CASH. And finally, Breslin topped them all when the Son of Sam sent him a letter from his room in Kings County Hospital. A NEW LETTER FROM DAVID BERKOWITZ was proclaimed by the *News*. Breslin had received what he wanted, a second note. David had issued him an invitation to come for a visit, anytime. Breslin couldn't have asked for more.

Popular psychiatry is the natural business of journalists. It is, after all, easier to vent an opinion than to find a fact. But pop-psych also seduced professionals. There was no shortage of free psychiatric opinion as Berkowitz ran his murderous ways in cold comfort.

The knife-wielding Berkowitz did not crawl out of a cocoon on Christmas Eve, 1975. His psychoses had been cooking, as it were, for many years. During those years, Berkowitz graduated from elementary and high school. He attended Bronx Community College. He served in the U.S. Army from June 23, 1971, to June 24, 1974 (and qualified as a sharpshooter with the M-16 rifle).

In the service one presumably is subjected to psychological reviews. The Army assures us that its own psychological testing program is "of a very high order, so that as far as is reasonably possible, we don't put guns in the hands of psychopaths."

But until he killed, until he killed repeatedly, he had slipped through the nets society sets to separate psychopaths from the rest of us. Why? The disquieting answer is that our vaunted fabric of psychological testing is flawed.

Mental health professionals at once plead that psychology is an inexact science. Indeed. But once David was captured and we knew his life story, we could all spot points of crisis. With even a casual background in psychology, we can make diagnoses—one hardly needs a medical education for that. Once David was captured, the points of crisis and his responses were so obvious that you and I and Jimmy Breslin could stand with Sigmund Freud.

Cold comfort. In fact, no comfort at all.

AFTER his Christmas-Eve assaults, Berkowitz resumed work as a security guard for I.B.I. No one who knew him on the job reports any detectable change. "He was just a heavy, hulking guy," someone says, "who once in a while would smile a Mona Lisa kind of smile."

Within, David Berkowitz was highly agitated. He left the littered Bronx apartment in January 1976 (what could the next

THE MAKING OF A KILLER • 33

tenant there have thought?) and moved to a more comfortable place in a two-family home at 174 Coligni Avenue, New Rochelle. His new landlady, sixty-two-year-old Nann Cassara, found him "a polite young man." She accepted a two-hundred-dollar deposit and gave him a two-year lease.

A two-family house moved David closer to family life. Both Jack Cassara, a sixty-five-year-old retired mechanic, and Nann had a casual knowledge of David's wanderings in and out of the apartment. They were not prying; such awareness is in the nature of life in two-family homes. Now someone would be aware of David's home existence. The Cassaras would know, and be concerned, if he fell ill.

But David's psychosis had passed beyond the help of casual attention. The Cassaras owned a German shepherd; it barked and sometimes howled. Other dogs in the neighborhood responded with baying of their own. That is the way of things around New York. Live in the city, and you hear grinding garbage trucks at night. In the suburbs, you have to listen to dogs.

Berkowitz decided the dogs were demons. Or, rather, demons lived inside the animals. The howling was the cry of demons, shrieking for the blood of women. "In the day, after my job at night," Berkowitz says, "I'd come home to Coligni Avenue like at six-thirty in the morning. It would begin then, the howling. On my days off, I heard it all night, too. It made me scream. I used to scream out begging for the noise to stop. It never did.

"The demons never stopped. I couldn't sleep. I had no strength to fight. I could barely drive. Coming home from work one night, I almost killed myself in the car. I needed sleep. I started to fall asleep on my job. I almost got fired. The demons wouldn't give me any peace."

After only three months in the Cassara house, David moved again, this time to the high-rise at 35 Pine Street in Yonkers. He'd have his privacy back; and, he hoped, he would be free of the baying demon-dogs.

Nann Cassara says she was at a loss to understand why

Berkowitz left without asking for a return of his two-hundred-dollar security deposit. Berkowitz says "more pressing things" were on his mind. His irrational comments show how far he had fallen from the paths of sanity: "When I moved in the Cassaras seemed very nice and quiet. But they tricked me. They lied. They said they were good people and they were lying. I thought they were members of the human race. They *weren't!* Suddenly the Cassaras began to show up with the demons. They began to howl and cry out.

"Blood and death!

"They called out the names of their masters! The Blood Monster, John Wheaties, General Jack Cosmo.

"I was able to sleep only an hour a night."

The Cassaras have never howled blood and death in all their lives.

MOVING to Pine Hill Towers took David only a few hours. The date was April 28, 1976, and by nightfall he had placed blankets over his windows, which blocked a lovely view of the deep-gorged Hudson River and the Palisades. David put up the blankets "to prevent others from spying on me." The closest buildings with a view into his apartment lay a mile and a half distant, across the Hudson.

David appreciated the comparatively low monthly rent ($230) he would have to pay. He also liked to feel a sense of mobility, even freedom. When the demons rose, it was sometimes essential to mount his Ford Galaxie and drive, and Westchester's major highways lay within minutes of Pine Street. David could drive to the Sawmill River Parkway, which led south to Henry Hudson Parkway, the George Washington Bridge, and the West Side of Manhattan. Then the New York Thruway cut north to Albany and Buffalo, and south through the central Bronx. The Bronx River Parkway led toward the Whitestone Bridge and Queens. There was also the Long Island Parkway system. Even this early, three months before he murdered Donna Lauria, David was thinking of escape from the demons, of fast access to a variety of victims, and possibly of diverse avenues of escape from the police.

Mostly, David concerned himself with getting settled. What little furniture he owned had come as gifts from Nat Berkowitz. David missed Nat and wrote him frequently at the retirement village in Boynton Beach. He asked for guidance.

David was also fearful of contact with his neighbors. He made it a point to park his Ford a block away from the entrance to Pine Towers. Cheryl Preston, who lived in the building, remembers seeing David occasionally in the morning. "Instead of taking the elevator," Miss Preston says, "he would just rush down the stairs. He always seemed to be in a rush."

As David recounts his life, after his Army discharge he found it progressively harder to communicate with others. When he tried to talk to someone he had met in school or on the street, something seemed wrong. He is not sure what was wrong. But he knew he was different. Other people didn't like him. They never approached and began conversations with *him*. Well, if they were avoiding him, David thought, he might as well avoid them first.

Unfortunately, Pine Street was not free of dogs. One, a large black Labrador owned by a man named Sam Carr, who ran a telephone answering service, bothered and frightened Berkowitz. On May 13, David threw a Molotov cocktail into Carr's paved backyard.

The glass bottle shattered against the concrete, the flaming wick instantly igniting the gasoline that spread along the pavement. Black smoke filled the air. However, since there was nothing to burn on the ground, the fire died in a couple of minutes, long before firetrucks arrived. The smell of burning gasoline clung to the trees and walls in the house for days, then was gone. However, the fear lingered in Sam Carr.

Late in May, David decided to take a trip. He would drive to see Nat Berkowitz in Boynton Beach, a town thirty miles north of Miami. David liked driving, especially at night. He didn't have much money, but he could sleep in the car. His plan was to visit his fosterfather and then proceed west to Houston, Texas, and see an Army buddy. Besides, in Houston it was easy to buy a revolver.

He left Yonkers on Saturday morning, May 26.

In a 1975 photograph, David Berkowitz squints at the camera, one arm around his half-sister, Roslyn Falco, and the other draped over the left shoulder of his mother, Betty Broder Falco, who is standing stiff and uncomfortable. Behind the three subjects you can pick out the front entrance of Roslyn's garden apartment. The photographic composition would do no honor to Steichen. Just to Betty Broder's right stands a battered metal garbage can.

Eleven years before the birth of David Berkowitz (Richard Falco), Betty had been abandoned suddenly by her Italian-American husband, Anthony Falco. Betty herself was the daughter of indigent immigrant parents, William and Gussie Broder, from Poland and Austria respectively. Coming to this new and wondrous land, they settled in the Bedford-Stuyvesant section of Brooklyn. The household language was mid-European Yiddish.

In the hands of such masters as Sholem Aleichem and Isaac Bashevis Singer, Yiddish can soar, but it is often described as a bastard language. Yiddish vocabulary is drawn from German, Polish, the tongues of whatever lands to which Jews were driven during centuries of antisemitism. However, even in Czarist Russia, where antisemitism raged like Dostoievsky's nightmares, upper-class Jews spoke Russian. Everywhere Yiddish was a language of the poor and the oppressed, although people romanticized in the Broadway portrait of Tevye, in *Fiddler on the Roof.*

Betty Broder, born in 1913, was one of nine siblings. After grade school, P.S. 148 in Brooklyn, Betty was forced to find work. "It was expected of you," she explains with no remorse. "What with times as they were, we all had to bring money into the family in order to survive." In 1927, when Betty graduated, ghetto people already worried about a depression. The stock market crash was still two years away, but the bellies of the poor were said to be barometers for a coming storm. Her first job was packing powder puffs for a firm called Reich-Ash on Tiffany Place in Brooklyn. The pennies she earned put bread on the table. They were often the difference between her brothers and sisters going to bed hungry or not.

At nineteen, three years after the stock market crash, Betty met Tony Falco, six months her junior, at an outdoor dance in Brooklyn's Prospect Park. "On Sundays you would go with your friend to the park to dance. It was a wonderful time, everyone was happy, there was no crime." She describes Tony as "rugged, tall, strong, and very handsome." For young women shackled in hopeless jobs, a husband offered the promise of liberation, before *liberation* became a jargon word. The couple were married in Brooklyn's Municipal Building the first week of December 1935. Betty's Jewish congregation was strict. Her rabbi would not marry her to a non-Jew. Betty and Tony didn't take a honeymoon. "Unaffordable," she says.

The couple worked at separate jobs for four and a half years, scrimping and saving. One could say they lived close to the vest, but it isn't certain that Tony Falco could afford a vest at that time.

In 1939 they had saved enough money to purchase the fish store where Tony worked on Vanderbilt Avenue and St. Mark's Place. One part of the American dream was realized. The Falcos had moved up in class from laborers to business people. Within a month Betty became pregnant and on November 14, 1939, Roslyn Falco was born. Within the year, Tony Falco was gone. Betty says "I guess I got pregnant too quick to suit him. Anyway, he found another woman."

During the following year, which Tony spent with the other woman, Betty tried to keep the business from failing. But motherhood combined with long hours at the store led to disaster. In the end, the Falco fish business went bankrupt.

Eight years passed—"eight years of loneliness," Betty

says. Finally she met Joseph Kleinman, a middle-class Long Island businessman involved in the budding real estate and contracting explosion taking place in what had been potato fields. Kleinman, whom Betty describes as "good looking, five feet eight inches tall, with a grand red moustache," was forty years old, the father of three children. As Joe Kleinman put it, "I was saddled with a wife who just wouldn't hear of a divorce." In those days, the mid-1940s, the New York State divorce law was among the most Puritan in the United States. Adultery was the only grounds and, afterward, the offending party could not marry again without the permission of a court. Thousands of moneyed New Yorkers circumvented the law and the indignities inherent in its provisions. (Customarily, to please the New York courts, a man had to pose in his undershorts beside a hired model clad in bra and panties. This charade proved his worthiness to split.) The moneyed people simply flew to the Mexican state of Guadalajara, where one could be divorced on the simple, reasonable issue of "irreconcilable differences."

Joe Kleinman felt trapped in his marriage. Betty remembers that Joe said she—not his wife—gave him strength. He praised Betty's warmth and strong Jewish sense of family. But when Betty told him she was pregnant, Kleinman recoiled. "Look," he said, "you're pregnant, not me. I want to keep seeing you, but I'll be damned if I ever pay a cent for the child's support."

"He'll be your baby, too," said Betty Falco.

"If you want to keep seeing me," Joe Kleinman said, "you'll give the kid away."

Although such behavior strikes most of us as deplorable, it does not shock knowledgeable professionals. Commenting on illegitimate children, one distinguished attorney says: "A man tends to run from his illegitimate child. You find it all through legend, even in Shakespeare. The rejected bastard son is a classic murderer in myth. In my own practice, it's the exception, rather than the rule, to find a father willing to assume responsibility for a child born out of wedlock. A sorry comment, maybe, but the truth."

Even before Richard David Falco was born at Brooklyn Jewish Hospital, 555 Prospect Place, Betty had begun adoption arrangements through a neighbor. She was happy when she learned her unborn son would be placed with "a fine Jewish·couple who could not have a child of their own." She says she felt great pain at the moment she gave the clothed baby to a total stranger in the hospital. "I did it for Joe's children's sake and for mine," she says. "It had to be done. But I ran from the hospital, miles to my home. By the time I dragged myself up the apartment steps, I knew I was hemorrhaging badly. The bleeding got so bad I had to be taken back to the hospital."

What comments Kleinman might have made on his bastard son, metamorphosed into David Berkowitz, are lost. He died of cancer in 1965.

Betty resumed life with her daughter Roslyn, now twelve, and when she recovered from the trauma of childbirth, she also resumed her affair with gruff Joe Kleinman. They would meet during the week; Saturday and Sunday belonged to Kleinman's family. Betty says she never expected to hear of her son again.

THE superficial facts of the life of one lone driver crossing the George Washington Bridge on the morning of May 26, 1976, gave no hint of madness. He had entered P.S. 77 at Ward Avenue at 172nd Street in the Bronx in 1958. There a friend, Lenny Schwartz, comments: "David was a great baseball player. He could field and throw. Being a big kid, he could really hit the ball." He enrolled in Junior High School 123 at 1025 Morris Avenue seven years later and was bar mitzvahed—the Jewish ceremony celebrating one's entry into manhood—at Temple Adath Israel at 169th Street and the Grand Concourse in 1966, a holdout in a rapidly changing community. It was a small affair with only the close relatives invited. Noteworthy was the absence of David's peers. But David's parents hadn't made friends in Co-Op City, and neither had David. It is not unnatural that when Pearl Berkowitz died of cancer on October 5, 1967, the son was devastated.

Surely it is within the bounds of normal life to feel devastation on losing a mother when one is fourteen.

The lone driver was David Richard Berkowitz. He crossed the two-tiered bridge (the wags on CB radio call the top roadway George, the bottom Martha) and hooked left down the New Jersey Turnpike. He drove the cream-colored Ford Galaxie at a steady fifty-five for nearly an hour and a half. The car passed refineries and chemical factories spilling pollution into the air that would blow across Staten Island, Brooklyn, and New York. Then Berkowitz passed an exit sign, with a green marker indicating Fort Dix. He remembered his own Army basic training there and his skills with the M-16 rifle, an extraordinary weapon that can fire 600 rounds a minute. Thoughtful design cushions the recoil. The rifle does its work with virtually no kick. The effective range is 500 meters, longer than five football fields. Marksmen joke that "with an M-16 you can shoot the balls off a monkey on the horizon."

And David thought of dark-haired Iris Gerhardt. They had not been lovers, but she is one of three women with whom Berkowitz had a warm, even a healthy relationship. Another was Pearl Berkowitz who died in the obliterating agony of cancer. The third was a black postal worker David would meet a month after beginning his short-time postal career, working in the main Bronx Post Office in 1976. He steadfastly conceals this woman's identity.

On the superhighway, driving south at an orderly fifty-five, Berkowitz thought of letters he had written to Iris Gerhardt:

> I am not really unhappy at all that I enlisted. Even though this life is very hard. I felt I just had to go. I always wanted to be on my own. I wanted to take up some responsibilities. There was nothing for me to do back home anyhow. I was growing up at home. . . . It was time for going into the world. And see all the different things so quickly. It's very strange, very different.

Forty-five minutes later he stopped for food, standard drab roadside fare, and then moved the Ford into a line for fuel.

He had to wait five minutes to reach a pump. He says he felt that he was always on line, at school or in the Army—even here. He bought ten gallons of regular gas.

David spent the night in Washington, D.C. He toured a bit, passing the monuments and memorials, parked in a garage within walking distance of the White House, gulped a fast-food supper, and returned to the car. He would sleep there and in the morning pay an attendant $4.50. Berkowitz is frugal. He was proud that he had escaped the cost of a motel.

CEMETERIES fascinate Berkowitz. An automobile seems to symbolize home. After his fostermother died on October 5, 1967, he visited her grave at a Jewish cemetery "every four months or so, on Sunday mornings for a ride. I just used to have the urge to go. Just hang around, talk. I used to visit all the graves there. I knew a couple. I don't remember the names. I used to have paper and mark down at what spots the people I wanted to visit were buried. Mostly young girls. A lot of young girls buried there and some young kids, young guys. I would, you know, talk.

"They couldn't hear me, I don't think. They were teenagers, young twenties. I don't know how they died. I always wanted to find out. I'm curious. Was it a car accident? A disease? It always intrigued me. The graves near where my mother's is, I felt like I knew the people buried there. People I have never seen.

"Girls that were there, whether they were pretty, I wanted to know. I felt akin to them. Everybody mourns more for pretty girls, more than ugly. Pretty girls always get more attention in life. Guys lay down their lives for them."

But David says he was sorrier for the homely girls who died. "I would feel that they missed so much. Like here she was, not pretty. She probably didn't have much social life or anything and she's dead at eighteen. It just doesn't seem fair for the homely girls. I mean some pretty girls at eighteen lived three times over, with all the attention they got. If a pretty one dies, what the hell. She had a good time."

David spent the morning of May 27 walking among the headstones at Arlington National Cemetery in Virginia. When he passed the Marine Corps Memorial and watched the honor guard in dress-blues march through a perfectly rehearsed changing of the guard, patriotism overcame him. The Marines looked more impressive than the draftees he had known in the Army. He remembered thinking when he himself enlisted that he wanted to serve his country. He wanted to be different from "kids who were hippies or into drugs."

"I was gung-ho," he says. "Almost straight. But later in Korea, it varied. The Army had a way of making you a nobody. You know. Impossible. I felt like I was going to make a revolt against them."

Among the graves of Arlington David mourned briefly for his old, simple lost patriotism. Then he returned to the Ford and headed south, resuming his search for his fosterfather and for a gun.

THE SOUNDVIEW section of the Bronx, a melange of six-story apartment buildings and middle-class homes, was "a friendly neighborhood" when Berkowitz grew up there in the 1950s and 1960s. Most of the families were Jewish or Italian, and the streets, Seymour Avenue, Fish Avenue, and Burks Avenue, were loud with children. But David didn't make any friends.

He grew quickly; by the age of ten he was bigger than his peers. Further, he seems deliberately to have chosen playmates who were younger and smaller and whom he would bully. One day in 1963 he tried to enlist another boy "to become a member of my girl-hating club." The *Daily News* reported that statement on August 11, 1977, the day after David's arrest. In the Son-of-Sam hysteria, this phrase was made to seem portentous although it is really nothing of the sort. Troops of healthy, normal ten-year-old boys boast that they dislike girls. To a ten-year-old, few epithets wound more than "sissy." But in the interplay between Berkowitz and the press, sensationalism rather than good sense frequently governed.

But certain aspects of ten-year-old David Berkowitz might have troubled psychologists, had any examined him. Bullying —whether its source be hostility, aggression, or just testing the limits of one's power—may be a phase. Children outgrow it. Or bullying may be a symptom of a variety of neuroses. Or, as with David Berkowitz, it may be a deadly warning siren. Behavior modification is a current vogue term in psychological circles. Bullying, even by a ten-year-old, can call for urgent behavior-modification treatment. No one on the staff of David's elementary school suggested he seek help.

David says he felt uncomfortable with his friends. "I was the only kid in the neighborhood who didn't have a brother or a sister." He says he always wanted a sister. "I couldn't quite understand why my parents didn't have one for me. I asked them a couple of times but they never answered . . . at least they never gave me an answer I could understand. It was that they were too old or didn't have enough money. But it wasn't true because other kid's parents had babies. I guess they just didn't want another kid. It was as simple as that."

David's boyhood in the Bronx is hardly comparable to Dylan Thomas' romantically remembered youth among the hills and apple farms of Wales. But, viewed objectively, David's childhood was hardly bleak. Nat and Pearl showered him with toys. His favorites were Carl Hubbell's baseball and a Chinese-checkers game.

His favorite sport was baseball. One acquaintance, Bruce Handler, says David was "a great baseball player, looked up to by the other kids." Berkowitz played first base. Surely another myth should tumble here. "Sports saved me," says the athlete on television.

"Yessir," says the interviewer, and we are swept into grandiose nonsense. Sport can indeed help young people find themselves. But for every one who does, at least one other plays the game and still finds ruin. Baseball and salvation are not synonyms.

Despite baseball, toys, and an adoring mother, Berkowitz is not now able to summon a pleasant memory from his early life. He also insists that he was always well-behaved.

During one of his psychiatric interviews at Kings County Hospital in Brooklyn, David said, "When I was a kid and we played soldiers, I was always the German." He says he *wanted* to be the German and adds, in a flurry of insight, that this foreshadowed a later tendency to "punish myself. I always wanted to be the guy who got shot down. When you play war, you know, the Germans always lose."

Berkowitz thinks, too, of his childhood in terms of imaginary monsters. "I used to watch horror movies on TV. All of them. Everything from Dracula to Godzilla. The other guys watched, too, but I was bothered more than they were. At eleven, you know, or twelve, the monsters haunted me. I couldn't sleep. I'd have to leave a light on. Sometimes I'd run out of my room. I was so scared. Then I'd go sleep with my folks. When I had to do that, they seemed annoyed and angry."

Berkowitz says that the monsters "stopped bothering me" before his thirteenth birthday. But at a later age—he cannot be specific—they reappeared. Thus Berkowitz refuses to see his childhood as a time of toys and baseball. Rather, he says, "the monsters planned to take me over, even when I was a kid. I'm almost certain that they're the same ones who got me later. Like they were with me. I think I was born so they could take me over. You know?"

WHEN DAVID was about thirteen and forced to take time off from baseball to study for his bar mitzvah, socioeconomic changes struck Soundview. The entrenched Jewish and Italian families began to flee—to the north Bronx, to Flatbush, or to tract housing springing up like dandelions along the Southern State Parkway in Long Island. The older families were replaced by blacks from Carolina dirt farms and Hispanics from many other cultures.

The change alarmed Nat and Pearl Berkowitz. They had seen Co-Op City advertised as "A middle income city within the city." It was Pearl, the Jewish mother, who wrote the letter accompanying the family application that is dated June

9, 1966. "We are most anxious to move into Co-Op City. It would be a fine place to raise my son. A fine place to live." The Berkowitzes had lived in the same apartment for nineteen years, and Co-Op City, with its starry promise as a middle-class paradise, seemed both an escape from a deteriorating section and a move to a better life.

On June 30, 1969, David and Nat Berkowitz moved into apartment 17B at 170 Dreiser Loop. Nat's down payment was $2025. But by then, the corpse of Pearl Berkowitz lay in a Bronx cemetery.

In 1950, three years before David's birth, Pearl had undergone a radical mastectomy. David says he never knew that she had lost a breast.

Cancer struck Pearl again in 1965, and by mid-1967, she was terminally ill. Nat checked Pearl into James Ewing Hospital in Manhattan, saying little to his stepson. For a long time David waited for his stepmother to come home. Then, in August 1967, with Pearl bedded in intensive care, David was allowed to visit her. The sight of his dying mother upset him. Cobalt treatments had made Pearl's face puffy. She had lost clumps of her silver hair. "She looked a mess," David says. But her appearance did not prepare him for what it portended. Pearl died October 5, 1967. She was fifty-two.

"David cried really hard at the funeral," says one of his old acquaintances. "I mean, he was *really* crying." For seven days Nat Berkowitz "sat Shiva," a traditional Jewish ritual of mourning. Each night Nat went to a synagogue and said Kaddish, the ancient, moving Hebrew prayer for the dead.

David continued attending Junior High School 123 but was not allowed to watch television during the mourning week. After that Nat drove him to the Cresthaven Motel at the New York State resort of Lake George, where they shared their grief far from familiar scenes.

Certainly, Pearl Berkowitz's death was a pivot point in David's life. Before, David's grades had averaged B-minus; now they plummeted. He failed some courses, in others he managed low Cs. (He would claim later to have been an "A student,'' something he might have wished but never attained.) He became a boy without purpose, spending long hours alone in his room or wandering the vast Co-Op City complex. Worse, he could never fathom why his mother had been taken away from him. He asked. There were no answers.

Again demonic interplay appears. David "supposes" that he "might" have become cynical or "angry at God," because his mother died. Then he adds that her death was not happenstance. "It was part of a master plan to break me down. It was no accident that she got cancer. My Dad doesn't know about it, but it wasn't a natural thing. They [the demons] had plans for me. Like you know. Kill. Everybody always circles around that."

What really happened to your mother, then, David?

"Somebody put something in her food. Evil forces. Poison."

Summing up his mother's death from cancer, David says: "She went out one day to eat and she never came back."

DRIVING south from Arlington Cemetery, Berkowitz proceeded to Interstate 95, the dull, crowded ribbon that runs down the eastern edge of the United States and has replaced older, more picturesque roads with such names as Pine-to-Palms Highway and the Tobacco Trail. For his second night on the road David found a truckers' motel near Smithfield, North Carolina, where he could rent a room with color television for $8.50.

In the diner he noticed truck drivers eating in groups and a couple seated in a booth. The woman was a platinum blonde, and the man was working his hands about her thighs. The blonde giggled. David took a seat at the end of the service counter, as far from the others as he could place himself. "There is a force," he says, "to turn other people away from me. Somebody wants me destroyed, makes people dislike me and makes girls be not attracted to me in any way. If I had close friends or girl friends, I would be able to resist the force. I would be able to resist, if I had people."

After eating he showered. "I keep my body clean," he says, "so I don't get sick. I hate to feel dirty, or when my hair is all dried or stringy with flakes."

The next night David slept in the Ford on a shoulder of Georgia Highway 204. He had extemporized a travel routine. If he spent night after night in the car, he would become filthy. So he alternated, one night in the car and another in a one-night-cheap motel.

On the fifth day "fairly clean because I'd been careful about that," he arrived in Boynton Beach and turned right, away from the ocean, toward his father's retirement home in the complex Village Royal on the Green. There is nothing royal about Village Royal, but Florida is rich in retirement communities with impossibly pretentious names: Apollo Acres, Suncoast Golden Arms, Happiness Dunes. Nat and Julia Berkowitz, who were married in 1971, lived in 2601, Village Royal on the Green, in a small apartment on the second floor. Berkowitz threw open his screen door and greeted his fosterson with a hug. Julia Berkowitz, a pleasant, slightly plump, intelligent woman, was more aloof.

David stayed in Boynton Beach for a week. He spent some evenings in singles bars at nearby Fort Lauderdale, where someone retains a bland remembrance of him. "He was a quiet listener, who would timidly attempt to join animated conversation. He'd interject a few comments, with his bemused smile, then quickly be cut out of the group as an odd duck. Then he'd retreat and try to strike up a conversation with others."

At his father's Florida apartment David relived the Soundview years. He had not thought much of Hebrew training, he told Nat. The rabbi was always "drunk."

The population shift had troubled Nat and David equally. As the Puerto Ricans came, some of the remaining white children tried to prove their *machismo*. They shot heroin, stole cars, and broke into apartments. So did Hispanic toughs.

"I didn't want you going to James Monroe," Nat Berkowitz said in his antiseptically clean and ordered Florida living room. "I know the school was nearby, but I heard a lot about drugs there and knifings. That's why I sent you to Christopher Columbus, even though it meant a long bus trip.''

"Two buses," David said, "and they were always mobbed. Everybody had to fight to get on.''

David admitted that he had cut some high school classes. ''I figured that the big people at the Board of Education didn't give a shit about the students. If the big people and the teachers didn't care, why should I?''

Nat said it was important that a young man have a girl, the right girl. This set David to musing. ''My social life at Soundview was screwed up by the long, lousy trip to high school. I'd say I was fifteen when I got, you know, real interested in girls. In the beginning, at Co-Op City I had friends. There were maybe five hundred young people there and I went out with a couple of girls. They came from neighborhoods that were more sheltered than Soundview.''

David's dates were few and far between. He found it difficult to sustain relationships with other boys, and even more difficult with girls. In the end he chose to fantasize; what might have been was more pleasing than reality.

''A lot of girls I hung around with came from Riverdale. We were all clumsy together. We didn't know how to do too much except kiss. If you wanted to make out, you just walked to the dark area.

''After a while, at Co-Op City there wasn't one girl who was a virgin. That whole group . . . everyone got older, eighteen, nineteen.

''So much freedom there. Drugs finally came in, you know. Pot and everything. I was still pretty straight. Like I wouldn't smoke any pot or anything. Everyone sort of became, sort of like turned into hippies. I still wanted the girls, but I didn't want the other stuff, the drugs or anything.''

David began to date. ''It was about . . . just a couple of months before I went into the Army on June 23, 1971. There was one girl there that everyone scored with. She was built, though not too good-looking. She would just come along and sit on your lap. Everyone used to tell stories about her, and then find out the other guys' stories were true. She was something else, but she's all right now. She changed a bit. She has a kid. Whose? I don't know? I don't think she does either, but she's got one.

"Then, there was a girl [Iris Gerhardt] before I went into the service. She was like thirty years old. Experienced. Wise. I mean she acted that way. But she was only eighteen."

David thought that Iris was very pretty, and that she was everything his mother could have been. From his fantasy he built a relationship he could daydream about. It was something he could tell the guys about.

But Iris meant far more to David than he did to her. Now married with a young family, Iris says, "I confess I liked him a lot. But then, I was only eighteen. It's hard to believe, but Dave was a guy who would do anything for you. We all hung around a local community club, and as for sex, Dave and I just kissed each other on the lips, in a building behind Co-Op City. Nothing more. We just kissed on the lips." Iris and David never had any real relationship. David made much more of it than it was, writing to her through his Army years, Iris choosing to answer only from time to time. In the end it vanished, as do most dreams, and young affairs that are one-sided.

Talking with his fosterfather in Florida, David remembered how he had liked calisthenics and weight lifting, and how he and other young people in Co-Op City formed the volunteer fire department. "I wanted to help people," David said to Nat. "A lot of kids were doing absolutely nothing. They just passed time in the local hangouts. They were high all the time. I wanted to help people, be important."

For all the reminiscing and the Fort Lauderdale singles bars, David describes Florida as "hot and boring." He thought briefly of moving to Florida so he could be close to Nat. "But there was nothing down there for me to work at. I mean, I needed a job and Florida has high unemployment. Got to be realistic. I had no money. I couldn't afford moving my furniture. Live with Dad? I couldn't do that because there was no way I could get along with his new wife. Julia and I could never live in the same house."

David did relish one aspect of Florida existence. The demons, he says, "bothered me less." He was not absolutely certain he would return to the New York area. If somehow he could find a place where demons could not reach him, there he might decide to stay.

Whatever, it was time to move on from Boynton Beach. Billy Dan Parker, whom he remembered from the Army as "tall, thin, short-cropped hair, twenty-three years of age," would be glad to see him in Houston, David thought. He would arrive in Houston on June 5, 1976.

DRIVING WEST toward Houston on June 4, David spent a night in Lafayette, Louisiana, where he found another one-night-cheap motel. He ate at a McDonald's across the street, went to bed, and heard the demons again. He was exhausted, he says. Even the demons could not block sleep. He awoke refreshed and made his way to a pay telephone. Then he called Billy Dan Parker in Houston.

Parker, who was now working as a construction worker, was surprised but pleased to hear from his old Army friend.

"How far away are you, Dave?"

"I think the map says, you know, 270 miles."

"Well, we'll be glad to put you up. My Mom likes to meet my Army buddies. Dave, she'll really make you feel at home."

By three o'clock on June 5 David would see the towers of Houston. The city rises dramatically from Texas flatland, much of it drained swamp. Before Houston became America's oil capital, before air conditioning made it a comfortable metropolis, it was described as "foul, pestilent, material." Even as recently as 1965, before the Astrodome was built, Sandy Koufax, the great Dodger pitcher, had trouble winning games there. "It's tough to concentrate," Koufax said, "under the assault of Houston mosquitoes. Only twin-engined mosquitoes I ever saw."

In an hour David reached Billy Dan Parker's home in a Houston suburb. It was a ranch-style house he shared with his mother, neat and orderly. David sat in his car and drank the scene in. It was everything he dreamed of.

David would stay in Houston for almost a month. He thought more seriously of settling there than he had thought of living in Florida. "I had the Texas newspapers. I was looking in the new employment section, you know? There were jobs, oil wells and stuff, but you needed a degree or training. The only jobs I qualified for were like the job I had. Security guards and stuff. I like that city, Houston. But I just couldn't move instantaneously. I wouldn't have known how to begin. How to get organized.

"I had no money. No money. No matter how much I wanted to move, I didn't have any money. I was just making enough to pay bills. I had no clothes or nothing."

He went to local bars with Billy Dan Parker. For the time, at least, he was not alone. But at Billy Dan's house he felt "underfoot."

"They were very hospitable," David says, "and they liked me, you know, but you don't overextend yourself for guests. I can't do that myself, overextend."

The demons continued to trouble him. "In Houston, I just about gave up fighting them. I knew I couldn't possibly get away. They had a hold on you. I knew they'd be back strong when I got home."

New York State and New York City officials boast (in election years) that "we have the toughest gun control laws in the country." Indeed, to buy a handgun in Manhattan you must first possess a pistol permit, then get a purchase order from the New York City Police Department. A legal purchase is time-consuming and difficult. You can also obtain a gun illegally, but David, psychopath, killer, and sometime patriot, did not like trafficking in contraband. Besides, at this point, he was not about to leave clean traces with those who might testify in a New York court.

"You know," David said to Billy Dan Parker, "it worries

me driving all the way back east without some protection."
Then he asked Billy Dan to buy him a pistol.

"It was my best friend asking," Billy Dan later told a
newspaperman. "I saw no reason not to help him out."

On Saturday morning, June 12, 1976, Billy Dan Parker and
David Berkowitz walked into the Spring Branch Jewelry and
Loan Pawn Shop at 8715 Longpoint Avenue in Houston. The
clerk, Bill Wheeler, ascertained that Billy Dan was a Texas
resident and requested that requisite Treasury Department
forms be completed. He says he barely noticed Parker's silent, hulking companion. He sold Billy Dan the Charter Arms
Bulldog revolver for $130. Then he sold Parker three boxes of
ammunition. Outside, Billy Dan gave the pistol to David.

FOR MONTHS, Berkowitz had wanted to acquire an arsenal. If he could not buy an M-16 (such arms are hard to come
by this side of East Asia, or Iran) he would do the best he
could. In November 1975 Berkowitz applied for a permit to
purchase a rifle in New York City. He paid $3, submitted to
fingerprinting, and the New York City Firearms Control
Board made its routine check for a known or wanted felon.
Berkowitz had never been convicted of a felony. There was
no history of mental illness. The board granted David a permit
on January 21, 1976. So much for the "toughest gun control
law in the land."

Five days later Berkowitz drove to Brooklyn and bought a
semiautomatic .45-caliber rifle, called the Commando Mark
III, from Mrs. Barbara Rutuelo at the Empire Gun and Coin
Shop, at Eighth Avenue and 56th Street in Bay Ridge. The
price was $152.50. David also bought four boxes of ammuni-
tion.

The Commando Mark III holds a clip of 30 steel-tipped
bullets. But marksmen disparage the weapon. Its effective
range is "limited" to about 65 meters. Its accuracy is described as imperfect. Although the manufacturer denies this,
hunters say that the only practical use for Commando Mark
III is "killing people at short range." D. E. Smith of Com-

mando Arms says: "The gun is used a lot as a home defense type weapon. It stores easily in a closet and women can use it because of its light recoil."

But David wasn't worried about the weapon's limited range. For his purposes, 75 yards would be more than enough. "I thought the Commando would do just fine. But it's hard to conceal and I knew I'd have to get a handgun."

The .44-caliber Bulldog pistol Billy Dan Parker bought for David Berkowitz is purely a "people" gun. It has no possible sporting use. It was designed in 1974 and manufactured by the Charter Arms Company of Bridgeport, Connecticut. The Bulldog was the first new .44 revolver introduced for public sale since the early 1900s. It is smaller and lighter than any of its predecessors, such as the classic Smith & Wesson single-action target .44. It is "a personal defense gun," intended mainly as a concealed weapon for police. The Bulldog combines maximum bullet weight and diameter with minimum weapon bulk and weight. The bullet used in the revolver is a .44 S&W Special, 246 grain, lead-nosed. It fires at a velocity of 675 feet per second from a 3-inch barrel. The total weight of the loaded weapon is 18 ounces. (The famous old western Colt .45 weighed 2.5 pounds *unloaded.*) In all, Charter Arms has manufactured 28,000 Bulldogs. Of that number, 667 have been reported lost or stolen.

David had no intention of registering the Bulldog .44 when he returned to New York City as section 265.05 of the New York State Penal Law requires. It is illegal to bring an unregistered handgun into either the state or city. He would have had to acquire a permit in advance and, as a general rule, permits are granted only to those who can make a persuasive argument. Diamond merchants often get permits. So do shopkeepers in high-crime areas. But even here the lawmakers tried to be careful. One class of permit allows an individual to keep a pistol "on the premises." It is more difficult to get a permit to carry a pistol on your person. (Quite beyond the law are a number of men and women who are licensed to carry handguns simply because they know the right people.)

The Bulldog .44 completed David's arsenal. Aside from the Commando rifle, he had been able to buy a 12-gauge Ithaca Deerslayer shotgun from individuals living outside New York City, which he would later use to kill two dogs in an alley on Barnes Avenue in the Bronx, two .22-caliber rifles, a Charter Arms AR-7 Explorer, and a Glenfield rifle with a 4-by-14 telescopic sight. So much, one is tempted to add, for gun control generally in the United States.

Late that Saturday afternoon, June 12, David said goodbye to Mrs. Patrick Parker and Billy Dan. The farewells were casual. There was no suggestion of fanaticism in Berkowitz that day.

He had a long drive home and it would be lonely.

He put the loaded .44-caliber pistol in the unlocked glove compartment.

Six weeks later, he would use it to kill Donna Lauria.

3

"After the First Death"

Soon after his return from Texas, on June 28, 1976, Berkowitz suddenly quit his job as a security guard. He had been working for I.B.I. as a night watchman at Universal Carloading's location at 60th Street and 12th Avenue in Manhattan, not far from the cultural delights of Lincoln Center. At the time he quit, his weekly salary was $128, just barely above the minimum wage scale.

Although David has described the job as lonely, he also remembers an aspect he enjoyed: a strange aspect, considering David Berkowitz, and a bewildering aspect for a man who heard demons wailing within hounds. Berkowitz relished working with guard dogs. Another I.B.I. employee, George Kelly, recalled that "David was the only one who could walk the guard dogs. A lot of others were afraid."

After quitting I.B.I., he signed on with the Co-Op City Taxi Company in the Bronx. This time he worked a twelve-hour day shift, beginning at seven in the morning. He says he liked spending time behind the wheel. Coincidentally, he came to know most of the streets and avenues of the Bronx and Queens.

In certain ways, his lifestyle seemed to be improving. After driving his taxi he would return to the apartment on Pine Street in Yonkers, wash, prepare dinner, and listen to phonograph records. He says his favorite performers were Peter, Paul and Mary, James Taylor, and Carol King. But he remembers nights when he could not sleep, when he mechanically played the same records over and over. Then strange voices carried above the music and he knew that he would lie awake till morning.

Insomnia often contributes to depression just as depression often contributes to insomnia. On Tuesday evening, July 6, 1976, David decided he could not lie sleepless and "cooped up" for another night. Voices, he says, urged him to act.

The Charter Bulldog .44 lured him to the dresser top, where it lay. He stuffed the gun into a paper bag. It was a hot, damp night and David slipped on a clean blue and white sport shirt over his jeans. Then, carrying the gun in the bag, he began cruising.

He followed the sloping Yonkers streets, Greenvale, Nepperhan Avenue, and drove south to the corner of Nepperhan and Lake. He looked about constantly at the people he passed. He was waiting for "some kind of signal to use the gun." It would be less difficult to shoot people than to knife them, but he says he did not think shooting would be easy. For all his months in service, and despite his sharpshooter's medal with the M-16, David had never fired a gun at a human being.

Where Nepperhan and Lake avenues met, a car in front of the Galaxie made a right turn. David saw two girls inside. Apparently they were returning from a happy evening.

David heard voices commanding "Get them!"

He felt reluctant. He says he did not *want* to kill. He says he tried to resist his compulsion. But he followed the young women's car. They pulled into a driveway. David parked farther down. He threw open his own car door and stepped out carrying the paper bag that held his pistol. He ran in his heavy lumbering way to the driveway. The girls were gone. No one knows their identity to this day. Presumably they are alive and unaware that no more than seconds saved them from murder.

David tired of driving a taxicab and quit on July nineteenth. (When later asked about "The Son of Sam," no one could even remember David. But then, that was the essence of David Berkowitz, a nondescript person with no real identity.) He then spent hot summer days looking for work. Each night he cruised, "looking for a victim, waiting for a signal." He cannot recall precisely how many times "I failed on the job."

Psychotic tension assaulted him, but late in the month his Uncle Sol helped David find yet another job. The firm of Wolf and Munier of Elmsford in central Westchester County hired Berkowitz for $175 a week to help install air-conditioning ducts in buildings under construction. The demons, David says, told him it was necessary for him to work. He had to maintain a routine, "a regular life." But he was to keep to himself as much as possible.

Jack Villetto, a foreman at Wolf and Munier, describes David as "quiet and a loner." "I had no trouble with David," Villetto says, "but he was just a body at a plant, not much of a worker. He didn't do good with tools. He was sometimes depressed and would break into tears."

David remembers July 28 as a day that was tiring and made him feel jumbled. It was not hot for summer—the temperature ranged from 70 to 90 degrees—but David was worn out. But not so worn he would not cruise again. Not too worn "to get someone."

After work, he lifted the Bulldog .44 and checked to see that it was loaded. He checked to see that it was loaded every night, although he never once unloaded the gun. He bagged it, left apartment 7E at 35 Pine, and descended the fire stairway rather than in the elevator. He saw nobody. He believes that nobody saw him.

He wanted to find new areas in which to hunt. In the old places, luck had been bad. The word David heard the voices shriek was monosyllabic—*Blood*.

The night was clear and pleasant. David drove his Ford to Broadway—the Yonkers street is a suburban extension of the famous boulevard that etches itself diagonally through Manhattan. David drove south, into the Bronx, proceeding south, always south, and angling east. Just after one o'clock on Thursday morning, July 29, he entered a wide asphalt-topped street lined with aging stores and apartment houses called Buhre Avenue. He believes he was driving twenty miles an hour. He was looking for women who could satisfy the demon's craze for blood.

He turned off Buhre, circled, and came back. On his second pass, he saw a blue Oldsmobile in which two young women chatted. One was Donna Lauria, the dark-haired eighteen-year-old medical technician. The other was Jody Valenti, a student nurse, who was nineteen.

"I was heading west on Buhre Avenue and I knew I had to get them. Those were my orders. I never saw them until moments before the shooting."

David turned the corner of Mayflower Avenue and parked. "At the first corner, I turned around. There was a space there. It was an accident. But there was a parking space all set up waiting. Probably the most convenient location you could ask for."

Berkowitz left his car, the .44 tucked in the paper bag. The bag, in turn, was tucked inside his waistband. He walked slowly around the corner and looked down Buhre Avenue. The young women in their car were still talking.

David says he knew what was "expected" of him. He says the fear and uncertainty of previous nights were gone. He looked straight ahead. His shuffling stride brought him closer to the two girls.

IT HAD BEEN a sad, rich, and demanding day for Donna Lauria. As an emergency medical technician, she was in some ways mature beyond eighteen. She worked amid agony and cries. She understood grief.

Earlier this night—actually on July 28—she had been urging her parents, Rose and Michael, to visit Giordano's Funeral Parlor on Crosby Avenue. Donna's uncle, Ralph Falcone, had died two days before.

At Giordano's, Rose Lauria remembers, "I met people I hadn't seen for years. It was crowded and sad, but loving, the way these things are for us Italians. Everybody who met Donna told me that she had turned into a beautiful girl. I was especially proud after all the sickness she had undergone."

At about nine o'clock the Lauria family walked into the evening and separated. Donna said she wanted to visit her friend Jody Valenti. Michael said he didn't want Donna walking the streets alone. Donna said she would be fine.

Rose and Michael went to the Chateau, a local steak house, where Rose met a friend she hadn't seen for twenty years. "She was a schoolgirl friend," Rose says, "from my old neighborhood, East Harlem.

"She hugged and kissed me, and began crying. She spoke about her children. I hadn't known that she and her husband were separated . . . divorced. She had turned her children over to her husband. I said, 'Madeline, you're crying twenty years too late.'

"She knew I was right. She asked about my children and if they were still at home with me and Mike. I told her we had a very happy home life.

"Finally, I looked at my watch and it was ten to one. I turned to Mike. We had to go to work tomorrow."

As the Laurias reached their apartment building at one o'clock, they saw Jody Valenti's blue Olds double-parked in front of the entrance. Mike Lauria parked his own Chevrolet alongside the curb behind it. He could see the two girls talking.

Mike walked over to the Olds. "How come so late, Donna?"

"I don't know, Dad. We went up to the Peach Tree and

played backgammon. They had some tournaments going. We stayed to watch. I didn't realize how late it was."

"Well, come on upstairs."

"I'll be along. I just want to finish telling Jody something. Why don't you take Mommy upstairs and get the dog and we'll walk him together."

Rose and Michael Lauria entered the building. "She's eighteen years old," Rose said to Mike. "You've got to make allowances for kids once in a while."

As David closed the distance between himself and the two girls he thought "I have a mission." He was not anxious to murder. But he would do it. He had to do it. He would do it "as a kind of joke."

It was precisely 1:10 A.M., July 29, 1976. David walked to the passenger side of the double-parked Oldsmobile Cutlass. He remembers noticing Donna's dark hair.

"Who is this guy?" Donna said to Jody. "What does he want?" Those were her last words.

David, who is right-handed, pulled the Charter Arms .44 Bulldog from the paper bag and assumed a semisquatting position. Then he fired five times. The car windows shattered.

Donna raised her hands as if to protect herself from falling glass. One of the Smith & Wesson slugs struck the right side of her neck. Blood spurted. She died in minutes.

A bullet crashed into Jody Valenti's thigh. She screamed in pain and writhed forward, striking the horn.

David continued to pull the trigger even after the gun was empty.

Then, terrified by Jody's screams, by the blaring horn, David ran back to his Ford Galaxie and drove away.

As an indication of the extremes of psychosexual theory that emerged during the months that followed was one postulated by a psychotherapist about his crouching position: "When Berkowitz assumed the position he did, he was not simply shooting the women. He was symbolically copulating with them, fucking them, if you will. Note that even his weapon has a canine name."

A commonsense marksman would disagree. David was a sharpshooter handling a difficult gun. The Bulldog fires a large, heavy bullet at 675 feet per second down a barrel only three inches long. The laws of physics being inexorable, this produces severe recoil and significant "muzzle jump." That is to say, the gun kicks like hell and the barrel tends to fly into the air.

Firing the Bulldog properly, you set your body as firmly as possible. You go into a semisquat to lower your center of gravity. (You also place your left hand over your right wrist to hold down the muzzle jump.)

What a psychiatrist read into David's shooting posture had nothing to do with symbolism.

David was handling a difficult weapon like a pro.

JODY's body convulsed and continued to press forward against the horn. David drove frantically away, then slowed down. He was not sure he had killed either girl, but he recalls experiencing the pleasure of "a job well done." He sensed that "Sam was pleased."

After he reached the Hutchinson River Parkway leading back toward Yonkers, he was careful to hold his speed at fifty. This was no time to get a ticket. He was home in half an hour. Only when he parked did he realize that the empty .44 was on the seat beside him. The collector at the center booth (a single manned booth was open in either direction at that hour) could have spotted it easily.

He ran up the fire stairs and, once inside his apartment, bolted the door. He felt that now he would be able to rest. He found the bare bed in the dark and fell onto it. He was totally spent.

He says he went to sleep fulfilled. He believes he slept unmoving until the midmorning summer sun filtered through the blankets on the windows. Even then no prying eyes could see him.

MIKE LAURIA had gone upstairs, planning to walk their toy poodle, Beau, with Donna, and had reached the doorway

of his fourth-floor apartment when he heard a "series of sharp
reports, screams, and a horn." By the time he reacted and
reached the window, Jody Valenti had regained a remarkable
measure of composure. She now stood in the street shouting
"We were shot. We were shot." The horn continued to blow.
Leaning against the car, Jody was keeping one hand pressed
against it.

Lauria ran down four flights. His two sons—Michael,
twenty-one, and Louis, fifteen—followed barefoot and in pa-
jamas. Rose stayed at the window, four stories from her dying
daughter. "I was in shock," she says. "I can't begin to tell
you the shock I was in. I still can't believe it."

The whole neighborhood was awake now. Someone dialed
911, calling the police, who in turn summoned an ambulance
from Jacobi Hospital.

Mike Lauria rode in the ambulance, holding the hand of
his dead daughter. A technician tried to revive her. A policeman who accompanied father and daughter, hoping for a
statement, at length placed a hand on Mike's shoulder and
turned him away. Gently.

Only then did Mike Lauria know his only daughter was
dead.

THE LEAD story in *The New York Times* of July 29, 1976,
was remote. The headline read:

VIKING SCOOPS UP MARS SOIL IN HUNT FOR LIFE

Donna Lauria's death went unreported in all the sixty-four
pages of *The Times* that day.

David rose late and went to lunch in a Yonkers diner. On
the front page of the *New York Post* he saw a headline:

BRONX GIRL SLAIN IN CAR

Until then he had not known that he had successfully murdered anyone, much less Donna Lauria's name. He describes
his first emotions as a mixture of curiosity and blankness. "I
never thought I killed her; I couldn't believe it. I just fired the
gun, you know, at the car, at the windshield. I never knew

she was shot." Then he felt "elated at my success." There was no sorrow, no pain, no remorse. For David it was an event worth reliving hundreds of times over in the next fourteen months, a strange but happy event.

"You just felt very good after you did it. It just happens to be satisfying, to get the source of the blood. I felt that 'Sam' was relieved. I came through."

In the next weeks David drew on that feeling time and time again. "It felt good a couple of weeks or so; I don't know." But, as time went on, the demons reappeared. By then, David says he ceased to have feelings "for people. I no longer had any sympathy whatsoever for anybody. It's very strange. That's what worried me the most. I said, 'Well I just shot some girl to death and yet I don't feel.'

"The demons were turning me into a soldier. A soldier can't stop every time he shoots someone and weep. He simply shoots the enemy. They were people I had to kill. I can't stop and weep over them. You have to be strong and . . . you have to survive."

David was developing a psychopathology to explain and justify his deeds. He called upon his Army experience and drew a parallel between war and what he was doing. "There are similarities. You're a soldier in both cases. In the United States Army you can't stop to feel grief. You desensitize yourself."

By mid-September the demons were pressuring him again, violating his privacy and peace. He couldn't escape them. Each night he found himself cruising the streets of Westchester and the Bronx. However, the stubborn demons refused to give him a signal. They were subjecting him to torture: "They broke me down. I felt sick, weak. They took a lot away from me. Things I can't get back any more, like feelings for people. I remember once I used to be an auxiliary cop, you know, with the rescue squad at Co-Op City beginning in October of 1970. I was risking my life then for another person."

Later, David called Donna Lauria his "little princess." Right after he killed her, Sam had promised her to him. He was supposed to marry her, he says. Sam told him that. But

Sam lied. He always lied. The six-thousand-year-old man never lived up to that promise. "I don't know," he says. "Maybe he would have given her to me, eventually?" David never complained, figuring that, in the end, Sam would give her to him. David would always have a "mystical attachment" to her. If he had known what cemetery she was buried in, he would have visited her grave; he even tried to find her grave. Somehow, he believed, Donna Lauria would rise from the dead, like Lazarus, to stand beside him for eternity.

ON THE AFTERNOON of July 29, newspaper reporters and television news crews converged on the Lauria household, pressing for details, driving for what editors like to call human interest. To the stricken parents, the "interest" seemed inhuman.

"I feel that when a victim—and we were victims just as Donna was—tells the press 'Please, I don't want no interviews,' " Rose begins. Her voice trails. "I mean you can't rehash. A person had just taken part of my life away. It's a part of my heart that was gone.

"Some of the people would say 'I'm sorry. It's my job.' But why do they have to keep prying and prying? Somebody was out there who had done a killing. A sick man. He killed a girl. A woman. A child. Whatever. Later when he killed again, the press kept coming back to us. I'd come off the subway train from work and they'd be there. After a while I thought the killer needed help. I thought he himself wanted to be caught. I thought he didn't want to live anymore himself. Because what would his life be? Nothing?

"But the same questions from the press over and over again. One fellow in particular. It was a circus."

MIKE LAURIA: "It's like my wife says. Donna had been the life of the party. We'd walk into a room and if Donna was there, she'd bring out happiness. She was a good girl, a proper girl.

"You take a writer into your confidence. You try to be

honest with them, but they can't print what you say or how you feel. There was one individual. He wrote a book with an associate. He made the girls who were shot look like tramps, every single one of them."

Lauria is referring to Jimmy Breslin, the *Daily News* columnist, and a television sportscaster named Dick Schaap. They collaborated on a novel called *.44.* The publisher promoted the book intensely, even offering book salesmen gathered at a convention in Atlanta a free boat ride down the Chattahoochee River with Mr. Breslin. Referring to the book, the May 22, 1978, issue of *People* magazine states "It's difficult to remember a more exploitative reach for the big bucks."

"Aw, forget about it," Mike Lauria says finally.

At 1:30 A.M. on July 29, Detective First Grade John Sheridan, forty-nine, was "next up" in the Eighth Homicide Zone in the Bronx. A six-foot, 210-pound, slightly balding man, Sheridan had spent twenty-seven years on the New York City police force. Because of the heavy caseload in the Eighth Homicide, which worked out of the Forty-third Precinct on Benedict Avenue, the Bronx, Sheridan had no partner that night. He would have to investigate the report—"Two women shot, 2860 Buhre Avenue"—by himself. He might have asked for a partner from a neighboring district, but he was a professional. He had worked alone before.

A former police commissioner named Patrick J. Murphy, known on the force as "a chilly-eyed theoretician," had been dismayed by the elitism of the detective division. During his three years as commissioner, Murphy restructured the division in 1972, cutting 1000 of the 3000-man force, putting the detectives under special commands.

Detective Sheridan began his investigation by talking to Jody Valenti in a treatment room at Jacobi Hospital. He began with quiet, easy questions. She was shaking with shock and horror.

Twice doctors insisted that Detective Sheridan stop his questioning. But since the best time for interrogation is immediately after an event, before details slip away or irrelevancies and imagination cloud the memory, he persisted.

After half an hour, Jody said that she had seen the killer and that he "resembled" one of her friends. The friend was not the killer, but perhaps his face could serve as a model for a physical description.

Sheridan made a note of the man's name. He would check him out. There were other questions, too.

Sheridan returned to Buhre Avenue at 8:00 A.M. Jody's blue Oldsmobile was parked within ropes designating a criminal search area. People on their way to work stopped to look. Patrolmen spread among them, asking if they knew anything, if they had seen anything, heard anything.

"Shots," some people said. No one could offer more.

Sheridan studied the scene, his feet grinding bits of glass into the street. Then he visited the Lauria apartment. He learned the name of Donna's boyfriend.

Vinney joined Jody's friend as a suspect. This is in no way a reflection on either man. Rather, it points up the fact that most times the killers know their victims. If Guinevere had been found hacked to death in Camelot one morning, the prime suspects would have been Arthur and Launcelot.

During the next twenty-four hours, Detective Sheridan devised a theory. The killing was possibly mob-related. A hit man had simply made a mistake. There had been several other mob-related shootings in the neighborhood. Detective Sheridan dismissed the possibility that a psychopath had pulled the trigger. Perhaps his theory would have been different if he had worked with a partner . . . but he had not.

Back at the Eighth Homicide, he typed the report. This was going to be a complicated case. Sheridan, who would take his pension in a few months, was thinking of retirement and did not want to undertake a protracted murder investigation.

He spoke to his Lieutenant, John Powers, and on Friday, July 30, the shooting of Donna and Jody was assigned to younger men: Detectives Richard Paul, thirty-seven, and thirty-nine-year-old Ronald Marsenison.

4

Soldier
of Misfortune

There is a theory, which Army recruiters and even certain judges do not discourage, that a term of military service straightens a bent youth. By the time David Berkowitz enlisted at the Army Induction Center on Whitehall Street in Manhattan on June 23, 1971, he regarded himself as not merely bent but battered.

He was still wounded by his fostermother's death. He felt wounded afresh when his father married Julia in 1971. "She meant well," David insists. "Dad was happy and that's all that mattered. I always told people that she was generous to me, but we didn't get along.

"She had a different set of rules. She didn't give me any freedom, as my Dad used to. I never got into trouble. I used to come up at eleven, eleven-thirty at night. I never did anything bad and she would say something like . . .'' Berkowitz gropes for specific words and finds none. "It was different, the way I just didn't do things right.

"She made a comment to Dad on things I did. She had older children, like married with kids of their own already. When they came, I'd say hello and nothing else."

David was far from the model youngster he'd like people to believe he had been. Even at play, he was somewhat unusual. One of those who remembers him during his high school days describes David as the one bully "who took the ball and wouldn't give it back." Mrs. Lillian Goldstein, who lived just below David, remembers that as a younger child "he was a strikingly good-looking boy—nice and tall with brown wavy hair. But he was hyperactive and his parents had a difficult time coping with him. The kids would complain he'd hit them without provocation."

David says he enlisted in the Army "for a lot of sound reasons." Nat Berkowitz did not think the reasons all that sound. He suggested that David go to college.

"I'm not ready for those demands," David said.

He acknowledges that his new stepmother's presence made the independence of Army life seem attractive. "I wanted some adventure. I wanted experience of life, something different, you know? I had no idea what to do in college, what to major in. I wanted to serve the country and get an education through the Army."

In 1971, with the American Vietnam disaster on so many consciences, the Army generally was out of favor.

BERKOWITZ: "I sort of lived like behind the times. I wanted to see some action, prove something to myself. It was rebellion then against parents, country and stuff. Kids were hippies and into drugs. I guess, then, I was very patriotic. Nobody else, except a couple of people, were."

David passed the Army physical and psychological tests in July. His Army psychological assessment was that he was a normal recruit who would fit well in infantry training. He says he wanted to fight in Vietnam, but that the war was winding down. Troops were returning from Southeast Asia, not going there. He applied for duty in Korea "because my recruiter told me I could get from there to Nam, which was not true."

He served as an infantryman, rising to the rank of Specialist E4, and he patrolled the Demilitarized Zone between North and South Korea. "We saw North Koreans, but while there was a potential for action, we never had any. There were some North Koreans by the fences. On patrols, we guarded the bridges over the Inchon River."

Although he says he adapted well to Korean barracks life, he was prone to minor problems in his garrison. His record indicates an inclination to be late. Once, with the Second Infantry Division, he simply missed a truck convoy he was to ride. On another occasion, he went AWOL overnight, missing a bus back to his unit. He was fined $50 and had his rank reduced from E4 to E3.

According to his fellow soldiers, Specialist David Berkowitz was nothing so much as an average guy. The one possible significant comment comes from Davi Zammit, who says "Whenever barracks banter about sex came up, David would back off."

When David talks about Korea, either to his counsel or to court-appointed psychiatrists, his statements are contradictory: "I got there in the unit and I was really, you know, just out of training. I was really gung-ho, super straight. Everyone who got there, changed. Wow! When we got exposed to everything, everyone changed. Almost everybody went crazy.

"There was all the women in the village [of Kumwa], you know, and we used to start smoking dope.

"There were prostitutes in the village. If you wanted. It only cost a couple of dollars. But you had to stay clean. It was important to me. You could only go so far with them. They were willing. We lived like millionaires there, every GI.

We had so much money. The women wanted so little. We really partied.''

The off-duty hours of the tiny garrison were spent in listless activity, smoking pot, indulging in harder drugs. The activity officer attempted to organize baseball games, with little success. Staging area CHARLIE had become the backwash area of an ancient conflict. The soldiers were merely pawns in a cold war game of chess being played thousands of miles away in Moscow and Washington.

"Drugs were very heavy. The guys there zonked out. They used alcohol. There was a group there called 'the juicers' that would stay with alcohol. Like Southern guys, Indians, Mexicans. They would constantly be going to the village and you would have to drag them back. They had Korean Champagne. That's a good name for it. It like cost fifty cents a bottle. Korean Champagne.

"If you weren't 'a juicer' you smoked dope. If you didn't do that you were just a redneck. You didn't do anything but fight. [David says he refused to be drawn into brawling.]

"The guys had all types of drugs. At first I tried to resist, but everybody else was doing all types. Guys came into the barracks really zonked. After a while I went into drugs, except for heroin. Speed. Uppers. Downers. Acid. Mescaline. Whatever was brought in. Stuff that everyone's using now. Stuff that sounds American. I liked pot best. I didn't do too much of the other stuff, very little, really. [It is questionable, suggest some who knew him then, that David ever indulged in anything stronger than occasional pot-smoking.]

"Since I got back from Korea, I had pot two or three times. As for acid over there, I only did it a couple of times. Maybe not even that often. They're not that bad, trips. Like —they used to have these little tablets. I never did a whole one, just about a half, *I never liked to be out of control.* Some guys would really—the whole place was just so drug-infested they used to come along every other week to raid the place.

"When I got back, I still had eighteen months to do at Fort Knox. At Fort Knox I didn't touch nothing. I was clean. Korea, that was the right place for drugs."

David's only experience with sex, he claims, happened in Korea. He later told one lawyer he had achieved penetration, but he refused to confirm this in other conversations with other lawyers or psychiatrists. The prostitute he knew best was a Miss Chet. He claims to have stayed with her on and off for a month, thanks to a series of overnight passes he was able to get. He paid her fifty dollars for that month, which was a great sum of money for a Korean. Usually, "I protected myself because we used prophylactics, but not with her. She was very clean. But, before I met her, I got gonorrhea once, when I first got to Korea. I remember being treated by the medics for it with big, two-foot-long shots of penicillin, one in each hip. I couldn't drink soda or alcohol. I just drank milk and was cured in about a week. [David's medical records for his Army years show no such treatment.] One of the guys, a friend of mine, had gonorrhea seventeen times."

Therapists, viewing David Berkowitz from the vantage point of hindsight, see his boasting as that of a ten-year-old. Knowing that David refused to participate in the usual banter in which soldiers indulge, they see his boastings as being that of an outcaste desperately attempting to be "one of the guys," and possibly even better than the boys.

While in service, David wrote frequently to Nat and to Iris Gerhardt. He had failed to pass his first marksmanship test in Fort Dix, but near the barren hamlet of Nieywah, Korea, he became a Sharpshooter with an M-16. A Sharpshooter ranks between Marksman and Expert and means the rifleman scored better than 44 hits out of 50 shots.

"They taught me how to fight," he wrote to Iris Gerhardt. "In Fort Dix, New Jersey, during basic training they taught me about weapons, demolition, riot control, self-defense, all of these courses will come in handy one day—I plan to use them—and it isn't going to be in the way of lifers [career Army men] want me to use them. I'll use these courses, these tactics to destroy them the way they destroyed millions of people through the wars they started. One day there will be a better world.''

When David saw this letter in Kings County Hospital, he said he was amazed that he had written it. He reacted as if someone had written the letter for him. To David, Korea had become a totally foreign experience. It was a classic case of someone who wants to forget a disturbing part of the past by simply having the mind block it out. Thus, his letter to Iris was no longer David's letter.

"I never knew I wrote that. At the time I was really gung-ho. At other times I really felt I was going to revolt against them [his Army superiors]. But it never turned out like that. In Korea there was no morale. Everybody was against lifers. Everybody was radical. *Everybody* wanted to revolt against the United States.

"I was fucked up! Being fucked up was the way you get in the Army. Everybody is down on you. Old lifers, you just can't please them. Petty stuff. Ask the other soldiers what it was like. They all felt the same way, all wrote the same stuff home. Lots of the guys wrote they were going to revolt.

"The black guys had their own thing. They were very rebellious. They used to have their own signs, and stayed with their own group all the time. We white guys had ours, but there were no hidden messages there.

"I wasn't religious in Korea. Maybe sometimes I felt that way from drugs and stuff. It's all so irrelevant.

"That was just the Army.

"One period of time.

"I was different.

"I had different views.''

Obviously, David is unclear about his Korean soldiering days. He learned to shoot well, but he would "get" the career Army men who taught him marksmanship. He was "ten thousand miles" away from imagined bad times in the Bronx but "the Koreans hated you and the Army lifers hassled you constantly." He had no sex but caught clap. Korea, where he sometimes says he learned and grew "was nothing but a bad dream."

He recalls writing letters home that were meant to be "shocking." Then, again, he says "It really wasn't that way."

Whatever Korea actually may have been for Berkowitz and for other soldiers there in 1972, the experience was not what Irving Berlin's jingle suggests. In reality, Army life is just as likely to create a "fuck-up" as make a man.

AFTER TEN MONTHS in Korea, Berkowitz was reassigned to Fort Knox, Kentucky. "I never saw the gold there," he says. "They had armed guards. They wouldn't let me go near it."(The U.S. gold hoard at Fort Knox was estimated at $200 billion dollars when David arrived, in January 1973.)

In Korea, Berkowitz had been a radio operator in an armored personnel vehicle. He had also been required to mop floors. At Fort Knox, he was made clerk-typist, which he describes as a "very responsible position."

"All my time at Fort Knox," he says, "I was an A-Number-One soldier.

"I didn't use drugs, just a couple of pills, occasionally. Maybe, once a month someone would have pot. It was very straight down there. You couldn't socialize. Louisville had bars, but Knox itself was a dry town. Elizabethtown, the other town, would have lots of booze, places all along Interstate 65. The guys used to drink a lot. I didn't have much money, so I couldn't go out like that much. I spent a lot of time on post doing nothing.

"Every day you would go back to the barracks. There would be a hundred guys there. It was all so ridiculous. If we went into Louisville, there would be one girl and about eight or nine guys with their hands on her. So you had to find other things to do. Sometimes you kept to yourself and masturbated.

"You could go to Louisville and get a prostitute, but it cost a lot of money. In Korea you could get a prostitute for a whole night, for a week, for fifty dollars. But in Louisville, it's like New York. They want forty dollars or fifty dollars. Ridiculous. I never bothered with them in Louisville. The prostitutes there were dirty too. The girls in Korea were pretty. The prostitutes I saw in Louisville were not attractive.''

Berkowitz's general conduct at Fort Knox was excellent and he received good efficiency reports. He was considered a prime choice for special Army efforts to get him to reenlist.

He even won back his former rank of Specialist E4. In off hours he "chummed around" with barracks buddies. He played softball, bowled, and went to post movies.

The outstanding event of this period in the life of David Berkowitz, born Richard David Falco, was spiritual. The former Bronx bar-mitzvah boy became a Baptist.

A POINT the distinguished theologian, Will Herberg, made during the years when David Berkowitz was growing up in an undistinguished corner of the Bronx was that American religion was becoming, so to speak, homogenized. The three largest organized faiths, Roman Catholicism, Judaism, and the central Protestant sects, were so influencing one another, so interborrowing ideas and even ritual that the conventional way of regarding U.S. religion no longer made much sense. We no longer had three separate faiths, drawing from heritages of Europe and Asia Minor. Rather, Herberg postulated, we had a single faith. He called it, perhaps cynically, "The American Way of Life Under God." At about that time, too, President Dwight Eisenhower voiced an unconscious echo of Herberg's theory. "I don't care what religion an American is," Eisenhower said, "so long as he believes in God."

Herberg's point, articulated in a small, brilliant volume called *Protestant, Catholic and Jew,* at once looses the wrath of many conventional religious spokesmen.

"What," one hears, "does a strict San Francisco Irish Catholic have in common with a Brooklyn Hasidic Jew?" Well, both regard birth control and abortion as sinful and both speak of rival social systems—say, the Soviet Union—with righteous apostolic hatred.

How do Arkansas Methodists and Manhattan Reform Jews emulate one another in places of worship? Both have adopted similar mixtures of sacred music and responsive readings.

It is not possible or necessary in the story of a killer wholly to summarize Professor Herberg's philosophical points. But one of his concerns that seems relevant to David Berkowitz is this: As Catholicism, Protestantism, and Judaism become more alike, each is diminished rather than enlarged. The American religious experience, Herberg suggested, was becoming interchangeable, convenient, superficial.

Before the advent of the catered commercial bar mitzvah —the pop-bar mitzvah of today—a boy was required to attain scholarship and truly to reach for faith before he could make the Jewish ritual passage into manhood. He had to read the Torah—the first five books of the Old Testament. He had to learn Hebrew. Teachers labored to instruct him in the Talmud, a long, difficult series of books considering God and man, good and evil, as propounded by Jewish scholars across twenty centuries. No Jew who underwent such training thought in Methodist or Roman Catholic patterns. He may not have been sure how to define a Jew (scholars are forever arguing definitions) but he would unquestionably have been certain of something else. As one rabbi puts it, "Whatever a Jew may be, it's me."

Growing up in a lower-middle-class household, David Berkowitz was Jewish in name and heritage but hardly in lofty aspects of Jewish spirit. Thus he casually dismisses one rabbi as "a drunk." He resisted serious religious training because he would rather have been playing baseball and also, one suspects, because he was lazy. When he was bar mitzvahed at Temple Adath Israel, David's total knowledge of Hebrew consisted of four paragraphs, learned by rote, to be repeated without understanding.

One cannot argue that a severe religious training necessarily brakes murderous inclinations. Indeed Torquemada, spearhead of the Spanish Inquisition, thought he killed in Christ's name. Josef Stalin was once a seminarian. But in the specific case of Dave Berkowitz, there was no real religious training at all. This may have contributed to his confusion, his madness.

"I began searching for a kind of religion at Fort Knox," Berkowitz says. "There was an emptiness there, you know, with God. The meaning of life. I used to read a lot. Soul-searching, you know. They had guys in the barracks, like really Christian. They used to go to church all the time. One of them, John Almond, used to ask if I wanted to go along. One day I did. I went to church. The service was really uplifting. Men, women, children, singing, holding hands. I never felt anything like that before in my life.

"I considered converting, I wanted to go to church. I used to go there quite a bit for a time. But not to lose my Jewishness. I mean, I still wanted to be a Jew. But I didn't want to miss church either.

"I finally converted." On May 18, 1974, David was baptized in the First Baptist Church, along with more than twenty others. "I went through the thing. They wanted to dunk you in water. Yeah. I went through it [the immersion] because you're supposed to, if you want to get in there. You know. Join. I didn't want to lose my Jewishness. But again, I wanted to be with these people.

"I told them I was Jewish. It didn't matter. What they wanted me to say was like the minister he was the Lord. You say 'I do.' It was a very warm feeling standing there. They accept you. They crowd around. I wanted to accept them. I knew that if I accepted Jesus, I was giving up my Jewish religion. But I didn't think it [sic]was related. I'm still of Jewish blood.

"After the baptism, the group accepted me. I continued to pray as a Christian. But, towards the end of my tour at Fort Knox, I began to lose interest in Christian stuff. I could never stay with anything too long."

QUESTION: David, can we talk about going from embracing baptism in 1974 to your feeling that you were a tool of demons only two years later? Have you thought about that?

BERKOWITZ: I just don't know. I don't know what happened.

QUESTION: There's a lot of talk in the Baptist belief about sin and repenting; in other words, of bad people becoming good.

BERKOWITZ: I didn't say I was bad.

On June 24, 1974, the Army gave Berkowitz an honorable discharge.

He returned to New York City a few days later. As far as he remembers, he never attended a Baptist service again.

IN DECEMBER 1975, armed robbers held up Nat Berkowitz's hardware store. Nat was sixty-five years old. He'd had his fill of the excitement and perils of New York. "The robbery was the final straw," Nat says. "That did it. I hadn't lived this long so a thug could shoot me to death." He packed up and moved to Florida.

Thus, with the fabric of his family life eroding, David found his job at I.B.I. Security and also enrolled at Bronx Community College on the old campus of the NYU College of Arts and Pure Science, "to better myself."

"I didn't study anything in particular," he says. "The first half I had to take all these remedial courses because I had been out of school so long. They started bugging me about making a decision on what I wanted to do. I put down plastics. I don't know just why. I didn't want liberal arts, because you have to mess with a foreign language. Stupid. I wanted to go to college to specialize in something, but I didn't know what."

David attended class sporadically at Bronx Community College, completing the year. Jessie Roberts, a fellow student, remembers David as someone who "sometimes sat in the back of the room, not participating. More often than not, he was absent."

An official at the college said: "There is nothing in the young man's college records to distinguish him from any other student."

His Jewish upbringing had not taught Berkowitz to do justice, love mercy, and walk humbly with his God. The Army had not made him into a recruiter's image of a man. His baptism did not bring him near the paths Christ is said to have trod. His time at college did not open the ways of culture.

But there is more than sad emptiness to these years. No rabbi, minister, teacher, professor, no Army officer or psychologist recognized that Berkowitz was developing into a madman.

"When I came home," he says, "there was this other Army. It was an Army of rank and rules. This was an Army that created chaos. This was an Army dedicated to battle."

His puffy face shows pain.

"It was not an Army of good."

5

Hounds of Hell

David looks at all life following his Army discharge as a season in Hell. People, specifically his fosterfather Nat; his Army friend Billy Dan Parker; and presently his natural mother, Betty Falco, possessed real and even coherent importance to him. But other individuals metamorphosed in his mind. These became phantasmagoric characters, part earthly and part supernatural.

As important as the people were the dogs.

David did not have a pet dog as a child, but growing up in a city, you see dogs more than other animals. You encounter them in streets, in empty lots, and classrooms:

> See Spot
> See Spot run.
> Spot is my dog.
> Spot is a good dog.

Perhaps a pious schoolteacher even points out that *dog* spelled backward is *God*.

David remembers being bitten by a dog when he was ten.

"There wasn't any blood. Just a scratch." He speaks of a Bronx friend, Glen Eapolito, who owned two German shepherds. Although "one was a real menace," David talks casually of playing with Eapolito's animals. He was bitten by a guard dog at I.B.I. Security in 1974. "This was a wolf with sharp teeth. I still have a scar from that attack. I had to show that dog something. I bit him back." Berkowitz smiles his slow smile to let you know that he is making a joke. "Actually, I took the chain to him. I wasn't afraid."

All this seems within normal bounds. David said he was surprised at how easy and pleasant it was to turn a tour of duty for I.B.I. Security with guard dogs. But even as he worked regularly with attack animals in late 1974, David began to observe his own variety of German shepherd from his apartment at 2161 Barnes Avenue in the Bronx. Peering around the blankets that draped the windows, Berkowitz looked into a concrete courtyard and saw "demon dogs."

"They looked like dogs, but they had many human qualities. They could talk. They acted human. But they weren't. They weren't human or dogs, either. They were demons. They began to howl things. Yell like maniacs. They threw tantrums. Strange things. It was vicious. Saliva used to drip down their mouths. They wanted to get at children, to tear them up. Young children!

"I had come under torment," David says. "There was constant noise, howling noises, howling, howling. Everybody heard it. I never spoke to anyone about it. But I know everybody heard it. They *had* to hear it."

At 2:00 A.M. on March 2, 1975, David decided to stop the howling. He slipped into clothes and workboots without socks and pumped a shell into the firing chamber of his Ithaca-Deerslayer 12-gauge shotgun (Serial #371494956). As he went down the stairs, the howling seemed to increase. He shoved open a fire door at ground level. The moon was full. He climbed two concrete steps and saw what appeared to be a muzzled German shepherd. The animal grew silent, turned, faced him.

It only appeared to be an animal.

In David's mind, other dogs were darting about, baring their fangs.

It was not an animal that faced him, David decided, and it was more than a demon. It was the leader of the other demon dogs.

David moved to within three feet of the muzzled shepherd. When he fired, he hit the dog dead on. The disfigured creature pitched backward, bounced against a wall, and flopped on the concrete courtyard. Bits of shattered bone, fur, and flesh lay atop a pool of blood.

David hurried upstairs. The leader of the demon dogs was dead. But back in the moist stagnant air of his apartment, he heard the howling start again.

WHEN DAVID moved into the two-story red-brick home of Jack and Nann Cassara in New Rochelle the following February, his fantasies extended to humans. Once again the demons had fooled him. They were intent upon causing him financial ruin. They had made him move twice already and the expense taxed his meager bank account. The Cassaras seemed nice enough at first but, after he moved in and had left his security deposit, "things" began again.

From February to April 1976 he tried to cope with the demons. David says "my one-room apartment above the Cassaras' garage was too confining." There was no shelter from the ever-present howling. Then, slowly at first, David says, he began to tie humans with the dogs. Of course the Cassaras were not part of any demon group, but in David's fantasies Jack Cassara was part of a mystical Army out to recruit him. Cassara became Jack Cosmo, General Jack Cosmo, commander in an Army of demon dogs that roamed New York, New Jersey, and Connecticut.

It was no use. They forced him to flee again, forfeiting his security deposit of $200. "I just couldn't go back. They would have been waiting for me. They had everything planned. Their dog's barking made things so bad that sometimes I couldn't come home to sleep. Finally, it became too much. It all was too much. Sometimes I had to drive around all night." Driving became David's way of trying to clear real and imagined noises from his mind.

"When I met General Cosmo," David says, "he looked like an average man. But he was deceptive. After I got my stuff moved, he let loose his demons in the yard. They tore my head off.

"They constantly yelled, constantly howled, threatened. They were nasty, belligerent, blaspheming everything, every-body. God, people, the mayor—Abe Beame!

"One night it was so bad I couldn't sleep. I stormed out of the house yelling. The general [Cassara] came out. He said 'What's going on? What are you doing?' I yelled at him: 'STOP!' He acted like he didn't know what was going on. He had a smirk on his face. But then he made it stop, just for a little spell. Until the next morning, until the next day."

In New Rochelle the demons began to explain what they wanted. "They called up to me from the yard. They came into my head. They told me what they were. Demons. Who Jack was. General Jack Cosmo, General of this region of demons. He wanted people to die. That's it. Pretty simple.

"The demons needed blood. The feeling of killing innocent people. The feeling of killing and defying God. It was war. They're still battling, still fighting. They need that blood.

"Me? I never needed or wanted blood. But after *I* shot someone, the demons would move in and feast."

As DAVID goes deeper into himself, his relocation from New Rochelle to 35 Pine Street in the Glenwood section of Yonkers on April 15, 1976, becomes no mere neurotic flight from imagined prying in a private dwelling. David describes the move in terms of a last attempt to escape the demons.

For a little while, he says, he eluded them in Yonkers. He knew quiet. He was even able to sleep. But his psychosis was out of control by then. By May the whole neighborhood of Glenwood seemed to have become a realm of Satan.

He met Sam Carr, sixty-three, a gaunt man and an incessant smoker, who lived two blocks from Pineview Towers at
316 Warburton Avenue. Carr, owner of Carr's Telephone Answering Service, had three children, including a daughter
named Wheat, twenty-six, who was a Yonkers Police Department dispatcher. To David, Sam Carr was a duality. There
was the visible person Sam Carr, but within him lived another
creature, also named Sam, who was "a high official of the
Devil's legion." This demonic Sam worked directly under
General Jack Cosmo.

In the "Devil's chain of command," Sam had recently
replaced Robert Neto, whom David refers to as Joquin, who
lived at 18 Wicker Street, a three-story one-family frame
home David could see from his apartment. Neto shared it
with another imaginary character, the Duke of Death. David
says General Jack Cosmo had "demoted Joquin for not following instructions."

To David the adjacent house, 22 Wicker Street, occupied
by one John Wheaties, was "a Holiday Inn for Demons.
That's where the demons stayed. These demons traveled
through the earth, you know. Like on different missions.
They stopped at 22 Wicker Street to rest."

Here then was a quiet suburban neighborhood and a smat-
tering of ordinary suburban people. But David saw the neighborhood as an outpost of Hell.

DAVID found the early hours of May 16, 1976, particularly
painful. The demons tormented him so fiercely that he decided he must destroy them.

How do you destroy a demon, David?

"You burn him in the fires of Hell."

A demon is first of all an "indwelling evil spirit." But in
some interpretations, demons move freely between earth and
hellfire below. Can you destroy a creature native to flames by
burning? David believed that he could.

Before sunrise—at 5:00 A.M. on May 16—David gathered
equipment. He emptied what little remained of a half-gallon

bottle of table wine. He then poured in a flammable product called Red Devil Varnish Remover. He tore an old undershirt and stuffed a strip of cloth into the neck of the bottle, leaving a little cloth extended as a fuse. At his sink David had created a weapon that sometimes stops a tank—a Molotov cocktail.

David walked into the predawn dark of Pine Street, carefully avoiding street lamps. At the end of Pine going north, he made a left on Glenwood. Then he turned left again, onto Grove Street, and found himself directly behind his apartment house, Pineview Towers, which rises on a steep hill. He proceeded half a block south on Grove, then made a right turn into Wicker Street, until he stood just outside the low chain-link fence at the front of the white house numbered 18. Joquin lived there along with the Duke of Death.

There was no wind, no passers-by. Nothing distracted Berkowitz. Nobody could see him. He turned the wine bottle upside down, so that the cloth from his undershirt absorbed the varnish remover. He held it that way until liquid dripped to the pavement.

He turned the bottle right-side-up and lit the wick. Then he threw his Molotov cocktail toward 18 Wicker Street and fled.

He did not stop running, he says, until he had returned to his apartment. He locked the door. He stood against the door listening for the death shrieks of demons, caught in an auto-da-fé.

Instead he heard sneering laughter. Immortal demons snickered at him for trying to destroy them with a weapon from the wars of mortal men.

There is no record that anyone reported the fire-bombing to the police. That was May 16. Exactly eleven weeks later Berkowitz murdered Donna Lauria.

A savagely tormented man had become a savage.

MURDERING Donna Lauria won David Berkowitz at best a couple of weeks of peace. He was insane by then, according to most reasonable definitions of madness, and when he saw

Donna's picture in the tabloids, he convinced himself that he loved her. Even so, the demons continued to play "sadistic" games on him, howling until he ran into the street at night to seek them out. Then they would simply laugh and hide in shadows. Sometimes he, in turn, would hide. But the demons made it a point not to emerge when he was watching.

On August 12, 1976, Berkowitz called 963-4900, the number of Yonkers police headquarters, to complain about Joquin. It was 4:00 A.M. when the dispatcher took the call. She listened and laughed, unable to discern whether or not the caller was drunk and simply bothering the police department. Because a tape records all telephone conversations that come into 963-4900, a report was taken down, then later disposed of. Ordinarily, an anonymous call obviously from an inebriated individual wouldn't have to be acted on. But this one was. Officers Chamberlain and Intervallo, on patrol in the area, were dispatched to look around just in case there was trouble. There was none. At least nothing visible.

ON THE NIGHT of October 19, 1976, a group of perhaps half a dozen young men who had never heard of David Berkowitz drank beer in the Taxcipo Grill in the Flushing section of Queens. It was a noisy, dark neighborhood beer joint, popular with young people in this mixed Jewish and Italian neighborhood.

"Hey, Carl," someone said. "The Air Force is gonna cut off all the hair you got."

Carl Denaro, who was twenty, grinned. He was six-foot-one, 180 pounds, and had long brown hair. He had graduated from high school and then, like Berkowitz, taken college courses part time. But Queens College, which he attended, was not, Denaro says, "my cup of tea." Neither were "a bunch of low-paying jobs." Also like Berkowitz, Denaro looked to the military "as an opportunity to learn." He had enlisted in the Air Force for a four-year term and he had been ordered to report for induction on October 27. Finally, like Berkowitz, Denaro had worked as a private guard. But Carl Denaro was not like David Berkowitz at all.

He and his friends looked back on the summer of 1976 in terms of Long Island beaches and girls who wore their bikinis well. One of those young women had been dark-haired Rosemary Keenan, eighteen, daughter of a New York City Police Department detective who was to work on the Son of Sam case.

October 19 was a stag night. "Carl," one of the young men said across his beer glass, "I hear they teach photography in the Air Force. You like cameras. Any chance they might let you take it up?"

"Maybe," Denaro said. "I'm gonna be in the Air Force for a while."

"Well, if they do and you get good, maybe you'll get to snap some *Playboy* models. And if you end up snapping some naked bunnies, remember who's buying your beers tonight. Don't forget all your old buddies here." Carl recalls this farewell party clearly, although today he has a steel plate in his skull.

Four days later, a Saturday night, Denaro was back at the Taxcipo Bar for a second, final farewell. He was selling his car, a 1974 Pontiac, for $1750. He had picked up a final paycheck, and Wednesday he would begin his Air Force career.

Good friends around him laughed and drank beer and danced to a jukebox that played "The White Room" and Frank Sinatra's "Strangers in the Night." The party broke up shortly after midnight, but Denaro stayed on for another beer. The bartender offered him one on the house.

Carl looked along the polished surface of the bar, glanced up, and saw Rosemary Keenan. He had met her in class at Queens College. Rosemary was sitting with another girl, but when Carl smiled and beckoned, she joined him. According to Denaro, they spent the next two hours "chatting and enjoying ourselves."

It was two-thirty. "If I get home this late," Rosemary said, "my dad says I should be escorted. You know. It's safer." Rosemary's father, Redmond Keenan, had twenty years' experience with the New York City Police Department.

"I'll take you home," Carl said.

"I've got my car," Rosemary said.

They drove eight blocks. Rosemary was at the wheel of her red Volkswagen. She braked at a stop sign and checked her rear-view mirror. A Ford Galaxie was behind them.

She proceeded up 33rd Avenue and found a parking space near the corner of 159th Street. They continued to talk. They did not touch. Rosemary remembers checking her rear-view mirror again. She saw a solitary jogger.

DAVID BERKOWITZ had been passing a miserable night. He heard the howling again. "It was the Blood Monster," he says, "Joquin the Joker."

For three hours he paced the studio apartment. At one forty-five he faced the dresser beside the bed. He picked up the .44 and caressed it. He made sure it was loaded. He put on clean underwear, soiled jeans, a striped shirt, and put the .44 under his belt on the right side. Then he donned a denim jacket that would conceal the gun.

He walked to his car and made his way down parkways, across the Bronx-Whitestone Bridge and into Queens. Just after 2:00 A.M. he was cruising through Flushing. At the corner of 159th Street and 33rd Avenue he pulled up behind a red Volkswagen at the stop sign. He noticed that the driver had long, wavy hair. He says he could not tell whether the driver was male or female.

"I drove around. I saw the two of them had parked the car. I pulled around the corner and parked and I just walked up behind them. I walked up on the passenger's side."

Berkowitz drew the .44 from his belt and fired five times. "Glass shattered," he says. "I stayed a couple of minutes watching." While firing, he noticed the passenger's brown jacket. He realized that one of the people at whom he was shooting was male.

Inside the Volkswagen, Rosemary screamed. "Let's get out of here." She drove back to the Taxcipo Grill and helped Carl Denaro into the bar, where he fainted.

She was terrified but unharmed. Carl, wounded by a slug in the back of his head, recovered after two months of treatment. Surgeons at Queens General Hospital had to replace shattered bits of his skull with a metal plate.

But his Air Force dream was dead. He would never become a photographer. He now works in construction in Long Beach, California.

THE NEXT DAY David Berkowitz studied the newspapers. The tabloids confirmed that he had indeed shot a man.

He also recalls a sense of surprise that the papers gave greater play to accounts of the final debate between Jimmy Carter and Gerald Ford.

Two candidates who shared flat speaking styles had stolen headlines from a man whose demons howled.

6

David and Betty

There is poetry, verse, and doggerel; each is different and only poetry is art. But any of them can be moving, as Noel Coward remarked with some disgust about cheap music.

For Mother's Day, May 12, 1975, David Berkowitz composed eight lines of doggerel. He had been searching for his real mother for nearly a year (or, as some will surely comment, all his life). Now he had found her. Reaching, trying to touch, he wrote:

> *So, as once before*
> *We've been Destined*
> *To meet once more.*
> *And I guess the time is now*
> *I should say hello—but how?*
>
> *Happy Mother's Day!*
> *(You were my mother in a*
> *very special way.) Love, R.F.*

Then, early that Sunday morning David Berkowitz, born Richard Falco, slipped the message into her mailbox.

THE DECAYING enclave of Coney Island lies between the affluent Brooklyn community of Manhattan Beach and the Atlantic Ocean. The tidal creek that once separated the island from the mainland was filled long ago to create a peninsula rather than an island. During the hot summers in the late 1940s and 1950s more than a million persons a day thronged to the beach and amusement area. Now the hundred-year-old resort has fallen into disfavor. Only the once-famous boardwalk and a scattering of food stands and amusement parks remain, spurred by the hope that casino gambling might arrive.

Betty Falco's three-room apartment on the third floor of a seventy-five-year-old building was immaculate. At ten in the morning she went downstairs and out of habit checked her mail. She found an envelope stuffed into the small metal box. It had been folded over many times, apparently pushed through the tiny slot rather than being delivered by the postman. It was marked. PRIVATE, MRS. BETTY FALCO (ONLY).

First things first. Betty visited a neighbor who was seriously ill. Thus it was noon before she sat down at her chrome-and-formica kitchen table and tore open the envelope.

Betty read and reread the enclosed poem. Under the initials at the end of the verse was a phone number. The initials R.F. meant nothing to Betty; nevertheless she dialed the number.

"Hello . . . hello" was the reply on the other end of the line, Betty remembers. "It sounded like a little boy."

"I received a note from you this morning. Who are you?" she questioned.

"I'm your son, Richard Falco," he answered. "You gave birth to me a long time ago . . . June first, 1953."

Betty's throat went dry. It was too much to ask. From a portion of her life she wanted never to remember, her son had appeared. "Richie, is it really you?"

"It's me, Mom. Richie."

Tears streamed down her face. She couldn't speak.

"Mom . . . Mom, are you still there?" the voice begged.

Finally she started anew. Her voice broke. "Richie, I can't talk now. I'll call back in a little while. Please wait."

"I will. Mom, I love you."

Betty dropped the receiver. Then she reached for it again. She dialed. "Roz!" she screamed into the mouthpiece. "I spoke to him. Richie! My son, Richie. Roz, he found me." Then she lapsed into uncontrollable sobbing.

Roslyn Rothenberg, thirty-seven, describes the next moments: "My mother was completely hysterical. She kept crying, 'My son. My son. My son. It's my son!' " When Betty grew calmer, the two women agreed to meet with David at Roslyn's home.

After speaking with her daughter, Betty Falco ran through her apartment building. "I was screaming," she says. "I called neighbors. I pounded on doors.

"They didn't even know I had a . . ." She cannot say the word *bastard*.

"And yet I was so thrilled I just had to tell."

Thus did Betty Broder Falco proclaim, in one small corner of P.~ ..klyn, that she had been found by her illegitimate son.

The following Saturday, May 17, Richard David Falco was reunited with his mother. The meeting took place at the home of Roslyn, his half-sister, who lived with her husband, Leo Rothenberg, and her two young daughters in the Glen Oaks neighborhood of Queens. Roslyn's house was only a mile away from where David would shoot another victim seventeen months later.

NAT and Pearl Berkowitz had told David that he was an adopted child when he was seven years old. It had started as a slip of the tongue on Nat's part, and David had persisted in asking what it meant to be adopted.

"If I'm adopted," he asked, "then what is my real name?"

"Falco," Nat answered reluctantly.

"That's a funny name," thought David. "It doesn't sound Jewish."

However, not until February 1975 did Nat show David the

Bronx Surrogate Court adoption papers. It was then that he decided to find his natural parents. He was not looking for a family tree so much as for a single root. But by this time David's sense of identity, and indeed his sanity, had begun to come apart.

David does not recall how he learned of the existence of an organization called ALMA (Adoptees Liberty Movement Association), which had been founded in 1971 by Florence Anna Fisher to help adopted children trace their natural parents. Every Tuesday evening ALMA met at Queens College and, in the early spring of 1975, David went to one of the open sessions. After about an hour, he turned to the young man sitting next to him. "How would I find out about my mother, even though she's dead?"

"How do you know she's dead?"

"She died in childbirth."

The young man laughed. "That's what they all say."

David got the idea to go to telephone books for the year he was born, stored in the Fifth Avenue branch of the New York Public Library. He started telephoning every single listing for Falco in Brooklyn. And so he tracked down his mother's new address.

Still, David was concerned that in years past his mother "really had no use for me."

Those who feel inexpressibly rejected may collapse.

Or take revenge.

"DAVID told me that he loved me," recalls Betty Falco. "He said that he understood that I must have had a good reason for giving him up. But most of all, he kept telling me that he loved me. That was everything to me. I never had hoped for something this wonderful."

David immediately became one of the family. It was something he longed for, something he had never had. As weeks passed, he made three to four trips on weekdays to his mother's apartment; on weekends he went to his sister's garden apartment in Queens. He always brought gifts: a present for Roz's girls or a cake for the family. "He fell in love with Roz's girls. Whenever the bell would ring, Lynn, nine, and Wendy, eleven, would race to the door to see 'Uncle Richie.' " David had found his roots.

But by mid-July 1976 his visits became more infrequent. When he did come, he stayed only minutes instead of hours as before.

On the morning of July 30, 1976, Betty Falco was shocked as she read in the newspaper that someone had slain a girl named Donna Lauria in the Bronx the night before and that a second girl, Jody Valenti, had been wounded.

On July 31, David visited his sister. He complained of headaches. "Richie," she asked, "have you seen a doctor?"

"Yes," he replied. "I've seen a couple and they tell me I'm very sick. One of them said I have a brain tumor."

Horrified, she pursued the matter. "Let me take you to someone, please." But her brother wouldn't hear of it.

Within a month, Nat Berkowitz called Roslyn. David had written him about some of the things that were bothering him. And David had complained on the telephone about headaches. Nat felt his son needed psychiatric help. He remembered "David standing in front of the mirror pounding his head with his fists."

But David had refused to allow his father to help him. In an act of desperation, Nat appealed to Roz. "Please, Roz. Try to help him. He has nowhere to turn."

"I've tried, Nat. But he won't let me."

"Please, Roz. Try again."

"I will. I promise."

In the early fall of 1976, David's visits all but stopped. "He claimed that he had a new job that kept him from coming," remembers Roz.

"We were sad he wasn't visiting us often, yet glad his new job was going so well. I knew once things became routine at work he'd come more often," recalls Betty Falco.

But she was wrong. His last visit was on Thanksgiving night—November 25, 1976—and when he started to return home, traffic was unusually heavy even at that hour. "Leo suggested that David stay over for the night," says Roslyn. "Wendy slept with my mother. David slept in the room with Lynn.

"David had a restless night. He finally got up and raided the refrigerator. He just couldn't sleep. He was like an animal on the prowl." Today Roz doesn't want to think about what might have happened. "David told me, 'I'd never hurt you or the girls.' I didn't know what he meant."

The next night David would pump bullets into two young girls.

THE evening of November 26, 1976, was cold and windy.

Donna DeMasi, sixteen, had planned to spend at least the first days of the Thanksgiving vacation at home, studying and completing all her high school assignments. However, just as during the previous Christmas holiday, her good intentions were sidetracked. A few words from Joanne Lomino, eighteen, on the telephone were all that were needed to postpone the night's study schedule. Both girls were normal teenagers, growing up, living their lives as a great adventure. At times their studies took a back seat to the world about them.

By 11:45 P.M. the girls had traveled to and from Manhattan to see a movie and have a hamburger. The bus dropped them off at the corner of Hillside Avenue and 262nd Street, less than fifty yards from Joanne's house. Joanne said: "Isn't that Maria?"

Donna looked across Hillside Avenue. "Yeah, it is."

Joanne called out to her friend, who was with two other girls: "Maria, come on over." The girls met on the corner. "How come you didn't want to join us in the city?" Joanne asked.

"My mother said if I went tonight I couldn't go tomorrow."

Donna checked the time; it was 11:55 P.M. She had a curfew, 12:30 A.M., and it was time to go. It was then that she noticed a figure standing behind a nearby lamp post. "Joanne, there's a guy watching us over there. He's kind of scary. Let's walk faster." They headed directly for Joanne's house at 83-31 262nd Street. The man followed. In thirty seconds they reached the bare concrete stoop of the Lomino home and hurried up the three steps to the front door. Joanne fumbled inside the pocket of her furry white coat for the key. In the excitement her fingers missed them. Donna turned to see if the man had followed. Not seeing him, she relaxed. "I don't think he's . . ." Her sentence cut off in midword as the man came into view.

The man had walked along the opposite side of the street, paralleling their movements. When the girls stopped at Joanne's house, he was already past them. He recrossed the street and started walking toward them, his hand groping at his waist. He took deliberate steps. He was in no hurry.

"I watched him step onto the sidewalk and come toward us," remembers Donna.

Recalls Joanne: "He walked at us from the right. It didn't look as if he was really going anywhere."

Joanne said to Donna "Just wait here with me until he leaves."

"Yeah. He looks kind of spooky," answered her friend.

The man stepped onto the gentle rise of grass that separated him from the girls. He began to speak. "Do you know where . . ." He never finished.

"He reached under his jacket and pulled out a gun. It was unreal," says Donna.

The girls watched in terror as the gun pointed at them. They turned toward the door, Joanne's hand tearing at the lock, the keys still in her pocket.

"And then he began shooting at us," says Donna.

The girls screamed, their voices lost in the noise of the exploding gun. Joanne felt a warmth come over her body as she fell. The first bullet shattered her lower spine and lodged there. The second shot struck Donna from the side, at the intersection of her neck and shoulder, passing within a quarter-inch of her spine, then exited the other side. Both girls fell off the small stoop, one on each side, into the low hedges Joanne's father, Charles, had planted a couple of years earlier. They fell into deep shadows.

"It all happened so fast," recalls Donna. "One minute I was standing; the next I had fallen into the bushes."

Seconds later three more "pops" went off. The man had emptied his gun at the house. The girls did not hear the sound of breaking glass. They were both in shock.

A few moments later a porch light came on at the house next door, 83-27 262nd Street, where off-duty police officer Ben Taormina had been watching a late-TV movie. He thought he heard a car backfiring and went to the door to investigate. It was dark and silent. He saw nothing on the street; cold air swirled around him. He closed the door, returning to the comfort of his living room.

"Donna . . . Donna. Are you okay? Please, dear God," cried Joanne. She was more concerned about her friend than herself.

Donna heard Joanne but was unable to reply.

In the Lomino home, everyone had been in their bedrooms. The sound of shots and breaking glass brought the family rushing downstairs, and Joanne's younger brother Charles, fifteen, found the girls. "Dad, something's happened to Joanne and Donna." Then "They've been shot!"

Charles rushed to the phone and dialed 911, the police emergency number. A squad car arrived within four minutes. Meanwhile Ben Taormina knelt beside the girls and took charge. Charles also called Donna's family. Her father, Maurice, and mother, Catherine, ran to Joanne's house, arriving just after the first police car.

An ambulance was dispatched. But before it arrived, the officers lifted Donna into their squad car and drove off to Long Island Jewish Hospital, less than two miles away.

"My God. You're shot!" Catherine screamed as she cradled her daughter's head in her lap.

"Please, Mom, don't let me die," Donna cried.

Her mother drew her close. "You'll be all right," she said. "You'll be just fine."

The officers radioed their dispatcher to alert the staff at Long Island Jewish Hospital that they were bringing a gunshot victim. On arrival, a trauma team lifted Donna onto a portable stretcher and wheeled her into the emergency room. Catherine was told to wait outside. She was drenched with blood.

"Do you feel your hands, Donna?" one of the physicians asked. "Your feet?" He poked a pin into the soles of her feet. The prognosis was good. No serious injury. Her nervous system had not been damaged.

By now the ambulance was at the Lomino home. Joanne still hadn't been moved. The attendants tied her onto a rigid stretcher and lifted her carefully. Joanne followed Donna to Long Island Jewish Hospital. After an hour the doctors told her family their initial prognosis. Joanne's spine was damaged beyond repair. She would be a paraplegic.

Her mother and father embraced, then sank to their knees.

"IT would be a night for hunting," David had thought as he walked to his car parked to the right of the entrance of 35 Pine Street. "It started right up, almost as if it knew I'd be looking again."

David drove across the Bronx-Whitestone Bridge and down the Cross Island Parkway south to Hillside Avenue. He chose to stay close to the Cross Island, for it would allow him to escape to his apartment quickly when he completed his mission.

At first he was driving aimlessly about his hunting ground, crisscrossing Hillside Avenue time after time. It was then he saw the girls.

"I saw them standing with their friends and I parked. By the time I was able to get back and hide behind the lamp post, they started to walk. I followed. They saw me and walked faster. By the time I'd crossed the street and got to them, they'd gotten to one of the girl's houses. They knew I was behind them and they tried to get in the door. One of the girls was wearing a maxicoat and calf boots. The other a white furry coat and black jeans. She had blonde kind of hair.

"I started across the grass to them. Everything was going right. They were right in front of me. I didn't want to get them frightened, so I began to ask them for directions. All the while I was getting closer.

"They turned back to the door for an instant, but it stayed locked. Then they turned their heads to me. I had the gun out and pointed it in their direction. Then I shot twice. They both were hit and they fell on either side of the stoop."

David watched with fascination as the girls tumbled like carnival dolls off the concrete platform. "It was just like it should be."

The entire action occurred in less than five minutes. Now it was like a movie, not like his clumsy attempts with a knife that Christmas Eve in 1975. "You shot them, and they fell. It was as simple as that."

In a burst of elation, David emptied the .44. He fired two shots at the front window of the Lomino home, shattering it. The last round was fired at the sky. David Berkowitz was happy. The demons wouldn't taunt him tonight.

QUESTION: Where were the girls when you fired at them?
ANSWER: They were face to face with me. They had gotten to the door, but it wouldn't open. They turned their heads to look at me, and I shot them.
QUESTION: Did you intend to kill them?
ANSWER: Yes.

7

"A Routine Homicide"

The police now had three seemingly unconnected assaults in two boroughs. Donna Lauria was dead. Jody Valenti had been wounded. Rosemary Keenan had somehow escaped the fusillade of bullets fired into her car. Carl Denaro was still in the hospital, as was Donna DeMasi and Joanne Lomino. Five people had been shot—all with a single gun—within four months. But the New York Police Department had not yet found, or even noticed, the link that joined the victims: David Berkowitz's Bulldog .44.

The problem was that in the three assaults, only one intact bullet was recovered. Meanwhile, like everybody else, the cops were noticing the cold. The winter of 1976–1977 attacked the city with an icy hand. Before its grip eased to warming winds in March, this winter would go on record as the second coldest in New York history. Snow fell first on November sixteenth. It didn't melt. Prices for fuel oil were starting to rise. The country was about to learn a new term: energy crisis. Amid such global concerns and the omnipresent cold, three unconnected assaults on young people were hardly front-page news.

David Berkowitz, still employed as a sheet-metal worker with Wolfe and Munier Co. in Elmsford, New York, spent warm, uneasy nights in his Yonkers apartment. He remembers his feelings of solitude and terror thus: "I am a sensitive person. I'm aware of things about me. I concern myself with something alive, like a bird or a plant. I love birds and plants; I always loved nature. People too. Yet I was never able to relate to people. I was always a loner. This was another thing that led to my downfall; I was a loner all the time!

"I had no defenses. It was my own fault for not seeking out friends. Without friends I had no defenses against demonic attack. I don't know why I was alone all that time.

"But," David concluded to psychiatrists Daniel Schwartz and Richard Weidenbacher in an interview two years later, "I don't want to be alone any more."

ON NIGHTS when he journeyed into the cold, David drove his Ford Galaxie in the Bronx and Queens, hunting. "On times I didn't hunt," he says, "Roz's family offered me the comfort of a life I never had. She had two daughters and her girls were everything to me. Also, there was my Mom . . . my real mother."

What did your real mother mean to you then, David? "She was my mother, that's all."

The cold was keeping people at home but neither bitter winter nor his real mother stilled David's demons. Like many schizophrenics David tends to repeat himself, to contradict himself, and to confuse his listeners. Indeed, he confuses himself. Classically, a schizophrenic—a crazy person—has lost touch with reality and with self. At times schizophrenics appear normal, even healthy, but a symptom of madness is the relapse into a reality-disoriented condition.

David's demonology is not controlled and calculated, like the demonology that slowly emerges from *The Exorcist*. That is a novel, inherently a controlled work, and the author, William Peter Blatty, is of course sane. David's demonology is wilder, less consistent than Blatty's fiction, more frightening. David believed his demonology was real.

According to David, for example, Sam, who inhabited the body of Sam Carr, "has been around for six thousand years. He's been around since the beginning of recorded time." (Earlier Berkowitz had learned, as we all did in school, that the world is much, much older than six thousand years.) "People should take me seriously," David says. "They should try to look into it. This Sam and his demons have been responsible for a lot of killing. The people should try to destroy Sam, if they can. It would be hard because Sam and the demons have been around for so long and they'll continue till the end, until God comes and destroys them in the last heroic final battle."

There is some altruism here and there is hopelessness. People should destroy Sam before he orders other killings. But people cannot really destroy Sam. Only God can, and even He will have to wait for Armageddon. In David's mind, who, then, is Sam?

Different things at different times, to be sure. David is a schizophrenic.

But who is the Sam who can be destroyed only by God, and only in the "last . . . final battle"?

A six-thousand-year-old man, as some tabloid journalists have speculated? Hardly. Sam is the Prince of Darkness, the ultimate fallen angel, the infinite evil. He is "a speck of evil cosmic dust that has fallen to earth and flourished."

Sam is the Devil.

"I am the Son of Sam," says David Berkowitz. Illegitimate, adopted David Berkowitz. Looking backward to the cold winter of 1976–1977, he says "It wasn't me. It was Sam that was working through me. I mean, me and the Son of Sam, there's just one body, but we weren't the same people. Sam used me as his tool."

Tool of the Devil.

What do you want most now, David?

"I want to be only David Berkowitz."

HE HAD GONE to bed at seven o'clock in the winter dark on January 29, 1977. He reached for sleep. Only in sleep now was he wholly free of baying demons. He lay in the dark and tried to sleep and he could not. He tossed in bed. He writhed. Three hours passed.

He rose to a sitting position and swung his bare feet to the chilly floor. He sat motionless. He recalls agitating thoughts. He dressed in the dark, slipping on jeans and a light jacket, although the temperature outside was 14 degrees. He walked to the dresser and broke open his pistol. The .44 was loaded. Then he ran down the stairway and into the street.

Hurrying toward the Galaxie, David fingered the gun tucked inside his waistband. Demons watched him from the shadows. If a demon sprang, David would use the gun right there.

It took David several tries to start the Ford. Then he sat for ten minutes waiting for the engine to warm and for the heater to start functioning. Meanwhile he contemplated the problems of good and evil. "People really don't know anything. They don't know what's happening in the world. Take the United States. Some people think it's the President that has his hand moving everything. Others think it's the rich people like the Rockefellers or the Kennedys. But it's neither of them, you know. It's forces, God and Satan. They have their hands in the world. One day God is going to bring peace into the world and there's going to be hope for mankind. I guess it was Satan's will for me to kill innocent people. It happens. Why? I don't know why. It just happened, but God will want to help people and in the end peace will win. People are dying every day in the most horrible ways. There's nothing we can do about it."

David perceived himself caught in a majestic cosmic battle, a pawn of occult forces beyond his control. "Without Sam I'm nothing."

He released the parking brake and drove to the top of Pine Street. Then he made a right turn onto North Broadway and proceeded to the intersection of Ashburton Avenue. From Ashburton he made a left onto Yonkers Avenue, which connects to the Cross County Parkway a quarter of a mile farther. He drove a mile and a half on the Cross County, passing over the New York State Thruway, and onto the Bronx River Parkway south.

David drove carefully. The roadway had patches of ice. In fifteen minutes he reached the toll booths at the northern side of the Bronx-Whitestone Bridge. The toll was seventy-five cents.

IN THE CONTINENTAL THEATER on Austin Street in Forest Hills, Queens, Christine Freund and John Diel sat holding hands, riveted by Rocky's gallant fight against heavyweight champion Apollo Creed.

Diel, thirty, worked as a bartender at a lounge in Ridgewood. He said he did not intend to spend his life mixing drinks, but he didn't seem to have any other specific ambition. That bothered Christine. She was twenty-six, a soft-voiced, slender, long-dark-haired Viennese woman whose good looks and gentle manner made her mother glow with pride.

After the movie they walked to a nearby restaurant called The Wine Gallery. The cold was so bitter that Christine's teeth were chattering.

Inside they found a table and ordered two glasses of wine. "I really liked Sylvester Stallone," Christine said. "Wasn't that a good picture?"

"Sure was," Diel said. "I liked it too."

"When he was fighting in the shorts . . ."

"Boxing trunks."

"I wondered how you would have looked up there."

They laughed. Diel was a sturdy, mustached man. Stripped down for the ring, he would have looked muscled enough to pass for a light-heavyweight boxer.

After a while, Christine felt warm enough to let her dark

coat fall from her shoulders to the back of her chair. She not only had relatives in Vienna but, eight years earlier, after graduating from Grover Cleveland High School in Queens, she had worked in Austria as a bilingual secretary for nine months. John Diel also had family and friends in West Germany.

They were comfortable with each other, loved each other, and regarded themselves as engaged to be married. They hoped to make the formal announcement in two weeks, on St. Valentine's Day. But as they drank their wine, Christine spoke of her parents, Olga and Nandor. "They're getting older," she said. "I worry about their health. It makes me uneasy to think of them getting sick. When I think of what they've done for me . . . the warmth of the home they've given me. I hope that I can do that for you, John, make as warm a home." They held hands and talked about having children; they weren't sure how many. It was a glowing evening for two young people in love.

They left The Wine Gallery at 12:10 A.M. for John's car, a blue Pontiac Firebird. He had parked it at Station Plaza, just off Continental Avenue. Other couples rushed by them as they walked under the tracks of the Long Island Railroad, a commuter line that cuts through the borough of Queens on its way to suburban redoubts in Nassau and Suffolk counties. Once through the underpass they turned left onto the small square called Station Plaza. The plaza was deserted; a darkened apartment building just ahead was flanked by a row of one-family houses. Just behind were the empty tracks of the railroad.

Diel unlocked the doors of the Firebird. Once inside the couple turned and embraced. After a moment Christine sat back. John started the car. Their breath began to fog the windows. The temperature outside was 5 degrees above zero.

DAVID BERKOWITZ had been cruising Queens in his cream-colored Galaxie. After a time, something suggested that Forest Hills was the place in which to hunt. He drove under the Long Island Railroad tracks, turned left at Green-way Terrace, and parked. Then he started walking.

He drifted about, with no set route in mind. He passed a pizza shop and looked inside. A wall clock showed 11:35. He kept walking. By twelve-fifteen he found himself near the Long Island Railroad tracks. At last he felt the extreme cold through his denim jacket. He pulled up the thin collar. Looking up, he noticed a couple hurrying toward him. "We just passed each other," he says. "We almost touched shoulders."

Berkowitz looked at the girl's face. She was extremely pretty. He noticed her long dark hair, flowing to her shoulders. He says he heard voices in unison uttering a command. "Get her. Get her and kill her." The voices repeated themselves and grew louder. Then David heard the voices say "Sam likes pretty girls and we do too."

David followed the couple at a distance through the Long Island Railroad underpass and quickly moved behind the trunk of a bare Norway maple. Its six-inch diameter did little to hide his bulky frame. But the couple were intent upon each other and hadn't noticed him. He stared as they entered the blue Firebird. He continued watching as the pretty woman pressed her body against the man.

He heard a din. Demons were clamoring for blood. He felt his heart pound. He stepped out from behind the tree and began shuffling toward the Firebird just as Christine leaned back to let John start the car. He hurried to the passenger side. He hurried toward the pretty girl.

"I don't remember what kind of car it was, a blue something. The engine was running and I just walked up from behind."

He wanted "just to kill her. I wasn't told to kill him. I aimed for her head, you know, quick and efficient. I guess practice makes perfect. I was able to control the gun, physically. After walking up, I stood in front of the window, crouched slightly. I brought the gun up with two hands. I opened fire. Three shots were all I had to use.

"The glass flew into the car and I hit her. I just wanted to kill her, nothing more. I only used three of the five shells in the gun. There really wasn't any reason to use them all. I knew I had hit her. I had to save my ammunition.

"After I shot her I began to run. I ran to my car. It was quite far away. It meant a long run for me. I ran past the Long Island Railroad and kept on going. I think I heard the car's horn blowing, and I think I heard the man get out. He began to scream. But by that time I was far away."

As he drove back to Yonkers, Berkowitz says, he knew that this time, as with Donna Lauria, he had not merely wounded a victim, but killed.

How could you be certain, David?

"The voices stopped. I satisfied the demons' lust."

JOHN DIEL remembers kissing Christine's lips. "Gently," he says. Then he turned and put one hand on the steering wheel and the other on the shift lever. He was still feeling the afterglow of the kiss when his world blew up.

He heard the frightful explosion of shots. He saw the right front window shatter into a shower of razor-sharp glass fragments. He heard Christine scream as two bullets hit her. She was struck in the right temple and in the neck. The third bullet spent itself against the dashboard.

John turned in panic. A trickle of glistening blood ran from Christine's head, through the soft, dark hair, and down the front of her coat. He put one hand on her head, as though to stop the flow of blood. It was warm and sticky. He pressed his other hand on the horn. He was crying in fright and shock. He called her name. There was no answer.

The midnight horn sounding on Greenway Terrace drew no response. Had nobody heard the shots? Was everyone asleep or dead? What the hell. Wouldn't anybody help?

Diel released the horn and groped for a door handle. Christine's body was silent and bloody and limp. He let her slump until her head rested on the driver's seat. John didn't know if he himself was wounded. (He was not.) He ran down deserted Greenway Terrace toward the Avenue, the empty tracks on one side, dark houses on the other, screaming for help.

Headlights shone and John ran toward the car. John was not aware of how he must have looked to the driver. Slivers of glass showed on his coat. His right sleeve was dark with Christine's blood. Seeing him, the driver neither slowed nor stopped, but sped away.

A second car approached. Diel tried to flag it down. This driver accelerated, almost running down the stricken man.

Suddenly Diel remembered Kitty Genovese. Thirteen years before a twenty-eight-year-old Queens bar manager named Kitty Genovese was attacked and murdered in an area called Kew Gardens. At first the killing was reported as a casual deed of violence. Later investigative reporting brought out something else. Kitty had screamed when she was assaulted on the street, at knifepoint. For thirty minutes she screamed her life away. At least thirty-eight people admitted they had heard her shrieks. During the first thirty minutes no one called the police. Nobody wanted to "get involved." No one left his or her apartment.

A third car appeared. Desperate now, Diel stepped into the center of the street and blocked its path. "My girlfriend has been shot," he called. "Please, please call the police!"

The driver surely heard him, but when John stepped aside, the car drove off, turning onto 71st Avenue.

Of course, people in the two-story houses on Greenway Terrace heard the shots. They heard Christine scream, then the horn and John Diel's calls for help. No one dared enter this suddenly violent street, but someone did dial the police emergency telephone number. And promptly, too. But time dragged for John Diel in his grief and shock.

Alone in the cold, Diel heard the far-off sounds of sirens. The noise drew closer. He ran back to the car and placed his face close to Christine's. He remained there until police tugged him away so that they could move Christine into an ambulance. The police had arrived four minutes after the shooting.

Christine's life hung in the balance. Within ten minutes an ambulance sped her to St. John's Hospital at the intersection of Queens and Woodhaven boulevards, a mile and half away. Doctors worked feverishly on her, but she never regained consciousness. At 4:00 A.M. she died.

"IT STARTED OUT as a routine homicide," Detective Sergeant Joe Coffey, forty-three, remembers. "I was seated with the Inspector, Richard Nicastro [fifty-seven], who was in charge of the Queens Detective Area, and he asked me if I'd be willing to go over and work with Captain Joe Borrelli of Fifteenth Homicide. I agreed and myself and another detective, Marlin Hopkins, began a thorough investigation. We came up with two theories quickly. One was that something in Christine Freund's past would explain the homicide. The other theory was that we were dealing with a psycho."

Joe Coffey, six foot three, has a handsome, chiseled face. Some of his colleagues say that he looks more like a movie actor than a cop. In reality, he is an experienced, rugged police officer.

When Coffey graduated from the Police Academy in 1964 he was assigned to the Tactical Patrol Force. To understand the TPF, you have to recall the 1960s, the decade of Vietnam, assassination, and rioting. Organized in 1959, the TPF was a band of physically imposing policemen trained in close combat. Tactical Patrol officers worked in high-crime areas, mostly black and Hispanic neighborhoods. One squad leader explained their mission to Coffey's squad in 1965: "Look, if the young blacks want to burn and riot, we can't stop them every time, but we can sure try to control the situation where it exists. We got the strength and the know-how to keep the situation contained. If they want to burn something, they'll have to deal with us."

Joe Coffey spent sixteen months on the Tactical Patrol Force, patrolling the most dangerous corners of New York City. He is said to have made a name for himself as a cop who was "bright," "energetic," and who "would certainly rise some day to a position of command." Coffey subsequently worked as a detective in the office of Manhattan District Attorney Frank Hogan. Later he was promoted to sergeant and transferred to Harlem, supervising twenty-five patrolmen. He knew investigative techniques, and when a Puerto Rican Nationalist group, the FALN, frightened the city by bombing historic Fraunces Tavern in the Wall Street area, Coffey was shifted to the Arson and Explosion Squad. He stayed there until January 31, 1977, the day after Christine Freund was killed.

That afternoon Sergeant Coffey was switched to a new unit under Captain Joe Borrelli's command. The group was called the Homicide Task Force.

ON JANUARY thirtieth—just minutes after midnight—the detectives in the Fifteenth Homicide heard about a shooting in the 112th Precinct. Detective Marlin Hopkins was working the 4:00 P.M. to 1:00 A.M. shift. Since he was "next up," he was assigned the case and raced to the scene. When he arrived, he found patrolmen attempting to question John Diel, who was walking about in shock. "Did you see anyone?" Diel was being asked over and over.

"I turned toward where the shots were coming from," Diel said, over and over, "but there wasn't anyone there."

There were no witnesses to the shooting. One couple in a building across Greenway Terrace had heard noise but, Hopkins discovered, "they had been partying and were unreliable."

The next day Hopkins was joined by Coffey; together they would reconstruct the evening with Diel. Later the two officers found people who had seen John and Christine at the movies and at The Wine Gallery. But nobody, except David Berkowitz, had seen the killing.

At first it seemed like one more unpleasant, difficult, but —from the point of view of a police professional—routine homicide. Since there was no weapon and no witness, Coffey could not be sure how many shots were fired. "It could have been five, two, or some other number. We recovered one slug from Christine's skull. The one that passed through her neck, like the one that missed, we took out of the dashboard.

"I put in an inquiry to all homicide zones to see if they had any unsolved yet similar cases. I didn't believe that the bullets came from a normal-caliber gun; they were just too big." He regards .25s, .32s, and .38s as normal. "From a preliminary check of the bullets, we felt they could have come from a .44, a .45, or maybe something even more powerful, like a .357 or .44 Magnum."

At nine the next morning, Detective Ron Marsenison of the Bronx Detective Area gave Coffey a call. "Joe, we have something that sounds similar to the one you guys got. On July twenty-ninth of '76 we had a shooting in our zone. Two girls late at night, one just getting out of their car. It was a large-caliber slug. I don't think it's your guy. This one looks like a professional hit by mistake. But I'll send you what I got if you want." Marsenison had been investigating, without luck, the .44-caliber killing of Donna Lauria.

"Thanks," Coffey said. This was a small link, but better than no link at all. Two murders, six months apart, with large-caliber weapons. Coffey called the office of the Chief of Detectives and asked for information on any large-caliber murders anywhere in the city during the last six months.

The answer came back quickly: one in Brooklyn, a false lead. Then they had an assault, but not a killing, in Bellrose, Queens. The victims' names were Joanne Lomino and Donna DeMasi.

Coffey called Borrelli, the Commanding Officer of Queens Homicide Detectives, to report his suspicion that a single madman, using a large-caliber handgun, might well be stalking victims throughout the city. A day later, February 2, a special Homicide Task Force was ordered created by Acting Chief of Detectives Martin E. J. Duffy. The sixteen-man unit would work out of the 112th Precinct, at Yellowstone Boulevard and Austin Street in Forest Hills—three blocks from the scene of the Freund killing. In command was Captain Joseph Borrelli.

No conclusive evidence linked the four attacks, thus Captain Borrelli did not include the Bronx detectives in his original unit. However, it was the first step toward an organized investigation of the shuffling Army vet who was beginning to think of himself as "Son of Sam."

CHRISTINE FREUND's bloody death was not enough for Berkowitz's demons. "They kept needing blood and if I didn't give them more blood when they wanted it, Sam would have done something real bad. Like kill multitudes. Once I remember his demons were howling all night long and I didn't do anything. The next day there was an earthquake. Where? Turkey, I think."

THE POLICE ballistics report was disappointing. The slugs fired into Diel's blue Pontiac were too badly fragmented to reveal the specific weapon from which they had come. But the weight of bullet fragments equaled those of a .44. That told something to Detective George W. Simmons, a ballistics expert. "I say you got yourself a psycho here," Simmons told Joe Coffey.

"Why do you say that?"

"The gun," Simmons said. "It looks like a .44 Charter Arms Bulldog, and that's a pretty rare weapon. I have three shootings here. Two girls in the Bronx: Donna Lauria and Jody Valenti. Two more girls named DeMasi and Lomino in Queens. And now this one, Christine Freund. I have all three, all with the same type gun."

The same *type* gun, but not the same gun. Not yet. Theories come more easily than evidence. Although Simmons and Coffey both suspected a single psycho, they lacked the evidence to support their belief. "With the little we had," Coffey said, "I had to run the string out." That meant an intensive investigation of John Diel.

First Coffey won permission from Olga and Nandor Freund to search the bedroom of their dead daughter. There he found a draft copy of a letter Christine had written to a German woman with whom John Diel had been having an affair.

"Christine's letter couldn't be classified as blackmail or extortion," Coffey said, "but it was close. I mean the tone of the note was, 'Okay. Either knock it off, or I'm going to inform your husband.' " The police filed the letter and Coffey remembers several thoughts. The German girl became a possible suspect. She might have flown to New York and shot Christine to preserve her own marriage. How serious was Diel about his "engagement"? Was he living a Captain's Paradise —loving two women in two countries simultaneously and being truly committed to neither? If that was so, then his engagement to Christine Freund could be a sham. And if it was a sham, couldn't Christine have turned on him in hurt and anger? And couldn't John Diel, provoked, have killed his girl?

The police questioned Diel for two months. He underwent hypnosis several times and took a polygraph test. "He was very cooperative," Coffey says, "and very emotional. Understandably emotional, considering what he'd been through. Still, you have to be suspicious. That's part of the job. There may have been a moment or two when I wondered if Diel's emotions were false. It turned out they were true, of course, perfectly true.

"But it was just about at the point when I was doubting John that Detective Simmons from ballistics told me his psycho theory. It wasn't so much of a theory as a gut feeling. Good detectives usually have that second sense. My own feelings tended to go with Simmons'. That would put Diel and the German girl out of the picture. But we had to satisfy logic, not feelings."

IT IS IRONIC that being murdered deprives a victim of all privacy. Not only is the body violated, but the spirit is also laid bare.

To this day, Olga Freund will not acknowledge the part of her daughter that wrote a threatening letter to a woman in Germany. Instead, she speaks of Christine as though the dead woman were still a child.

"She was very cute, quick and smart. She liked to sing. She spoke early and always had a song. She went to Catholic school and had to make the first year twice. When she got there, you see, she couldn't speak English.

"But in high school, her English was so beautiful that a teacher asked Christine if she was going to attend college.

"I still expect Christine to phone from work every day, the way she did. In the morning, I want to go into her room to wake her up.

"Christine was happy when other people were. . . ."

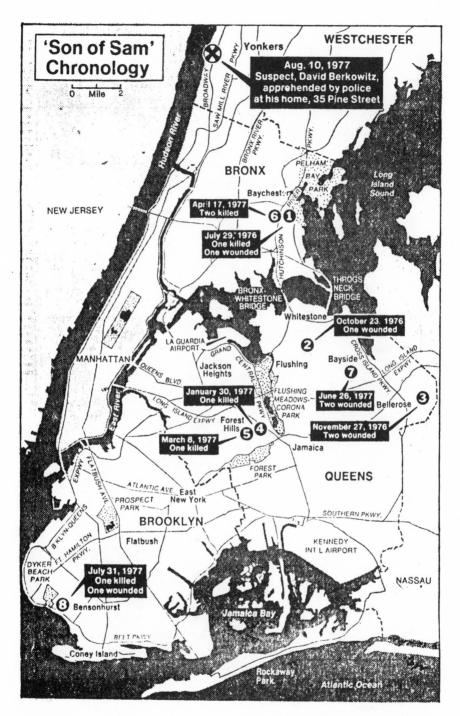

'Son of Sam' Chronology

0 — Mile — 2

Aug. 10, 1977
Suspect, David Berkowitz, apprehended by police at his home, 35 Pine Street

WESTCHESTER

Yonkers

BROADWAY

SAW MILL RIVER PKWY

Hudson River

NEW JERSEY

BRONX

BRONX RIVER PKWY.

PELHAM BAY PARK

Baychester

HUTCHINSON RIVER PKWY.

Long Island Sound

April 17, 1977
Two killed **6** **1**

July 29, 1976
One killed
One wounded

THROGS NECK BRIDGE

BRONX-WHITESTONE BRIDGE

Whitestone

October 23, 1976
One wounded **2**

CROSS ISLAND PKWY

LONG ISLAND EXPWY

Bayside **7**

June 26, 1977
Two wounded

Bellerose **3**

November 27, 1976
Two wounded

LA GUARDIA AIRPORT

GRAND CENTRAL PKWY

Jackson Heights

Flushing

FLUSHING MEADOWS-CORONA PARK

MANHATTAN

QUEENS BLVD.

LONG ISLAND EXPWY

January 30, 1977
One killed

Forest Hills **5** **4**

March 8, 1977
One killed

Jamaica

EAST RIVER

FOREST PARK

QUEENS

ATLANTIC AVE. East New York

PROSPECT PARK

SOUTHERN PKWY.

FLATBUSH AVE. EXPWY

B'KLYN-QUEENS

FT. HAMILTON PKWY.

BROOKLYN

Flatbush

KENNEDY INT'L AIRPORT

DYKER BEACH PARK

July 31, 1977
One killed
One wounded **8** Bensonhurst

NASSAU

BELT PKWY

Coney Island

Jamaica Bay

Rockaway Park

Atlantic Ocean

(*The New York Times*)

Donna Lauria, age eighteen. (Inset) Donna Lauria, age two.
(*Courtesy of the Lauria family*)

(Top) Rosemary Keenan, age eighteen. (Bottom) Jody Valenti, age nineteen.

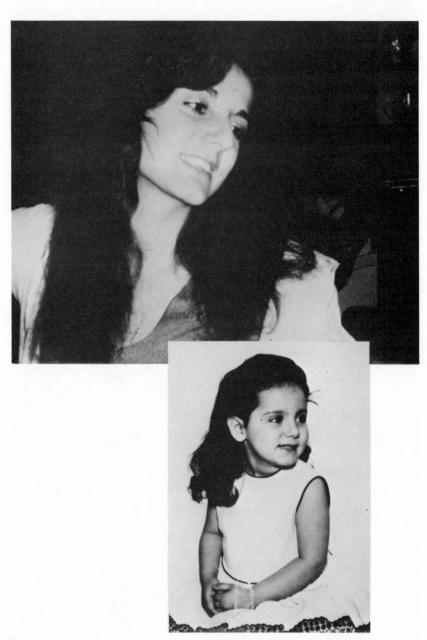

Donna DeMasi, age sixteen. (Inset) Donna DeMasi, age three.
(*Courtesy of the DeMasi family*)

Christine Freund, age twenty-six, the summer before her murder.
(Inset) Christine Freund, age one. (*Courtesy of the Freund family*)

DAILY NEWS

DAILY NEWS, FRIDAY, AUGUST 12, 1977

Ticket to the solution

Five More Pages on Son of Sam Featuring:

Myths Gone; What Drove Sam

Psychological Mystery Remains

Will He Ever Stand Trial?

(Daily News)

(Top) The view of Sam Carr's house as seen from David
Berkowitz's apartment. (Bottom) Front of the Carrs' family home
with David Berkowitz's apartment house in background. (*Photos
by Nadine Novis*)

Drawing by David Berkowitz

8

Broken Flower

During the year just past David had become increasingly unenthusiastic about his construction job. When he seemed sad and other workers asked why, he would say that he had "problems at home and bills to pay." Once he even went so far as to suggest "I'm having troubles with women."

David didn't say he had found his mother or that in June 1975 he had taken a civil-service examination for a position with the U.S. Post Office. He had concentrated hard and scored 80.5 percent—"a high mark," says Bronx Postmaster Frank Viola, "for a man with Berkowitz's limited education." In addition, David qualified for a veteran's bonus of an additional five points. Thus, in February 1976 he received a notice to come in for an interview at the Bronx General Post Office on the Grand Concourse, at which time he was told that he could begin work on March 15. His starting salary would be $13,000 per year—the highest pay he would ever earn.

And so one day at a union meeting in early March 1976 David called some workers over to his Ford and opened the trunk in which he stored his tools. He sold ten-dollar hammers for two dollars. He all but gave away screwdrivers, clamps, chisels, and wirecutters. That was a signal. Berkowitz was quitting the construction business. As someone else put it, "He simply walked away from the job during that union meeting. He walked away and he never came back."

His first job in the Post Office was as letter sorter, scanning addresses and zip codes from 4:00 P.M. until half an hour after midnight. Most postal workers consider this an undesirable shift. David says he didn't mind. He would have the early morning hours to himself.

He is remembered as being conscientious. He adjusted to Post Office routine. He bought new clothes. But he was not outgoing, not a joiner. Fellow employees say that he ate alone in a corner of the cafeteria, and he generally spoke only after someone had first spoken to him.

George Moffa, twenty-three, says that David did sometimes join in conversations. Moffa remembers that on several occasions workers chattered about "the .44-Caliber Killer."

"They gotta get that guy," Berkowitz would reply. "He's really doing bad things. He should be caught."

David continued working at the Post Office, his last job, until Friday, July 29, 1977, the first anniversary of the murder of Donna Lauria. During five months of being a clerk, David remained "just another face" in a building where new faces turned up all the time. Theresa Graziano, twenty-four, says David didn't seem to be the sort of person who would harm anybody. "He talked like the rest of us, mostly about work, and how difficult the job was."

ON TUESDAY, March 8, 1977, a suggestion of spring came to the New York area. The temperature climbed to fifty degrees. The withering winter at last was vanquished.

In his studio apartment at Pineview Towers in Yonkers, David Berkowitz felt restless. He had spent his day off, Tuesday, alone. He was spending most of his days off alone. Where most of us who have both friends and family look forward to days off, to visits, to parties, or even bowling, the loner finds a day off more difficult to cope with than a day at work. His sense of solitude is reinforced, sometimes unbearably.

Clinically speaking, David had trouble "letting people in." This is a depressive condition attributed to a schizoid personality. David felt he was alone. Someone reached out. He refused to let himself be reached.

"Say, some of us are going to a roller rink tomorrow. Want to come?"

"No, thanks. I've got things to do."

"Ah, come on."

"No. Dammit! Leave me alone."

To those comfortable with labels, this is neurotic behavior. You are not saying what you mean. You are not comfortable with your feelings. Yes, you would like to join a group at a rink. But you don't skate well. You may look foolish. Besides, in the camaraderie of roller skating, you may let down your defenses. People may see more of what you really are. Will they like what they see?

You are afraid they won't. You are afraid that others won't like you. You aren't sure you like yourself. You put up a wall, politely at first. *No, thanks. I've got things to do.* Pressed in a friendly way, you become angry. *No. Dammit. Leave me alone!*

Actually, you need friends, but your neurosis blocks your need. It drives you to build a wall of anger. Later, when you realize what you have done—*if* you realize what you have done—the anger evaporates and you want to cry.

Thus it was on one level of David Berkowitz. He was not comfortable with his adoption or the fact that he was born a bastard. He was psychotic, hallucinating, and had difficulty controlling himself. He was isolated before the psychosis and it simply got worse as he deteriorated. At length we see him as a sheet-metal worker in Westchester weeping with sadness on the job.

But on another level David was psychotic. His murders, an outlet for psychotic tension, set up a ruinous circle. Once he had killed, he could not possibly accept the hand of friend-ship. He could never let down his system of defenses. If he did, he might have said "I've got these howling thoughts, and they make me do wild things, and look, I've been shooting people. It scares me." To say that is to court a life in prison.

Loner and murderer, David Berkowitz felt restless at the touch of spring. The demon dogs began to wail within his head. In the apartment—furnished with a bed, a couch, two chairs, a television, a bureau on which the pistol lay—he pulled on clothing. It was warm outside, but David was not responding to reality. Before leaving he zipped on a heavy new ski jacket and pulled a brown knit stocking cap toward his ears. In ten-degree temperature he had dressed lightly when he hunted and found Christine Freund. Now, in pleas-ant weather, preparing to hunt once more, Berkowitz dressed as if he were setting forth across a tundra.

He would drive to Queens again, to Forest Hills. "I picked Queens because there are a lot of pretty women there. It seemed to me that Forest Hills was where the prettiest ones were."

He felt for the gun and found it in a pocket of his jeans. It was a little after six o'clock. Berkowitz was starting to hunt earlier than was his custom, but he had his reasons. On cer-tain early evenings he had seen a crush of pretty girls pressing out of the subway kiosks onto Queens Boulevard. They were secretaries, receptionists, even models returning home after a day's work in Manhattan. On March 8, Berkowitz wanted to shoot a pretty girl.

He parked the Galaxie on Tennis Place, a narrow winding street just to the west of the tennis club. Familiar ground. Stepping from the car, he considered where he was. The West Side Tennis Club and the Forest Hills Tennis Stadium lay to his right. Chris Evert, a pretty girl, had won the U.S. Women's Open there the preceding fall.

Up an embankment just ahead he saw the tracks of the Long Island Railroad. Moonlight shone on the street where he stood, mingling with the beams of street lamps. It was early evening. Still it was dark. David had grown more calculating. He left the Galaxie unlocked. If he had to make a quick getaway, he would not have to fiddle with the key to the car door.

For an hour he roamed a small expensive community called Forest Hills Gardens. The private homes were mostly Tudor-style, secure half-timbered houses built in the 1920s, when pseudo-Tudor had its greatest vogue. They still suggest solidity and warmth. Houses in Forest Hills Gardens now sell for $150,000 and up. A number of well-known New Yorkers live there, including journalist Jimmy Breslin and his family.

Looking into the houses, David thought they were privileged and secure. He remembers thinking that he would like to have grown up in this community. Berkowitz was wandering down Dartmouth Street, on the perimeter of the Gardens, heading east away from the tennis courts. Then he saw a slight, attractive young woman walking toward him. She had a rather long face framed by dark-brown wavy hair. She wore a tan maxicoat and dark boots, so he could not see her legs. Although the light came from behind her, David saw that she was carrying notebooks and what he took to be school texts.

THE YOUNG WOMAN'S NAME was Virginia Voskerichian. She was indeed a student, as Berkowitz surmised. She was walking to the family's home at 69-11 Exeter Street after a day of classes at Barnard College, where she was a junior majoring in Russian-language studies. Her average was 3.5, the numerical equivalent of A-minus.

Born in Sofia, Bulgaria, in 1956, Virginia was the youngest of the three children of Armenians Yolanda and Garo Voskerichian. The father had worked as a watchmaker in Sofia, dreaming of the day he could leave the Communist state. In December 1958 Garo applied for permission to emigrate to the United States; he would wait ten years for his turn to come up. When it did, Yolanda and Garo Voskerichian didn't hesitate. They packed whatever they could carry, leaving their home and furnishings behind. Their property would revert to the state.

Settling in Queens when she was ten, Virginia picked up English very quickly. She was a bright girl, popular with friends, whom she often helped with homework. Virginia was disciplined and had a healthy ambition. She became a naturalized American citizen on July 29, 1975. Virginia would use her degree in Russian to become a political specialist. Then, she often said, "I would be able to relieve mother of the burden of supporting the family." The mother worked as a housekeeper; Virginia's older sister Alice was a student teacher; her brother Dikran was working in an auto-parts store in Glendale, Queens.

"I know Virginia would have become a valuable citizen," says the strikingly beautiful Alice Voskerichian. "With her intellect and talent, she would have brought a great contribution to society. It's a very big loss, not only to us, the family, but to American society. She can never make her contribution now."

Yolanda cries when she talks about her youngest child. "When she was small and we would go outside, she'd look at flowers. She would like them, love them, but never touch them. When I would reach to pick one, she would say 'Mommy, let it live. I don't want to have a broken flower.'"

BERKOWITZ thought the young woman approaching was "really beautiful." He closed his palm around the butt of his revolver. They were walking toward each other on Dartmouth Street beside a row of one-family attached houses facing Forest Hills Gardens. The girl noticed him when they were twenty-five feet apart. If she felt alarm, she concealed it. Her stride was constant.

When they were a step apart, David pulled the .44 out of his pocket. Virginia Voskerichian stopped and made a soft cry of terror. She raised her schoolbooks in front of her face as if to protect herself.

David fired once and hit Virginia "somewhere in the

face." He was becoming more professional—which is to say more deadly—with his gun. "I only fired once, because once was all I needed."

Virginia tumbled into the bushes that bordered the sidewalk. She died instantly.

David began to run back to his Galaxie. He saw a man in dark clothing—a fifty-nine-year-old civil engineer who was the first witness to see David leaving the scene of a murder.

"Hi, mister," David said.

The startled man did not respond.

THREE plainclothesmen were riding in a tan Plymouth on 69th Avenue, which intersects Dartmouth Street three blocks from where Virginia Voskerichian lay. According to one of them, they noticed a young man running, then slackening his pace when they came into view. They thought he was trying to look inconspicuous, which made him an immediate target of their interest. But they were assigned to street anticrime, not to Borrelli's task force, which meant that they were not on the lookout for anyone who might be linked to a series of killings. Besides, the killer did his violence after midnight and it was only 7:32. If such a man would prowl that evening, it would be closer to midnight. The plainclothesmen weren't attuned to the possibility that this figure and the murderer might be one and the same. They were on the lookout for purse-snatchers, muggers, car thieves.

The Plymouth edged toward the curb and stopped. "Might as well check him," said a plainclothesman, indicating David Berkowitz. Coincidence—the kind that is hard to believe when we encounter it in nineteenth-century novels—now worked in behalf of David.

The officer seated in the rear swung open the door of the Plymouth. He was about to step out to question Berkowitz. The policeman and the killer were within ten feet of one another. Suddenly the plainclothesman froze. A call was coming in over the police radio:

"Report woman shot on Dartmouth Street, near 71st."

David was so close that he could hear the voice of the woman dispatcher.

The plainclothesman scrambled back into the car. A siren sounded. The tan Plymouth accelerated away.

The plainclothesmen had not associated the man in the ski jacket on this mild March night with a woman who had been shot three blocks away.

David does not remember feeling fright. Rather, he says, "Satan was creating illusions." The police had sensed something when they stopped the car, he says, but failed to react because they must have decided what they saw—himself— "was an illusion."

By the time Berkowitz reached his Galaxie he felt secure. Tomorrow he would go back to work at the Post Office in the Bronx and no one would suspect what he had done.

CAPTAIN JOE BORRELLI and Detective Jim Gallagher were sitting in the squadroom at the 112th Precinct at about 7:40 P.M. when the call came in. A girl had been shot on Dartmouth Street. The two policemen ran downstairs to Borrelli's Ford.

Borrelli drove hard, and the conversation was clipped but intense.

"It's not far from where the Freund girl was killed," Gallagher said.

"January 30," said Borrelli.

"Think there's a tie-in, Captain?"

"Who the hell knows?"

Lying in the bushes, Virginia Voskerichian was no longer pretty. Berkowitz's bullet had struck her squarely, entering at the upper lip. It knocked out teeth and disfigured her face.

As far as Borrelli and Gallagher could tell, there was only one gunshot wound. Such matters are checked by a coroner, who in New York City must be a licensed physician. But, considering the wound on the scene, Gallagher said, "It looks to be a smaller-caliber bullet than was used in the Freund killing." There are so many variables—angle of entry, point of impact, distance from which a shooting takes place—that final determination of the caliber of a killer's bullet is a job for skilled technicians. From what Borrelli and Gallagher could tell at first, this murder was not related to the killing of Christine Freund.

Gallagher left the death scene with Captain Borrelli for the Voskerichian house on Exeter Street. It was more modest than the Tudor homes of Forest Hills Gardens, but still comfortable. He found a family wild with sorrow.

Virginia's brother Dikran was punching a wall. He had run two and a half blocks to Dartmouth Street and identified his sister's body, and now he was pounding a fist against a wall and bellowing his grief. For a few moments Gallagher thought he might have to restrain Dikran for his own good.

The parents, Yolanda and Garo, wept with Virginia's sister Alice. Gallagher began speaking gently, and the family regained a measure of composure. Even Dikran settled down a bit.

They spoke of Virginia's intellect, her promise. Gallagher asked if possibly, just possibly, she might have known anyone with criminal connections.

Impossible. She was a model young woman, an honor student at Barnard.

Trouble with a boyfriend, perhaps?

Absolutely not. Virginia was involved in her studies. She wasn't in love. Besides, she got along with everybody.

Leaving the Voskerichian home, Gallagher wondered: "I can't figure why this girl was shot, unless maybe there's some connection with the .44-caliber guy."

Back on Dartmouth Street, Gallagher decided to renew his feel for the neighborhood. He had worked out of the 112th Precinct House for more than fifteen years, and he had driven through these streets a thousand times. Still, he would walk to the subway station at Continental Avenue and Queens Boulevard and retrace Virginia's path to Dartmouth Street. It might give him a clue.

He found nothing. There weren't any clues to find. By the time he had finished following Virginia's steps, her body had been removed. A chalk and ribbon outline indicated where she had fallen. Other detectives were trying to recreate what had happened.

Virginia was carrying books and a 1977 calendar. To protect herself, she lifted them in front of her face. The bullet drove through books and calendar, leaving a distinct powder burn on her lip and her front teeth before lodging inside her skull.

What a waste, Jim Gallagher thought. "Just a pure waste. A young girl so small she looked like a high school kid. A bright young girl."

Gallagher hoped her end was quick.

Then Detective James Gallagher turned away from the outline of what had been Virginia Voskerichian.

He had been a policeman for more than twenty years, and he had worked a hundred homicides. Still, this one touched him. He felt sick.

JOE BORRELLI remembers this shooting, too. "If you watch detectives at any homicide, you'll notice that they go about their jobs unemotionally. Sometimes, like when a couple of kids, along with their babysitter, were killed a few years earlier in that same area, you watch the guys holding back their tears. There's something about kids. Maybe it reminds them of their own kids. Anyway, at this one, they didn't want to look at her. They knew it was senseless. She was someone beautiful and she was laying under the sheet, a bullet in her face had destroyed her. It began to grab at them, in the guts, and they just turned away. These were veterans and they couldn't take it."

9

The General's
Wife Needs Sex

ixteen detectives and plainclothesmen met in the crowded office of Captain Joseph Borrelli on March 9, 1977. They stood around their new commander, whose face showed the tension he was under. He had taken over a portion of the 15th Homicide Zone's office space on the second floor of the 112th Precinct at Yellowstone Boulevard and Austin Street, just three blocks away from the last two shootings.

Borrelli called the meeting to order. He was feeling frustrated. "I think we've got a psycho here," he said.

Detective Sergeant Joe Coffey agreed. "Yesterday the Voskerichian kid gets killed in Forest Hills. The bullet goes to ballistics. Bingo! A match. It's from the same gun that killed Donna Lauria in the Bronx last July. This guy's going to hit again. This isn't a barroom brawl."

"What?" someone said.

Coffey shouted at them: "It's our job to stop him from killing. But where are our leads? Nobody can tell us what we're looking for. Who the fuck is he?"

"Do we have a car?" Borrelli asked quietly. "No, we don't. We don't know what he drives. Do we have a firm general description? Do we know what he looks like? No. Then what the hell are we looking for out there?"

"It's vast," Jim Gallagher said. "It's a mountainous type thing. Jesus Christ. We've got the whole damn city to cover."

"He's done some jobs near parkways," Coffey said. "If someone at the scene just sees him leaving. If we find out it's a green Buick, or a blue Dodge, then maybe we could get him on a parkway."

By the end of the meeting, Captain Borrelli was making changes in his helter-skelter task force. First, he would ask that it be expanded from sixteen to thirty men. Half the men would work on investigation, talking to victims and the families of victims, going over old ground, hoping for something, for anything. Was there a tie between the victims? Was there any link? "The truth," says one detective, "is that we had nothing, except a certain type of gun."

The other half would "work the field." They would ride about in unmarked cars, patrolling areas already hit or areas that seemed likely to be hit. They would cover the Bronx and Queens, concentrating on streets that led to parkways.

"He tends to hit on weekends," Borrelli said. "We have to be especially alert then, Joe," Borrelli said to Coffey. "I want you to head up the weekend detail."

ON THE AFTERNOON of March 10, 1977, New York City Police Commissioner Michael Codd held a formal press conference at One Police Plaza in Manhattan. He announced that a positive link existed between the Donna Lauria and Virginia Voskerichian killings. As camera flashes went off, he went on to say that a .44-caliber handgun, a Charter Arms Bulldog revolver had been identified as the weapon used in at least three separate incidents in the Bronx and Queens. His words struck hard as a sledge hammer.

When he finished his prepared statement, the press closed in on him.

"Commissioner Codd," one reporter began, "how can you be so certain that there was a single gun used in all the attacks?"

The Commissioner responded as all cops would have, with the simple facts: "The Police Lab, our Ballistics Unit in particular, has positively linked the bullets used in the Lauria and Voskerichian killing to one another. Through an exhaustive process of weighing the fragments and comparison of the striations peculiar to the weapon used, a .44 Charter Arms Bulldog, my men have concluded that the same weapon was used in both of the previously mentioned killings. Armed with this conclusion, we were able to make further comparisons and feel that we can say for certain that this same .44 was used in the other attacks."

Flashbulbs popped all around as Commissioner Codd recognized Jeff Kamen of WPIX-TV. The slender reporter looked down at his pad and began, "Commissioner Codd, I believe everyone would like to know what the police department is doing to catch the individual or individuals responsible for the attacks."

"First," Commissioner Codd answered, "we believe that the shootings have been the work of a single individual. Second, this morning a warrant has been issued based upon the statements of available witnesses and surviving victims. It names a white male, twenty-five to thirty years old, six feet tall, medium build, with dark hair." The reporters pressed closer. "We have increased our patrols in those areas we feel have been targets of this killer and hope the public will cooperate with the police in their efforts to apprehend this individual."

Immediately following the press conference and through the evening of March 10, 1977, the police brass struggled to head off further attacks by the unknown killer. They were spurred onward by the afternoon's media barrage; like all public servants, the cops are afraid of—or at least uncomfortable with—the press en masse. They worked through the night expanding the tiny task force with detectives awaiting new assignments.

The Commissioner also met with his new Chief of Detectives, John Keenan, and told him to find someone above the rank of captain to command the growing task force. The choice would not be easy. Keenan first had to establish order in his own office. He then began reviewing candidates. Some men couldn't be taken away from their current assignments; others refused the job. Finally he chose Deputy Inspector Timothy J. Dowd and set a date of April 19 for the official announcement of the organizing of the task force.

The Deputy Commissioner for Public Information, Francis J. McLaughlin, who had watched interdepartmental crises over the years, predicted to Captain Borrelli: "Joe, this one's going to be the biggest case in the history of the department."

DEPUTY INSPECTOR TIMOTHY J. DOWD had become a New York City policeman in 1940. While the clouds of war hung heavy on the horizon, Dowd's first assignment was walking a beat in Astoria, Queens, for a salary of $24 a week. In 1977, he was sixty-one years old. He had been on the force for thirty-seven years, and as a deputy inspector he earned $40,000 a year. "He is no 'spit-on-the-squadroom-floor cop,' " wrote a *Newsweek* reporter, "and he never watches *Kojak*." His colleagues looked on Inspector Dowd as a hard-nosed pragmatist, a man who kept his serenity amid confusion, and as a master of practical police-department politics.

Dowd was born in Ireland. His parents emigrated to Boston when he was four. He moved to New York at seventeen to study at City College, where he majored in Latin and English. He supported himself at odd jobs as other college students did. He was not certain of a permanent field. Dowd thought of the priesthood. He went on to take a master's degree at the Baruch School of Business, part of the City College complex. But for whatever reasons—he may not be sure himself—from the day he first put on a blue, silver-buttoned coat, the police department was his life.

Gradually he moved up through the civil service ladder until, in September 1973, Tim Dowd was appointed Deputy

Inspector in charge of a major precinct. Then, at the hands of Commissioner Donald Cawley, Dowd suffered a setback that would have driven a weaker man from the force. Cawley had instituted a program called "produce or perish." Supervisors at or above the rank of Deputy Inspector were to be held responsible for both their own performance and those under them. In 1973, fifteen officers thus reviewed were demoted. Tim Dowd was one of the fifteen. He was broken back to the rank of captain, the highest possible civil service rank. As a commander, Dowd had been held responsible for "cooping" (sleeping on the job) by various patrolmen under his command. He had fallen victim to the axiom "A ship's captain is always responsible for the actions of his crew."

Eleven demoted men, many younger than Dowd, chose to resign and take pensions amounting to as much as two-thirds of their salary. Dowd and four others elected to stay and fight. They hired counsel and petitioned the New York State Human Rights Commission, charging they had been discriminated against because of age. (Dowd was then fifty-eight.)

A year passed. The four men waited. Then, with the appointment of Michael Codd as Police Commissioner in 1974, the four officers were given back their ranks. It was a quiet victory. Newspapers had played up stories about Cawley's "get-tough" program and the demotions. Tim Dowd's victory went unreported.

In mid-1976 Dowd was supervising a force charged with investigating extortion in Chinatown. It was a hard case, in which his men had to penetrate a secret society called The Flying Dragons. By reputation, the society could not be penetrated by occidentals, and some policemen felt Dowd was given the case to make him look bad, to punish him for fighting the police-department system. But in February 1977, Dowd announced that Michael Chen, twenty-seven, had been arrested on the charge of murdering David Wong, seventeen. Chen was the leader of the Flying Dragons, Wong a member of the rival Ghost Shadows. The brutal extortions of local businessmen practiced by these junior tongs was stopped.

Thus, on April 19, 1977, in a carefully planned conference at City Hall, Chief of Detectives John Keenan publicly named Timmy Dowd to lead the growing search for the .44-caliber killer. Within the ranks of the police department, it was known simply as Omega Group.

With Timothy Dowd as commander of Operation Omega, Captain Joseph Borrelli became his deputy. The veteran policeman had been pushed into the background.

"It had to come," Joe Borrelli told his friends. "The case is too big for a captain. Two boroughs are already involved and it's growing every day. Sooner or later they'd have to give it to someone with more clout than I have. It's a logical decision, and the department runs on logic."

DAVID BERKOWITZ remembers that day. "I read about this group they had started to get me. It was in the papers and on television. I remember Borrelli and Dowd. I followed them from that day on. Whenever anything was written about them, I read it. I also listened to the radio when it came up. I knew that they'd get me some day. The only question was how . . . and when."

David also had mixed emotions about seeing on the front pages of the *Daily News* and *New York Post* that the authorities believed his attacks were the work of a single individual. He clipped the stories and started saving them. He also began to believe he'd never be caught because "The police couldn't see me. I was an illusion . . . someone other than David Berkowitz." This belief had been heightened by a second bizarre incident shortly after he had almost been caught by the officers in the unmarked squad car following the Voskerichian killing.

As David drove home to Yonkers after firing a single bullet into Virginia's face, the police had put out a "Code .44" call over the radio. Two policewomen were assigned especially to patrol the toll booths at the south end of the Bronx–Whitestone Bridge. Their instructions were to stop all cars containing a single white male. The officers were just about to end their tour of duty when David drove up to the toll plaza. He was only third in line, the .44 loaded and lying in full view on the seat beside him, when the two policewomen decided to quit a few minutes early. He couldn't believe it when he saw them turn and walk away.

David had no feeling of guilt, no compassion for those he had killed. "After the shootings," he says, "I thought I might weep for some of the people killed. But I couldn't. It was all puzzling, you know. You hear so much news about victims, all the sob stories. In the United States, they show sob stories on TV so much. Women in tears. After a while you don't feel anything at all."

And now he was beginning to feel a warped sense of mission. He wanted, he says, to enlighten the world about "a conspiracy of evil." He wanted to tell his fellow humans about "Sam, who was Satan, and Joquin the Joker, and that wretched building on Wicker Street in Yonkers which was a Holiday Inn for demons, who traveled around the world."

He followed newspaper accounts of his killings. He read and reread the stories. He tried to imagine what the police officers might be like. He noticed repeatedly the name of the head of "the helter-skelter task force," Captain Joseph Borrelli. He would wait about five weeks for his next attack. During that time, he would organize his thoughts into a four-page letter to Borrelli. In that letter David would reveal his true name: Son of Sam.

ON APRIL FOOL'S DAY David began to compose the letter. It took two days to complete. He printed it in large block letters, like a child. There would be two distinct differences in Berkowitz's method of operation when he next went forth to murder. First, he would carry this letter with him. Second, he would try to shoot not only a woman, but a man as well.

His madness exploded on April 17, a balmy evening. He put the pistol in the belt of his jeans. He put the letter in a pocket of his dungaree jacket. He intended to begin his hunt in Queens. His luck there had been good.

David left his apartment in Pineview Towers about 8:30 P.M. He cruised about until ten o'clock. Then, at the intersection of Bartow and Baychester avenues in the Bronx, he was stopped for a routine traffic check by police officers of the 45th Precinct. This was less than two miles from Co-Op City. One officer asked Berkowitz for his license, his registration, and the proof of a current auto-insurance policy that New York law requires. Berkowitz had no insurance card. Officer Jose Pinero issued a summons, ordering David to appear in Bronx Traffic Court on July 6, or his driver's license would be suspended. (There is normally a one-month delay between the issuance of a traffic summons and the offender's scheduled appearance in court.)

David accepted the summons from Pinero without protest, made a mental note of the appearance date, and drove away.

VALENTINA SURIANI, eighteen, and Alexander Esau, twenty, were youngsters in love.

Valentina was dark-haired, with a chubby face and carefully plucked and penciled eyebrows. Friends called her "cute" and talked of her warm, quick smile. Esau had a boyish face, framed by a rich halo of dark hair that fell over his ears and almost touched his shoulders, making his face seem smaller than it was.

Valentina was petite. She hoped for a career on stage or as a model. She was studying acting and was looking for a photographer to take a series of photographs for her portfolio.

Alexander was an operator's helper on a towtruck. Unknowingly, in recent weeks, he had ridden the same parkways as David Berkowitz.

The couple left Valentina's home that evening at nine o'clock with the promise to her parents that they would return before 3:00 A.M., which would give them time to go to Manhattan for a movie in the Times Square area and then dinner and drinks. Valentina had just received her driver's license, and, as she usually did, when the couple began their journey home, she asked if she could drive. She knew that Alexander had borrowed the 1968 Mercury Montego from one of his three brothers, and he was worried about getting a scratch on it.

Upon reaching Upper Manhattan, they turned right onto the Cross-Bronx Expressway and continued east to the Hutchinson River Parkway, some five miles later. They took the Hutchinson north a short distance, and Valentina finally exited at Tremont Avenue, staying on the service road. Just one short block from the high-rise apartment building at 1950 Hutchinson River Parkway where she lived, the young woman nudged the car to the curb and brought it to a halt. She had chosen a parking place only three blocks from the home of David's first victim, Donna Lauria. Valentina and Alexander turned toward each other in a last embrace.

At 3:00 A.M. Sunday, four shots shattered the passenger-side window. Two shots struck each of the lovers. Valentina died in that first minute, Alexander within two hours, at Jacobi Hospital.

THE SUMMONS had not discouraged Berkowitz from cruising. He drove across a bridge into Queens and proceeded down Queens Boulevard, a broad, divided thoroughfare lined with shops and restaurants and movie theaters. He heard no signal from his demons.

Berkowitz turned right into Woodhaven Boulevard, and drove south to a community called Howard Beach, which lies adjacent to Kennedy International Airport. He drove down quiet streets. No signal.

He began to lose track of time. The hunting was poor tonight. He made his way down unfamiliar streets. At 3:00 A.M., he says, he found himself in the Bronx, driving along a service road that parallels the Hutchinson River Parkway. He was within two miles of Co-Op City. He noticed row houses to his right and realized he was within half a dozen blocks of the site at which he had murdered Donna Lauria. David remembered Donna from her picture in the newspapers. She was his "pretty princess," the girl he would have married had not the demons intervened. The girl he might have loved. The girl he murdered.

Abruptly he saw a couple in a maroon Mercury Montego. They were embracing. Berkowitz had found his victims.

David passed the Montego, then made a right turn and parked his Galaxie a block away, near the corner of Milford and Lowrey. He retraced his path on foot. As he walked, he began to sweat. He opened his ski jacket.

The necking couple never noticed him. Berkowitz walked to the passenger side of the Montego, pulled his gun, and crouched as he had crouched the night he murdered Donna Lauria. He fired four times.

Esau, in the passenger seat, slumped toward the dashboard, comatose. Valentina slid slowly backward. David could hear her moaning. He raised the pistol again to fire a final shot, but suddenly he noticed approaching automobile lights on the street.

The man was dead. The girl was probably dying. Better not linger, Berkowitz thought. He took the letter from his ski jacket and dropped it in the center of the service road, about ten feet from the car, and ran back to his Galaxie feeling, he says, "flushed with power."

He drove two blocks to Buhre Avenue, where he "could catch a glimpse of Donna Lauria's apartment building." Ten minutes later he stopped at a White Castle Restaurant on Baychester Avenue, where he gorged on twenty-two-cent hamburgers and chocolate malts.

DISCUSSING this double murder with psychiatrists later, Berkowitz is embarrassed by the fact he killed a man for the first time. He admits the demons had demanded he kill a man as well as a woman, but is reluctant to say more.

But why, David? Why would the demons suddenly want a man?

"General Jack Cosmo had a wife."

I don't understand.

"General Jack Cosmo had a wife named Nancy Cosmo."
(Jack Cassara, Berkowitz's landlord in New Rochelle, was married to a woman named Nann.)

And?

"Nancy Cosmo wanted some action too."

Action? What kind of action?

"You know," Berkowitz says. "Sex."

The word loosens the flood of madness: "When the soul of a victim leaves the body, demons are right there. They snatch the souls and take them to the attic of 316 Warburton Avenue [Yonkers], or to the houses at 18 and 22 Wicker Streets. They chain the souls and have sex with them forever. The demons take the victims' souls and drag them into houses and rape them and molest them. It's messy. It's brutal. There's no sleep for the victims' souls, no resting, no peace.

"Not now.

"Not for a while."

TRUE to his basic modus operandi, David had murdered again on a weekend—it was three o'clock Sunday morning. The helter-skelter task force had been deployed in the Bronx and Queens on the orders of Detective Sergeant Joe Coffey. From the 112th Precinct, at Yellowstone Boulevard and Austin Street, Coffey sent detectives into areas that seemed likely to be attacked. Sergeant Freddy DeLuca, thirty-five, of the Bronx Sex Crimes Unit, was patrolling close to the Hutchinson River Parkway. "We figured areas near the highways were prime targets," Coffey says, "because the parkways gave the killer a quick getaway." DeLuca's tour was to end at 2:00 A.M. He lingered for another forty-five minutes, however, talking to Detectives Richard Paul and Ron Marsenison, who were still assigned to the Lauria homicide. The three chatted in a car, parked opposite 1873 Hutchinson River Parkway, almost exactly where Berkowitz would kill Esau and Suriani less than fifteen minutes later.

As Coffey recalls it, there were more than two hundred

stakeouts in all. When nothing had come from any by 2:30 A.M., Joe Coffey decided to call it a night. Leaving the precinct, he met another officer coming off duty and the two detectives went to a Chinese restaurant-bar at Queens Boulevard. Coffey was weary and depressed. A drink or two wouldn't hurt.

The two men talked about the .44-caliber killer and how frustrating it was to try to find a single psycho in a metropolitan area of fifteen million people.

"You'll get him, Joe," the officer said.

"Yeah," Coffey said wearily. "Yeah. But when?"

At the 4:00 A.M. closing time for the bar, Joe Coffey drove home to Levittown. His family was safe, asleep in the modest white Cape Cod house.

The telephone rang. It was a detective from Queens homicide. "Sarge," he shouted. "We've got a homicide in the Bronx. It's similar to the other ones we're working on. I'm on the phone to the guys there, and the more I hear the more it's got to be him."

"Run it down for me fast," Coffey said.

Within seconds, Coffey ran for the door. He drove to the murder site in the Bronx. Valentina Suriani's body had already been taken to the city morgue. Alexander Esau was alive but dying at Jacobi Hospital. A detective sat at his bedside, hoping that Alex would regain consciousness.

Coffey then drove to the city morgue at 520 First Avenue, at 30th Street, on the East Side of Manhattan. He was tired, angry, upset. The goddamn killer was wearing him down.

THE NEW YORK CITY MORGUE sits as a small appendix next to the massive structures that make up the Bellevue medical complex on First Avenue at 30th Street. Its white block façade is set off by a powder-blue tile entrance that is continued in the structure's interior. All corpses from Manhattan and the Bronx are brought here for examination if the death is in any way suspicious. Set on the main floor is the Chief Medical Examiner's autopsy room, equipped with a stainless steel table and a set of microphones for recording commentary during autopsies. In all, the autopsy room looks like an operating room. Except that all the patients are dead before they go under the surgical knife.

Coffey shuddered as he walked into the autopsy room. He had come here, or to rooms like this, a hundred times, to view the shattered corpses of murder victims. He never liked it. He never got used to it. Bodies upset him.

The corpse of Valentina Suriani lay under a thin white sheet on a stainless steel table. Coffey walked up and gently lifted the covering from her face. An attendant removed the sheet completely.

"In a way," Joe Coffey says, "the girl was gorgeous. Young. A classic. She was one of the prettiest girls I'd ever seen. But she was covered from head to toe with caked, dried blood. It was her own blood and later we'd find it was the blood of her boyfriend, too."

Another morgue attendant appeared, carrying a large kitchen knife. Coffey felt utter, helpless anger. This girl had been a beauty. He felt that part of himself had been destroyed also.

Professionalism and detachment are fragile shields. But this case, this .44-caliber psycho, was shaking Coffey as nothing else in his dozen years on the police force. This case and the naked corpse of a beautiful blood-caked child.

The attendant lowered his knife toward Valentina's wrist.

"What the fuck do you think you're doing?" Coffey shouted.

"I'm going to cut off the jewelry, like I always do. You know. To get the body ready for the doctors."

"Like hell you are," Coffey roared. "You're not going to cut anything off her. Get the hell out of here and give me that fucking knife."

Coffey shoved the morgue attendant from the tiled room. He threw the kitchen knife to the floor. Clatter and echoes filled the room. Three other detectives stood by. They never moved.

Joe Coffey walked to the corpse and tenderly worked the jewelry from the body. He removed every bracelet undamaged.

He had blown up. He knew he had blown up. But, as easily as this kid, it could have been his own daughter lying there. Or himself. Hell, as a kid he'd liked to sit in cars with girls.

The kids this psycho was murdering were just young people trying to grow up. This one, Donna Lauria, Virginia Voskerichian, were all innocent. "Innocent to beat the band," Coffey says.

Well, he had blown up. But he felt calmer now. If he never did anything else on the force, he would catch the killer.

SERGEANT JOE COFFEY left the morgue and returned to his precinct. In spite of the hour, he called Detective Fred De-Luca at home. "Freddie. He's hit again."

"Where?" asked DeLuca.

"Just outside 1878 Hutchinson River Parkway at a couple of minutes past three."

There was prolonged silence. "Joe," DeLuca said finally. "Tell me it wasn't there, please. Tell me it was somewhere else."

"Why, Fred?"

"I was sitting on that exact spot until two forty-five in the morning."

"Freddie, did you see anything at all?" Coffey pleaded.

"Not a fucking thing, Joe. Nothing!" He could hear Freddie begin to cry at the other end of the line.

DETECTIVE MARLIN HOPKINS was working with Sergeant Joe Coffey and Captain Joseph Borrelli. He was in charge of the Freund investigation. "Finally we established that we were dealing with the same person or persons going from

Queens to the Bronx," he says. "There were thoughts at the time that we had a possible conspiracy—a group of people, who, for whatever reason, wanted to go out and kill lovers. Possibly killing anyone who was merely seated in a car as a kind of initiation to a club or cult. But we mostly leaned to one person, a psychotic individual.

"At this point I was getting all psyched up. I found myself talking about it to my family, friends, everybody. Maybe I spoke about it to get it out of my system? I don't know. There was so much notoriety about this guy."

But soon after Christine Freund's death, the investigation was no longer the exclusive domain of the local homicide-zone detectives. "It became a citywide thing. Lots of people became involved. Hundreds of phone calls flooded in, letters came in. People suspected their neighbors. Someone passed someone on the street who didn't look just right, and that was called in. They were turning in members of their own family: police officers, firemen, city officials, people from every walk of life. But we found that the great majority of the phone calls and letters that did come in were about people who did actually have psychological problems.

"Each one of the people who were reported had an investigation done on them," Detective Hopkins claims. "We got a rounded-out opinion of the person, using most of the time the detective's gut reaction. Was he the man or wasn't he? Many of the people we spoke to, especially in Forest Hills, were people who frequented bars there because of an underground reputation that neighborhood has. The psycho-capital of the world." (Members of the police believe Forest Hills has the greatest concentration of psychiatrists and psychologists per capita in the nation.)

BY NOW, Dr. Martin Lubin, the former Chief of Forensic Psychiatry at Bellevue and Chief of Psychiatry at Booth Memorial Hospital, had created a profile for the police. It was conjectural but expert. "Dr. Lubin gave us a fairly accurate profile of the person as a psychotic individual," says Captain

Joe Borrelli. "But we talked to other doctors. We went to a meeting of forty-five psychiatrists held by Dr. Bernadelli at Creedmore. Each psychiatrist had his or her own individual viewpoints."

The meeting lasted three hours. At the end Borrelli recalls the words of a short, slight German psychiatrist who spoke with a heavy accent. The doctor came into the aisle, waited for silence, then began. "Gentlemen. Every time he shoots his gun, he's ejaculating!"

"All forty-five psychiatrists laughed," Borrelli recalls, "along with the handful of cops who were there.

"We all needed a laugh. And, in a way, maybe this guy was right. But, in the end, we had to get back to the basic investigation. We were evaluating each of the phone calls and letters as they came in. We gave some top priority and some the least priority. We acted on those that sounded the best to the investigator who took it first. I'll say some of the suspects looked pretty good. Some looked so good that we followed them; we stayed with them from when they went to work in the morning until they went to bed at night. We virtually tucked some of them in at night."

THE SPARK that turned the manhunt into a totally emotional confrontation of man against city was provided by the letter David had so carefully written to Captain Borrelli.

One of the first uniformed patrolmen to arrive at the scene of the Suriani–Esau killings noticed an envelope lying in the middle of the street, about ten feet from the victims' car. He picked it up, read the name of the addressee with surprise and passed the envelope on to his superior—who in turn passed it on to his superior, until there were so many fingerprints on the envelope that David's were lost forever.

The only fortunate occurrence was that no one opened the letter—and someone, no one remembers who, finally placed the message in a glassine envelope. The letter was opened later in the morning at the Fingerprints Section of the NYPD. A check for fingerprints revealed bare traces on the four pages of paper, as though someone had held the pages between the very tips of forefinger and thumb. There was no identifiable whorl that would allow detectives to race to the computerized fingerprint files.

Then, and only then, did Captain Borrelli read the letter:

Dear Captain Joseph Borrelli,

I am deeply hurt by your calling me a wemon
hater. I am not. But I am a monster.
I am the "Son of Sam." I am a little brat.
    When father Sam gets drunk he gets mean. He
beats his family. Sometimes he ties me up to the
back of the house. Other times he locks me in the
garage. Sam loves to drink blood.
    "Go out and kill," commands father Sam.
    "Behind our house some rest. Mostly young—
raped and slaughtered—their blood drained—
just bones now.
    Papa Sam keeps me locked in the attic too. I
can't get out but I look out the attic window and
watch the world go by.
    I feel like an outsider. I am on a different
wavelength then everybody else—programmed
too kill.
    However, to stop me you must kill me. Attention
all police: Shoot me first—shoot to kill or
else keep out of my way or you will die!
    Papa Sam is old now. He needs some blood to pre-
serve his youth. He has had
too many heart attacks. "Ugh, me hoot, it hurts,
sonny boy."
    I miss my pretty princess most of all. She's
resting in our ladies house. But I'll see her
soon.
    I am the "Monster"—"Beelzebub"—the chubby
behemouth.
    I love to hunt. Prowling the streets looking
for fair game—tasty meat. The wemon of
Queens are prettyist of all. I must

be the water they drink. I live for the hunt—
my life. Blood for papa.

Mr. Borelli, sir, I don't want to kill
anymore. No sur, no more but I must, "honour
thy father."

I want to make love to the world. I
love people. I don't belong on earth. Return
me to yahoos.

To the people of Queens, I love you. And I
[the letter *m* was then crossed out] want to wish
all of you a happy Easter. May God bless you in
this life and in the next. And for now

One more page of the letter was withheld from the press
so that a positive identification could be made if Son of Sam
was caught. The last page of the letter was released and the
newspapers reproduced it in the killer's own handwriting.

If the letter deserves reproduction in a textbook of abnor-
mal psychology, then David's explanation, his skeleton key
given to the author, may belong there, too.

"I am a little brat," Berkowitz says, seems an appropriate
way of "describing myself." He was "Sam's child . . . not
by birth, but by possession." He was "Sam's little boy. Sam
guards me, he's like authority . . . like father. . . . He's always telling me what to do. . . . I don't feel like a man next
to him—he's so mighty and powerful."

The comment in the second paragraph, "Sometimes he
ties me up to the back of the house," is Sam's dog speaking.
"But it becomes me. The dog says this on repeated occasions.
He begs to be released. He howls in terrible pain." This is a
reference to the dog David shot on Christmas Eve 1977 at the
Netos' home. "They say I shot a dog, but it looked like an old
woman to me."

"Papa Sam keeps me locked up" describes David's disturbed state of mind. Sam "makes me feel . . . locked in the
attic." David had never been to Sam's attic, but he thought
his "soul" went there. "He [Sam] has my soul . . . in the
attic. I remember the attic. It's dingy and dark and there is
never any lights there."

I SAY GOODBYE AND GOODNIGHT.

POLICE: LET ME HAUNT YOU WITH THESE WORDS;

I'LL BE BACK!

I'LL BE BACK!

TO BE INTERRPRETED AS - BANG BANG BANG, BANK, BANG - UGH!!'

YOURS IN MURDER
MR. MONSTER.

"Ugh, me hoot, it hurts, sonny boy" is Sam speaking. "Hoot" means "heart"; Sam Carr is complaining. The real Sam Carr had suffered a heart attack.

"My pretty princess" is the girl David was promised by the demons. He was to have married her. "I never knew her. Sam promised her to me. That's Donna . . . Donna Lauria. . . . He didn't give her to me . . . I don't know why. Maybe he would have eventually?" David never asked for Donna Lauria, for "I figured in the end he [Sam] would give her to me."

"Beelzebub" and "Chubby Behemoth" are names David believed the demons had chosen for him.

It "must be the water they drink" that makes them so pretty: "I had to write something. I had a message. It was an important message . . . to let them know what was happening, a warning."

"Yahoos: It's like utopia, a land of peace. . . . It's not heaven or hell, it's just a place."

"To the people of Queens, I love you: I loved them, I want to love them. . . . Sometimes I have to kill them. . . . I don't know. It's all so mixed up."

DAVID SAYS the purpose of the letter was not to win him publicity. He stoutly denies that he was dropping a clue in the hope that somehow he'd be caught and stopped from killing. No. He wanted the police to capture Sam!

As far as Berkowitz's reasoning was coherent, it went: The police would find this letter and seek out Sam. They would catch Sam Carr and with him they would capture Satan. David would then be free. Sam's hold on him would die. David would be able to stop killing.

Hopelessness invades his further comments. If he, a new postal worker, had chosen to *mail* the letter to Borrelli, "it would have been somehow lost." Further, the letter had to be futile. "Nothing could hurt Sam. He knew the letter wouldn't hurt him. You see he knew the police. I thought the police would be able to piece things together. Sam knew they wouldn't. If he thought they could, something would have happened. I'm telling you my car would have been smashed up."

Two significant things happened to that letter. First, the police handed it around. Perhaps eight people touched it before it was sent to a laboratory for fingerprint tests. The tests would then prove futile. This mistake made Joe Coffey rage.

Second, the letter was leaked to the press.

So if the letter served no purpose as evidence, it still was not without effect. Once the Sunday, June 5 *Daily News* appeared, the old nemesis, the .44-caliber killer, was dead.

Son of Sam was born.

10

Operation Omega

The morning after the name *Son of Sam* was coined, Mayor Abraham Beame called in Police Commissioner Codd and his top aides and ordered them to throw the full resources of the Police Department into the search for the killer. "I'll never forget that morning," says the former mayor. "I knew the press was going to have a field day. Son of Sam. I even liked the name and that in itself was terrifying. I knew it would stick . . . would become his trademark. There had been six attacks, all laid at the feet of a single individual, and you could see it all building, the fears of the people, including my own, and the headlong rush of the press to create a personality, someone they could build a story around.

"The killings were a horror. The police were under terrible strain. Everyone was beginning to question their inability to capture the gunman. The letter fused everything together. It was a man against an entire city. He had written this one policeman, but I knew it wasn't that captain he was writing about. It was every cop who was after him, all twenty-five thousand of them.

"I knew sooner or later I'd be asked to respond to some reporter's question about the name, the Son of Sam. What response would I give? I just didn't want to be drawn into a web created by someone who was looking for headlines. And at the back of my head was the thought that whatever I'd say, whatever was either written or said on either radio or television, would be either heard or seen by the killer. I couldn't afford to make him strike out at another innocent pair of kids. And I knew there would be many more sleepless nights before this thing was over."

At the March 11 news conference, held at the 112th Precinct in Forest Hills, Mayor Beame stood by as the Police Commissioner announced that all the shootings were the work of a single individual. The choice of the 112th, in the heart of Forest Hills, was symbolic—for the two prior attacks were in that area and residents were up in arms, a fact attested to by their institution of a civilian patrol. "We had fears that the situation was escalating," Beame says. "I never liked vigilante groups of any sort, no matter their intention. The police are trained to do their jobs; civilians aren't."

The mayor saw that the first signs of hysteria were building. That evening the *New York Post* ran a headline CO-ED'S KILLER MAY STRIKE AGAIN. After reading the article, His Honor ordered a police detail be assigned to the Voskerichian funeral. The *Post* had revealed that Virginia would be at rest at the Edward D. Jamie Funeral Chapel, 141-26 Northern Boulevard, Flushing. It went on to say that the burial would take place at Maple Grove Cemetery. "I had to do something to try to shield the family from the curiosity-seekers. Maybe it was guilt at our inability to catch him. Anyway, I ordered that detail."

On the afternoon of June 1, 1977, *Daily News* reporter Jimmy Breslin received the first shocking communication written to a member of the press from the .44-caliber killer. The Mayor wouldn't learn of that letter until the story broke on the front page of Friday's paper. It was as if the Mayor had been forgotten, the entire case passing him by. Perhaps it was a foreshadowing of the fact that the Democratic Party was about to pass him by as well.

Once the Breslin letter was reproduced in the Sunday, June 5, edition, public response became overwhelming. Calls flooded into the new police hotline number, 844-0999, and into the local precinct switchboards. Captain Borrelli offers an explanation: "Everyone had their own suspect and they were certain their man was the Son of Sam."

THE TASK FORCE itself became a clearinghouse for all the nuts and well-meaning citizens in the city. With its still-limited manpower, it was nevertheless able to follow up three hundred separate investigations a day.

On the morning of April 14 a police sergeant attached to the Midtown South zone called in a report that a man living in Maspeth seemed a likely suspect. A trusted source had confided to the sergeant that the man owned a .44-caliber handgun. The source also said the suspect was "somewhat psychotic."

Detective Marlin Hopkins ran a check. The suspect had never been arrested, but he had been issued a pistol permit by the New York Police Department. The permit allowed him to have in his home a .38 and a .45, but not a .44. "Since we were told he had a .44," Hopkins says, "and he didn't have a permit for it, we were going to have to confront him and find out."

Along with another detective, six-foot-three-inch John O'Connell, Hopkins drove to the suspect's home. A neighbor said the man wasn't there.

Where was he?

"In some bar on Metropolitan Avenue, probably the one just north of the Long Island Expressway in Queens," answered the neighbor.

Hopkins looked at the photographs of the suspect that they had found on copies of his permit application. Then he and O'Connell drove back to Queens. They would check out the bars on Metropolitan Avenue.

They found the man in the fourteenth bar they entered. "He had that look," Hopkins says, "of the type of person we wanted.

"It was like he was there, but he wasn't. There was a kind of feeling there—hard to describe."

Hopkins felt hopeful and nervous. He was about to nail Son of Sam. He put a hand on his service revolver in his trouser pocket and walked up to the man.

. "Police! Don't move!"

The man turned slightly. Hopkins saw a gun in his waistband. Moving quickly, he slammed him toward a wall, disarmed him, and threw the pistol to the floor. He handcuffed him, spun him around, and said "Where's the .44?"

"I have it at home," the man said.

Hopkins remembers thinking "I've got to do this legal now. I've got to get a search warrant." "You're under arrest. Come on. We're going to the station house," he said. Then O'Connell recited the suspect's legal rights.

"Okay," the suspect answered.

"I'm going to check out your house," Hopkins said, "but first I'm going to get a search warrant."

"You don't need one," was the answer. "You can come over to the house without one. I'll take you there if you'd like."

Hopkins "made out a paper" saying that the man was freely granting permission for his home to be searched without "any form of duress." Still in handcuffs, the suspect signed the release.

Hopkins and O'Connell drove back to Maspeth with the suspect. There they found a .44 and lost their case. The .44 was a black-powdered gun, a replica of a Civil War weapon. But the detectives found eight other handguns, thirteen rifles, and a target nailed to the back of a door. The suspect had been shooting a high-powered rifle at the target. Each bullet drilled through the door and carried into a cemetery across the street.

The man was "somewhat of a psycho," but he was not Son of Sam. He was arrested and charged with illegal possession of twenty-one guns. Subsequently a court fined him and released him.

The incident went down hard for Detective Hopkins. He could have lost his life arresting a gun nut. He had thought he was arresting a psychopathic killer. He was wrong, but he had found an unstable character obsessed with guns.

He had risked . . . and what did the damn courts do? Convict, fine, then set free an unstable man who might, in time, acquire a new arsenal. And then . . .

"It was frustrating," Hopkins says, "putting your neck on the line for nothing, for absolutely nothing at all."

ON APRIL 10, Sam Carr of 316 Warburton Avenue in Yonkers had received an anonymous letter complaining about Harvey, his black Labrador retriever. Carr had once worked for the City of Yonkers. Retired now, living on a modest pension, Sam and his wife Frances ran a small telephone-answering service from their white-shingled three-story frame home. The family also included a daughter, Wheat Carr, employed as a dispatcher in the Yonkers Police Department; their eldest son, John, serving a tour with the Air Force in North Dakota; and Michael, a freelance advertising stylist, working out of the Carrs' home. It was a close-knit family: Sam, Frances, John, Wheat, Michael, and a black Labrador named Harvey.

Sometimes Harvey barked. The anonymous letter complained that Harvey was a public nuisance. "Our lives have been torn apart because of this dog," the letter read. It was signed, in bold script, *A Citizen*. The Carrs didn't know what to make of the letter, yet for some reason they decided to save it.

On the morning of April 19, two days after the slaying of Valentina Suriani and Alexander Esau, the Carrs received a second anonymous letter. The handwriting on this one seemed to match that of the first:

I have asked you kindly to stop that dog from howling all day long, yet he continues to do so. I pleaded with you. I told you how this is destroying my family. We have no peace, no rest.

Now I know what kind of a person you are and what kind of a family you are. You are cruel and inconsiderate. You have no love for any other human beings. Your selfish, Mr. Carr. My life is destroyed now. I have nothing to lose anymore. I can see that there shall be no peace in my life, or my families life until I end yours.

Frightened, the Carrs called the police. The sector officers, Tom Chamberlain, thirty-one, and Pete Intervallo, twenty-six, investigated and filed a report for the Yonkers detective division. Technically, the anonymous letters were classified as "citizen harassment," a minor crime. The detective division noted the case and left it in the hands of Chamberlain and Intervallo.

AT NINE-THIRTY on the foggy morning of April 27, the calm in the Glenwood section of Yonkers was broken by a single shot. Sam Carr rushed from his house toward his backyard. He saw Harvey, the Labrador, on its side. Carr rushed to the animal and saw a trickle of blood on its flank. The animal had collapsed with shock, but would recover. The bullet was never removed.

He also saw a man—the back of a man—running away. He wore jeans and a yellow shirt. "Stop!" Carr shouted. But David Berkowitz, who had killed another demon-dog, kept running until he was out of Sam Carr's sight.

Carr dialed the police. Tom Chamberlain and Pete Intervallo responded. They checked out the scene and reread the two anonymous letters. Then they decided to gather what else they could about curious happenings in the area.

It would be difficult to prove that the man in the yellow shirt had deliberately shot Harvey. But if they could find him, and the gun, he could be arrested for "firing a weapon within city limits"—a misdemeanor.

The two policemen were determined to find their man.

TASK FORCE OMEGA was beginning to fill out. More than a hundred detectives were being assigned by Sergeant Coffey for nightly patrols of the Queens and Bronx areas considered likely targets for the killer.

Stakeouts (two or three a night) were restricted to hours of darkness, with patrols of plainclothesmen in unmarked cars, two or three to a vehicle. Within a month, the Omega Force was expanded to two hundred detectives, making it the single largest combined operation in the history of the New York City Police Department.

Almost as if on cue, the press made note of the expanded police force. Reporters have their sources within the department, and word quickly leaked out that the Mayor had ordered all available manpower into the search. After all, this was an election year, and voters just might remember the Mayor who was instrumental in the capture of the killer. (In the case of Abraham Beame, it was not to be.)

Meanwhile, merchants began to complain. More and more young people stayed away from restaurants and discos in Queens. Later, as the fear spread throughout the city, establishments everywhere felt the absence of usual evening clientele. Discos that usually drew fifteen hundred young men and women on Friday and Saturday nights now were deserted. Food spoiled in restaurant kitchens. New York was becoming a disaster area. At The Wine Gallery, where Christine Freund and John Diel had eaten just before Berkowitz attacked them, the owner was contemplating closing down and going to Florida. Forest Hills was particularly hard hit. The Son of Sam had struck four times in succession in Queens and had killed twice within a one-block area.

One segment of the retail trade, however, reported a boom. Beauty parlors were doing a stand-up business as women queued up to have their hair cut, or dyed blonde. Rumor had it that the killer didn't strike blondes or girls with short hair.

The murders became an ever-increasing topic in the conversation at the cafeteria of the Main Post Office where David worked. Like everyone else, David expressed indignation. He agreed that the police had to catch the killer. But, as the days went on, he became angered. "Son of Sam, Son of Sam. They were making jokes, you know. I told them, 'Don't make jokes, 'cause he'll get you, man.' The Son of Sam could say you're welcome. . . . There was power there. There was a force. You see, they jump around, you know. It's like making fun of the devil. You just can't fool with this black magic. You can get hurt. This is a tremendous force of evil, you know. Evil forces. You just can't play with these things. They warn you to stay away from them—dabbling in the occult. They do that for a reason, because . . . there are forces there and you all can get hurt. These guys were joking about the Son of Sam, and they shouldn't, because these demons can get awful upset."

No one knows whether or not David actually voiced his warnings. If he did, nobody seems to have noticed. His co-workers continued to treat the subject lightly. This caused David further anguish, for he was convinced that harm might befall those who belittled Sam's power.

11

Killer Taunts Cops

The two hundred men in Operation Omega were recruited from precincts in every borough of the City of New York. As the *Daily News* put it, the policemen came "from the pockmarked battlefield called the South Bronx, from the neon sleaziness of Times Square, from the alleys and street corners, the darkened bars that were their hunting ground."

Some of the detectives who assembled at the command post, the 109th Precinct in Flushing, Queens, had known one another years earlier as patrolmen. They joked and looked for signs of age on the faces of colleagues. Those who were strangers felt joined in an elite fraternity. Their emblem was the gold detective's badge.

Some had been drafted to Omega. More had volunteered. They all knew, although few spoke of, the rewards that lay ahead. The men who captured Son of Sam would not only save the city from a psycho. They would win promotion, an instant measure of fame, a better salary, and recognition throughout their careers in the department.

It is an irony of the New York police force that homicide detectives have a particularly hard time making ends meet. In certain divisions, one hears, policemen supplement their salaries in shabby ways. Some cops who recover stolen goods expect a tip, a modest or not-so-modest percentage of what they recover. Shakedowns of drug pushers and pimps persist, despite the efforts of honest cops to end these practices. But the homicide detective, like Sherlock Holmes, has to live on what he legitimately earns. You can't go around "fixing" murders (although some have tried). A pragmatic morality works here, which one old homicide hand sums up nicely: "When I was a traffic cop, could you get me to fix a ticket? Yeah, if I was broke enough that day. But now can you get me to fix anything? Hell, no. Listen, murder isn't exactly running a stop sign."

Force Omega, then, was joined by personal ambition, by altruism, and by one final communal sense. The detective division would show what it could do. According to someone who was there, the detectives felt that "in the last few years they'd been stripped of power and glamor and personnel. But, by God, when the city was in trouble, who did it turn to? The detectives. The detectives in Operation Omega felt pretty good. This was the big one and they were on it."

THE BOSS was Tim Dowd, whose high-cheekboned ascetic face was a reverse of David Berkowitz's soft features. Under him was dark-visaged, young, and promising Joe Borrelli.

"Borrelli was the best," says Sergeant Joe Coffey. "He was the necessary catalyst, the buffer between Inspector Dowd and the squad." Dowd tended to be aloof. He made snap decisions and left the handling of his troops to Borrelli, Lieutenant John Powers, and Sergeants Richard Conlon and Joe Coffey.

One detective had a special, personal motivation. He was Redmond "Red" Keenan, fifty-one, who normally worked out of the office of the Queens District Attorney. Detective Keenan was the father of Rosemary Keenan, Carl Denaro's date at the Taxcipo Bar on the night of October 23, 1976, when David Berkowitz fired a bullet into his head. "It might have easily been my kid," Keenan commented. "I know he was aiming for her. So let's just say I put a little more than I had to into this case."

Every evening the brass distributed "hot" information on what had been gathered by the day men from a flood of calls. In addition, the police Intelligence Division forwarded information gathered from leads being supplied by officers who were working on their own time. Intelligence became the clearinghouse for leads supplied from other police agencies throughout the tristate area and from as far away as California and New Mexico.

There were also the composite sketches drawn by police artists from the vague statements of witnesses and surviving victims. Although the drawings varied greatly, no single one closely resembled David Berkowitz. No witness thought the police artists were able to capture exactly what the killer looked like.

Police artist William F. McCormack explains the difficulties in getting an exact likeness of a suspect: "First you have to remember that the witness or victim was under great stress at the time they saw the attacker. Second, the lighting conditions, due to the nighttime hours, were usually poor at best. And then time would pass. Time isn't a police artist's best ally. It works against you. Given too much time, people tend to allow things to distort that somewhat clouded image they've tried to retain.

"So you get what you can quickly. After a point, you sense that you've gone far enough with someone. Work more, and you come up with less. You're never going to come up with a perfect likeness. It's something you realize and you make do. No witness is ever really completely satisfied. In fact, when they are, you can be sure they have some other person's image etched in their mind. It might be a movie star, or someone they grew up with. It isn't something they intended to do, it just happens."

Time and time again, Sergeant Coffey warned his men not to rely on the sketches. "They're supposed to help, but they don't. In all the time I've been on the job, I haven't seen a composite picture work. They don't work because they always wind up looking like someone else. After all, you can get a dozen trained observers to see something, and they'll come up with a dozen different descriptions. So don't lock in on them. Let your gut talk to you. If your gut says 'bag him,' then bag him.''

Following the killer's M.O., 85 percent of the Omega Task Force was put on a rugged shift, working from 8:00 P.M. to 4:00 A.M., concentrating on those days of the week when he had already struck. The Voskerichian killing, coming on a Tuesday, was discounted as being a part of that pattern, for the killer was thought to have a job that enabled him to have his nights free. The killing on March 8 was considered to have occurred on a day off for some unknown reason. When he killed Alexander Esau and Valentina Suriani, it was believed to be because he had returned to his pattern of night attacks.

The men began staking out the subway stations in Forest Hills, hoping to spot the killer lurking about. On one particular evening, Captain Borrelli was on patrol when he saw one of his men hiding behind a tree in an area near the Voskerichian and Freund killings. He double-parked his car and tried to inch up as close as possible, snapping his fingers to catch Detective John Clark's attention. Finally the detective motioned him forward. Borrelli ran and crouched. "What have you got?" he asked.

"Cap," Clark responded, pointing just down the block, "see that guy with the shopping bag. He's been hanging around the station. Then he walked here looking into cars. Rudy is in the alley working his way ahead of him." The man was indeed carrying a partially filled shopping bag. Clark had been instructed that the killer might be carrying the .44 in just such a bag. Thus the bag and the man's suspicious manner made him a target. As he moved down the block, the detective and his captain kept him in sight. Suddenly a hand came out of the darkness and grabbed the suspect by the neck and pulled him into the alley. The detective and his supervisor sprang forward and drew their weapons, running to the spot where their suspect had disappeared. From the alleyway came a series of screams, which grew louder as they ran. They turned into the opening to find the man up against the side of the building in the classic frisk position. He had been apprehended by Detective Rudy Gregorvich and had been virtually stripped by the burly officer. The suspect was screaming over and over "Please, don't rape me."

The three policemen tore open the shopping bag. It contained toilet goods. They turned the man around, let him dress, and identified themselves. "At any other time," says Captain Borrelli, "this guy would have been down at police headquarters the next day, yelling his head off. But once he knew we were after the killer, he forgot about everything else. In fact, he seemed relieved that we were there."

FOR THE MAJORITY of the men of Omega Force, the investigation had become an all-consuming preoccupation. Most of them gave up their home lives and usual routines. Cots were placed in the back of the precinct house where they could grab a few hours of sleep, only to rise, brush their teeth, and get out on the streets once again.

"There were days on end that I just never got home," recalls Sergeant Coffey. "Something always was breaking, some new angle or suspect. The drive back to Levittown became a luxury I just couldn't afford. I began putting in twenty-hour days. We all did. Finding him became the most important thing in our lives. Our families just had to understand."

Even when they did go home, the detectives' minds never left what they were working on. Sometimes they'd wake in the middle of the night to rush back to the precinct with a new slant. They were grasping at straws; their supervisors knew it. It became the sergeants' jobs to keep them on the right track, hoping that the killer would make a mistake. Vacation plans were canceled, marriages were on the rocks. Some wives didn't understand their husbands' obsession. Most did, however, and supported them when they needed it most.

"My wife Veronica took it in stride," says Hopkins. "She was a cop's wife and understood what was going on inside me. The shootings, the killings were all against young kids. As a father you came to look on each killing as an act against your own kids. I'd look at my two boys and I thought to myself, What if they were the ones? That made me push a little harder. But Veronica was always there when I needed her with a smile, a meal, or a word."

The detectives' kids were hit the hardest. Little League teams throughout Nassau and Suffolk counties went without their coaches, but other fathers stepped in, understanding just what was going on.

More frustrating was that despite their Omega assignment, many of the officers still had to make court appearances because of prior arrests that were just coming to trial. Thus they were forced to get up at 7:30 A.M., sleeping just three hours, rush to court, then drag themselves back to their homes sometime in midafternoon. Despite their new 8:00 P.M.-to-4:00 A.M. schedules, they worked on, not getting or caring about overtime pay. They'd see their kids and wives for just a few minutes—after school and when their wives returned from work or between napping, showering, and getting ready to go back to work.

"I'd get home in the early morning and fall right into bed," says Hopkins. "The boys, Danny, twelve, and Johnny, nine, would have left for school long before I'd get up. When everyone got home, we'd catch a few minutes together. But those minutes were too short. Even though I had to report at 7:45 P.M., I'd go in earlier. So I'd catch a bite with the family and run. Veronica became both mother and father to the boys.

"The other guys I worked with, John O'Connell, Rich Conlon, and Erwin Jacobson, had the same problems and the same support from their wives and families. Looking back on it all, I don't know how our families survived."

At the 109th, the coffee machine never stopped working. Over cup after cup of steaming coffee and amid the noise of ringing phones, the detectives speculated endlessly about the killer who was eluding them. Tempers began to fray. Fights broke out. Men had to be separated by fellow detectives, with Coffey and Conlon finally having to order some of them to take a couple of days off. The fighters always apologized and begged to stay, but the sergeants knew they had to take the time off or they wouldn't be good for anything.

BY NOW the Omega investigation had become—as already noted—the largest single operation in the history of the New York City Police Department. More than $90,000 a day was being spent in trying to capture the Son of Sam. Even more telling was the fact that the reduction in the overall detective force was beginning to be felt throughout the city. Other areas of investigative work were suffering badly.

Supplementing the task force was a psychiatric team of doctors who, in the past, had helped the police department on similar cases. While not officially employed by the police department, these doctors received certain "perks" and gave of their time in an effort to come up with a workable profile of the killer.

On May 26, 1977, the Police Commissioner released a psychological profile that described the killer as "neurotic, schizophrenic and paranoid." Included in the profile was the heretofore untouched notion that, possibly, the killer regarded himself as a victim of demonic possession. Commissioner Codd added: "He is probably shy and odd, a loner inept in establishing personal relationships, especially with women."

When asked why he released the profile to the press, Inspector Dowd said he felt that the killer would make a mistake. A simple slip "that would trip him up." Another letter would be handled better. Next time there might be fingerprints that could be checked.

Meanwhile, there was routine work to do. Dowd ordered four detectives, including Redmond Keenan, to find all fifty-six Bulldog .44s registered to owners who lived in the metropolitan area. He also ordered a test firing from each. It took four weeks and led nowhere.

Then Dowd insisted on a search for every one of the 28,000 Bulldogs manufactured by Charter Arms of Bridgeport, a complicated task. Many of the guns had changed hands after their initial purchase. Some new owners had not reregistered with the Treasury Department's Bureau of Tobacco and Firearms. Adding to the problem was the fact that 667 of the guns had been stolen from the manufacturer before reaching firearms dealers.

This investigation took another ten weeks and turned up nothing.

An average of 250 calls flooded into the emergency hotline number each day. They came from kooks and from concerned citizens. "Hello. I'd like to report that I know who the killer is."

"Please give me your name and address."

The caller would usually cooperate. Only 5 percent of the calls came from anonymous sources. This was an unusually small number, far less than the typical ratio of police tips, 25 to 30 percent anonymous. "There's this neighbor of mine who is suddenly sneaking about at night. He never did that before. He's leaving the house at eleven, twelve o'clock, always carrying something."

"Anything else?" the responding detective would ask.

"Well, he's always carrying something when he goes out. That's something he never did before. You know, something in a small paper bag. And one thing more. That new sketch you guys released. He looks a lot like it."

After some further evaluation, the officer wrote the information on a card and put it in one of the three boxes on the sergeant's desk.

It was a time, first, for organization. Every call was recorded and typed into an official summary. Each was then classified into borough of origin and further sorted as "high, middle, or low priority." This last was done viscerally. Detectives relied on gut reactions to distinguish a caller telephoning because he wanted to "get someone"—perhaps a hated neighbor—from a caller offering a serious lead.

Gut reactions are fine—indeed, essential. They are part of

almost all professional work, whether it's making an elusive medical diagnosis or deciding how to try a case before a jury. But because gut reactions are imprecise, they can lead you to second-guess yourself. Scores of detectives, marking a call "low priority," found themselves reconsidering days later, then hunting for their first report and leaving the 109th Precinct to seek out the caller personally.

In the case of the tipster whose neighbor was keeping strange hours, the man had changed shifts in a bottling plant. The bag was his lunch; the hero sandwich shop across the street was closed at night.

No one was above suspicion, not even police officers themselves. The highest security stack at the 109th was a compilation of reports suggesting good suspects from their own ranks, and the cards in that pile were saved after the case was broken. According to Borrelli, "Some day someone in one of those cards may go off the deep end, and we'll at least have a head start on him." As far as can be learned, there are at least a hundred names in the secret stack.

Against Berkowitz's method of operation, the police were developing an M.O. of their own. From 8:00 to 11:00 P.M., detectives read through daily complaint sheets. Each detective paid particular attention to complaints from his own borough, then he went out into the field. The search ranged from Tottenville, on the southern tip of Staten Island, to the northern border of the Bronx. Before David was caught, after making a simple slip, as Inspector Timothy Dowd foretold, police would closely investigate 3,167 suspects.

Omega men consulted psychiatrists, psychologists, hypnotists, numerologists, handwriting analysts, astrologers, exorcists, and biorhythm specialists. Detectives studied time spans between the killer's attacks, looking for cycles.

Eighty-six days had passed between the time a .44 bullet killed Donna Lauria and another wounded Carl Denaro. Thirty-five days lapsed between the Denaro and Lomino–DeMasi shootings. Then there were gaps of thirty-seven days and forty. Was there a rhythm here, a progression of any kind? It was worth considering—although, as one detective said, "How do we know the killer hasn't been prowling other nights, looking for a victim and failing to find one? Or being scared off before he pulls the trigger?"

To Tim Dowd, as to most experienced cops, psychiatric reports are something less than tablets from Mount Sinai. He had seen too many earlier psychological profiles of unknown killers miss the mark. But, for Dowd, the reports on this case were convincing on at least one point: The murderer was a man who led a double life. "He's the kind of guy," Dowd said, "who probably goes to work every day. Maybe he does something with statistics. An accountant or a clerk. He just kind of melts into the city scene. He doesn't *look* crazy."

In the Fingerprint Identification Unit at One Police Plaza, a brown and rather formless brick fortress on the lower end of Manhattan Island, Lieutenant James Ghericich, and Officers Robert Craft and James Chillis were putting in seventeen-hour days, seven days a week, working with three fingerprint tips from the letter Berkowitz had left for Joe Borrelli near the Hutchinson River Parkway. As Coffey puts it, "Whenever they caught the killer, those prints would match and could possibly be the strongest piece of evidence we'd have to tie him to the killing of the two kids." But the fingerprints were providing little help in finding the killer.

Thus what the police possessed were only the building blocks of a future prosecutor's case. And they still lacked a good suspect.

JIMMY BRESLIN of the *Daily News,* forty-seven, was covering the Son of Sam case with a particular passion. Breslin had first drawn notice with sports stories in the 1950s, which he wrote in a vivid later-day Runyon style. He liked rebels and misfits. A club-throwing professional golfer called, in sports-page argot, The Terrible-Tempered Bolt. A brooding, angry jockey named Bill Hartack. Breslin was never better than in his description of an extremely intelligent, extremely corrupt basketball player named Jack Molinas who attended

Columbia University and is thought to have fixed games for
the underworld. Molinas threw games himself and bribed
other athletes as well. He was killed mysteriously, an apparent victim of the syndicate for which he worked.

A generally cheerful sports book about the New York
Mets, *Can't Anybody Here Play This Game?* won Breslin a
job on the old *New York Herald Tribune,* whose publisher,
John Hay Whitney, was the brother of the Mets' principal
stockholder, Joan Payson. Soon Breslin moved out of sports,
with columns about politics, chicanery, and mobsters. He
published a successful novel about a semicomic, wholly
deadly gang of Brooklyn killers.

Crime attracted Breslin. Crime stories eased his pathway
to success. The same subject also attracted his employers at
the *Daily News.* As *The New York Times* is global (even inter-
planetary, comfortable with soil samples from Mars), the
Daily News became successful with local New York stuff,
much of it local blood and gore. "Yeah, we're common,"
concedes one *News* columnist, "and we do better with common people than all those Princeton Ph.Ds. But you know
what Abraham Lincoln said about God and the common man.
He must have loved the common man. He made so many of
them."

Writing about a psychopathic killer is a Breslin specialty.
And the Son of Sam was a very special psychopath. He had
killed twice in Forest Hills, within a mile of the small attached
brick house where Breslin lives with his wife Rosemary and
their six children (twins James and Kevin, Rosemary, Patrick,
Kelly, and Christopher).

On Friday, June 3, splashed across the front page of the
New York Daily News was the headline:

THE .44-CALIBER CASE
NEW NOTE: CAN'T
STOP KILLING

News reporter Richard Edmonds went into great detail
about how the Son of Sam wished the detectives "luck" in

their hunt for him. Edmonds gave an analysis of the symbol scratched on the letter. The reporter also quoted that "Breslin could forget about writing about the Son of Sam because the killer doesn't want any publicity."

Edmonds was careful to include the reference to David's first victim, Donna Lauria, whom Berkowitz had singled out for mention. "Don't forget Donna Lauria, whom he described with warmth and affection." The article ended with a warning that the killer didn't intend to stop.

The buildup had begun for two things: first, the publishing of the killer's letter, mailed from a drop box just across the George Washington Bridge in Englewood, New Jersey, and second, in a tortured twist of journalism, Jimmy Breslin's reply. The public, and press, were in suspense until Sunday. As a Saturday filler, the *News* proclaimed in bold, block letters:

.44 KILLER: I
AM NOT ASLEEP

Reporter Donald Singleton had worked for two days on preparing a teaser. The article opened with a piece of the original letter:

"Don't think because you haven't heard from (me) for a while that I went to sleep. No, rather, I am still here. Like a spirit roaming the night. Thirsty, hungry, seldom stopping to rest; anxious to please Sam. I love my work. Now the void has been filled."

Singleton wrote that the police had confirmed that both the Breslin letter and the note left at the April 17 killings of Valentina Suriani and Alexander Esau were the work of the same individual. Taking great care to continue the buildup of the coming Breslin reply, Singleton dropped this tidbit: The killer looks forward to meeting Breslin, "face to face someday or perhaps I will be blown away by cops with smoking .38's." The article ended with the statement that Breslin planned to answer the Son of Sam in the next day's edition. The ending was written in the best tradition of Saturday-morning cinema serials, when the hero was about to be blown up or the girl about to be run over by a train. "Come back next week and see . . ."

By Saturday midnight, thousands of New Yorkers were lined up at their newsstands awaiting the heavy *News* trucks that dropped ninety-pound bundles on the streets. Vendors sold the papers without all the color sections that usually comprise a Sunday edition. People cared little for anything else than news about this crazed destroyer of young people.

Breslin and the planning brains who sit in plush offices at the *News* Building on East Forty-Second Street had mapped their strategy well. They were out to get a killer, but weren't opposed to selling papers.

The entire first printing was sold out within an hour of hitting the streets. The pressmen were ordered to keep on printing, and, by the end of the day, more papers had sold than ever before. (This record, 1,116,000 copies, was broken on the day David Berkowitz was caught.)

What the entire city—the world—had been waiting for shouted from the front page:

BRESLIN TO .44 KILLER
GIVE UP! IT'S
ONLY WAY OUT

On page three the article began by quoting from the killer's letter: "Hello from the gutters of NYC, which is filled with dog manure, vomit, stale wine, urine, and blood. Hello from the sewers of NYC which swallow up these delicacies when they are washed away by the sweeper trucks. Hello from the cracks in the sidewalks of NYC and from the ants that dwell in these cracks and feed in the dried blood of the dead that has settled into the cracks." This was the extent of the letter published for this edition, but more was surely to come. Breslin and his editors at the *News* knew what they had. They intended to milk the letter for as long as possible.

The article jumped to page 51, with Breslin issuing a subtle challenge to the Son of Sam: "If he wants any further contact, all he has to do is call or write me at the *Daily News*. It's simple to get me, the only people I don't answer are bill collectors.''

The Monday edition continued the yellow journalism with the headline:

COPS: '.44 KILLER
IS TAUNTING US.'

The article gave the impression that the police were baffled by the case—and also that they had confided in the *News*. Perhaps the *News* was in contact with the Son of Sam? This vague relationship placed the police under immense pressure, making them unsure what item would next appear. The situation was rapidly becoming one where control was bounced back and forth between the media and police. Many times the press knew the police game plan before the officers who were coming on duty received their assignments from their superiors. What was leaked with the knowledge of the department and what was not was never clear in the minds of many.

"I wrote Mr. Breslin because he had an obsession with the shootings," Berkowitz says. "That was evidenced in his columns and how he wrote about them. I also wanted him to write about Donna Lauria because the newspapers did not cover her properly. They just had Donna down as a name. The pattern of the shootings was not figured out until much later—that all the shootings were connected—and after that, when people were shot they got all the publicity. Before they figured out the pattern, nobody wrote that much about the victims, and I didn't want Donna to be forgotten. I felt a mystical attachment to her that I can't explain.

"I didn't think Mr. Breslin would ever publicize what I wrote him," Berkowitz says. "But I wanted him to remember Donna Lauria. I wanted him to write about Donna. It wasn't because of any feeling of sorrow on my part. I simply don't know what sorrow is."

Why did you use different handwritings, David, when you

wrote Captain Borrelli and Mr. Breslin, as opposed to how you wrote to the Carrs?

"The reason I printed the letters to Captain Borrelli and Breslin was for effect. I wrote those two out first in longhand. Then I wrote them again in print without any changes, I thought the printing was more ghoulish-looking."

To thwart his hunters, David had driven to Englewood, a New Jersey suburb just across the George Washington Bridge, on the morning of Memorial Day, May 30. Because of a mix-up in the holiday schedule for box pickups, David's letter was not collected. Two hours later a second truck was especially dispatched to that single corner drop. All mail from the box was hand-stamped at a substation rather than at the main branch. Thus, the Son of Sam letter was traceable to a specific box in Englewood.

The "ghoulish letter" made its way slowly through the holiday mails, arriving at the *Daily News* nearly three days after it was mailed. When it arrived it was opened by Breslin's secretary, read (her fingerprints were later found on the pages), and passed on to the reporter. Although Breslin told the police that only he and his secretary handled the document, reporter Pete Hamill's fingerprints were also found on the sheets by the police laboratory.

This is the Breslin letter as printed by the *Daily News*.

Hello from the cracks in the sidewalks of New York City and from the ants that dwell in these cracks and feed on the dried blood of the dead that has settled into these cracks.

Hello from the gutters of New York City, which are filled with dog manure, vomit, stale wine, urine and blood.

Don't think that because you haven't heard from me for a while that I went to sleep. No, rather, I am still here, like a spirit roaming the night. Thirsty, hungry, seldom stopping to rest; anxious to please Sam.

Sam's a thirsty lad. ("Lad sounds better than man," David would later tell psychiatrists.) He won't let me stop killing until he gets his fill of blood. ("They need the blood, need the killing of innocent people. They're in the air. They don't have to be physically present, they can change. Move in quickly and feast. They follow, they take the blood they're there.") Tell me, Jim, what will you have for July 29? You can forget about me if you like because I don't care for publicity. However, you must not forget Donna Lauria and you cannot let the people forget her either. She was a very sweet girl.

Not knowing what the future holds, I shall say farewell and I will see you at the next job? Or should I say you will see my handiwork at the next job? Remember Ms. Lauria. Thank you.

> In their blood
> and
> from the gutter—
> "Sam's creation" .44

A single page of the Breslin letter was withheld from publication by the *Daily News* at the police department's request. It contained specific police jargon and hinted at a professional knowledge of police procedures. It included a reference to the NCIC (National Crime Information Center), a semisecret clearing house of information used by law enforcement agencies across the country. Later, when questioned by police and psychiatrists, David gave them the explanations and missing clues he had omitted from the text, which read:

Here are some names to help you along. Forward them to the Inspector [Dowd] for use by the NCIC Center. They have everything on computer, everything. They just might turn up, from some other crimes. Maybe they could make associations.

Duke of Death.
Wicked King Wicker.
The twenty-two Disciples of Hell.
And lastly, John Wheaties, rapist and suffocator of young girls.

P.S., drive on, think positive, get off your butts, knock on coffins, etc.

David was also giving the police a hint of what was tormenting him. After his capture, he told them: "The Duke of Death lives at 22 Wicker Street along with Wicked King Wicker. The King is over the Duke, but still just an officer under Sam, much lower than General Cosmo. It's no accident either, Wicker . . . wicked. Do you notice the connection? It's just what they are, wicked, wicked demons. They changed the name to Wicker Street. The Wicked Wicker. And John Wheaties, he lives in the same house as Sam Carr, at 316 Warburton Avenue. There are lots of women. There are a lot of men there, dozens."

Had David's letter given the police the addresses where his demons lived it would have been simple for the detectives to locate the community where such streets existed. But Son of Sam had no desire to be captured, at least not yet. The police had nothing concrete to go on. Once again they were forced to wait for the killer's next move. The former New York City auxiliary cop (from 1970 to 1973) had learned his trade well.

"I got into trouble for writing the letter to Mr. Breslin," Berkowitz later told psychiatrists. "They [the demons] didn't want me to write it. But truth comes out in the end, and it got through. I wanted to tell people about the demons.

"But nobody listened.

"Nobody cared."

THE THREE police fingerprint specialists, James Ghericich, Robert Craft, and James Chillis, spent nearly six weeks running tests on the letter to Breslin. In the end they lifted two separate partial whorls of fingerprints which later would match Berkowitz's prints taken the night of his capture. These traces were on the last page of the letter, in the lower right-hand corner, from David's left thumb and ring finger, and to a lesser degree on the other pages.

Now they could link the Esau–Suriani and Breslin letters, but the police were still unable to match those partial prints to any they had in their files. They never got to examine the right thumb print left with the New York Firearms Control Board in December 1975, when David applied for a rifle permit. (It would have been the wrong thumb, anyway.) The Control Board has more than three million prints on hand, and the police were pushing those of known criminals. Known criminals usually do not apply for permits.

These three officers worked seventeen-hour days hunched over magnifying glasses, looking at rows of prints, and trying to match tips of individual prints to their fragments. Because they didn't know whether or not they were the tops or sides of the fingers, the fingerprint men were forced to turn each specimen 360 degrees while comparing it to those on file. They were working with NYCPD files and then would turn to the state and then federal files if nothing developed. It was estimated by knowledgeable officers that three men might labor a lifetime without even getting through the city and state prints. As for the federal prints on file, it would have been an impossible task. The federal system works on a computer which assigns each specific pattern a code. Partial prints without direction couldn't be assigned an identifying code, hence couldn't be run through the computer. Any trace of federal files would thus have to be done by hand, and with almost 250,000,000 sets of prints on file in a single agency (the FBI), tracing that agency alone would require an army of experts with no certainty of success.

AFTER he dropped his letter in that solitary mailbox in Englewood, David went out and bought the *Daily News* every morning. Finally the *News* broke the story and on the following Sunday, June 5, he was mildly disappointed when the letter wasn't reproduced in its entirety. Perhaps the *News* was withholding a portion of the text for another occasion, or the police had so ordered it. "It didn't matter. The people were finally learning the truth. They'd have others to read." But the Son of Sam never did communicate with Breslin again, at least not when he was at large.

David had other correspondence on his mind. On June 6

he wrote another letter. He had been brooding about Jack Cassara, his former landlord in New Rochelle, the General Jack Cosmo of his fantasies. "I understood," David says, "he had fallen off the roof of his house. I was happy and sad when I heard about it. I had mixed emotions when I wrote to him."

How did you know he fell off the roof, David?

"This demon dog told me. That's how I knew."

On June 10, Jack Cassara, who had not fallen off his roof, found a get-well note in his mailbox. On the upper left-hand portion of the envelope he saw the name Carr (he didn't know anyone named Carr) and an address in Yonkers.

Cassara opened the envelope and found a get-well card with a picture of a German shepherd gazing at him. Within, he found a letter that confused him:

> Dear Jack,
> I'm sorry to hear about that
> fall you took from the roof of
> your house.
> JUST WANT TO SAY
> "I'M SORRY"
> BUT I'M SURE IT WON'T BE LONG
> UNTIL YOU FEEL MUCH BETTER,
> HEALTHY,
> WELL AND STRONG:
> Please be careful next time.
> Since your [sic] going to be confined
> for a long time, let us know
> if Nann needs anything.
>
> Sincerely:
> Sam & Francis

The postmark was Yonkers and the return address was 316 Warburton Avenue, Yonkers, the Carrs' home. The Westchester telephone directory provided the Cassaras with the Carrs' number. They called, and the two families agreed to meet at the Carrs' house early that same evening.

At 7:30 P.M. on June 10 the Cassaras met the Carrs in the three-story white frame house owned by Sam Carr. Shown into the living room, the Cassaras didn't know what to expect. Carr's Victorian house, set back from Warburton Avenue, had an eerie quality to it. Sam Carr, sixty-four, balding, thin, with a sunken face, asked "Did you bring your card with you?"

"Of course," responded sixty-three-year-old Nann Cassara, taking it out of her purse. "If you look at the return you'll see that someone has copied your name and address. We thought you could offer some explanation." She handed the card to her husband Jack, who passed it to Sam Carr. No one in the room noticed how much Sam Carr and Jack Cassara resembled each other. Both were approximately the same age, had the same build and coloring. In a crowd they could easily be mistaken for each other.

Sam Carr studied the card and envelope. After a few moments he lifted his head and looked at the couple opposite him. "Mr. and Mrs. Cassara, I have no real explanation. I can only say that I've been getting some strange letters also."

The Cassaras straightened up. "Strange letters?" they responded almost in unison. "You, too?"

"Yeah, I've gotten two letters. They were unsigned. Both of them threatened me and complained about our dog, Harvey. When I got your call last night I began thinking. And when I put your card together with the two letters I've received, along with the fact that Harvey was shot in the leg in April, I began looking at some of the other strange things that have been happening in the neighborhood." Carr stood up and stepped into the light of the overhead fixture.

"Last Christmas Eve, one of my neighbors had his dog shot also. It was a German shepherd. And then there was the fire in the backyard. Together they added up. So, this afternoon I called the Yonkers Police Department. My daughter, Wheat, is a dispatcher for them. Two officers came over and I gave them all the information I had on the letters and the other things. They already knew some of the stuff, and they were very interested in it all.''

Mrs. Cassara broke in. "I called the New Rochelle police also. I think they will be contacting the Yonkers cops about my letter." (In fact, the New Rochelle Police Department turned over Mrs. Cassara's statement to the Yonkers Police Department, believing it to be a Yonkers case.) "It's all very strange."

"Yes, strange at the least," agreed Sam Carr.

After another ten minutes, the Cassaras agreed to inform the Carrs if anything else occurred and began the twenty-minute drive back to their home on Coligni Avenue. In the car, Mrs. Cassara was thinking. Finally she spoke up. "Jack, I think there's something more than meets the eye here."

When later they told about their meeting with Sam Carr to their son, Stephen, nineteen, he immediately came up with the solution. "Mom, remember the guy who rented the room over our garage in the beginning of last year? He never came back for his two-hundred-dollar deposit when he left. Well, he was always bothered by our dog, too. And the card you got had a picture of a German shepherd on it. It all fits. That guy . . . Berkowitz. There was something strange about him. Remember how we'd hear his car in the middle of the night? Well, he could be the one who's writing to us. Maybe he's trying to get back at us?"

Stephen had figured it out.

The next morning, Nann Cassara called Sam Carr and told him of her son's suspicions. Carr agreed that the police should be informed. Mrs. Cassara promised to call the New Rochelle police to inquire what action they'd taken on her original complaint. She did.

"Mrs. Cassara," began the detective, "we've turned over the file to the Yonkers detectives. It's really their case."

Nann Cassara made another call to Sam Carr, informing him of the news.

"Let me take care of it," said Sam Carr. "My daughter will talk to one of our detectives before she goes on duty today."

Later that afternoon, Wheat Carr cornered the Yonkers detective. She told him the entire story and ended with the statement "Officers Chamberlain and Intervallo know all about what's been happening. Ask them. They'll be able to fill you in on everything." But with nothing to go on other than the unsigned threats, the detective would have little to charge Berkowitz with. Even the shooting of the Carrs' dog couldn't be laid at David's door. The next day, June 12, Sam Carr called the Yonkers Police Department and was put through to the same detective. He ran through his suspicions, paralleling the story Wheat had given the day before.

"But, Mr. Carr," the officer protested, "what do you really have? I mean, what proof? We can't go around making arrests, or even questioning without proof of some kind."

"But what about my dog being shot?"

"And? Can you identify Berkowitz as the one who did it?"

"No, not really. I mean I didn't see him. But he's got to be the one."

"So you really have nothing, do you?"

Sam Carr had to agree. There was no proof. As in the case of the Cassara letter, there was no proof.

That afternoon, Nann Cassara decided to follow up her call to the New Rochelle police with a call to the Yonkers authorities. The detective she called was out, but the desk man took her name and number, promising that the detective would call back. But it was not until August 6, two months later—that the detective called her back. By then she was certain that David Berkowitz and the Son of Sam were one and the same. She had seen the *Daily News*. That was all she had needed to convince her that what she believed was correct.

The detective was polite, yet asked her for proof. "Mrs. Cassara, do you know someone named Craig Glassman?"

"No. Why?"

"It seems that Glassman is a neighbor of Mr. Berkowitz. He's also a deputy sheriff with the county force. He's also received a letter . . . unsigned. It seems that your husband, Jack, has been mentioned in that letter."

"What?"

"And, what's more, the letter tells about some kind of group, a demon group made up of Glassman, the Carrs, and you people. Let me read it to you: 'I know that the Cassaras and Carr are out to get me and they put you [Glassman] here.' But there's still no proof that Berkowitz has had anything to do with any of the letters. So far it's all only conjecture." The rest of the conversation was polite and quick. She had been given the brushoff, but it merely served to reinforce her belief that David Berkowitz had to be the killer all of New York was looking for. As other people have found out, however, knowing something and making someone in authority act on your knowledge can be two very different things.

DAVID's explanation of these events is intense and not wholly coherent. Somewhere in his chattering about Sam and Satan and General Jack Cosmo, another character appears. He is a six-foot, 225-pound man named Craig Glassman. Craig Glassman, twenty-six, had separated from his wife in March 1977, the month David murdered Virginia Voskerichian. Glassman moved into apartment 6E at Pineview Towers, directly under David Berkowitz. He was a registered nurse. His father, Sam, was a doctor. Craig worked at Montefiore Hospital in the Bronx. He was also a part-time auxiliary deputy sheriff in the Emergency Services Unit of the Westchester County Sheriff's office in White Plains, a volunteer cop.

Craig Glassman worked in traffic control, patrolling school sites in the evenings and during public functions. As a part-time peace officer, Glassman wore a forest-green uniform issued to him by the County Sheriff and carried his licensed pistol. At other times he carried his automatic under his shirt.

The presence of a uniformed officer a floor away upset Berkowitz. According to his fantasies, who could Glassman be but another accomplice of Satan, another soldier in the legions of hell? Of course the Carrs and Glassman were not part of any demon group but in David's twisted mind the Carrs and the Cassaras had placed Glassman there to torment him. David walked about his apartment in stocking feet. "I was afraid master Craig might hear me and be angry." Once again the demons had followed him, intent on ruining his life.

"He just came—he just appeared one day—this Craig. He remained hidden in the walls and in the floor. He made funny screams all night long. I used to beg him to stop yelling and screaming, but he'd never listen.

"His real name was Gregunto Lacinto. He was one of *them*. He's got power to go into my mind. There was no doubt about who he was. Downstairs in the apartment below, it was always quiet, as if no one ever lived there. Then all hell broke loose. Someone constantly yelled and howled in that apartment. The noise was deafening. The house, my room, shook, trembling. I don't know where it came from. When he moved in, he must have done so quietly. When he entered that apartment, underneath, alongside. There were some strange people. I don't know who they were—very weird. They'd break me down, you know, so I'd be ready to fight them. They constantly had to be on top of me or alongside me, you know."

David began to write messages on the walls of his apartment. The messages had very specific meanings:

"As long as Craig Glassman is in the world, there will never be any peace, but there will be plenty of murders.

"Craig Glassman worships the devil and has power over me.

"My name is Craig Glassman and I shall never let a soul rest."

"I wrote those things," Berkowitz says, "because I *became* Craig Glassman; he entered me. He never lets the people rest."

ON JUNE 6 and 18 Craig Glassman received threatening, anonymous letters. Rambling and obscene, they were written on blue-lined notebook paper in a nearly illegible childlike scrawl. They contained puzzling references to demons, Satan, and "the streets running red with blood at the judgment."

The writer was "the slave"; Craig "the master," or "Craig darling," who "drove me into the night to do your bidding."

Meanwhile, Officers Chamberlain and Intervallo had a good suspect in the shooting of the Carrs' dog. The circumstantial evidence developed by the Carrs and the Cassaras seemed to point toward David Berkowitz. The problem was that, even if the charge could be proved, it would simply become a case of harassment and the firing of a weapon within the city limits. And they couldn't even prove that. It was all based on circumstantial evidence. If Officers Chamberlain and Intervallo were to make the case stick, they'd need more —much more.

12

You Can't
Stay Home Forever

On Saturday night, June 25, 1977, David Berkowitz's studio apartment was a hotbox. A heat wave had struck the city, yet the windows were still sealed tight by gray blankets. The temperature in the apartment was pushing a hundred. David remembers thinking "I just wanted to live a nice happy life. I wanted friends, a good job, a future, maybe an education." Then he began to think of Sam.

David walked to the double windows, parted the blankets, and stared down at the Carrs' house and backyard. "I was watching for movement," he says. There was none. His mind wandered to girls, the girls of Queens. "The demons wanted girls," he insists. "Sugar and spice and everything nice. That's one of Sam's favorite sayings. Then they began to yell in the yard."

Who began to yell, David?

Berkowitz raises his voice. "You just don't understand what was happening!"

He dressed, putting on a baggy denim shirt, faded jeans,

and worn work boots. He carried the .44 in a paper bag, as he had the night he murdered Donna Lauria. He stood at the door of the studio, looking back to its disarray. It was 10:00 P.M. The apartment was a single rectangular room with an entranceway containing the chrome-and-formica dining-room set his father had given him. A mattress lay on the floor against the north wall, blankets covering the windows to its left. A single off-white sheet was tangled in an army blanket that partially covered the bare mattress. The shiny orange bedspread lay thrown back, showing a drawing in magic marker of a man's bearded face smoking a pipe. In block letters under the picture, David had written the words NEED and ZIG ZAG, a popular brand of rolling papers. A single wire record stand pushed against the bed but held no records. Against the opposite wall sat a thirty-inch-wide wooden bench. Dirty clothing was piled high in the apartment's entry. David waited to do his laundry until he had no clean clothing left.

Just in front of the tiny kitchen's entrance were three cardboard boxes in which he stored magazines and newspapers. All around were discarded papers, bottles, and beer cans. Only a single red-plastic rose air freshener gave the wall any color. The kitchen itself was as sloppy as the remainder of the small studio apartment. Garbage was piled on every available surface. The kitchen window was also covered with a blanket, effectively shutting off the outside world. The walls had no adornment except for those peculiar scribbles he had chosen to inscribe on them:

> Hi.
> My name is Mr. Williams
> And I live in this hole.

An arrow pointed to an eight-inch hole David had made in the wall.

Under the hole was another inscription, this one in red magic marker:

I have several children
who I'm Turning
INto Killers. WAIT
Til they grow up.

"I ran downstairs to my car. It was cooler in the early
evening. The fresh air always seemed to clear my mind." He
was going to hunt again. He drove down parkways, entering
Queens via the Bronx–Whitestone Bridge. Soon he was cruising on Northern Boulevard, the busy four-lane thoroughfare
that runs through the northern neighborhoods of Queens and
continues as route 25-A toward Gatsby country—such fash-
ionable Nassau communities as Sands Point.

In Bayside, he slowed as he passed a disco called Elephas,
a low squat building of cement blocks. Its customers, mostly
young people, pay a five-dollar entrance fee and receive two
tickets that can be exchanged for two drinks at the bar. The
interior design is based on revolving multicolored lights, ac-
cented with blinding strobes. "Tony C," the Elephas resident
disc jockey, spins nonstop music from 9:00 P.M. to closing
time at 4:00 A.M.

That hot Saturday night, the small crowd of young people
was lost in the vast interior of Elephas. The music seemed
even more frenzied than usual, almost as if it could keep away
the specter of the killings that had plagued the city this past
year. The manager, Mike, remembers, "The place was like a
cemetery. It was the same all over Queens, the whole damn
city. No one would go out any more. I was scared. I used to
look over the faces of different guys, thinking to myself if he
could be the one? Who the hell knew? All I knew was that if
the cops didn't catch the killer soon, we'd have to close. It
takes a thousand people a night to make a buck in here, and
we weren't getting three hundred all weekend."

Berkowitz parked the Galaxie two blocks south and two
blocks west of Elephas at the Clearview Expressway. He took
the .44 from the paper bag, stuck it in his waistband, and
slipped on the denim jacket to conceal the gun. He walked to

Northern Boulevard and turned right toward the club. His steps were regular, military, as if he were on parade.

His walk must have appeared strange. At one point he made a sharp turn and then continued. He says he was trying to follow the cracks in the pavement.

He rounded the corner of 45th Road. He was one block from Elephas when he saw a red Cadillac sitting in front of 45-39 211th Street. It was a red Caddy with a red top. Two people inside the car were talking. He saw that one was a girl.

"I saw her long hair," David says. "I looked about. The street was deserted. I then began to approach the car from the rear, keeping just behind the right rear fender. When I reached the car's trunk, I stopped to get out the gun. Then I stepped onto the curb and took a few steps forward, which brought me directly in front of the passenger's side. I could see them clearly in the front seat. The window was closed. They weren't looking in my direction. I crouched down to bring myself level with the girl, and I fired."

JUDY PLACIDO was a pretty girl, slim, with long hair. She lived in Pelham Gardens, the Bronx, a community less than two miles from the Bronx–Whitestone Bridge. Her widowed father, Aldo, had been lonely ever since Judy's mother, Anne Victoria, died of Hodgkin's Disease in 1968. In 1972 he remarried and moved a short distance away to Pauling Avenue, and Judy went to live with her aunt, Judith Carioscia, and her grandmother, Domenica. Her older brother, John, twenty-nine, and her sister, Donna, twenty-five, had made lives for themselves outside the city.

On the evening of June 25 her family celebrated by having a graduation party for her at their home. Judy had graduated from St. Catherine's Roman Catholic Academy in the Bronx the preceding Saturday and was looking forward to entering Pace University in the fall. (A year earlier, Valentina Suriani had completed her high school education at St. Catherine's.)

After the party, Judy called her friends Debbie Volpe, eighteen, Angela Delfino, nineteen, and Antoinette Coiro, nineteen, and they decided to have their own celebration.

It was a damp, muggy night, with intermittent showers falling after sundown. The temperature hovered in the eighties with a seven-mile-an-hour southerly breeze, giving little relief from the high humidity. At about 9:30 P.M. Angela suggested that they drive to Queens. On the spur of the moment, the group set off for the Elephas.

The girls were cheerful and excited. The warm rain had stopped. Judy said, "I picked that particular disco because I'd been there before." In their clique it was considered the "in" place to be. They didn't feel any undue fear of the murderer now called the Son of Sam.

As Debbie said to Judy, "He won't come out in weather like this. He likes clear nights."

The four girls piled into Angela's blue Buick Regal and drove across the Whitestone Bridge and down the Clearview Expressway. They got off at Northern Boulevard and headed west the twenty blocks to the disco. They found a parking spot on 213th Street and walked two blocks on the wet streets. The girls paid the five-dollar admission charge and received their two bar tickets. They hadn't been asked to prove their ages. Business was bad. Almost anyone could get in. "The crowd was almost nonexistent," recalls Judy. "It picked up a little around ten forty-five. It must have been because of the rain and maybe the killer."

Between dances, the girls used their tickets to purchase Black Russians, a mixture of Kahlua and vodka. Tony C kept the music going loudly. "I wanted them to forget fears of the killer." Two guys in conversation eyed the girls, then walked to the bar, continuing their discussion. Judy overheard bits and pieces about a trade the New York Mets had made ten days earlier. Gone were Dave Kingman, known as "King Kong," and the pride of Queens, right-handed pitching ace, Tom "Terrific" Seaver. "Without them, the Mets are nothing," said one of the young men, Sal Lupo.

Judy turned to the boys and began to talk to them. "You guys Mets fans?"

"Of course," replied Lupo. "You a baseball fan?"

"Sure. Yankees. I'm from the Bronx."

"The Bronx?"

"Oh, so you've heard of it?" They laughed.

Sal Lupo had come to the disco because his friend, Ralph Saccente, was the bouncer. He could get in free and drink free, too. He had left his house in the Maspeth section of Queens and had driven in with Ralph. Sal had been in the club for a couple of hours before the Bronx girls came in. On seeing them, he walked over with another young man whom he knew. He was quick to join in the conversation with Judy.

For the next two and a half hours, roughly from midnight to 2:30 A.M., Judy and Sal danced and drank Scotch and Black Russians. Judy liked the way he looked. His hair was styled, and he dressed smartly. Their conversation revolved around records, fashion, and the summer.

At a little before two o'clock, Judy's three girlfriends decided to call it a night. They had a twenty-five-minute drive ahead of them and had agreed to leave at two.

"Why don't you stay?" Sal Lupo asked Judy. "I'll drive you home when the place closes. My friend Ralph has a car. . . . When he's finished, we'll drive you right back to the good old Bronx."

Judy thought briefly. She turned to her girlfriends and told them of Sal's offer. After a moment of discussion, she turned back to him and smiled. "Okay." A few minutes later the other girls left, walking back to Angela's car. (They wouldn't learn that Judy had been shot until four the next afternoon, when her aunt called Debbie from the hospital.)

"Another drink?" offered Sal.

"Oh, why not."

"Sal seemed like a real nice guy," remembers Judy. "It all seemed okay because the guys would all drive me home. Sal was bright and unafraid of the killer. We'd been talking about it on and off, and I kind of trusted him."

It was 3:00 A.M. and the sparse crowd at the Elephas had thinned. "When do you think we'll be able to get going?" asked Judy.

Sal looked around, and spotting his buddy Ralph the bouncer, he excused himself, walking toward him. After a moment, he returned and told Judy that Ralph said he'd be finished a bit early. "In the meantime he's given me the keys to his Caddy. We can wait in it until he finishes. Okay?"

The two left the Elephas, walking directly to where the car was parked, opposite 45-39 211th Street, one and a half blocks south of 45th Road. On the way to the car their conversation again touched on the .44-caliber killer. Sal didn't seem afraid, and that lack of fear kept Judy at ease.

Sal opened the passenger door with Saccente's key. Then he ran around to the driver's side and let himself in. He didn't want to stay on the street longer than necessary. He felt, he says, he would be safer inside the car—as though car windows could protect him from .44-caliber slugs. He was not thinking clearly, but Sal had had some drinks. The bravado of minutes before had faded.

"This Son of Sam is really scary," Judy said. "The way that guy comes out of nowhere. You never know where he'll hit next."

Sal looked at Judy's hair. "Did you notice how few people were at the club? People are afraid to go out."

"But what are you supposed to do?" Judy said. "You just can't stay home forever."

Judy had been glancing toward the window, at the dark, deserted street. She turned to talk to Sal.

"All of a sudden, I heard echoing in the car," she says. "There wasn't any pain, just ringing in my ears. I looked at Sal, and his eyes were open wide, just like his mouth. There were no screams. I don't know why I didn't scream; I'll never know why, I just didn't.

"All the windows had been closed. I couldn't understand what this pounding noise was. After that, I felt disoriented, dazed."

Judy looked at Sal. Fear twisted his face.

"What happened, what happened?" Judy said.

"Somebody threw rocks . . . through the window of the car," Lupo said.

Sal climbed out of the car. He had been hit in the right forearm. He ran to Elephas for help. Judy Placido found herself alone in the Cadillac.

She sat there for perhaps five minutes, hurting, frightened, but mostly dazed. Then she suddenly looked into the rearview mirror.

She saw herself. "Blood was all over me." She tried to open the passenger door, but something was wrong with her right arm. It wouldn't move. She reached across her body and opened the door with her left hand. She got out of the car, but paused for a moment to pick up her pocketbook.

She ran toward Elephas, two blocks away, passing a man who stood open-mouthed in shock. When Judy reached the corner of 45th Road and 211th Street, she collapsed—about a hundred yards from Elephas.

By now Sal had run to a nearby apartment house, where he screamed at the doorman to call the police.

Judy never lost consciousness. Within a minute, a crowd gathered around her as she lay on the sidewalk. She tried to get up, but the people wouldn't let her. Within two minutes the first police units reached the scene, including members of the homicide task force. One Omega unit had passed through that exact area only five minutes before.

Only when Sal Lupo returned did he notice blood pouring from a wound in his right forearm. A half hour later, after both victims had been rushed to Flushing Hospital, calls were still coming in to the police emergency number, 911.

Judy Placido is now a prelaw student at Pace University and looks back on June 26, 1977, with horror but also with remarkable detachment. "I was injured near the temple," she says, "and near the spinal cord, and in my right shoulder. Yet I was able to run.

"But at the time I had no idea what had happened. I didn't even know that I'd been shot. I didn't think for a second I'd been shot by the .44-caliber killer."

Her smooth face shows the beginnings of a smile. "And that's funny, isn't it, because just before the shooting what were we, Sal and I, talking about? It was the .44-caliber killer!

"It's funny," she says, "but it didn't click at the time."

One bullet had struck the back of her neck, tearing through and narrowly missing her spine. The second passed through the intersection of the shoulder and neck. The third struck her in the right temple and spun across her forehead just beneath the skin, then stopped just above her eye. No one can explain why she wasn't killed.

ONLY two weeks earlier, at Task Force headquarters, after a particularly frustrating tour, Deputy Inspector Dowd articulated an educated guess to Sergeant Coffey. "The next place he's going to hit is the Elephas. It's a set-up for him, all those kids all over the place." The inspector drove home to Douglaston, Queens, from the 109th Precinct every night, passing the Elephas on purpose.

Coffey agreed. "Yes, sir. We've already got it covered with extra sweeps. Every time I get a chance, I swing by the place. Sometimes we'll go around the block, near the small homes on 211th, and sit for a while. So far, nothing."

"Well, Joe, just keep it up," Dowd responded. "Sooner or later something's going to break."

DAVID BERKOWITZ looked into the Cadillac with dismay. He had meant to kill the girl, but "I didn't intend to kill the guy, the driver." He could see two things had gone wrong. First, the girl was still alive; then a bullet intended for Judy Placido had struck Sal Lupo.

"The window," he said, "the window deflected the bullet. It wouldn't go through the window right. I mean, I tried."

Berkowitz saw two shocked, injured people in the car. He remembers that Lupo had been simply sitting, looking at Judy. Then Berkowitz began to run. He ran along Northern Boulevard, east for one block, and made a right turn at 211th Street.

The Galaxie started at once. David drove down the street to come to the Clearview Expressway. Along the Clearview access road he passed a squad car. He remembers the blue-and-white markings. He says that he remained calm.

"The demons were protecting me," he says. "I had nothing to fear from the police."

SIX DIFFERENT CALLS to 911 reported the shooting within two minutes. The sector car was ordered to respond: "Shots fired." Because of the area, Omega Force picked it up at that exact instant and radioed to its cars on patrol. Their plan went into action with the words "CODE 44."

Deputy Inspector Dowd was notified immediately. After confirmation that the M.O. of the attack fit the Son of Sam, he telephoned Chief of Detectives Keenan at his home, waking him. "Chief, I think we have another shooting by the .44. It looks like his trademark, that damn gun."

DETECTIVE SERGEANT Joe Coffey and his partner, Detective George Moscardini, had been outside the Elephas Discotheque at 2:45 A.M., and they patroled the area until just after 3:10 A.M.

The pair was driving along the service road of the Clearview Expressway at 3:24 A.M. when the unmarked car's radio crackled "Shots fired. Intersection 2-1-1 Street and 4-5 Road." Sergeant Coffey ordered George to stop and turn around. With siren screaming, they headed back to the site of the shooting.

"Holy shit, we just left there! That guy had to be there when we were circling around. It's incredible!" the sergeant screamed over the sound of the siren.

"How do you know it's . . . ?"

"I know, George. It's got to be him. It's the right place."

While Moscardini was backing up in order to turn around, David's car passed them as it went up the entrance ramp of the Clearview Expressway. "I saw this unmarked car headed along the service road in reverse," David said later. "Then it spun into a side street. One of the cops put their red light on the roof and they sped away. By now I was watching in my rear-view mirror. They must have been going to where I had just shot the guy and his girlfriend.''

WHEN COFFEY and his partner arrived at the scene, Judy Placido was still lying on the concrete. Someone had placed a jacket over her to keep her warm. She still didn't know she had been shot. No one had told her, fearing what the shock might do to her. A couple of minutes after Coffey's arrival, Sal Lupo reappeared. Blood was running down his hand from beneath his shirt. At Coffey's insistence, a uniformed officer hustled him into a patrol car.

Detective Moscardini pushed through the growing crowd and spoke to another detective who had arrived only seconds earlier. "Eddie, got anything?"

"I just got here, George. All I got was her name, then you guys showed up."

An emergency medical technician knelt beside Judy, applying a compress to her neck. He turned his head and called to his partner: "Get the stretcher. We can move her." In another minute they put her in the ambulance and the doors closed.

Moscardini spoke to the attendant, then ran back to where Coffey was. The sergeant was looking over the crowd, hoping to spot something. "Sarge, she's been hit in the right temple, shoulder, and neck. But, she's lucky. She'll make it. The boy's been hit in the forearm. One of our guys is going with the girl to the hospital. I'll send the boy in a patrol car."

"AM I going to die?" a tearful and frightened Judy Placido asked one of the nurses at Flushing Hospital.

"No, of course not. You'll be just fine." The nurse began going through Judy's purse.

"Please don't," Judy pleaded. She had taken her girlfriend's sister's driver's license as ID just in case they asked for proof of age at the Elephas. They hadn't asked. Now, in the hospital, she was worried that they'd find it and call her girlfriend's mother saying her sister had been hurt.

Meanwhile, doctors removed the bullet from Sal's right forearm. "Well, officer," the intern said, "whatever caliber it is, it sure is a big one."

Detective Moscardini dropped the bullet into an envelope and sealed it. "It's a .44."

"A .44? Are you sure? It's gotta be the. . . ."

Walking out, Moscardini said, "Yeah, we've seen it before."

Judy Placido was seriously injured. After attendants removed her blood-soaked clothing, she raised her left hand and touched the bandage taped to her right temple. Her fingers pushed at the lump under the skin on the right side of her forehead. It felt hard. A nurse pulled her hand down, saying, "Leave it, please. The doctors will take the bullet out in a few minutes."

A bullet! Only then did she realize she'd been shot. The loud, echoing noise hadn't been rocks: it had been the noise of bullets crashing through the window and striking her. Was she going to die? Probably. After all, she'd been shot. No, no, she must not think that; she was lucid; she must try to remain calm. She was young and healthy, and she would heal. Judy knew she must convince herself she wasn't dying. She concentrated on the overhead lights. The movements of the doctors, nurses, and police became a blur as she tried to fight off the comfort sleep would bring. It was nearly 4:30 A.M., June 26, 1977.

"DUE TO the poor quality of the .44 Bulldog," says Captain Borrelli, "its trajectory is sometimes unpredictable. The shot that struck her in the right temple had lost a great deal of its force passing through the windshield of the car. It merely penetrated the skin and then deflected along the bone of her forehead. It stopped under the skin of her forehead an inch above her right eye. The two other slugs tore through her body and lodged in the car's front cushions. One of them missed her spine, entering the right side of her neck and exiting the left by less than half an inch. The second carried through the fleshy portion of her shoulder, adjacent to the base of her neck.''

Neither Placido nor Lupo was able to give any description of the attacker to the police.

13

Donna's
Anniversary

On June 7, 1977, David Berkowitz failed to answer the summons he had received for driving an uninsured vehicle. The court automatically suspended his driver's license and notice of the suspension was forwarded to the computer at the DCJS (Department of Criminal Justice System), a centralized information bank that services local police departments within New York State.

Three days later, on June 10, police officers Tom Chamberlain and Pete Intervallo interviewed Sam Carr, who gave them David Berkowitz's name as the possible sender of the mysterious letters and the possible shooter of the Carr's dog. Returning to Yonkers police headquarters in the former Consolidated Edison garage building at 10 St. Casimir Avenue, the officers went to their local DCJS computer link and requested information on David Berkowitz. Within ten seconds the screen began its printout in green lettering. It gave Berkowitz's address, which caused the officers to look at each other in excitement, and then stated that Berkowitz's driver's license had just been suspended. The officers punched another key. The computer gave them the license number and vehicle registration number for David's Ford Galaxie. On their next patrol through their sector, the officers drove past David's address and tried to spot his car. Under the law, it was all they could do.

Chamberlain and Intervallo knew Berkowitz had no right to drive. But no warrant had been issued when David failed to appear in court. Thus, only if they could catch David driving his car could they arrest him. And if they arrested him, David's car would be available for them to make a routine inspection.

By now both officers suspected that Berkowitz was not only strange but might also be somewhat violent. There was even the possibility that the Son of Sam and Berkowitz might have some connection, and they increased the frequency of their patrols around the Pine Street area.

On some days Tom Chamberlain truly hated his job. He had talked to his wife, Beverly, about quitting the force and perhaps joining the New York City Fire Department. He had passed that test at the same time he'd passed the test for the Yonkers Police Department. Only two weeks after he'd begun at the Police Academy, the New York City Fire Department had called him and now he was having second thoughts about having turned them down. On the other hand, Pete Intervallo always said he wanted to be a cop. At this point in his short career, he was still excited about the job. "Yeah, there were days that got you down," says Pete, "but then there are the good ones also."

One of those good days both officers remember was in June 1977. They had driven to the home of a fifty-five-year-old woman, less than a mile from Pine Street. It wasn't *Dragnet* stuff, just everyday police business. Ida Wilson lived alone and she reported that her four German shepherd puppies had been stolen the night before. "Those dogs meant everything to her," remembers Chamberlain. "The woman lost it all when they were taken. With no family, the dogs had

194 · SON OF SAM

replaced her sons and daughters." The officers drove her around the neighborhood looking for the animals. After an hour they drew a blank. "Finally we had to bring her back to her house and go back to our regular patrol. You had to see her standing at the curb. Her world had just folded up around her."

"Please find them. Please," she pleaded as the officers drove away.

The balance of the tour had been uneventful. Then, just before they began their drive back to the station, Intervallo spotted a teenager walking a couple of puppies on a rope. Tom pulled the patrol car around and slowed down to match the boy's pace. "Hey," said Intervallo. "Nice dogs you have there."

The teenager stopped and turned to the officers. "You want to buy one?" he asked.

The officers got out of the car, walking toward the boy. He was edgy. "They yours?"

"What you mean, mine? Of course they're mine. They're nine weeks old and ready to get away from their mother."

Tom knelt down, as the dogs came to him. "Nine weeks old? They don't look that old. They don't look . . ." The boy cut him off.

"I said they were nine weeks old. I know. And besides, if you don't want one, there are other people who do." His voice was rising.

"Where do you live?" Officer Intervallo asked.

"What do you mean where do I live? I ain't done nothing wrong."

"Didn't say you did. But we got a report about some dogs being stolen a couple of hours ago. These could be the ones."

"They're mine."

"Well, then, how about us going home with you and seeing where you kept them. Maybe we'll talk to your mom?" That did it. The boy knew he'd been caught. The officers took him into custody. Ten minutes later they recovered the other two dogs from the people he had sold them to. The sixteen-year-old was charged with possession of stolen property. He was under age and the charge was eventually dropped. But of greater importance was the fact that the woman got her family back.

Watching her as the dogs licked her face gave the officers a sense of accomplishment. "It was times like these that make being a cop worthwhile."

Officer Chamberlain felt sorry for the Carr family. He sensed that Sam Carr was a victim. Chamberlain hoped he'd be able to crack this case, even if it was only a minor one. "I knew the family. They were hard-working and didn't deserve this kind of treatment. It was tough on them, the letters and their dog being shot. It seemed so senseless. But, with the law placing so many restrictions on police action, our hands seemed tied. I was hoping to catch Berkowitz driving his car. I'd have loved to arrest him, but after all, what charge could be proved aside from driving without a license? There really wasn't anything that would stick. You can have that gut feeling, but it won't hold up in court."

DAVID BERKOWITZ had fallen prey to yet another demon. It was, he says, a "Mr. Williams. I think he lived next door in apartment 7D." Actually, the tenant who lived next door was Manuel Garcia.

"I never saw Mr. Williams," Berkowitz said. "He just made a lot of noise. Nothing coherent. I think he lived next door, or maybe in the wall."

David remembers one especially hot night when "Mr. Williams" was tormenting him. "I kicked in the wall. I jumped and kicked. I tried to kick his face in. Nothing happened. It just didn't have any effect. I could hear deep in the wall a lot of sounds. Voices, thousands of them. Screams. Funny sounds. Music. Like drums.

"The demons came into my apartment and went through everything and looked at things. They liked to see my writing on the walls.

"It showed them loyalty. You know. Admiration.

"I tried to do what they said, but they were never satisfied. Sometimes I argued with them, asking why they were making me do these things. But they never answered. They just laughed at me. I wasn't a bad person, but they were making me do bad things. I didn't want to. I did everything they said to do, and still they weren't satisfied."

THE JUNE 27 issue of *Time* magazine featured an article entitled "Human Rights: Confrontation in Belgrade." The story contended that the issue of human rights had now become President Jimmy Carter's "centerpiece" of foreign policy. This issue had won him popularity at home and admiration abroad.

As for the city, the Mets, New York's National League baseball team, had made headlines for their trading of Dave Kingman and wonder pitcher Tom Seaver. And if one thought things couldn't possibly get worse, the Financial Control Board passed the city's beleaguered budget. Yet United States Secretary of the Treasury W. Michael Blumenthal informed the Mayor that he intended to put any further request for additional federal short-term loans under a microscope.

TWO DAYS after the Lupo–Placido shooting, the police still seemed unable to pick up the killer's trail. In an article published in the Tuesday (June 28) issue of *The New York Times,* Deputy Inspector Dowd, and a key assistant, Sergeant Conlon, both admitted what Sergeant Coffey had feared all along. If the police were to catch the Son of Sam, he would have to keep up his pattern of attacks. "We don't like it, but we're stuck with the situation. Whenever he makes that one mistake, we'll be on him," said Sergeant Conlon. The statement did little to calm the fears of the populace.

The article, headlined T.V. FINDS NO KOJAK OR COLUMBO AT 109TH PCT. and written by Francis X. Clines, went on to say that the police were merely able to eliminate some suspects after the Placido–Lupo attack. However, the detectives had not been able to come to grips with the more important issue, the killer's identity.

Both Dowd and Conlon also granted a series of television interviews, stating that the killer's capture was still a long way off—"unless," Dowd said, "he makes a mistake."

"Will he make a mistake?" asked an anxious television reporter.

"AS A POLICE OFFICER, you always wondered just when he was going to shoot that gun again," said Detective James Justus of Brooklyn Robbery. "When is it going to happen next? As a cop, if you weren't in a panic, you were a damn fool."

BY NOW, SERGEANT COFFEY was emotionally drained. He had stopped eating regularly and, from a 220-pound frame, lost twenty-one pounds. "I was riding with other detectives for ten hours a night whether or not the schedule called for it." The men talked incessantly, trying to figure an angle they had missed.

One night Detective John O'Connell said "I bet the bastard comes from Queens."

"No!" shot back Coffey. "He comes from the northern Bronx or Westchester. I'll take that bet . . . a bottle of good Scotch that I'm right." (He's still not collected the bet.)

ON JULY 10, after a meeting with Police Commissioner Codd and his political advisers, Mayor Abraham Beame went before the television cameras to announce that on the anniversary of Donna Lauria's death he was adding more detectives to the task force. He also added: "I've instructed the Police Commissioner to increase patrols in key areas, and to place the entire New York City Police Department on the highest alert."

"The Mayor's statement tended to reinforce the growing —but the highly speculative perception—that the killer was planning an anniversary attack," reported *The Times*.

Meanwhile, New Yorkers and their police reeled before other events:

Thursday, July 14th . . . New York Daily News . . . Headline . . . BLACKOUT! LIGHTNING HITS CON ED SYSTEM
New York City was blacked out in the wake of a major loss of power due to lightning striking a transmission line.

Friday, July 15th . . . New York Post headline—24 HOURS OF TERROR. It took more than 6,000 cops to arrest 3,481 persons during the looting that lasted 25 hours yesterday.

Friday, July 15th . . . New York Times . . . Headline . . . NEW YORK'S POWER RESTORED SLOWLY; LOOTING WIDE-SPREAD, 3,360 ARRESTED; BLACKOUT RESULTS IN HEAVY LOSSES.

Saturday, July 16 . . . New York Daily News . . . Headline THE PRICE TAG—BILLION DOLLAR BLACKOUT

Monday, July 18 . . . New York Post—100° AND THREAT OF A BROWNOUT.

Wednesday, July 20 . . . New York Daily News . . . AT 102° WE'RE A BAKED APPLE.

Thursday, July 21st . . . New York Daily News . . . Headline . . . DEATHS RISE 10% IN HEAT WAVE. The city sweltering in a mass of hot humid air can look forward to some relief tonight as a mass of cool Canadian air should pass through by midnight.

Friday, July 22nd . . . New York Times . . . President Carter, in a firm, yet conciliatory speech in Charleston, called for Soviet-American Arms Control. He pleaded for the Soviets to limit their deployment of big missiles.

On July 28, under a headline TO THE .44 CALIBER KILLER ON HIS 1ST DEATHDAY, *New York Daily News* columnist Jimmy Breslin asked: "Is tomorrow night, July 29th, so significant to him that he must go out and find a victim? Or will he sit alone, and look out his attic window to be thrilled by his power, this power that will have him in the newspapers and on television and in the thoughts and conversations of most of the young people of this City?"

The next day, July 29, both the *News* and *Post* saw fit to mark the first anniversary of Donna Lauria's death with a barrage of stories recapitulating all the attacks of the past year. Not satisfied with merely recounting the grisly events, the tabloids went on to tell of "fearful neighborhoods" and futile police efforts to apprehend the killer.

The headline sprawled across the front page of the *Post* read GUNMAN SPARKS SON OF SAM CHASE. The story was about a Nassau County police officer's nighttime pursuit of a man reported to have a gun, walking along the Cross Island Parkway. The last paragraph revealed that "police say the mystery gunman was definitely not the Son of Sam."

The New York Times decided to take no special notice of the anniversary. However, in the July 31 issue, the newspaper printed an article describing mounting police efforts and the extra patrols on the anniversary night. The story noted that the warning issued by Jimmy Breslin had gone "unfulfilled."

SERGEANT JOE COFFEY made an unconventional move. He telephoned Al Seedman, former Chief of Detectives of the New York City Police Department, now chief of security for the Alexander's department store chain. As a young detective Coffey had worked for Chief Seedman and the Chief had seen that the officer had potential. It was almost as if Seedman had taken Joe under his wing. Now, nearly ten years later, Coffey was turning to his former boss to propose something that not only was irrational but also possibly deadly.

"Chief, I'd like to borrow a couple of mannequins. I want to put them in cars as decoys to try to flush this guy out."

"But they won't move," said Seedman. "He'd know they were fake in a minute."

"Chief, only the girl would be fake. One of us will be the guy in the car."

"You have bulletproof cars for this, Joe?"

"Nope. It's going to be us against him."

"You have to be crazy. You'll be a sitting duck."

"We have to do something, Chief. We can't wait around for him to make his move. Maybe we can force it this way."

The Chief agreed. It was something only a cop could understand. And, although retired, Seedman was a cop. "All I can say, Joe, is that I'll pray for you."

Finally, after checking out the equipment and the procedure, Coffey acted. On the night of July 3, 1977, Joe Coffey parked on a deserted street near the Continental Avenue subway station in Queens—in the area of the Freund–Voskerichian killings. In the darkness he turned to the dummy (which everyone called "Gretchen") and pretended to kiss it. It was anything but humorous.

Coffey was kissing with his eyes open. Watching him were Detectives John O'Connell and George Moscardini in their back-up vehicle, half a block away. Coffey was the target, and they all knew it. The sergeant was holding two guns, a .38 Detective Special in one hand, a .38 Smith & Wesson in the other. Hour after hour he sat kissing the blonde. "I was always partial to blondes. Sometimes I wondered what my wife, Pat, would have looked like as a blonde. You know, after a while, that dummy began to look good to me."

Behind the bad joke there was deadly seriousness. Coffey couldn't discount the fact that some jerk would simply look into the car and try to mug him and "Gretchen." Coffey didn't know how he'd react. "I wasn't wearing a bulletproof vest and I hoped that I wouldn't just start shooting." Officers O'Connell and Moscardini had the same fears. "They were afraid for my life, and I guess I was too."

After a week of this duty Captain Borrelli and Sergeant Coffey went to Chief Keenan. Borrelli was concerned for Coffey's life and told the Chief of his fear. The Captain asked that Coffey tell the Chief of a new plan. "Chief, if the department will get us five bulletproof cars we'd blanket the areas where he's already struck. Right now, with me alone it's a hit-or-miss operation. But with five cars out every night, we'd have a hell of a chance to get him before he can strike again."

But with the city's budgetary considerations before him,

Chief Keenan hedged about the cost. Finally he agreed to provide a single bulletproof car. The vehicle arrived at the task force the day Berkowitz was caught.

"THERE is a kind of brotherhood in the police department," says Captain Borrelli. "It's unwritten, yet there. You're a cop first above everything else. Like when an officer gets shot, anywhere in the city and you hear about it. You go to the hospital to give blood . . . or just to be there. It doesn't matter if you're black or white, you're a cop.

"And when one of us gets killed, you're at the funeral too. You let his family know that you understand it might just as easily been you. And I've been to those funerals, those inspector's funerals. You can look at the faces of the men. They might have never known the officer, yet they're there. Sometimes cops from all over the country are there, and you know they never knew the guy. But they're cops too. And you cry, if not outside, then inside.

"If anyone ever says that putting on that silver badge doesn't mean anything, they are wrong, dead wrong."

THE OMEGA Task Force kept changing personnel. New men came into the unit to relieve those who had been working without rest. On one particular night, Detective Marlin Hopkins found that for the next two shifts, he would draw a black partner. "I never met Carl before. But I liked him at once. We related to each other because of our backgrounds. I came out of East New York, a section of Brooklyn, and he came out of there too."

The first night the pair patrolled together proved to be uneventful. The second was not. Late in the evening, the two detectives were answering phones in the second-floor office of the task force. All five buttons were lit on the phones, indicating calls still coming in. Hopkins pressed one of the buttons and said "Homicide Task Force. Detective Hopkins. Can I help you?"

On the other end of the line the excited voice of a young

male replied, "I don't know if you guys can use this, but less than an hour ago the guy I relieved at work walked over to two girls and showed them a gun he was carrying inside his jacket. He said he was the .44-Caliber Killer. You should have seen the girls. They began to scream and ran."

"Are you sure he had a gun?" Hopkins asked as he motioned Carl to grab a phone and listen in.

"Man, I tell you it was a gun, a big mother. I never saw a .44, but this one was bigger than a .38."

"OK. Just stay calm," Hopkins said. "I'll need your name and address." The officers asked more questions and learned that the caller knew the home address of the man with the gun. With that, they ran to their car and sped off to Brooklyn. This tip looked as promising as anything they had, and they were instructed to follow up immediately on just such calls.

The address given for the suspect was a two-story frame house in the Italian neighborhood of Bensonhurst in Brooklyn. The front door faced the street, as did a terrace and bay window. Hopkins whispered to his partner, "Carl, you cover the door; I'll get the window." Carl nodded that he understood.

Carl stood by the door. The six-foot-seven-inch officer looked into the small glass rectangle in the center of the panel. Everything was dark inside. He knocked. A moment passed. He knocked again, this time more forcefully.

From the second floor came a response, "Who's there? I said, who's there?"

The officer responded, "The police!"

"OK, wait a minute." It was several minutes before a light went on inside the house. A sleepy-looking middle-aged man walked toward the door, then froze. He had seen Carl's face framed in the tiny window. A black man. In an Italian neighborhood. At that hour. He began to scream. "They're here to kill us! They're here to kill us!" The man turned and ran into a back room. A moment later he reappeared with an axe, running toward the door.

Detective Hopkins could see the man through the bay window and he screamed, "Carl, get away from the door! *Move!*" Carl jumped back just as the door opened. At the same time, someone upstairs opened the window, saw the black officer, and began to scream. Someone else dialed 911.

The two officers began backing down the steps followed by the man with an axe. "I tell you," yelled Hopkins, "we're the cops. Really. See our badges." He took his gold shield from his pocket and held it out. The man didn't believe him. He raised his axe as the officers' hands found their guns. They didn't want to shoot, so they began to run.

At that moment two police cars came around the corner, their lights flashing. "You're not the police," the man continued, axe raised. The officers ran directly to the police cars.

The vehicles came to a halt in the middle of the block. Officers piled out, guns in hand. The second call they had received was "Man with a gun."

"Stop! Police! Drop your guns!" frightened uniformed officers commanded.

"Hold it," the two detectives called out. "We're the police. We're the good guys."

"*Freeze!*" yelled the uniformed officers, pointing their guns at the detectives.

"*Freeze!*"

They froze.

"Like I said," said Detective Hopkins, "this was a real staunch Italian neighborhood."

The uniformed officers took the detective's guns, then checked their identification. In a moment the tension was broken. Everyone began to laugh. The guy with the axe was embarrassed and invited everyone inside for a drink.

The detectives had been given the wrong address. The young suspect was found two days later, minus the weapon.

IN THE COURSE of the Son of Sam investigation, detectives uncovered people who had committed crimes not related to these specific murders. When this happened, they quickly referred the specifics to whichever division handled the crime in question. They turned in rapists and petty crooks, child-molesters and pickpockets. But they kept to the Son of Sam case. "There were people we could have arrested, but we didn't," says Hopkins. "We just didn't want to get involved in arrests."

"One time we got onto some boy who molested a girl. He appeared, psychologically speaking, like the type of individual we were looking for. Joe Coffey and I went to his apartment and we got invited in. We sat in his apartment for four hours, talking to him, and the longer we stayed the more interested we got in him. After four hours, we knew we had him on the girl-molesting charge. Later on, when the Sex Crimes Unit got involved, he was positively identified, and then arrested on the charge."

Sometimes, responses to questions weren't what the detectives had bargained for. "Sometimes you'd ask people questions just to get their reactions. If it hit home, many times the people would turn around, it would kind of set them back, and they'd say—Why are you asking that? They'd get very excited, wanting to know the reason for your line of questioning. One individual responded much the same as others had. When it finally came to pinning him down to a particular time, he answered 'No, of course not. I left work an hour after that.'

"It became evident that he was an unstable individual, but he wasn't our man. We didn't have the time to pursue the matter any further. Maybe after we typed up the report, some other unit would get around to him. When we left, he seemed kind of agitated, restless, on edge. But, we'd been working almost twelve hours and we just called it a day."

They went back to the precinct and signed off. Half an hour later the detective walked in the front door of his own house. "I was just sitting down at the dining-room table, having a drink with my wife when the phone rang. It was a call from John O'Connell. He told me that I'd better call this phone number right away. 'It's a psychiatrist, he's just called us. It seems that the guy you two just talked to, he's on a ledge—twenty stories up, and he's going to go off any second. The doctor wants to know what you two said to him to make him go off the deep end.'

"I couldn't help him at all. I thought he might be looney tunes, but what I was really interested in was the killer, not some guy with scrambled brains who wanted to kill himself."

Another facet to the case appeared. Detectives associated with the investigation found their names in the press. They feared that Sam might retaliate against them or their families.

This fear remained with Captain Borrelli throughout the investigation. At the scene of the Suriani–Esau killings, David had chosen strategically to drop a letter written specifically to Borrelli. It was something he had to live with, but did his family? Every detective knew Borrelli to be the father of four young girls, and the men under him were concerned. The captain was more than a detective or their boss. He was their friend. The men came forward and volunteered to escort his wife and kids around on off-duty time. They wanted to start watching his home around the clock, unofficially.

Borrelli answered them by simply saying "No! I'm a cop. My family understands that." But he was concerned. The Lynbrook, Long Island, police were informed, and they gave special attention to the street where the Borrellis lived. Each sector car did an extra turn down the block, very slowly, just in case.

Even more detectives joined the task force. Men who normally would have been working on other homicides signed on. They all believed the killer had settled into a pattern that would be unbroken until his capture.

Says Hopkins, "It was a crime that had to be solved sooner or later. It wasn't going away. We all knew he was going to hit again . . . we all thought along the same lines."

Hopkins had worked on another string of cases where three women were killed. There was no doubt in his mind that there was a single individual responsible for all three murders. "Everything pointed to it," says the detective. "But for some strange reason it stopped there." The cases remain unsolved to this day. There were no leads, no more killings. But with the string of shootings in the Son of Sam case, the killings weren't going to stop, no matter how much the men wanted them to.

Hopkins had "caught" the Christine Freund murder. It was his from beginning to end. It might take him his entire career, but he'd stay with it until the end. It held overtones similar to another case, in which an elderly woman had been killed in a Queens apartment house. She was seventy-three years old, and penniless. After an intensive investigation, the detective believed that three local toughs were responsible, although he couldn't prove it. "Every time one of the guys involved got locked up for something, I went to the can to interview them."

"Get out of here!" they'd scream. "What the fuck are you bothering me for? I don't have to talk to you about nothing!"

But the detective kept at it. Four years passed before he got a break. Eventually, one of them was arrested for something he couldn't get out of. Then the conversation changed. "OK. What have you got to trade?" the man asked.

"Nothing," replied the detective. In the next hour, the man confessed to his part in the murder, implicating the other two. Hopkins had broken this one. The Son of Sam case was parallel in that if Berkowitz had not been caught, Marlin would still be on it.

Hopkins spent his days reading report after report, trying to make a connection. When he was finished with the forms, he'd turn to a mountain of newspapers published within a fifty-mile radius of the city. "Maybe he lived further out than we thought," says the detective. Soon he'd even go beyond that, turning to out-of-state newspapers. He was always looking for a similar type of crime. Finally he'd place calls to other jurisdictions when anything, no matter how insignificant, turned up. "What were your particular characteristics?" he'd ask. "I have a case that looks like this . . . could it be?" He was grasping at straws, hoping against hope.

On June 30 Deputy Inspector Dowd received ten more men for his Omega Force. He had requested a hundred more, but the Police Commissioner's office was hard-pressed. All other commands were now skeleton squads, the men working extra shifts, covering for each other. They couldn't continue at this pace. Worse, summer was approaching. Kids would be out of school and, with their newfound freedom, street nuisance crime would climb. Merchants would demand action. Ten was the best Dowd could hope for.

There were now more than two hundred officers working directly under Dowd's command. Leads constantly ended in nothing more than frustration. Reporters screamed for something new to print, for an exclusive. On July 27 Inspector Dowd finally called this particular constituency together, issuing a new profile of the killer. The profile had been put together by police, doctors, and social workers familiar with other crimes that fit into the pattern created by the now-infamous Son of Sam. The profile created was a montage of a person, white, male, quiet (possibly a loner), who worked in a regular job. In short, there would be nothing so strikingly different about the killer as to make anyone in contact with him even suspect that he might be the Son of Sam.

July 29 came and passed. The massive police effort that had been mounted in an effort to catch the elusive gunman failed. With their energies all but spent, the police had no alternative but to await the killer's next move. They knew he'd strike again, but where?

14

The Final Shots

Brooklyn a generation ago was first of all a punch line for cheap comics.

"What else did you expect?" the comics said. "I come from"—pause, oafish grin—"Brooklyn!"

Audiences broke into laughter.

The real Brooklyn, as opposed to the comic's labored creation, was a place of foment, conflict, vibrant life. Although San Franciscans and Colorado mountain men would argue, there is perhaps no more glorious vista in America than the night scene from the Belt Parkway looking toward Manhattan. The Wall Street towers rise under the twin monoliths of the World Trade Center. Closer to shore, ships ride into the Port of New York. The Statue of Liberty beckons from a distance.

Brooklyn has a rich history. George Washington made a strategic retreat there during the American Revolution, after a holding action from Lookout Mountain in what is now Prospect Park. As the Bronx once housed Edgar Allan Poe, Brooklyn was home to Walt Whitman, who edited the *Brooklyn Eagle* and wrote his free-form verse. Later the borough was home base for the Dodgers, who, after losing for decades, became a baseball dynasty and—more than that—Jackie Robinson's first team. Proof, if proof were necessary, that black and white together could make a winning baseball team came first from Brooklyn.

At length, tempted by small suburban plots, the middle class began to desert the borough. No Brooklyn blight rivals South Bronx devastation, but areas are dying or decayed. The middle class (and indeed the wealth) remains in specific neighborhoods: Brooklyn Heights and Park Slope, Flatbush and Cobble Hill, Sheepshead Bay and Bay Ridge and Bensonhurst.

It was in Gravesend Bay, where people look across calm water to Staten Island under a vast span called the Verrazano Bridge, that Berkowitz struck for the last time.

STACY MOSKOWITZ, bleached-blonde, brown-eyed, and immediately attractive in a flashy effervescent way, lived with her parents, Gerald and Neysa, on the second floor of a three-story house at 1740 East Fifth Street. The building was in the Bay Ridge section on a street of one- and two-family homes. The Moskowitz home, the newest on the block, was brick.

Gerry Moskowitz worked long hours as a deliveryman for Dolly Madison Ice Cream. Neysa was a housewife who delighted in her own parents, Esther and Nat Rome, her fifteen-year-old daughter, Ricky, and in Stacy, her pride and joy, who was twenty. Mrs. Moskowitz had lost another child years earlier, and Stacy had become everything to her. Stacy did well at Lafayette High School but dropped out in 1974, seeking a career in the fabric industry. She then went to Adelphi Business School for a year.

"Stacy was an open kid," Gerry Moskowitz says. "Really an open kid. At the office where she worked, she used a Telex machine, a direct line to Europe. She was working with people who were over there in shoe factories. They'd never met her in person, just over the machine, yet they knew her. Or, they wanted to know her. There was joy in her messages."

Stacy would Telex orders to factories in Frankfurt, Paris, and London, and she'd end each one with the weather in New York, or a report on what new movie she'd seen, a new record she had liked. "When the managers came to America, they all wanted to meet the girl on the other end of the Telex line," says her father.

Hans Müller, assistant manager of Munich Sales, Ltd., remembers, "When I got to the Empire State Building and the Minella Corp's office where she worked, I walked right in. I was able to pick her out immediately. She shone out from the girls who worked there like a lamp in darkness."

Stacy loved to live life to its fullest. Unlike the other young girls who had been David's victims, Stacy had a lively neighborhood reputation. But rumors have a way of building on themselves until they become a great deal more than the truth. She was outgoing, yet sexually cautious. On an airplane coming back from Puerto Rico, she was having a good time and she let everyone know it. But when one of the boys suggested she stay with him in his apartment in New York City for a few nights, the young woman would have nothing of it. A good time, yes, but she'd prefer to sleep at home with her parents. At twenty, she still had a lot of life before her.

ROBERT VIOLANTE, who had turned twenty that July, had shoulder-length hair, a closely trimmed mustache, and the somewhat swaggering manner of a young man who knows how handsome he is. He had graduated from New Utrecht High School in June 1975, where he was voted best dresser.

Bobby was living on Bay Ridge Parkway in the nearby Bensonhurst section of Brooklyn. He liked clothes and, since high school, had worked at a number of jobs that were all in the retail end of the clothing business. Most recently, he had sold men's suits and shirts at a respected men's shop called George Richlien's, on Bay Parkway and 86th Street, not too far from his home. He was taking the summer off, but planned to return to work for the busy fall season. During the slow summer months, Bobby Violante was spending time at the

End, the Place, and at other area watering spots. As his father Pasquale says, "Bobby was just drifting about. He was like lots of other kids his age. Trying to find a place for themselves."

On Thursday, July 28, Bobby had gone to dinner at a franchise restaurant called Beefsteak Charlie's at 3121 Ocean Avenue in Sheepshead Bay. A hail-fellow-well-met character proclaims the virtues of Beefsteak Charlie's on New York television. "Come on in," he says, "and we'll feed you like there's no tomorrow." At the restaurant, Violante was seated at a table with two friends. He noticed both Ricky and Stacy Moskowitz just inside the entrance. Stacy's tomorrows were running out.

He kept his eye on the girls, who were quickly seated at a table nearby. Finally he approached Ricky, who looked older than her fifteen years. He introduced himself and asked if he might join them for a few moments. The girls looked at each other and then invited him to sit down in one of the wooden captain's chairs with red leatherette padding. The restaurant's motif attempted to be San Francisco 1890 but succeeded in merely being U.S.A. plastic 1970s.

"I've been watching you girls since we came in," Bobby said. "You're both very pretty." His eyes didn't leave the younger girl.

Ricky knew almost immediately that this young man was much too old for her, so she directed the conversation away from her to her sister. "What's your name?"

"Bobby . . . Bobby Violante. What's yours?"

"I'm Ricky, and my sister is Stacy."

Bobby finally noticed Stacy and realized that she was more his age. "Do you live close by?"

Stacy now took the lead. "Yes, on East Fifth Street. Know where it is?"

"Sure."

"What do you do for a living, Bobby?" she asked.

"I'm in men's clothing."

Stacy was interested. The shoe and clothing businesses

are a good mix, and the two youngsters found they had something in common to talk about. Young Ricky kept discreetly out of the conversation until she broke in to say "Bobby, your friends are motioning to you. I think the waitress is bringing your meal."

Bobby left, saying "Hey, after you girls finish eating, I'll meet you at the bar for a couple of drinks? Okay?"

The girls agreed, and he excused himself and returned to his table. When he finished, Bobby threw ten dollars down on the table and told his friends, Ralph and Vinny, "You guys figure out the bill. I'll be in the bar with the girls."

The bar's atmosphere was more subdued than the dining room. The girls sat at the far end, sipping wine, waiting for Bobby. In the next hour, the three of them were joined by some friends of Stacy's. Ricky remembers, "Stacy liked Bobby from the beginning. They were good together. Even in the first few minutes, it seemed like they knew each other for a long time." Finally it was time to leave, and Bobby nervously asked Stacy for her number. "How about going out to a movie or something on Saturday?"

"Bobby, give me a call tomorrow. I think I already have plans with my grandmother. But I'll see if I can arrange something. If not, we'll make it in the next couple of days."

Bobby wrote down Stacy's number in an already full address book. He'd make a special note for her. "Stacy," he says, "was the type of girl who made you feel like you knew her and she knew you all her life."

Almost blind now, Violante concludes "It was incredible, the vibes she gave me."

When Stacy returned to the Moskowitzes' second-floor apartment, she rushed to tell Neysa about the new man she had met at Beefsteak Charlie's.

"He has turquoise eyes, Mom," she began. "He was different than all the other guys. You'd like him. He's handsome, and very polite. Like he holds your chair when you sit down, and lights your cigarette and says please. I know you'll just fall in love with him."

Her mother was interested in this new encounter, for Neysa and Stacy were more than mother and daughter. They were like sisters. Stacy told her mother about work and the people she'd met. And her mother loved to hear her daughter's stories, for it reminded her of her own youth. "Mom, he's slim and tall. He's Italian, but not in that rough kind of way. And before we left, he asked me out. I'm going to go if I can put Grandma off."

Neysa stopped her daughter there. "No, you can't. Your grandmother has been looking forward to this. It isn't fair to her. If this guy is all you make of him, tell him the truth. He'll wait another day or two, or maybe just end a little early with Grandma and see him in the evening."

STACY MOSKOWITZ spent much of early Saturday shopping with her grandmother. They traipsed through the women's clothing stores in Kings Plaza at the very end of Flatbush Avenue, just north of the Belt Parkway. By the end of the day, Stacy had bought two pairs of designer pants with matching blouses. She'd bring everything home to show Neysa, and they'd decide which outfit to keep.

At home they settled on a pastel blouse and light-blue pants to wear on her date later that evening. The outfit was perfect for the warmth of summer. It was sexy but not flashy.

Her grandmother Esther commented, "Stacy, it looks like it was made for you. I'm sure he'll love it."

Stacy's mother didn't have to add anything to what Grandma said. It was as if she had somehow moved into her own past. It could have been her own date. The same anticipation of youth was there.

Stacy glanced up at the plastic kitchen clock. She didn't understand where the time had gone. Bobby would be there in less than an hour, and she hadn't showered or put on her makeup. The young woman rushed to her room at the rear of the apartment, closing the door behind her.

Her room was small and neat, filled with mementos of trips she had taken to the Caribbean. Atop her wooden dresser was a mirror. Next to it, a box filled with makeup and perfumes. There also was a plastic photo cube filled with snapshots of her girlfriends frolicking on the beach.

When she had finished showering and applying her makeup, Stacy slipped into her new outfit. The final touch was a new scent, Ciara. Dressing had taken the full hour, and Stacy heard her mother call out that her date was parking his car in front of the house at the fire hydrant. Her clock radio showed it was 7:55 P.M. Bobby was on time, something Stacy was certain her mother and father would note with approval.

BOBBY VIOLANTE pulled into a parking space in front of 1740 East Fifth Street. He was driving his father's car, a 1969 four-door blue Buick Skylark. Gerry Moskowitz was sitting on the small terrace on the second floor and he watched Stacy's date closely. The young man opened a black iron gate and walked along the concrete apron to the front steps. He rang the bell of the left-hand door and waited for the buzzer to free the lock. He walked in and up the single flight of stairs and turned right. Mrs. Moskowitz opened the apartment door and was waiting to show him in. "Good evening. I'm Stacy's mother."

"Good evening, Mrs. Moskowitz." Bobby walked inside. He followed her into the living room. Stacy's father had come in from the terrace. "Hello. I'm Mr. Moskowitz."

Bobby took Stacy's father's large hand and grasped it firmly. It was a gesture Gerry would remember, for he believed it showed strength, not weakness, as was the case with some of Stacy's other dates.

"Nice to meet you, sir." Another point for Bobby Violante. It had been some time since Gerry Moskowitz had heard the word *sir*.

Before anything else was said, Stacy appeared in the hallway behind Bobby. "Bobby, I'm glad you've already met my family. Won't you sit down?" she said, patting the cushion next to her.

Bobby walked to the couch. He felt odd before Stacy's parents. It seemed as if he was about to get the third degree. He began, "Lovely room you have here, Mrs. Moskowitz."

"Oh, you think so? We're going to paint it after the summer. Right now it's just too hot to think of it." (The room would finally get that painting eighteen months after Stacy's death.) Mrs. Moskowitz took a seat opposite the young couple. "Stacy seems to think a lot of you."

Bobby looked at his blonde date, smiling. Her eyes dropped as if she were embarrassed, but she wasn't.

"Where are you planning to go tonight?" her mother inquired.

Bobby answered, "We'll go out for a bite, and maybe to see *New York, New York.*" He began to rise.

Mr. Moskowitz, who had been quiet all the while, sensed Bobby's discomfort. He hadn't taken a seat, but was standing framed in the terrace doorway. "Wherever you kids go, remember that crazy guy, the .44-caliber killer, is still on the loose. Don't go parking anywhere, please."

Stacy turned to her father as she stood up following Bobby's lead, "Don't worry, Daddy. I'll call as I usually do. And, besides, I'm a blonde and everyone knows he doesn't like blondes." She laughed, taking Bobby's hand and leading him to the stairs.

Bobby turned back to Stacy's parents. That would be the last time he'd be able to see them.

Stacy's parents walked out on the small terrace and watched as Bobby opened the door of the Buick for Stacy. By now, Stacy's sister Ricky had joined her parents on the terrace. She had stayed in her room when Bobby was upstairs. The fifteen-year-old caught a last glance of her sister as Bobby closed the car door on the passenger side.

"I just have to keep looking at *Superman,*" Neysa Moskowitz said lightly to Ricky. She paused. "They look a little like Mutt and Jeff." Stacy was five feet one inch tall, Bobby six feet two.

Gerry Moskowitz watched Bobby Violante open the car

door for Stacy. "I haven't seen that in years," he said, with enthusiasm. "It's a chivalry you don't see today."

"He's treating Stacy like a woman," Neysa said. "She likes having doors opened for her and cigarettes lit."

BOBBY STARTED the car and put on the air conditioning. He turned to Stacy. "How about something to eat? Like I said on the phone, we can go to the ten o'clock showing of *New York, New York*. Would that be okay with you?"

"I don't think I'd like to eat just now. I had a lot of junk food this afternoon. I'd rather not see *New York, New York*. Maybe we could go to the Trans-Lux East in Manhattan?"

"Impossible, on a Saturday night, what with the traffic into the city and then the parking. Better try to see something nearby. I hope you're not disappointed."

Stacy wasn't. Being with Bobby could be the start of something good for her. She could feel it.

"Look, Stacy," Bobby said, "let's go to the movies at the Kingsway Theater. In the meantime, we have an hour to kill. How about driving over to Gravesend Bay and watch the ships?"

It was still light, and she answered, "Sure. Just remember, I want to get to the movies."

The couple drove to the parking area. The Verrazano Bridge and the shoreline of Staten Island stood etched in the sunset. They talked for a while. Music from the car's radio created a romantic mood. Bobby lit a cigarette for Stacy, and she sank back into the auto's cushions. It was a good time to be young.

Violante looked at the dashboard clock. The movie started in fifteen minutes. He drove to the theater, at Kingsway Avenue and Coney Island Avenue, and found a parking place less than a block away. It was so easy that he commented to Stacy: "Look, it's Saturday night and this .44 killer has everyone staying home." Stacy just smiled.

While Violante bought the tickets, Stacy went into the theater lobby and called her mother.

"Mom," she said, "I'm at the Kingsway and having a great time. He's everything I thought he'd be. He's a real gentleman." Stacy went on to tell her mother that they'd be going out for something to eat after the show, and that she needn't wait up. "I'll be just fine. See you in the morning."

Stacy and Bobby were disappointed by the movie. The music was the only saving grace. The couple walked out of the theater into the coolness of the summer's night. They'd have a bite at a local diner. "Stacy, how about driving over to Jasmine's, over on Third Avenue?" She agreed. But the club was virtually empty, and after forty minutes they left.

It was 1:37 A.M. and Stacy wanted to be alone with Bobby, so she agreed to go back to the lover's lane. "Sure, Bobby. I love the bridge at night. It's a real romantic place. Could we walk down to the water, across the parkway?"

Bobby Violante led Stacy back to the car and helped her in and then hurried around to the driver's side. Stacy leaned over and opened the door for him. The engine started and Stacy slipped next to him, placing her arm around his shoulders as he drove back to the parking area facing Gravesend Bay.

Violante found a parking space under a street lamp on the service road at Bay 17th Street. The other spots in darker areas had been taken. Stacy moved against Bobby as the young man turned off the car's engine. They embraced for a moment, then sat back. Stacy spoke first, "Bobby, how about that walk over the bridge [the pedestrian bridge across the Shore Parkway] to the park at the water?"

Bobby decided to play things cool and agreed. He stepped outside the car and went around to her door and opened it. He helped Stacy out and the couple walked toward the bridge, twenty feet away. There was a slight breeze, and the young man took his jacket off and slipped it around Stacy's shoulders.

TOMMY ZAINO, nineteen, five feet nine inches tall, 155 pounds, was part owner of Zaino Brothers and Company,

Corvette body specialists, of 2727 Stillwell Avenue in the Coney Island section of Brooklyn. He and his date, pretty seventeen-year-old Debbie Crescenco, of Bay Ridge, were parked in a metallic powder-blue Corvette directly under a mercury vapor street lamp on the service road of the Shore Parkway at Bay 17th Street. Zaino had borrowed the Corvette from one of the workers at the shop. "It was polished like a diamond," he says, "with all kinds of extras on it." Zaino wanted to make a good impression on Debbie because it was their first date. "She was tall, slim," he remembers. "She was the kind of girl I liked. You know, she was someone you wanted to show off."

But she was nervous about parking, especially in a lover's lane during the night. Her parents had repeatedly warned her not to go to that kind of place, yet here she was. Debbie had dark shoulder-length hair, which made her a target, newspaper stories said, for the Son of Sam. They had spoken about the shootings at the Queens disco Elephas earlier that evening. She said, "The killer hadn't struck yesterday on the anniversary of the first killing, as the newspapers said he would. Perhaps he would wait till tonight?"

Tommy Zaino and Debbie Crescenco left the Corvette at 1:20 A.M. and walked across the footbridge to Gravesend Bay. When they stepped off the iron steps on the far side, Debbie started to complain that it was cold, and they promptly turned around and walked back to the Corvette. The temperature had dipped into the low sixties, and they rolled up the windows of the sports car against the fresh sea breeze.

Tommy turned to the young girl and put his arm around her, drawing her near. His lips moved against her cheek and down to her lips. "Tommy, someone will see us and tell my folks."

Tommy didn't care and pulled her closer. She protested again and he moved away. She looked at him and said, "Tommy, how about moving down the street away from this light?"

Tommy didn't have to be told twice, and he started the car

and shifted into first as soon as the engine caught. He drove about fifty feet farther south, into a darker area, adjacent to a bent cyclone fence that bordered the Shore Parkway with its speeding traffic.

Once again Tommy began the ritual of putting his arm around his date and drawing her close. She pulled away. "I had time," recalls Tommy. "I sat back and we listened to the stereo. The car was loaded with equipment and she loved to play with all the gadgets."

In a few minutes he began the game once again. Tommy was going to give it one last try.

"Hey, cut it out, Tommy."

Just then the headlights of a car hit the Corvette's rear-view mirror. Another car was pulling into the space behind them, directly under the street lamp. Tommy glanced down at the Corvette's clock. It was 2:15 A.M. Bobby Violante and Stacy Moskowitz had just taken the spot behind them.

At 5:30 P.M. on Saturday, July 30, apartment 7E, 35 Pine Street, was a hot box. By six David Berkowitz decided to leave the apartment, to get something to eat. He showered and put on fresh clothing, denim shirt, faded dungarees, and work shoes.

At a Spanish-American food stand at Tenth Avenue and 31st Street, Berkowitz ordered a taco and fries and a large Coke. He asked for a large dish of chocolate ice cream as dessert, paid the bill, and left a fifty-cent tip. Then he drove across town on 14th Street, and continued onto the Williamsburgh Bridge to the Brooklyn–Queens Expressway. Fifteen minutes later he was in Queens, where David says the girls are so pretty.

But this night he drove through Queens and into Nassau County. By 7:30 P.M. he found himself in Huntington, a middle-class suburb of 65,000 people on Long Island's north shore. Things "didn't feel right" in Huntington. It was too neat. At eight o'clock Berkowitz left the quiet suburban

streets of that village, returned to the Long Island Expressway, and headed west, back toward the city.

As he drove, he listened to the voices of Sam and the
demons. They instructed him to kill. "I purposely drove out
to Long Island to kill someone," he says. "It didn't matter
who I'd kill, whoever I'd come across. When I'd find the right
one, I would be told.

"Sam would tell me through his dog, as he usually did
when the night would be right. But the dog's not really a dog,
it just looks like a dog. It's not. Sam just gave me an idea
where to go. When I got the word, I didn't know who I would
go out to kill, but I would know when I saw the right people."

A mile into Queens on the Expressway, David veered onto
the Cross Island Parkway south, past Kennedy Airport toward Brooklyn. Just beyond the airport he left the Belt Parkway, entering Howard Beach.

A small enclave of apartment houses and two-family
homes, Howard Beach is the area he had cruised through the
previous March on the night he murdered Virginia Voskerichian. David drove through the streets of Howard Beach for
an hour. The demons remained silent.

It was now 9:30 P.M. David returned to the Parkway going
west and drove an additional exit until he entered Brooklyn.
He went past Pennsylvania Avenue, getting off at exit 13,
Rockaway Avenue. Now he was in Canarsie.

He drove north along Rockaway Avenue, past frame one-
and two-family homes constructed in the 1940s, and turned
left onto Flatlands Avenue. After three blocks he made another left onto 94th Street. David now followed each block
from 94th, to 93rd, to 92nd Street, going down one street
four blocks, then coming back the same number on the next
street. "I'd driven them before, a month earlier. I also drove
through that area when I worked as a guard near Kennedy
Airport."

At about 1:50 A.M., Berkowitz arrived in Bensonhurst.
The area is different from Canarsie in that the buildings here
are a mixture of one- and two-family brick homes and are set
against a backdrop of six-story apartment houses. He finally

parked next to a fire hydrant on Bay 17th Street, between Shore Road (the service road for the Shore Parkway) and Cropsey Avenue. "I'd driven all the way through Queens and out to Huntington, then back to the South Shore along the streets of Brooklyn. When I got to Bay 17th, I knew I had the right spot."

As he walked away from his car, a blue-and-white police car turned the corner of Cropsey Avenue onto Bay 17th. It began to cruise down the street in his direction. "I had the feeling they would go by my car." But Patrolmen Jeffrey Logan and Michael Cataneo of the nearby 62nd Precinct did not ignore the illegally parked Galaxie. They stopped alongside Berkowitz's car. Patrolman Cataneo got out and wrote a summons, numbered 906953 2, to the owner of a white four-door Ford, license plate number 561-XLB, carefully printing the offense. "HYDRANT." (In fact the car was a faded yellow.) It was 2:05 in the morning, July 31.

"I watched them write the ticket," David says. "I waited till they left. Then, I went back to my car and took the ticket off the windshield and placed it inside, on the dashboard. I wasn't worried by the ticket. It didn't matter. I'd pay it, of course, in a couple of days."

Berkowitz began to walk around the area. He walked south along 17th Street alongside a row of apartment buildings, finding an opening between the buildings, then walked through. On the other side of the buildings was a park (the Bay 17th Street Park) enclosed by a chain-link fence. There were handball courts to his right and a softball field directly ahead. A rectangular passageway had been cut into the fence, and he walked through onto the ball field. He looked ahead and saw that the park stretched for two blocks. Intersecting the park was a pathway lined with trees. There were concrete and wooden benches on either side. At the northern end of that lane, an abandoned car sat overturned, casting a shadow from the two lamps midway down the lane. As he walked across the field, he could see a fenced-in children's play area with swings and slides. Next to it was a bocci court.

David continued walking through the green belt until he reached Shore Road. At its entrance he stopped, first looking at the pedestrian bridge straight ahead, then at the lineup of cars along the roadway. The smell of marijuana reached his nose from the Volkswagen closest to him, and he stared at the couple inside. They didn't even know he was there. Barely fifty feet ahead, Tommy Zaino's borrowed Corvette was parked under the street lamp. David's hand felt for the gun at his belt, and he grasped the handle. The sports car's occupants were moving about, oblivious of the killer watching them. David crossed the street, catching a glimpse of Debbie Crescenco's long brown hair. He began to lift the gun from his belt. His eyes focused on the couple's movements through the small rear window of the car, noticing them sit back suddenly. By now David had reached the right rear fender of the car, his left hand running across its smooth surface toward the passenger-side door.

Suddenly the car growled as Tommy started it. David stopped, frozen in place. "I wasn't sure that they had seen me. I couldn't move, so I just stood there waiting for someone to scream out at me. But nothing happened, only the car just began to move. I turned away and walked along the street alongside the parkway. When I looked back, the sports car was about fifty feet further away. I didn't know what to do, 'Should I follow them, or shouldn't I?' " The killer sought refuge in the semidarkness of the park's interior. He shuffled to a bench at the far end of the walkway to a point opposite the overturned car. From time to time, David glanced back to the vacated spot under the street lamp, staring at its emptiness. "I knew they had got me to this spot to kill. I couldn't understand why they let that couple get away? Maybe I was there to get someone else?"

David didn't have to wait long. At 2:15 A.M. a 1969 Buick pulled into the spot the Corvette had vacated. There were many other cars around but the only spot open on the lover's lane was under the street lamp.

"You know, Bobby," Stacy said to Violante, "it's much

nicer here when it's dark. It's really much more romantic. Don't you think so?''

Bobby Violante and Stacy Moskowitz had returned to the exact spot where they had parked six hours earlier. The light from the overhead street lamp cast an artificial halo around their car. It was as if they were actors on center stage in some grand production and the kleig lights were shining their way. Stacy looked straight ahead at the Corvette parked in front of them. Violante blinked on his car's bright beams to see what was going on inside the Corvette. "Hey, Bobby. Cut it out," Stacy laughed. "How would you like it if someone did that to us?''

Bobby turned to his blonde companion, drawing her close. Violante liked Stacy and didn't want to rush anything, and he sat up straight, asking "How about taking a walk in the park?''

Stacy protested mildly, "It's pretty dark in there. What if the Son of Sam is hiding there?''

"Are you kidding?" he said. "This is Brooklyn, not Queens. Come on,'' and he stepped out of the car and hurried over to her side, opening the door for her.

The couple walked hand in hand across the street and onto the concrete lane that bisected the park. Stacy joked and laughed, suggesting that they run over to the swings. "Come on, Bobby. I love to be pushed on the swings.''

"I remember her having such a good time," Bobby Violante says. "I especially remember the moonlight playing through her hair. There was something about her, something so different from the other girls I had dated.''

Bobby finally stopped the swing and leaned forward to kiss Stacy again. When she opened her eyes she caught sight of a man looking at them just outside the fence. "Bobby, someone's looking at us.'' Violante turned and caught sight of David. Their eyes met for an instant, then Berkowitz turned away and walked across the concrete path and behind the abandoned car.

"Bobby, I think that's the same fellow I saw when we

walked into the park a little while ago!'' There was a sense of urgency in her voice.

Bobby felt her fear and he said, "Hey, don't worry. He won't bother us. Anyway, you're with me. Come on. I'll swing you again."

"No, Bobby. Maybe we ought to get back to the car."

"Okay. But don't worry." He helped her down and put his arm around her.

The couple walked back to Bobby's car. Stacy looked about for an instant, but the man was gone. She returned her attention to her date. In another minute they had reached the Buick. Once again he opened her door first and helped her in. He ran to the driver's side and got in, turning to her immediately. He moved toward her; his hands found her face, cradling it in his palms. His lips found hers. It was 2:35 A.M.

The kiss ended, Stacy said: "Bobby, let's leave. Let's leave right away."

"No, Stacy. We'll spend just another five minutes here." He could see she was nervous, but the thought of any possible danger was far from his mind. "We'll hang out for another five minutes." They were sitting close together, facing each other, Bobby smiling and Stacy trying to force a smile in spite of her fears.

DAVID HAD WATCHED Bobby rolling the windows up as the young couple got out of the Buick and walked into the park. He remained seated on a park bench as they approached and then walked past him. They turned left into the playground and he got up and positioned himself behind the abandoned car, always keeping them in sight. "She looked at me, but didn't say anything."

While Stacy was on the swing, David left the cover of the car and moved to the bordering fence. It was then that she saw him for a second time. She pointed him out to Bobby. David sank into the shadows. Minutes later, the couple walked back to the Violante car, and David followed, staying close to the fence as he walked. He stopped, still inside the park, and watched as the boy held the door open for the girl, then ran to the car's other side and got in. There were other cars in the street, and David quickly eyed them. No one seemed to be paying any attention. He stepped from the shadows to the sidewalk and then into the street itself. He was now in the light from the overhead street lamp that hung directly above the Violante car.

"I walked straight to the car. When I got to the rear of it I looked around, then stepped onto the sidewalk. I moved right to the driver's side and pulled the gun out. The voices began again. They began to howl. I knew I'd have to go through with it this time. I didn't care if anyone saw me. It didn't matter, I had to shoot them." David crouched over and held the pistol with both hands. He pointed the barrel into the car, at the heads of the couple, and pulled the trigger.

FOUR YOUNG PEOPLE were sitting in cars on Shore Road at 2:32 on the morning of July 31. Stacy and Bobby were facing each other in the 1969 Buick. Fifty feet away, Tommy Zaino noticed a middle-aged blonde woman walking a white dog along the park fence. Curiously, her presence reassured him. Zaino turned back to Debbie. Her delicate profile was framed against the right car window as she sat back in her seat.

Zaino looked at the rear-view mirror. He saw a Buick parked behind him. He could tell it was a Buick by the car's distinctive grill. It's not that easy to distinguish one make of eight-year-old car from another for most people. However, Tommy's business was cars. "I noticed there was a guy and a girl inside," he says. "They were sitting close together. I mean they weren't apart, like Debbie and me."

Zaino looked around. A man came shuffling out of the park. Another dog-walker, Zaino thought.

Except where was the dog?

He watched the man in a denim jacket cross the street and approach the Buick from the rear. Probably this man knew the couple in the car. Maybe he was going to climb in with them? A threesome. Hell, that happens. And this guy in denim was decent enough to go for a stroll all by himself so that his buddy could make out a little bit.

The man "got even with the car," Zaino says, "and bent forward unexpectedly. Then he drew a gun." Tommy watched in the rear-view mirror. "It was just like a movie," he said.

Debbie, hearing the popping report of the .44, turned to Tommy and cried out, "What's happening?"

Tommy said, "Shut up . . . there's someone shooting at the people in the car behind us."

Debbie tried to turn around, but Tommy pushed her down onto the floor of the car. "Keep down!" he yelled as he started the car. "I think it's the .44 killer . . . the Son of Sam."

Debbie couldn't hear him as the car's engine fired up. "What? What is it, Tommy?"

BOBBY's lips had just found Stacy's. After the kiss, Stacy spoke first. "Bobby, I knew it was going to be this way between us." Her eyes met his.

"Stacy," he began, "sometimes you meet someone who you . . ."

"All of a sudden," Bobby Violante says, "I heard like a humming sound. A humming. A vibrating.

"First I thought I heard glass break. Then a humming. Then I didn't hear Stacy any more.

"I didn't feel anything, but I saw her fall away from me. I don't know who got shot first, her or me.

"Gradually—it seemed like years—the hum began to subside."

Violante had been shot twice in the face. Physicians explain the humming sound as an implosion of the eardrums. The pressure clogs one's ears.

Stacy Moskowitz slumped backward; she had been shot once in the head. She moaned.

Bobby heard her, but he could not see her. Berkowitz's bullets had left him blind.

"Stacy," Bobby screamed. "Stacy. He killed us." Then Bobby thought, "But how could he have killed me? I'm still conscious. And Stacy can't be dead. If she were dead, she couldn't be moaning." His hand found the car's horn, and he hit it a couple of times. Then, blind Bobby Violante staggered from the car. He wrapped his arm around the lamp post. He thought the attacker might be close by, might shoot again. He didn't care. He screamed into the night: "Help us. We're shot. Help. We're shot. Please, somebody, help us."

He felt his way into the Buick and pounded the horn once again, this time not stopping for a full minute.

Then he collapsed onto the sidewalk.

No ONE from Task Force Omega was in Brooklyn when Stacy Moskowitz and Bobby Violante were shot. And because 3:00 A.M. was sign-out time, the Omega patrols assigned to the Shore Parkway had begun to make their way back to the 109th Precinct around 2:20. The officers would all check out at three and needed time for the ride back to Union Street in Queens and for their sign-out procedure. As it was, only two Omega cars had been assigned to Brooklyn, one to the Shore Parkway, near the Kennedy Airport–Pennsylvania Avenue area, the other to the Brooklyn–Queens Expressway. On the orders of Deputy Inspector Dowd, the main thrust of the task force was deployed through the Northern Boulevard disco area, Queens Boulevard, and the approaches to the Throgs Neck and Whitestone bridges.

"Dowd just didn't believe that the Son of Sam would hit in Brooklyn," says Sergeant Coffey. "He'd called it correctly when Berkowitz hit on Northern Boulevard, and now he'd guessed that he'd go back there, or possibly to the Bronx once again. We therefore covered the bridges connecting the two boroughs and left Brooklyn's main roadways to the Highway Patrol operating out of their Flatbush Avenue Headquarters."

RICHARD SHEEHAN, a thirty-year-old policeman for the Port Authority of New York–New Jersey, had returned to his home at 311 Bay 14th Street after attending the wedding of a friend. His brother-in-law, Christian Cecere, dropped him off at his home just five minutes before the shooting.

The sounds of gunfire, the blasting horn, screams alerted him, and he threw open the window of his rear bedroom and looked across the park. Bobby Violante was grasping the lamp post and hitting the horn, screaming. Cars were pulling out of their spaces and flying away.

Officer Sheehan quickly slipped his pants on, ran out of his house, down the block, and made a left onto Shore Road. In front of him, seventy-five feet away, Bobby Violante was on his knees, holding his face, screaming for help for someone called Stacy.

Officer Sheehan reached the kneeling boy and bent over him. "Are you okay, son?" he called out.

"Not me, look after her," Bobby answered.

Officer Sheehan tried to take Bobby's hands away from his face. There was blood streaming through the spaces between the boy's fingers. The officer stood up and looked into the car. There he saw Stacy, her blonde hair matted with blood. He reached inside and touched her. She moaned. "It was a good sign," he later told the police, "both of them were alive. There was glass everywhere, and I knew she'd been hit, but she began to talk. I thought that since she didn't look so bad, I'd get back to the boy. He'd been hit in the face, and I knew he was losing a lot of blood. I looked into the rear seat, and there was a blanket there, and I leaned over the seat and grabbed it. I wanted to cover him, and I started to when I heard this sports car come down the block."

Tommy Zaino was returning to the scene of the shooting. He cruised by slowly. Officer Sheehan stood up and called to the driver to stop. He did, but left the car's engine running. "Come over here and help me get him covered." Together the patrolman and the frightened Zaino got Robert Violante to lie down on the sidewalk. In another minute, people from the houses on Bay 14th Street began to rush to their neighbor's assistance. In a couple of minutes, Officers Cataneo and Logan responded to the call of "Shots fired." They sped to the scene and immediately called for assistance and an ambulance. They were afraid that the gunman might still be hiding either in the park or in the heavy growth that lined the Shore Parkway.

TOMMY ZAINO was recalling what he'd seen to the patrolman.

"I saw him hold the gun with two hands and fire it. He was close to the car, but not that close because of the way the gun was going up into the air. I mean, if he had been that close, the gun would have hit the car, so I'd say he was a foot or two back.

"I heard four shots, I know he didn't empty all of it, not like all six. After he shot about four, very fast, he just ran. He ran back from where he came from, right back into the park. He didn't throw the gun away, he just held onto it, keeping his hands low to the side."

Later Zaino told his story more fully. "As soon as I saw him run back, I looked for the key to the car. I grabbed for it and started the engine. Then I just took off! As I took off, I was thinking to myself, 'people had to have heard the shots. Maybe these people thought I shot them? 'Cause I took off just as he had shot them.' And I burnt out, it sounded bad with my car. I went up the block and made the first right and headed up that block, Bay 14th Street. I got to that corner and made another right onto Cropsey. I went towards the front of the park, and I looked down the block to see if there were some headlights or if someone was running up the block.

"But I didn't see anything and I took off for the 62nd Precinct, which was two or three blocks away. There was a cop on the corner of the station entrance. I had gone through all the traffic lights and everything. He was watching me coming real fast. I pulled up and I couldn't really talk that good, I was so nervous. But, I yelled out, 'Somebody got shot. I heard shots, and I seen somebody get shot at.' That's what I kept saying. All he answered was 'Okay, I'll get a car there.'

"I told him it was at Shore Road right near the 17th Street park. He just walked into the station house. Maybe he thought I was lying or something. I really don't know. But, he didn't sound as crazy as I was that night. Anyway, I just sped off as he walked into the station house. I went down 18th Avenue, back to the parkway.

"I just had to get back there to find out what happened, even though I was plenty worried. When I got there I kept low in the seat, just to look around. But, there was somebody there already, some guy was helping. He had a blanket and he called to me. He yelled he was a cop and told me to stop. And I did. But even when I got out, I left the engine running. I was having trouble with the car that night, and if I turned off the engine, I wasn't sure I could get it started again.

"I left Debbie in the car and ran over to the [other] car. Robert was on the ground. He had gotten out and held onto the pole and then had fallen to the ground. We put the blanket around him.

"He was a mess. His face was just filled with blood, and he was holding his eyes. But, he wasn't really holding his eyes, because he had a hole there. He was holding his face almost like he was crying. He was yelling out, 'Why me? Oh, God, why me?'

"After the blanket was around him I just walked away. I walked to the car and looked in. It was then that I saw the girl. Her head was back and I didn't notice that she was shot until her head fell forward. She just fell forward and was trying to say something, 'Something moving around.' But she kept falling, slumping down. I turned away and got sick.

"It was then that the cops began to come. I told them what happened and how the guy went running into the park. But I was pissed 'cause all the cops started running into the park. I yelled at them, 'He ain't gonna be in there now! He was there fifteen minutes ago.' They just came too late."

Zaino stood and walked back to his car, its engine now in

danger of overheating as he hadn't turned it off the entire time. He began to get in, then backed out, walked five steps to its rear, and vomited for a second time.

EIGHT PEOPLE who had heard the shots and screaming telephoned the police emergency number, 911. Four additional calls came into the 844-0999 Omega Task Force hotline.

The first police to reach the scene were two officers assigned to the local sector car. They had been only five blocks away during the attack, and received the call "Shots fired," at 2:37. Officers Michael Cataneo, thirty-six, and Jeffrey Logan, thirty-five, worked out of the 62nd Precinct at 1925 Bath Avenue and had been driving west on Cropsey Avenue when the call came in on their squad-car radio. They immediately spun their car around and headed back to the park area they had patrolled only recently.

"When we got there we saw that some guy was on the ground covered by a blanket. There was blood pouring from his face. One of the people helping him got up and showed us his shield. He was a Port Authority cop, and he asked that we call an ambulance. Officer Logan was already doing that, seeing the situation. Then this Port Authority cop informed us that there was a second victim in the car. I looked in and saw this blonde kid. She looked like she'd been hit in the back of the head. She was still moving and I yelled to Jeff to call in that there were two victims.

"This kid who was helping the Port Authority cop was yelling something about the Son of Sam, and that he'd run off into the park. It was then we added to our call for help. We requested assistance because we didn't know if he was still around. I was nervous, but I tried to help as best I could. I kept looking over my shoulder at the people coming out of the houses. I hoped they were only neighbors trying to help. I sure hoped that guy wasn't waiting around."

WITHIN TEN MINUTES the officers at the 109th Precinct belonging to Task Force Omega knew there had been a shooting in a lover's lane. Many wanted to get back into their cars and rush over. But Sergeant Conlon stopped the stampede to the doors and ordered them to get their tails out on the streets and go to the assigned spots at the bridges and parkways. "Pick him up if he heads over the Throgs Neck or Whitestone. Don't make any mistakes. I don't care if you back up the traffic clear down to Belmont Raceway, get him!"

BY NOW, eight marked cars had responded to Officer Logan's call for assistance. They were all from the 62nd Precinct. Officers, service revolvers in one hand, flashlights in the other, fanned out through the park and along the undergrowth alongside the Shore Parkway. Each succeeding minute would bring another screaming police car to the already crowded scene. It was then that a call was placed to the 62nd for detectives. Slowly, organization began to come out of sheer chaos. Zaino could be heard shouting at the cops still searching the bare park, "He ain't gonna be there now. You guys . . . where the hell were you ten minutes ago?" He got no response, just some dirty looks.

As other units arrived, officers began cordoning off the area.

Sergeant Joe Coffey of Task Force Omega arrived at 3:03.

BERKOWITZ had fired five shots, not four as Zaino reported. But it took a thorough investigation by the forensic and ballistics units of the police department to determine that fact.

"I shot the last three times at the both of them." He says he isn't sure why he did. "I really wanted the girl more than anything. I don't know why I shot the guy. But they were so close together."

The shots tore through the Buick's windows, shattering glass. Stacy screamed. Bobby didn't move. His hands grabbed for his shattered face; blood began pouring out of the massive wounds. Instinctively he dropped one hand and pounded at the car's horn as a trumpet in answer to the rolling thunder of the shots. The entire sequence took four seconds.

David watched with wonderment. Here was everything right in front of him, framed in the light of the overhead street lamp. And then there was complete silence, if only for an instant. Somehow, time had stopped for everyone: the couples in the other cars, Tommy Zaino and Debbie Crescenco, Robert Violante and Stacy Moskowitz, and the Son of Sam. It was as if a movie director had chosen this moment to freeze everything, to etch the finality of this act in the minds of an audience.

David turned. In his rear-view mirror, Tommy Zaino watched him shuffle off quickly toward the center walkway of the park. Tommy turned, but lost him as the rear window of the Corvette was so small.

David kept the gun in his hand and ran across the cobblestone walkway and past the overturned car, turning right through the opening in the fence and onto the softball field. He ran along the fence that was the right-field wall until he reached the second opening. He didn't stop there. He continued directly across the bordering street and between the apartment houses and out onto Bay 17th Street and slowed down. He was out of breath, and had to walk. The gun never left his hand. He finally turned it upside down and placed the barrel in the sleeve of his jacket. He reached the car and fell in.

Berkowitz waited in the Galaxie about five minutes to catch his breath, and still there was no sound. He heard neither sirens nor screams. Sounds were blocked off by the apartment buildings and the noise of speeding traffic on the Shore Parkway further masked the cries from the scene of the shooting.

At 2:38 A.M., Berkowitz says, he simply started the car and drove away. "I was on a one-way street, and I simply drove northeast on 18th Avenue as far as it went. It was a pretty big street. I could see that it went pretty far. I wasn't going any place in particular."

He continued onward. "I followed 18th Avenue to where it met Coney Island Avenue and turned left. I entered a big park [Prospect Park]. I took the drive around the park and got out at Grand Army Plaza, where the library was. Halfway around the plaza there was an all-night newspaper stand, and I bought the Sunday *News*. I put the paper in the car and took Flatbush Avenue north a few blocks, and then made a left onto Atlantic Avenue, where I was able to traverse Brooklyn and head towards the water [New York Harbor]. There was a park. It might have been Sunset Park. But I rode instead down Fifth Avenue in the direction I had shot the couple. I kept on riding until I approached the Verrazano Narrows Bridge, and there I saw another park. I was now less than a mile from the shooting scene. It didn't matter because I was tired. I just parked my car. It was four thirty or so in the morning. [David had made a complete circle of western Brooklyn.]

"I walked out to the park with the newspaper and found a bench. I sat on it for a long time. I sat there for the rest of the night. When the sun rose, I read the news."

THE LEAD headline of the *New York Sunday News,* July 31, 1977, was PROBE FIX RING IN N.Y. COURT. It was over a story written by reporter Claire Spiegel about widespread case-fixing in the Manhattan Supreme Court.

At 8:00 A.M. Berkowitz returned to the car and began to drive again through Brooklyn. At 8:50 A.M. he crossed the Williamsburgh Bridge into Manhattan. David had spent the entire night in Brooklyn. The East River bridges had been closely watched by the police from about 3:25 A.M. on. But, because David had stayed off the bridges and had chosen not to use the parkways, the operation failed.

DETECTIVE SERGEANT JOE COFFEY had spent an uneventful evening with Detectives John O'Connell and George Moscardini cruising the Forest Hills Stadium (West Side Tennis Club) area. He had a feeling that there might just be another attack in the area. Already Virginia Voskerichian and Christine Freund had been killed there. He was worried that their unmarked brown 1976 Plymouth would stand out like a sore thumb amid the neighborhood cars. "You could spot us as being a police car a mile away," Coffey laments. "Who the hell buys a car without any chrome at all?"

At 2:35 the call came over the citywide police band: "Shots fired, Bay 17th Street at Shore Road, Brooklyn." The officers listened intently. Within a minute, a second call came in on their second radio, the one tuned to the detective band: "Possible homicide, Shore Road at Bay 17th Street, Brooklyn. Possible single gunman." That was all the trio had to hear. No one had to give an order. Detective Moscardini put the revolving red light on the vehicle's roof and Detective O'Connell drove off onto Queens Boulevard, switching on the piercing electronic siren.

"I got on the communicator as we drove and called back to the Task Force headquarters at the 109th," recalls Coffey. "I wanted to speak to Dowd, who had made it a habit of staying there until about three A.M. on weekends. I asked about the call on the detective band and he said it wasn't our man. I asked him how he knew, and he said 'Because it was in Brooklyn.' I requested that he let me go there and after a couple of seconds he agreed."

Their unmarked car swung around and headed back to Continental Avenue, then made a left until it hit Queens Boulevard, three blocks later. They didn't stop for the traffic light, but spun right onto the Boulevard and sped at seventy-five miles an hour east to the entrance to the Van Wyck Expressway and headed in the direction of Kennedy Airport. Just before the airport entrance they turned onto the Belt Parkway (Shore Parkway) and sped the remaining eight miles to where the shooting had occurred.

"We'd made the trip that normally takes forty-five minutes in less than thirty minutes. When we got there, we were one of the first units on the scene. The other guys were the Night Duty Team from Brooklyn Detectives. The homicide men go off duty at one A.M. and after that there are only nine detectives left to cover the entire Borough."

Detectives from the Brooklyn night-duty team were getting statements from the uniformed men and from Port Authority Patrolman Richard Sheehan. John O'Connell and George Moscardini moved into the assembled crowd looking about. The chance that the killer had hung around was always there, and the two detectives scanned each person's eyes, seeking that sign of fear or glee. Coffey went to the Violante car. He looked in and peered at the steering post. "There was no doubt in my mind," he says. "There it was, right in the center of the hub, a .44 slug. I'd seen them before. It wasn't a .38."

He walked back to his police car and called through to the 109th. "Inspector Dowd, it's our man," he said.

"How do you know?" replied his commander.

"Because it's a .44 and because of the way it went down. It's our guy, I'm telling you."

"Can't be. He wouldn't move into Brooklyn."

"Inspector, come down here and see for yourself," the sergeant suggested.

"No!" Dowd answered. "Get ballistics first. Then we'll know for certain."

A few minutes later, after another tour of the area and further examination of the Violante car, Coffey made a second call to Dowd. "Inspector," Coffey said, "it's definitely our guy."

"What makes you the expert?" Dowd answered. He was becoming irritated.

"Inspector, I've been on this case since January. I know what I'm talking about and I'm telling you it all fits. It's him!"

"Impossible—Brooklyn?—Impossible!" Coffey waited. Dowd came back on the communicator. "I think we should wait, like I said before, for the ballistics guys to check it out."

It didn't really matter. Dowd felt he could coordinate operations from his headquarters in the 109th more easily than from the field. And it was up to ballistics to prove him right or wrong.

AT NEYSA and Gerry Moskowitz's apartment Neysa was waiting for her eldest daughter to return, although Gerry had gone to bed half an hour before. "I always waited for Stacy to come back from a date," says Mrs. Moskowitz. "I probably am going to do the same when Ricky dates, too." She paced the living room floor and walked to the kitchen. "I just made a cup of coffee and sat down when I realized that it was later than I'd thought. Stacy had said she'd be home by two thirty, and when she didn't return by three, I got very nervous."

The Moskowitz kitchen was bathed in harsh incandescent light radiating from a single ornate fixture set over the corner dining booth. She cast a shadow against the wall behind her as she sat down.

Unable to sit, she walked to her bedroom. There she undressed and put on a nightgown and a patterned housecoat.

It was then that Neysa heard a car stop in front of the house. There were footsteps. She glanced at the clock. It was 3:15 A.M. The outside chime sounded and she walked to the buzzer. "I wondered why Stacy didn't use her key," Mrs. Moskowitz remembers. "I rang back to let her in." The footsteps coming up to their apartment sounded heavy. They weren't like her daughter's.

"Gerry," she called, "there's someone at the door. It doesn't sound like Stacy." The chime hadn't awakened Gerry, but the tone of his wife's voice did. He quickly slipped out of bed, donned a bathrobe, and began walking through the narrow corridor to the side door. He was still in the hallway when the knock came.

"Who is it?" Neysa said hesitantly.

"The police. Mrs. Moskowitz?"

"Yes?"

"I'd like to speak to you. There's been an accident."

Neysa threw open the door. There, framed in the dim hallway light, was a middle-aged patrolman from the 61st Precinct, police cap in hand. "There was sweat running down his face," says Neysa.

"Mrs. Moskowitz, I think you know me. I was the crossing . . ."

He never finished his statement. Gerry Moskowitz broke in. "Is it Stacy? Has something . . . ?" He fell to his knees. He suddenly remembered the daughter who had died years before. His words came as a cry. "I've already lost one daughter, Jody. Please, I don't want to lose Stacy too."

The officer stepped inside and knelt over, grasping the older man and lifting him from his knees, "Come, stand up, please. Sir, something's happened to your daughter. She's . . . she's been shot. I don't think it's too bad, but they want you both at the hospital as soon as possible."

"Shot?" Neysa screamed. "Was it him? Was it her date? It had to be him, the Violante boy," she brought her hands to her face.

"No, Mrs. Moskowitz. I don't think so. Two kids have been shot in a car. He's probably the other one."

Without another word, Neysa ran to her bedroom to get dressed. "Take us there," begged Stacy's father as he looked at the policeman. "I'm going to get dressed. Don't go away."

"I'll be here."

Within minutes, both Gerry and Neysa were dressed. They returned to the hallway, followed by Ricky. She recognized the patrolman, who had been a crossing guard at her junior high school. "Hi," she said, not understanding what was happening.

"Ricky, you stay here," Neysa said. "Stacy's been hurt. Just stay here in case Grandma calls. Please, baby."

Valentina Suriani, age eighteen, and Alexander Esau, age twenty.

(Top) View of the interior of David Berkowitz's apartment.
(Bottom) The wall in David Berkowitz's apartment that he broke
open trying to get at the demons he believed to be hiding inside.
The writing is David's.

Sketches of the alleged murderer prepared by police department artists with the assistance of witnesses.

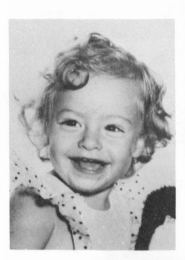

(Top) Robert Violante, age twenty.
(*Courtesy of the Violante family*)
(Left) Stacy Moskowitz, age
nineteen months. (*Courtesy of the
Moskowitz family*)

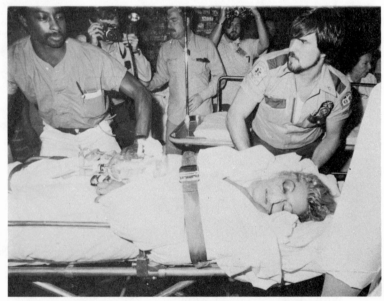

Stacy Moskowitz, age twenty, during transfer to Kings County
Hospital after being shot by Son of Sam. (*Wide World Photos*)

NASSAU
SUFFOLK
FINAL
Vol. 59, No. 39

DAILY ◎ NEWS

New York, Wednesday, August 10, 1977

Price: 20 cents

Cloudy, showers, 85.
Cloudy; tonight, 60s.
Sunny tomorrow.
Details, page 79.

WANTED

Son of Sam

This is new sketch released by police hunting for Son of Sam. Drawing is based on descriptions by witnesses to shootings of Stacy Moskowitz and Robert Violante and previous shootings.

Stories on page 3

Description: Male, white, 25 to 32, 5'8"-5'9"; 165-175 lbs, good athletic type build, clean shaven, dark almond-shaped eyes, dark wavy hair, sensuous mouth, high cheekbones.

Clothes: Jacket—blue denim
Pants—blue denim, slightly flared
Shirt—bluish grey Guava with small kidney-shaped design spaced 3" apart
Shoes—blue denim with narrow white band.

Notify special homicide task force at 109th Precinct with information on suspect: Call 961-9613 or 844-0929.

(Top) Front page of the *Daily News* with new police sketch of Son of Sam. Police Officer Mike Speros was cleared as a potential suspect (note the similarity of his photograph to the sketch that appeared in the *Daily News*). (*Lawrence D. Klausner*)

The arresting officer, Detective 2nd Grade John Falotico, leads murder suspect David Berkowitz into the Yonkers police station. (*Gil DeLorenzis, Gannett Westchester Newspapers*)

TODAY
Partly Cloudy, 85-90
TONIGHT
Partly Cloudy, low 70s
TOMORROW
Sunny, 90s
Details, page 2

TV: PAGE 34   THURSDAY, AUGUST 11, 1977   25 CENTS   Vol. 176, No. 215   © 1977 The New York Post Corporation

LONG ISLAND

DAILY PAID CIRCULATION 2D QUARTER 1977   609,390

CAUGHT!

Post Photo by Nury Hernandez

Son of Sam was on way to kill again

'I wanted to go out in a blaze of glory'

By CARL J. PELLECK

The man police say is the Son of Sam was on his way to claim more victims when he walked into the arms of waiting detectives.

David Berkowitz, 24, had already written a letter—his third—addressed to Suffolk County and New York police and the press. He was going to leave it alongside his latest victim. It had no stamp on it.

In questioning after his arrest last night, Berkowitz said he hadn't quite made up his mind whether to stalk his next victims in Riverdale or in the Hamptons.

And he told police that he wanted to "go out in a blaze of glory" because he felt the cops were closing in on him. Sources said the letter made a similar claim.

'DID IT FOR SAM'

A pleasant-looking, slightly chubby young man, Berkowitz remained calm throughout the many hours of questioning at Police Headquarters.

He gave no reason why he started his killing spree on July 29, 1976 other than "I was doing it for Sam . . . Sam can do anything . . . I was driven to do it by Sam."

He gave cops the answer they had long been seeking: Sam is a man who lives in a building behind Berkowitz' Yonkers apartment house.

He identified the man as Sam Carr of 316 Warburton Av.

When Berkowitz was grabbed, he had the dreaded .44-caliber pistol with him. He had two dozen extra bullets in a brown paper bag he had

Continued on Page 8

Full coverage: Pages 2, 3, 4, 5, 7, 32, 33.

This front page made the circulation of the *Post* jump from 609,000 to one million copies.

David Berkowitz stands before Judge Corso for sentencing.
Defense counsels Leon Stern and Ira Jultak on left. (*Marilyn
Church*)

15

Night of Hell

It was a hellish night.

Members of the press were quickly informed of the shooting by young reporters monitoring police radio calls on the graveyard shift at the *News, Post,* and *Times.* Local television stations WPIX, WOR, and WNEW, along with those of the major networks—WABC-TV, WNBC-TV, and WCBS-TV— also alerted crews to rush to Kings County Hospital, where the victims had been taken.

Son of Sam had struck again.

Meanwhile, John Falotico, fifty-four, had only had a couple of hours' sleep after completing his night's tour of duty at Brooklyn's 10th Homicide.

It was quiet outside his 58th Street bedroom window, a world away from the violence he lived with as a homicide detective, when the telephone rang a little before 3:00 A.M. The drowsy detective picked up the receiver.

"John? This is Bill." (Sergeant William Gardella, Falotico's supervisor and chief of the borough's night-duty team that had responded immediately to the report of the shooting.)

"We've got a multiple shooting at Shore Road and Bay 17th. You'll have to get yourself right over here because you're going to catch this one."

"How many shot, and how many dead?" Falotico asked.

"Right now there's no one dead, but word's come down that the docs expect them to die, both of them."

"Who were they?"

"Maybe you'll know one of them. It's two kids. One's Robert Violante; he's from your area. The other is a girl— Moskowitz, Stacy Moskowitz."

"Sergeant, got any idea who did it?"

"Looks like the .44!"

"I kind of sat back," Falotico says, "I just couldn't believe it. The bastard had come into Brooklyn!"

As the conversation ended, Falotico was throwing off his pajama bottoms. He washed and dressed quickly. Last, he put on the tools of his trade—a set of handcuffs, his two-inch snub-nosed service revolver—and placed his leather-encased gold shield in his jacket's breast pocket. Falotico then hurried to his 1967 yellow Chevy and raced to the scene.

The detective was "the next man out," meaning he was the next detective to get a case in the 10th Homicide. As cases came in, the duty officer would assign them to the detectives coming on the next tour of duty.

As he drove, he thought to himself, "Damn, why can't I get some sleep? My squad is down to one guy—me!"

Falotico belonged to a twelve-man squad that was the entire 10th Homicide Zone team. It was divided into three squads of four men each. In theory, on a rotating basis, four men were always on duty. But things never went entirely by the book. Right now Falotico was the only officer available, even though he wasn't on duty. Lieutenant Robert Kelly had taken his vacation; Falotico's usual partner, Joe Polizzi, was assigned full-time to a major case (the John Quinn–Shelly Golden homicide); and only the day before, "Big" George Donovan had gotten a hernia picking up an office typewriter.

But it was more than vacations, or injuries, or the reassigning of detectives to cover homicides outside the zone's area that worried John Falotico. The real problem was the attrition rate within the ranks of detectives throughout the city. Divisions were undermanned, squads almost devoid of personnel having to work long hours with far too little manpower.

Statistics never told the truth; it was the guy in the field who knew the truth. As Falotico put it: "We are giving the city over to the criminals not because there's more crime, but because there's less of us."

Falotico was wearing his trademark, a white jacket long enough to cover his gun, its brown polka-dot pattern obvious against the fabric's whiteness. "You have to make your wardrobe go a long way, so I wear jackets with a neutral color so I can combine them with lots of different pants. It helps."

He had devoted his life to the job, his preoccupation with police work being a major element in the breakup of his marriage in 1970. His ex-wife lived in New Jersey with her second husband. One daughter had decided to remain with her mother while the other two came to live with him in Brooklyn. Somewhere along the line, John Falotico felt the Roman Catholic church had all but abandoned him. All that was left was his job. While he was more than eligible to retire, anyone who knew John, knew that he'd die with that gold shield pinned to his sports jacket.

Only five feet nine inches tall, he didn't remind you of a cop. His speech and air suggested someone from the other side of the fence. Only two months earlier, Borough Commander Bill Fitzpatrick, two years younger than John, had called him to his office and offered to promote him to homicide detective in any of the five Brooklyn homicide zones. John felt good when the Chief said, "John, with your background, because you're Italian and you look like one of the bad guys sometimes, you'd make a natural for the tenth." And so, after thirty years on the force, Detective Second Grade John Falotico was starting a new career as a homicide detective in Brooklyn, where he had lived all his life. It would be here on the morning of July 31, 1977, that he would "catch" a hot potato—the most sensational attack and subsequent homicide in the history of the New York Police Department.

He reached the scene at 3:30 A.M. It was impossible to park close to the site; news trucks, neighbors, police vehicles, and the curious mixed in a madhouse of confusion. Falotico pushed through the police lines on foot while pinning his gold shield to his lapel. A uniformed officer from the 62nd Precinct lifted the rope barrier to allow him to pass.

Bill Fitzpatrick, Borough Commander, was there. So were John Keenan, the thin white-haired Chief of Detectives, and another member of the brass indicated by his captain's badge (later to be introduced as Joe Borrelli). Off to one side, giving orders to detectives John didn't recognize, was Sergeant Joe Coffey. John walked over to Coffey, whom he'd worked with years earlier at the Manhattan DA's office.

"What happened, John," Coffey asked as Falotico approached, "they finally decided to retire you from the DA's squad?"

"They need us old pros to teach you young guys the ropes, Joe. Hey, what have you got?"

Coffey outlined what had occurred earlier that morning and gave the detective an update on the victims' condition at Kings County. "The docs at the County think the boy has had it. The girl looks like she'll pull through."

As the detectives continued talking, Falotico's eyes drifted toward a distinctive, tall man standing near the blood-stained street lamp Robert Violante had used to support himself. It would be another hour before Falotico would learn that the man was Captain Joseph Borrelli. "I guess he had lots of things on his mind. Maybe he was thinking about that letter?"

Coffey ushered the detective to the shattered, blood-stained car. They walked across the street and looked in, Coffey pointing to the steering wheel. "See, John, the slug's still in the hub of the wheel. It's a big one, larger than a .32 or even a .38. It has to be a .44. I've seen enough of them lately."

Falotico looked inside and confirmed Coffey's analysis. "It's him, then," he answered. "It's that .44."

They walked back to the huddling brass, Falotico taking notes. Coffey introduced Falotico to Captain Borrelli. It was the first time they had met, and John liked him almost immediately. He thought Borrelli looked and acted as a supervisor should. This respect for the captain would be invaluable as the next few days passed. Borrelli would back the 10th's operations, allowing its detectives to plunge ahead with the investigation that resulted in the ultimate capture of David Berkowitz on a lonely street in Yonkers.

Falotico learned that there was a witness to the shooting, a young auto-body man named Tommy Zaino. Later that afternoon, the detective would drive to the 60th Precinct at West 8th Street and Surf Avenue, near the city's Aquarium, to get his first talk with the witness. Meanwhile, Tommy was trying to get a police artist to put on paper what he had witnessed in his rear-view mirror that early morning. Zaino would, in Falotico's mind, become the best witness the police had come across. This would later be disputed by other members of the 10th, Detective Strano claiming that Cacilia Davis had actually encountered the killer from a distance of less than three feet while walking her dog. Throughout the investigation, these two detectives would pursue different avenues in their quest for the Son of Sam. In the end, each would bring valuable elements into the search.

In the meantime, a temporary headquarters was being set up in the 62nd Precinct by the brass, and Falotico began to canvass the scene. He took notes on the position of the cars and the names of the first officers on the scene, not caring to trust official versions of what had happened, as they were usually inconsistent. He worked until dawn. Later he returned to the scene to follow up with interviews of all persons who could possibly have seen something—including the Port Authority patrolman who was the first person to aid the stricken Bobby Violante. He would continue questioning witnesses until night closed in again.

As THE NEWS of the Moskowitz–Violante shootings spread through New York, police officer Tom Chamberlain was asleep in his split-level home in Irvington in Westchester County. His partner Pete Intervallo was also asleep, in his home in Mahopac, north of Westchester in Dutchess County. Both officers were family men and they lived outside the suburban city of Yonkers, which they believed to have crime problems similar to New York's. They learned of the shooting while driving to work the next morning.

DETECTIVE SERGEANT JIMMY SHEA had gone to bed early in the quiet Queens community of Rockaway Point. Asleep long before their father were his children: Carol Ann, seventeen; Jimmy, sixteen; Kevin, fifteen; Maribeth, thirteen; and Kieran, twelve. Shea first learned of the shootings the following morning at 10:00 A.M. at the 10th Homicide Zone.

DETECTIVE JOE STRANO and his wife Eileen were driving home over the Verrazano Bridge from Staten Island after a family gathering when they heard the news flash over New York's twenty-four-hour all-news radio station, WINS. The location of the shooting was given as the 10th. Strano turned to his wife and said: "Eileen, he's made his mistake coming to Brooklyn. That's going to trip him up."

MICHAEL AND ROSE LAURIA had spent a quiet night at home in their apartment on Buhre Avenue in the Bronx. The anniversary of the death of their daughter Donna was past. It left them feeling hollow: it robbed them of sleep. They did not go out any more. People always were pointing at them as being the unfortunate parents of "Sam's" first victim. At 3:22 A.M., Michael switched on the radio to get the next day's weather report and heard of the shooting in Brooklyn. He shuddered. He thought of the parents of the kids involved, understanding all too well what they would go through. Michael waited until morning to tell his wife. She needed any sleep she could get.

OFFICER LOU MARCHINI was on patrol in the Bronx, operating out of the 43rd Precinct. He completed his tour at midnight and left the station house at 12:30 A.M. Going down the stairs in front of the building, he commented to one of the sergeants, "Looks like a good night for a shooting. This Son of Sam hasn't struck in some time." It was a morbid joke. In the back of his mind he knew that his longtime friend, Officer Mike Speros, was suspected of being the Son of Sam by other cops of their own precinct. The fact irritated both men, perhaps Marchini more than his partner, for he knew the absurdity of it all.

Marchini made his statement, believing that Mike was still away in Cape Cod on vacation with his family. "If anything were to happen this night," says Lou Marchini, "at least Mike would be nowhere near New York City." Three hours later, while watching an early-morning movie on television, Officer Marchini's hands went cold. A news flash broke across the screen telling of the shooting. His premonition had come true.

POLICE OFFICER MIKE SPEROS had lived under extreme mental pressure for months. Speros had seen other officers look at him with suspicion. They felt he had all the characteristics of the killer as depicted by the police sketches. He had been off duty when all the killings were done. He was left-handed. And the fact that he was an artist didn't help. The Son of Sam was supposedly artistic. Finally, close to the boiling point, Mike Speros decided to take some vacation time. He packed his family and drove to the artists' colony at Cape Cod. It was something he'd done on successive summers. This time it was an especially welcome respite.

Speros and his partner, Lou Marchini, had their own suspect in the Son of Sam case. But now it was up to his partner to follow up on the leads they both developed. Cape Cod was away from the city and the distance gave him a sense of security. As fate would have it, it was false. There was no rest from his thoughts, from his anger. "I just couldn't understand how the guys at work could believe I was the killer. They knew me—or at least I thought they did," says Speros. "I knew there was nothing I could do to change their minds. So I hoped he would be caught while I was away." But the Son of Sam was not.

Finally, a week before schedule, he decided to return. He packed his family into his yellow VW bug, with its peculiarly ominous license plates GRK 44 (GRK stands for Greek), and drove back to his home in the Bronx. When the Moskowitz–Violante shooting occurred, he was back in the city and a prime suspect once again.

JUDY PLACIDO was lying in her bed, eyes glued to the small television screen in front of her. At 3:22 A.M. she saw the same news flash that Michael Lauria did. She touched the back of her neck. A bandage still remained nearly six weeks after she was shot on the morning of June 26. "I couldn't breathe for a moment. Then I said a prayer for the kids. I never went to sleep."

DETECTIVE JAMES JUSTUS was on his way to Massapequa after having worked into the morning hours on a loft burglary. He was juggling two assignments at the same time. His regular tour in Brooklyn Robbery was to investigate industrial break-ins. He was also putting in time with the Queens Special Task Force, patrolling residential streets on weekends. He was emotionally involved.

He had just passed through the toll booths in Valley Stream, at a point where the Belt Parkway turns into the Southern State Parkway, skirting the south shore of Long Island. His radio was preset to WINS 1010, and he turned on the all-news station. Suddenly the announcement that the .44-caliber killer had struck again came over the airwaves. He was tempted to turn around and go to the scene, but he forced himself to continue home. He needed sleep. He knew the killer had made a fatal mistake. "He had come to Brooklyn," says Justus; "that was going to be his undoing."

He smiled as he drove on through the early morning mist. "This is the finish line," Justus thought. "Whoever it'll turn out to be, the guy just outsmarted himself. The guys in Brooklyn will get him!"

MAYOR ABRAHAM BEAME went to sleep early on the night of July 30, 1977. The summer hadn't brought any vacation to the beleaguered politician. The city's budget was still under fire from the United States Treasury and, as usual, street crime was up. One saving grace was that crime statistics showed an increase far below the projected one. "Perhaps this Son of Sam thing was keeping the rapists and muggers inside."

It wasn't until 6:30 A.M., his usual waking hour, that aides told him of the shooting. The Mayor first called Kings County Hospital to ask about the condition of the two victims. His second call was to One Police Plaza, where Police Commissioner Codd was already at work.

"It can't go any further, Mike," the Mayor said. "He's got to be stopped. The cost doesn't matter."

A YOUNG copy editor who was watching the shop in the early morning hours called Jimmy Breslin at home. The *News* had its sources at One Police Plaza. Less than five minutes after the shooting was tentatively reported as being the work of the .44-caliber killer, an unidentified policeman called the paper. On hearing the sketchy details, Breslin shouted into the phone, "Thanks, kid. I'm on my way." The reporter ran out of his Queens home and drove toward Coney Island Hospital. Midway along the Van Wyck Expressway, his radio-telephone rang. The victims were being moved to Kings County Hospital. Breslin changed his route. He arrived there only minutes after the victims' families.

REPORTERS PETE HAMILL of the *News* and Steve Dunleavy of the *Post* learned of the newest shootings by such mundane methods as the morning radio and telecast. Both columnists immediately raced to their respective publications. They knew they'd be pounding out columns for the afternoon and next day's editions. Later that afternoon, Hamill would confer with his friend Jimmy Breslin in order to get the latest scoop from the hospital and, hopefully, from Breslin's private sources at the police department.

ALL THROUGH the night, two detectives had been watching the home of a Queens garbage collector to whom, for obvious reasons, we will give the fictitious name of Mario Swift. He had become a suspect in the Son of Sam killings a month earlier, just before Judy Placido and Salvatore Lupo had been wounded, and for some unexplained reason the detectives who were assigned to tail him had lost him just before the Placido–Lupo shootings occurred.

The detectives were furious at themselves. When they returned to the 109th and reported to Sergeant Conlon, the sergeant raged: "Well, you guys call yourselves pros. Pros? You're boy scouts! If I wanted him lost, I would have assigned a couple of rookies!"

"But, Sarge . . ."

"But Sarge, your ass! You guys make me sick. How the hell do we know if he was the one or not? You've blown it! Now get out of my sight. Tomorrow you go back out and tail him. And if you lose him again, you'll be pounding a beat so far in the boondocks that the rats won't even be there."

The sergeant walked back to his desk and reviewed the file on the suspect. Everything fit. This Swift guy was a real loner, no known female companions. He had lost his temper, according to some of his fellow workers, and had ripped out pages that dealt with the shootings from newspapers he'd found in the garbage. He refused to make small talk about the killings; he got excited when anyone pressed him.

For the next month, Conlon assigned the detectives to tail Swift every Friday and Saturday night. He hoped either to pin the killings on him or to eliminate him as a suspect.

As Captain Borrelli puts it, "The public is used to programs like *Kojak*. They show the cops always sticking like glue to their suspect. But out on the streets, it's anything but that. You can't get too close or he'll see you. If you get too far away you give him the opportunity to disappear into an alley or a subway station or restaurant with a back door. Of course, something simple like a red light or everyday traffic will screw you even if your guy doesn't know he's being tailed. It's not unusual for detectives to lose their man. It's frustrating, but part of the job."

Thus, while Stacy Moskowitz and Bobby Violante were being taken to the hospital, the two detectives stood outside Mario Swift's two-story home in Rego Park. Their man had remained home that night. But had he really remained home? He could have slipped out a rear window. With the news of shootings in Brooklyn, the detectives would have to make sure, and there was only one way to check; they'd have to confront Swift face to face. The detectives walked up the steps and pounded on the door. No sound could be heard inside. For all they knew, the response might be a bullet coming back at them through the wood. One detective then hid in the space alongside the brick steps beside the garbage cans, .38 in hand. The second officer took his service revolver out of its holster and placed it inside his pants pocket.

Minutes passed. The detective pounded the door again. This time he heard movement in the house. Lights went on and he heard the sound of footsteps. The detective at the front door stepped to one side, putting brickwork between himself and the house's occupant. "Who's there?" came the voice from behind the door.

"Western Union," answered the detective, "telegram for a Mr. Swift. Sorry about the time."

"Okay," came the answer as the locks were undone. The door opened and out stepped a sleepy, pajama-clad Mario Swift. He was obviously drunk. "Okay, where's the telegram?"

One detective simply blew up; there wasn't time for Swift to have done the shooting in Brooklyn and to have made it home. Only ten minutes had passed. The distance was just too great. The detective took his hand off his gun and stepped back. His fist shot upward, striking Swift flush in the nose, knocking him on his back on the floor of the apartment. The two detectives looked at each other in shock. What had they done? Then they ran to their car and took off. As they looked back, they could see the suspect standing in the doorway, his hand holding his bloody nose.

"What the hell did you do that for?" one of the detectives said.

"Why? Because we wasted so damn much time on him. I could have sworn he was the Son of Sam."

ANOTHER SUSPECT was a policeman in the 72nd Precinct in Brooklyn. He too could not account for his whereabouts at the times killings had occurred. On the evening of July 31, this patrolman was in the process of booking a robbery suspect. He'd never know it, but that arrest saved him a lot of grief.

Other cops were suspect, too, and were cleared, either through checking their duty charts or through personal interviews. Sergeant Coffey comments, "When we talked to these guys, they weren't mad or anything. They always tried to help. They were as anxious as we were to make certain that Son of Sam wouldn't turn out to be a cop."

AS THE NIGHT turned into dawn, various units assigned to tail suspects began to call in to Omega headquarters. Suspect A had been here, suspect B there. None of them had been anywhere near the scene in Brooklyn. By the morning of David's final attack, all the suspects had been accounted for. The police were left with nothing to go on. Somewhere in a city of nine million people there was a killer. But where was he? Who was he?

"Even so, we knew we'd get him sooner or later," says Captain Borrelli. "The real fear was that we'd have to wait for him to go on killing until he'd make that one real mistake that would point directly to him. We didn't like it, but we had to live with it. I lost thirty pounds during that investigation, and most of them came off during those last ten days. Sometimes I didn't want to go home, waiting for that break; sometimes I didn't want to stay. All the guys felt it, each of us showing it in a different way. It was beginning to eat at us all. Sometimes I'd have to order a guy home for some rest, and they'd plead for just a few more hours. They always thought that this one, this guy would be the killer. How do you tell a guy to stop on a case like this? I couldn't."

NEYSA and Gerry Moskowitz had hurried to the police car outside their home and were on the way to Coney Island Hospital.

"Please, does your radio work?" asked Gerry Moskowitz. "See if you can get some news about our daughter."

The officer next to the driver turned to the frantic parents in the back seat. He spoke loudly over the wail of the siren. "Can't. It only goes to police headquarters."

"Please," Mrs. Moskowitz asked again. The officer faced the direction of the speeding car. It was futile, but he tried.

"61 Adam to central."

After fifteen seconds, the reply crackled over the radio set: "Central to 61 Adam." The Moskowitzes sat forward in the rear seat straining to hear the conversation.

"61 Adam. Can I get any further news on. . . ." His question was cut short as his partner turned off the siren and swung the patrol car into the emergency ramp of Coney Island Hospital. It was no longer necessary to ask for news. They were there. The patrol car was waved on to the emergency entrance, where two ambulances were backed up to the automatic doors.

The Moskowitzes jumped out and ran to the entrance. Stacy was being wheeled out of the emergency exit, plastic tubes taped to her arm. Neysa Moskowitz ran to her daughter. Stacy was moving, her eyes were open.

In the meantime, Gerry questioned, "Where the hell are they taking her now?"

One of the attendants answered. "To Kings County."

"Kings County?" Gerry said. "Why the hell Kings County?"

One of the doctors on duty raced over to restrain the Moskowitzes. "Because we just don't have the facilities here to handle head wounds," he said.

"Head wounds?" inquired Gerry, staring at the young doctor.

"Yes! . . . Officer, get these people out of here!"

The officer responded, "Doc, these are the girl's parents."

The doctor stopped, and the tone of his voice suddenly changed. "Oh, I'm sorry. It's just that Kings County has better facilities for these types of wounds. We've got the victims stabilized. They're all right now. Officer, why don't you get them over there now?"

"They're okay then Doc?" Gerry asked.

"I think so," answered the young doctor.

With that, Gerry ran to his wife and grabbed her by the shoulder. "Come, let's meet them at Kings County." There was nothing else to do. The ambulances were leaving the parking area. Gerry and Neysa Moskowitz ran back to the police car and climbed back into the rear seat. The officer tried to back up and found that he was boxed in by other police vehicles that had raced to Coney Island Hospital.

"Move the fucking cars!" he yelled. "I got the parents here. Now move them!"

Two uniformed men raced to their cars and quickly swung them out of the way, but by the time the patrol car reached the street, the ambulances were out of sight. The driver hesitated until Gerry Moskowitz yelled, "Take a right. I know how to get there! Just follow how I tell you to go."

The revolving red-and-white dome lights were switched on. A block later, away from the hospital quiet zone, the siren began its wail. "Move!" Gerry screamed. "Keep on Ocean Parkway. I'll tell you when to turn right. You got a long way to go. It's before Church Avenue." Mr. Moskowitz knew Brooklyn as a truck driver should. The shortcuts he told the policeman to take were the ones he used to save time on his regular delivery route. They arrived at Kings County Hospital along with the ambulances.

The Moskowitzes jumped out as they came to a stop behind the lead ambulance, and ran to where the attendants were placing Stacy on a portable stretcher. One attendant pushed them away.

"Hey, leave her alone. We have work to do here."

The parents backed away, watching their daughter disappear behind the closing doors. They looked at each other, then followed the stretcher into the emergency room. Stacy was taken behind a curtain. They could see physicians scurrying about, working on her. Standing to Gerry and Neysa's left was another older couple. In the midst of this, a police officer was writing information into a small book. The Moskowitzes instinctively realized the other couple were the Violantes. "I saw Bobby's mother and walked over to her," Neysa recalls. "We didn't speak. There were tears in her eyes as she looked at me. I guess she knew I was Stacy's mother." The two women embraced. Pat Violante and Gerry Moskowitz embraced also.

"I felt terrible that I had thought Bobby had been the one who shot Stacy. Here he was, in the next treatment room fighting for his life." Neysa drew Theresa Violante closer to her. "I'm sorry. Terribly sorry," she whispered to Bobby's mother.

"Please," Mrs. Violante answered, not understanding the guilt Neysa felt. "They'll be all right. I know they'll be . . ." She couldn't continue. She began to sob.

IN MINUTES an army of doctors, nurses, and attendants descended on the two curtained trauma areas. Suddenly a nurse walked out of one of the cubicles carrying a white brassiere. It was covered with blood. "That's Stacy's! I just know that's Stacy's!" Gerry Moskowitz grabbed his wife by the shoulders, keeping her from running to the nurse.

The nurse kept on walking. This scene was enacted for her

254 · SON OF SAM

all too often. It was something she was used to; parents screaming about their children, husbands crying over murdered wives. It was part of the commotion of every inner-city hospital emergency room. Doctors and nurses enveloped themselves with a protective shield, trying not to show emotion.

"Mommy," a voice cried out from behind the curtain. "Mommy, please. It hurts."

"Keep screaming, baby," Neysa Moskowitz shouted. As long as her daughter screamed, Neysa thought, she had to be alive.

Neysa was still wearing her housecoat. She hadn't bothered to change. She had no makeup on. It had all happened so fast. Abruptly she tore away from her husband and rushed toward the sound of her daughter's shrieks.

Gerry rushed after her, grasping her waist a step before the curtain. He dragged her back to a bench by the far wall. "Neysa. Let them do what they have to," he said. "They're doing everything they can." A police officer walked over with two cups of coffee.

Five minutes later the screams began again. "Mommy! It hurts so much. Please, Mommy."

Neysa Moskowitz stood up. Her husband got up too. Together they walked to where the sound came from. "I parted the curtain and stepped inside. I walked directly to her. One eye was terribly swollen and puffed. The eyelid was an ugly purple." A Levin tube disappeared into Stacy's nose, which was coated with bandages. IVs had been inserted into both arms.

"Hey, get that woman out of here," said one of the doctors, who was working on the back of Stacy's head.

A nurse gently took hold of Mrs. Moskowitz and guided her outside. "Please. Don't come in here again. We'll let you know," she said as she closed the curtain in Neysa's face.

Neysa stood facing the white curtain. She was frozen with horror. "There was so much blood," she said.

Meanwhile, Dr. Jeffrey Freedman performed surgery on

Bobby Violante. His left eye was completely shattered, and the doctors worked frantically to save the right one.

Stacy would need surgery too. A team headed by Chief Neurosurgical Resident Dr. Ahmet Oygar and Dr. Jamed Shahid scrubbed. After their initial examination, they called Dr. William A. Shucart, Chief Neurosurgeon at Downstate Medical Center, who was at home in Westchester, and briefed him about the situation. Upon completion of the call, Dr. Shucart dressed and drove to Kings County.

THE DETECTIVES requested that a special room be set aside for the parents. They had to be kept away from the throng of reporters. Ira Clark, the hospital administrator, helped settle the two families in. The parents kept asking about their children. "What about my Bobby?" asked Theresa Violante. "Will he live? Will he be able to see?"

"Is Stacy going to live?" asked Mrs. Moskowitz.

"I've spoken to the doctors, and their preliminary prognosis is that the girl . . . Stacy . . . maybe she won't make it. She's been struck several times in the head. The wounds are extremely serious, so serious . . ."

Neysa remembers listening to him and thinking only that Stacy would need some physical therapy and possibly a wig.

Sadly now, reflectively, she says, "I guess everyone was telling me that Stacy wouldn't make it, but I didn't hear that. I heard what I wanted to hear."

Ira Clark went on, turning to the Violantes. "And, Bobby . . . I'm afraid the news isn't too good for him either." Theresa Violante crossed herself. "Bobby has absorbed an extremely serious injury. He's also lost a great deal of blood. The doctors are doing everything they possibly can for him. There seems to be a fairly good chance they can save him. But, on the other hand, they believe he's going to be permanently blind." Theresa Violante looked up at Mr. Clark, then slumped into the cushions of the couch. She had fainted.

Gerry Moskowitz left to find a pay phone. Reporters were arriving in the waiting room and a television crew from

WNBC-TV was setting up. The reporter was talking to a detective, trying to find out what he could about the condition
of the two kids. Mr. Moskowitz slipped by unnoticed, found
an unoccupied booth, and placed a call to his daughter Ricky.

"Ricky, she's in the emergency room, honey. They said
she's . . . she's going to be fine, just fine."

"Daddy, is she?"

"I hope so," he answered.

At that moment his name was called out by a detective.
Almost as if on a Hollywood set, all the reporters ran to the
booth. He hung up immediately.

"Mr. Moskowitz, Mr. Moskowitz," a reporter from the
Post shouted. "Tell me, how is she doing?"

Gerry Moskowitz pushed him aside. "Get out of my
way!"

"Mr. Moskowitz, is she going to live?" the reporter asked
as he followed Stacy's father down the hallway.

"Get away from me," growled Gerry as he turned to face
the persistent man. A uniformed officer stepped between the
two, spreading his arms out and allowing the father to return
to the area the hospital had set aside.

As he walked in, he saw Jimmy Breslin speaking to the
Violantes. Somehow Breslin had slipped by the police officers. Gerry stepped back into the hallway and motioned to a
policeman. "Officer, there's a reporter in here. I don't know
who the hell let him in. But I think he ought to be removed,
either by you or by me." His face was flushed. The officer
understood and hurried inside. Breslin was hustled out amid
a flurry of protests.

Fifteen minutes later, Ira Clark returned to the doctors'
lounge. "The next forty-eight hours will be critical for
Stacy," he said. "If she survives them, she should pull
through with minimal damage to her motor system." Then he
turned to the tearful Violantes. "Bobby is going to live. The
doctors have stopped the bleeding."

"What about his sight?" asked Pat Violante.

"We're hoping that they'll be able to save one of his eyes.

It's much too early to tell, but there is a chance. I'm afraid that the other eye was so severely damaged that it was impossible." After answering their other questions, Clark left. The crush of reporters and media people was taxing the small waiting area, hampering other emergency procedures. He had to find some other place for everyone.

BY 4:50 A.M., all the networks had sent camera crews to Kings County. WINS, WOR, and WPIX radio were there too, plus reporters from *The Times, News, Post,* and Associated Press. Each time a detective left the doctors' lounge, a score of newsmen pushing mikes in his face surrounded him. They wanted a statement. Any statement. But the Chief of Detectives, John Keenan, had passed on the word: "Absolutely no comments!" The police department was determined not to turn it into a circus, and additional uniformed men were sent to the hospital to control the growing crowd.

Officer Connie Jacobs, twenty-eight, recalls the scene. "My sergeant told me to keep the corridor clear for other emergency cases. It was impossible. Every time we'd clear it, a doctor or nurse would walk out into the hall and everyone would rush toward them with a barrage of questions. I must have been on a thousand feet of film that morning."

If a member of either the Violante or Moskowitz families poked a head out of the lounge or attempted to use the outside telephone, pandemonium broke out. The police finally told both families to keep inside the lounge.

"Questions were flung at anyone with a white uniform," remembers Johnny Wilson, twenty-three. "I was coming on duty, and suddenly a whole group of reporters cornered me. They kept calling me 'doctor' no matter how many times I told them I wasn't. After a while I kind of enjoyed it. I mean all the fuss."

Wilson was an orderly. All he did was handle towels. He tried to tell them, but the reporters wouldn't take that for an answer. They thought he was a doctor sneaking in. They believed what they wanted to believe.

IRA CLARK returned to the doctors' lounge. Theresa Violante and Neysa Moskowitz, seated side by side, started to rise. "Please sit," he said. "You all must be exhausted. I just wanted to tell you that Stacy has been stabilized. It's a good sign." Neysa Moskowitz sat back. She closed her eyes and said a prayer. Her husband smiled for the first time. Maybe she'd pull through, he thought. She's too young, too beautiful to die.

The news Mr. Clark had for the Violantes wasn't as good.

"Mr. and Mrs. Violante," he began, "the doctors have repaired Bobby's right eye as best they can. There has been an extreme amount of damage. Hopefully, Bobby will have some degree of vision in that eye."

"Does that mean he'll be able to see?" questioned Pat Violante.

"I don't know. Bobby will live, but he'll probably be blind."

"I could feel the life go out of them for a moment," Clark recalls.

Then Theresa Violante stood up. "Please," she said. "I'd like to see the doctors who saved my son."

"But . . . ," the administrator began. Then he took her by the hand and walked out a special exit to another hallway and through the swinging doors to where the doctors were waiting. Mrs. Violante stopped just inside the room, Clark remembers: "She looked at each one of them. She just stared at them. Then Mrs. Violante walked over to where the doctors were standing, shifting their weight from foot to foot, and gave each one a kiss on the cheek, thanking them for what they'd done. There were tears streaming down her face when she turned away from the last one. I looked at their faces, the doctors, and they were crying too.

"Her husband, Pasquale, shook each doctor's hand and silently thanked them, trying to hold back the tears."

Neysa Moskowitz walked to the Violantes, embracing them as if Bobby had been hers. Gerry Moskowitz shook Pat Violante's hand. It was cold.

FINALLY the time came to operate on Stacy. A doctor broke the news to Neysa (Gerry was on the phone talking to Ricky), and the doctor took her to the operating room's entrance.

Neysa had put her hair up into a ponytail. Still in her housecoat, the woman who took great pride in her appearance hadn't noticed how she looked.

As Stacy was wheeled along the corridor on a portable stretcher, Neysa ran to her. She leaned over, whispering into her daughter's ear as the stretcher rolled along the tile floor. "Stacy, baby. Mommy's here. Can you hear me?"

Stacy opened one eye, looked at her mother, and smiled. "Mommy . . . Mommy."

Neysa got closer to Stacy's ear. "How do you feel, baby?"

Stacy answered in a low whisper, "Mommy, I have a terrible, terrible headache. I'm so tired."

"Are you in any pain?" Neysa asked as she grasped her daughter's hand while walking along with her. "I love you, baby."

"Mommy, am I going to be all right?"

"Yes, Stacy. You're going to be just fine."

In her shock and agony, Stacy still didn't know she'd been shot.

AFTER THE OPERATION, Stacy went to the recovery room. Clark told Neysa and Gerry to return home. Stacy wouldn't need them until after she would awaken in recovery. Avoiding the reporters, the Moskowitzes discussed how they would cope with the problems of Stacy's shooting on the ride back to their home.

"She'll need physical therapy," Gerry said.

"Whatever's needed, we'll provide."

"And another thing. I've said it before, but this time we're going to do it. I'm getting all of us out of the city. It isn't a place for any of us. It's just become too damn dangerous."

16

A Chance to Say Goodbye

Detective John Falotico had a "hard witness" in Tommy Zaino, who had seen the shooting and the killer from his rear-view mirror. At 5:30 A.M. Tommy was still busy answering questions. His date, Debbie, hadn't left the passenger seat the entire time, and she was desperate to get home. Tommy was also nauseated and nervous. He was known in the neighborhood and was afraid that he could be recognized as the person who would be able to "finger" the killer. Tommy didn't know if he should ask for police protection or what. All he could think of was to get out of there with his young date. Finally, John told him to go home. The detective would be around to pick him up the next afternoon. Tommy got into the Corvette and tried to leave, but the sports car stalled. It took a crew of officers to push the vehicle down the block so he could pop the clutch. Zaino arrived home at 7:00 A.M. The full effect of the shooting was just beginning to set in.

ON MONDAY, AUGUST 1, 1977, the *New York Daily News* headline was:

44-CAL KILLER SHOOTS 2 MORE
Wounds B'klyn Couple in Car
Despite Heavy Cop Dragnet.

It also featured "Jimmy Breslin with the Parents."

LATER THAT NIGHT, Ira Clark called Gerry Moskowitz's home. "Gerry, I'm afraid there's been a complication. I'd like you back here as soon as possible."

"What's happened?"

"The doctors have told me that they're afraid there's been some swelling of the brain stem."

"What does that mean?" the father questioned.

"The next twenty-four to forty-eight hours will be crucial."

Mrs. Moskowitz took the phone from her husband. "Ira, what's happening?"

"A problem. I'd like Gerry here. You stay home and get some rest."

"Rest? I don't know if I'll ever have any rest. Is Stacy going to live?"

"I hope so. But there are no guarantees. The doctors are doing everything. . . ."

"Ira, I'm coming too. I never had a chance to say goodbye to Jody. If there's a chance that Stacy is going to die, I want to be with her. Ira, if it were your child, where would you be?"

THIRTY-EIGHT HOURS after the attack, at 5:22 P.M., August 1, 1977, Stacy Moskowitz died. It was one year and two days after the killing of Donna Lauria and the wounding of Jody Valente.

BOBBY VIOLANTE is in recovery. An operation to attempt to save his severely injured right eye seems to have been successful. However, doctors are waiting until his strength returns to tell the young man that his left eye is shattered and that at best he can only count on a 20-percent recovery of vision in the right eye. This means that what a person normally can see at four hundred feet, Violante only will be able to see at twenty feet at best.

The surgery has closed off the blood vessels around the left eye and beneath the nose. Apparently, the bullet that injured his right eye first struck Stacy, then passed under Bobby's eye. It went through the bridge of his nose and shattered his left eyeball, exited, and continued out the window on the driver's side.

As if in a haze, a doctor approaches the heavily sedated Violante and whispers into his ear, "Son, you're going to live. Can you hear me?" Violante nods a couple of centimeters. His mouth tries to say something, but words don't follow the movement. "Your eyes. I know you want to know about your eyes. We've tried to save them; I think we've succeeded on one. Get some rest, son." The doctor begins to move away.

Bobby's lips form the word *Stacy*. The doctor returns. "She's fine, just fine. She'll live." Bobby Violante allows the medication to take hold, and slips into sleep.

It was days before doctors thought Violante had gained enough strength to tell him. Behind the bandages, Bobby wept.

"When I found out about me, how badly I was hurt, it really didn't register. It was hard to react because of all the dope they were pumping into me. But I was awake and alert when I found out about Stacy, and that was the worst. It was something I knew I would have to live with forever. Then it began. I asked myself, 'Am I human? Am I so cold that I don't even feel for myself?' I looked toward where I thought the doctor was. 'Are you telling me that I've lost my eye; that I may never see again? Or what?' It was hard for me to believe what I was hearing.

"In the beginning I was numb to the whole thing. Like I couldn't even imagine it had happened. I was always asking about Stacy. For a time I was under such heavy sedation that every time I asked, it seemed like a day had passed. But, when things started to come together, I realized that the time between questions wasn't days, but merely minutes, five minutes or so.''

By September 15, 1977, six weeks after the shooting attack, Bobby Violante's recovery would be as complete as it would ever become. He would later endure other operations to repair facial damage, but his disco days were over. As predicted by the doctors, he had lost his left eye and had regained less than 20-percent vision in his right. Bobby Violante was legally blind.

SERGEANT JOE COFFEY was furious. ''We knew that all the publicity had served to drive this killer into Brooklyn. If everyone had just kept our game plan under wraps. We had the Bronx covered and Queens blanketed; we would have had a shot at getting the guy. But, the department had given everything away. The newspaper guys were everywhere gathering bits and pieces, and putting them together.

''When I got to the Moskowitz–Violante shooting, I knew it was Sam. It had all the earmarks. Then I saw the hole in the steering column. It was a goddamn cannon that did it. No doubt about it, ballistics or not. I was fuming. Brooklyn . . . and here we were all over Queens!

''Our biggest beef was the press. They knew everything. Some of those reporters have friends on the top floors of One Police Plaza. Favors were commonplace. At the 109th, reporters were always looking over our shoulders. It was impossible to keep anything secret. It got to a point, like a joke, we'd all say that we'd look in the *News* or *Post* for just what we were going to do the next day. Sometimes the papers were right.''

Question, Sergeant Coffey. What about the responsibility of newsmen to cover the news?

''They have a job to do, I suppose,'' he answers, ''but doesn't the press also have a responsibility of not giving away what we as police are doing? Their deadlines become all-important to them. The TV guys have to have their film or tapes back to the studio by 5:00 P.M. in order to make the evening news shows. And this stuff was hot news. People were hanging by their sets waiting. So some of them pushed, pushed too much. Some were gentlemen. But when they got something that we had asked them to keep off the air, only to see another station put it on? How the hell could we ever ask them again?

"It was all so impossible. Those yellow press passes were more powerful than our shields. And I lay that at the feet of those at the top of the department. They should have ordered those guys out of the 109th, out of the hospital. But they didn't. For whatever reasons, they didn't."

Do these same newsmen have any responsibility to you guys, the police?

"Sure they do. They have a responsibility to the public not to hinder our investigation. There was a killer loose and we were breaking our balls to find him. The .44 was killing innocent kids whenever he wanted to. So we came up with a game plan. Dowd released just enough information to the newsmen so that they'd print how we had Queens covered tight as a drum, so that if he tried it again, he wouldn't escape.

"I believe that all that information served to drive Berkowitz into Brooklyn. It's something we'll never know for certain, but that's how I see it."

As for David's feelings about the Brooklyn attack, he says, "All that stuff in the papers. It didn't matter too much. The demons told me just where to hit and I did just what they said. That night I had driven out to Huntington, then back to the city. I was in Howard Beach, Canarsie, then I drove toward the Verrazano Bridge. I don't remember how, but I wound up alongside the Belt, near a park. I remembered it from before. I'd been there before. I'd sometimes drive along the Belt Parkway, so I knew the area.

"But there was no real reason for me being there other than the demons. They'd tell me where to go."

No interrogator fully understood the implications of David's statement: "I'd been there before." What they did not know was that David may well have been a fire bug. In fact, no one had any idea that the Son of Sam was setting fires until two hours after he was arrested and detectives began to search and inventory the contents of his apartment. Among David's possessions were three stenographer's notebooks. Two were filled with page upon page of detailed notes and descriptions (the third was half full) of 1488 fires which were set from September 28, 1974, to December 23, 1975.

The notebooks were photocopied and sent to the district attorneys of Queens, Brooklyn, and the Bronx. One copy went to the New York City Fire Marshal. Both the police and the fire departments checked to see if one of the fires had caused a fatality. None did. So no charges were brought against Son of Sam for arson, although he had once been given a summons by the Fire Department for a false alarm. The Fire Marshal believed it unlikely one man could have set so many fires by himself. Yet the possibility that a single person did in fact set the fires could not be ruled out. The Fire Marshal concluded that David must have been listening in on the Fire Department's radio bands, and simply copied down the calls. However, David did not have a radio capable of such reception. Furthermore, any such radio would have required special crystals, one for each recorded borough.

When the author checked with both the Fire Department and the district attorneys' offices of Brooklyn and the Bronx, they confirmed the notations were correct down to the individual call box numbers. And call box numbers are not broadcast on the Fire Department's radio net.

No one from the Police Department or the Fire Marshal's office ever questioned David about his "fire diary." By the time the Fire Marshal's investigation was complete, David had pled guilty to murder. He would never stand trial. And neither the police nor the Fire Marshal wanted to open the Pandora's Box that David's fire diaries represented. Thus, the issue died.

Three years later, the author obtained a copy of the diaries from a member of a district attorney's staff. He noted that most of the 1488 fires (and false alarms) were harmless, if any fire could be considered harmless, and caused little or no damage. However, a handful of fires were major structural fires resulting in injury to civilians and fire fighters. They weren't just routine trash can-type blazes, or fires in abandoned cars, or fires in vacant lots. Nor were they like the fires set in the rear yard of 316 Warburton Avenue (the Carr family home), or at the front door of apartment 6E (the Glassman apartment) at 35 Pine Street.

For example, the diaries show that on September 28, 1974, David set a fire at West End Avenue and West 60th Street in Manhattan. The time: 12:30 A.M. This was a major structural fire. Then, on October 13, 1974, David returned to the same location and set a second fire. This time it was at 9:40 P.M. Once again, it was a major blaze. Two firemen were injured fighting this fire.

On September 8, 1975, David set a fire at the Waring Nursing Home at 2000 Gun Hill Road in the Bronx. It was a two alarmer that sent elderly persons into the street at 4:32 A.M. Fortunately, there were no injuries.

On October 16, 1975, David set three fires in Queens at Northern Boulevard and the Little Neck Parkway. The blazes came in rapid succession, at 12:29 A.M., 2:30 A.M., and at 3:32 A.M. He set another fire in the area on April 2, 1977. These fires were within fifteen minutes' walking distance of the Lupo–Placido shooting on the morning of June 26, 1977, near the Elephas discotheque.

In making a final review of the diaries, acting on a hunch, the author turned every page. The third notebook was about one-half full. The remainder of the notebook appeared to be blank, but, sandwiched in between a score of blank pages in the back of the book were three additional pages that apparently had been missed by official investigators.

David's fire logs were written in the following manner (see accompanying reproductions):

Date of Occurrence—Fire Box number—Location of the fire
—Borough of Occurrence—Work designation—Time—
Weather. The Official N.Y.C. Fire Department radio code
signals, in use during 1977 were also used in David's "Work"
designation.

They are:	10-2	Return to your quarters.
	10-18	Return all companies except engine, ladder and B.C. present at scene.
	10-19	Return all units except those at scene.
	10-21	Brush fire.
	10-22	Outside rubbish fire.
	10-23	Abandoned derelict vehicle fire.
	10-24	Auto fire (with plates).
	10-92	Malicious false alarm.

David noted all the preceding, leaving out the 10 designation. Thus, a 92 would be 10-92, false alarm. These startling notations began April 2, 1977, and ended August 2, 1977, two days after the shooting of Stacy Moskowitz and Robert Violante. By checking the notations against a large-scale, citywide street map that shows power lines, sewers and hydrants, the author learned that on April 2, 1977, David sent in a false alarm from call box #6452 at the intersection of 61st Avenue and 262nd Street in Queens. This location is less than half a mile from where David had shot Joanne Lomino and Donna DeMasi on the night of November 27, 1976. The killer, it would seem, did return to the scene of his crimes.

Furthermore, in July 1977, David was setting fires in Brooklyn. In the early morning of July 3, 1977, David set three fires. At 3:40 A.M., he set a fire in an abandoned car at Shore Parkway and Bay 13th Street; twenty minutes later he set one in a second abandoned car at 13th Avenue and 78th Street; and ten minutes later he returned to Shore Parkway and Bay 13th Street to rekindle the fire that firemen had put out earlier (firemen say a new blaze in the abandoned car would have ignited immediately).

These three fires were within three blocks of the Bay 17th

DATE	BOX	Location	WORK	TIME	weather
4/2/77	6699	82 Ave. + 217 St.	Q 18-24	0025	cool clear
4/2/77	6452	61 Ave. + 262 St.	Q 92	0115	cool clear
4/2/77		Marathon Pkwy. + Thiebes Ave	Q 19-21	0125	cool clear
4/16/77	4373 (TA)	Adee + Edson	Bx * struc +2 vac comm	2230	warm clear
5/24/77	4361 (TAS)	E. Gun Hill Rd. + Mace	Bx 19-22	1200	Hot clear
5/26/77	3595	Webster bet. Gun Hill + E.233	Bx 18-23	0600	warm clear
5/26/77	*2245 (ERS)	River + E. 151 St.	Bx 19-23	2120	warm clear
6/2/77	4373 (TA)	Adee + Edson	Bx * struc 1+2 vac comm	0645	warm clear
6/16/77	4627 (TAS)	Ferry Point Park	Bx 19-23	1100	Hot clear
7/2/77	7139	40th Ave. + 11 St.	Q 92	0600	warm clear
7/3/77	2830	Bay Shore Pkwy. + Bay 13 St.	K 18-23	0340	warm clear
7/3/77	3848	13th Ave + 78 St	K 18-23	0400	warm clear
7/3/77	2830	Bay Shore Pkwy + Bay 13 St.	K 18-23	0410	warm clear
7/4/77	2248 (ERS)	Park + E. 151 St	Bx 18-22	2235	Hot clear
7/5/77	4426	Baychester + Darrow	Bx * 2+2 vac	0210	Hot clear

Date	Box	Location	WORK	Time	weather
7/8/77	2364	Hunts Point + Bruckner Blvd	Bx Struc 2+2, VAC	0650	WARM clear
7/11/77	3115	Cedar Ave. + W. 179 St.	Bx 19-23	0500	WARM clear
7/11/77	3151	Osborn + W. 179 ST.	Bx 18- Struc VAC	0547	WARM clear
7/11/77	2364	Hunts Point + Bruckner Blvd.	Bx 7-5 Struc VAC	0645	WARM clear
7/11/77	3151	Osborn + W. 179 ST.	Bx 18- Struc VAC	1328	Hot clear
7/13/77	4420	E. 222 ST. + Givan	Bx 18-23	2240	Hot clear
7/14/77	3151	Osborn + . W. 179 ST.	Bx Struc 2+2, VAC	0200	Hot clear
7/14/77	3227(TAS)	Lydig + Barnes	Bx 19-22	0300	Hot clear
7/14/77	2121(ERS)	Brown + 134 ST.	Bx 18-22	0245	Hot clear
7/14/77	3112	University bet. tremont + Burnside	Bx 18- Struc VAC	0445	Hot clear
7/15/77	3789	Palisades + W.247 St.	Bx 92	0135	Hot clear
7/20/77	4977	Blackstone + W.237 St.	Bx 92	0130	Hot clear
7/21/77	3730	Palisades + W.231 St.	Bx 18-23	0130	Hot clear
7/22/77	3787	Douglas opp. W.237 ST.	Bx 19-23	0136	Hot clear
7/23/77	3317	Ave S + E.15 ST.	K 18-23	0315	WARM clear

Date	Box	Location	Work!	Time	weather
7/23/77	*2124(ERS)	Park, No. est. Corner + 135 St	Bx 19-23	2300	warm clear
7/24/77	3115	Cedar + W. 179 St	Bx 19-23	0010	warm clear
7/24/77	4403(TAS)	Hammersley + Grace	Bx 19-24	0525	warm clear
7/24/77		Walton + 150 St.	Bx 19-23	0620	warm clear
7/24/77	3113	Burnside + Andrews	Bx 2-2, * struc Box 0645 YAC M.D. 2-2 0703		warm clear
7/29/77	3027(TAS)	Brush + Yznaga	Bx 19-23	0830	warm clear
7/29/77	2603	Clason Pt. Lane + Betts	Bx 18- struc VAC.	1135	Hot clear
8/2/77	2627	Newman + Compton	Bx 18-23	0135	warm clear
7/29/77	4103	Brush + Bruckner Blvd.	Bx 18-22	2300	warm clear

Street Park where David was to shoot Stacy Moskowitz and Robert Violante.

When asked to comment about the additional thirty-nine fires the author discovered, a police department spokesman said, "We don't have any copies of them. All our files were turned over to the District Attorneys."

When the Fire Marshal's office was pressed on this same question, officials simply said, "NO COMMENT." Yes, David could quite possibly have been a firebug.

OFFICERS Michael Cataneo and Jeffrey Logan had been tied up at both hospitals during the early morning. Being the first officers to respond to the call of "Shots fired," they had remained with the victims at Coney Island Hospital, then gone on to Kings County Hospital. It wasn't until midmorning that they returned to their precinct. Sergeant Coffey and Detectives John Cahill and Frank Pagiolla were waiting for them. The uniformed men entered the room and sprawled onto hard wooden chairs. They had been on duty for nearly sixteen hours and had returned to their precinct merely to check out. They weren't anxious to answer questions.

Coffey spoke first. He was standing by a huge coffee-maker. "You guys look like you could use a cup. Want any?" Steaming coffee was set before all five men. Coffey continued, "Now that things have kind of quieted down for a while, we'd like to find out just what you guys saw."

Officer Logan, six feet tall, 190 pounds, dark and muscular, answered, "Sarge, do we have to go over it again? We must have told the story a dozen times already."

Detective Frank Pagiolla, six feet one, 210 pounds and dark-complexioned, answered. "One more time, please." Pagiolla had his notes in front of him. They contained statements from Tommy Zaino and the off-duty Port Authority Patrolman, Richard Sheehan. Pagiolla was the logical one to question the officers as he had the best available information.

Jeffrey Logan answered, "We were working the sector as usual. In fact, we'd swung through the area ten or fifteen minutes before. Then came the 10-10 call,* and we responded. When we pulled up, we knew we had a shooting. I ran to the car, Mike took the guy on the ground. I looked in and this girl was on the seat with a towel around her head.''

''Conscious?'' Pagiolla asked.

''Yeah. She was kind of crying and looking around in a daze. I spent a minute with her and ran over to where the boy was. There were two other guys with him along with Mike. One of them identified himself as an off-duty cop.

''The kid on the sidewalk was face up, writhing in pain. He was screaming but not making any sense. You could still smell it in the air.''

''What?'' Coffey said.

''The smell of gunpowder. It was like when you shoot at the range. I knew we'd missed the guy who shot them by a minute or so at the most. It kind of made me look around, like maybe he was somewhere near, watching.

''The kid who was helping said he had driven his Corvette around the park when the guy took off, then to the precinct. He'd come back to see exactly what happened. You gotta understand it was a hairy situation.''

''Then what?'' Pagiolla asked.

''Then I went back to the girl. Mike ran back to the car and called in. The girl was talking pretty good and I asked her what happened. She said that she was with her boyfriend and had gotten sick. Then I asked her if she had heard any loud noises and she answered no. That was the extent of the conversation with her.''

''And what did you do, Cataneo?'' Coffey asked.

''Like Jeff says, I went to the boy, he went to the girl. When I saw what came down, I ran back and called everything in. I called for ambulances, supervisors, detectives. I guess I called for everyone I could think of.

''When I got a response I called Jeff and told him I was going to check out the park. He yelled out he was coming too.

* ''Shots fired.''

"We drew our service revolvers and walked into the park. Mike checked out the burned-out park house while I covered him. Then I walked into the back where the lights were out. There was no one there. By then we could hear and see the arrival of lots of patrol cars. I knew whoever shot them would be long gone so I motioned to Jeff and we ran back to the scene.

"As I got to the street the ambulance arrived, then another. The attendants took her first. They got her onto the stretcher and Jeff climbed into the ambulance along with the doc and the girl. I got into our car and followed the second one. It had the boy inside."

Coffey had run out of questions. The officers had added nothing to what the detectives already knew. "OK, you guys," Coffey said, standing up. "You deserve some rest. If we need you, we'll call."

"Thanks, Sarge," answered the pair in unison.

"By the way," Frank Pagiolla said. "Either of you guys give out any summonses tonight?"

The two uniformed officers looked at each other, then replied, "No."

"OK. We'll be speaking to you."

COFFEY REMEMBERS his reason for letting the sector guys leave. "They were beat. And they really had seen nothing. When they said they hadn't given out any summonses, there was nothing left to talk about.

"We'd get to the other summonses in the precinct as a matter of routine. Cahill would canvass the surrounding precincts the next day. He'd be on the lookout for any parking or moving violations in the vicinity of the 62nd Precinct. Anything might come up—be it parking at a crosswalk, bus stop, hydrant, double parking, or an accident—anything might turn into a lead. The Highway Patrol stationed at Flatbush Avenue was covered in the hopes that someone had seen something suspicious, either before or after the crime. All reports were negative."

In addition to the chaos of the moment, Coffey unknowingly had to contend with a totally unexpected foulup. Officers Cataneo and Logan had written a summons less than an hour before the crime, in a location two streets away from the shooting. It would be a member of the 10th Homicide who finally located that elusive summons locked away in the precinct's safe room.

DETECTIVE JOHN FALOTICO was dead-tired. The stress was beginning to show. He needed rest, and the department had robbed him of that opportunity.

In the dim light of dawn, Falotico had "caught" a potential homicide. "When I found out about the kids being shot, I guess I wasn't tired any more. I have daughters the same age. So right away I knew this case was going to mean something more to me.

"So, when I got to the scene, and saw the blood on the lamp post and on the car cushions, my hands began to sweat. As a father . . . a parent, it suddenly became something between me and him.

"I've had a lot of cases in thirty years; too many. I've been undercover, seen murders gangland-style and senseless, rapes and the like. But this one kind of hit me right in the chest, right in the first minute."

The detective surveyed the scene, noting the position of the cars and the park. He walked onto the footbridge to get an overview of the whole area. Then he got the names of the witnesses. "I immediately knew Tommy Zaino, the kid in the Corvette parked directly in front of the Violante car, would be the key." He arranged to see Zaino at the precinct in the afternoon.

Next, Falotico began compiling a list of officers at the scene, along with their arrival times. He'd interview as many as possible during the next ten days.

By this time the sun had climbed into the early morning sky. Shading his eyes, John looked up. It was going to be another hot day. He didn't like the heat because it drained him and he was going to need all the strength he had.

As he walked back to the lamp post, he watched a police towtruck hook up to the Violante car. He stopped a few feet away, looking in once again at the blood-soaked interior. His thoughts turned again to his three girls—Linda, Jean, and Jacinda. "I knew it had to stop, then and there," he says. "It could as easily have been any one of mine. The fact that this . . . killer was still free was a black mark on all of us as detectives, cops, and human beings."

He plunged into the crowd of curious who had gathered in the early morning. As he questioned people, he placed an asterisk next to names and statements he felt he'd like to double-check later. Right now he was simply gathering information while it was fresh. At 1:30 P.M. a young man walked toward the detective. Falotico watched him carefully. His movements were hesitant. The detective sensed that the man had something for him, yet was reluctant to get involved. "Hi," Falotico said. "I haven't seen you before. Are you a detective?"

The young man was startled. "No, no, I'm not a detective. I was. . . ."

"Yes. Have you seen something?" Falotico questioned, walking with the man away from the small crowd. "Why don't you tell me about it?"

The young man began talking. "Last night. I was parked right at the front of the park. Over there." He pointed to the park entrance, less than twenty yards from the spot where the Violante car was parked. Falotico knew the killer had to walk right in front of this parked vehicle to get at the Violante car. "I was with my wife. We were smoking some grass. Anyway, we heard what sounded like a bunch of M-80 firecrackers. You know, the really loud ones. A few seconds later, the screaming started and we looked up. There was no one around except the guy who'd been hit. He looked really terrible. And he started blowing the horn of his car and screaming. There was blood running down his shirt.

"Well, we kind of panicked. I didn't think. We had the grass and knew the cops would be coming. So I drove away." His eyes fell. "You can understand, can't you? What with the grass and everything, I didn't want to be involved.

"In the morning the papers had it, and I heard about it on the radio. I had to tell someone." His eyes came up to meet the older detective's. "What about the marijuana?"

Falotico tried to reassure him. "Don't worry about it. All I want is the killer, not you. The marijuana? What marijuana?"

Half an hour later another man came forward. He told about seeing a woman who was double-parked right before the shooting. "She had a light-colored car with a plate beginning with HW . . ." It was something for Falotico's notebook. Perhaps the detective would run it down later. Most likely, it was someone there just to make out.

FALOTICO scratches his cheek and lights a cigarette. "There's a practical reason to beware of information secured from underworld sources," he says. "If the police department gets information from them, what do you have? Information, sure. But something else as well. A debt. A criminal has given you something, and criminals don't give things away. They'll want the debt repaid."

How, John?

"Sometimes you have to give in order to get. It's not like you look away when something big's going down. It's more like a trade of information. Sometimes they give you what you want simply because it doesn't look good to have a cop around. Plenty of crimes have been solved because your presence has made them uneasy, and they give up someone, something, just to get you out of their hair."

Aware of all this, Falotico approached the man he knew as a local Mafia boss.

"Look," the detective said, "I've spent years in this area and I know the people who live here, and I know they know you. I need help. I need to talk to anyone who knows anything. I'm not after your background. I'm not after you."

"Okay, I'll help," the Mafia boss said.

Even if the Mafia couldn't supply the detective with the identity of the killer, the boss' presence made people come forward without fear of being branded police stoolies. By 5:00 P.M., Falotico was thoroughly convinced that his best witness was young Tommy Zaino. "I'd talked to this kid and there were discrepancies in his story, like position, gait, sequence, and some other minor things. But, in the excitement, that was to be expected.

"But he was scared, and how the hell could you expect a scared kid to remember everything? Sometimes even trained observers will give different versions of the same sequence," Falotico says. "When you think about it, it was amazing that he remembered things as well as he did after going through what he did."

Tommy was worried about Debbie, and for himself, that their names would be revealed. He felt that if someone wrote a column mentioning their names, perhaps calling it "Debbie's Night of Terror," he and Debbie would be through. He was sure the killer could find them and seek retribution.

The police somehow managed to keep the reporters away from Debbie. Partly because she wasn't known in the area too well, and because she never left the Corvette that night. Her name would show up on the pad of only two detectives, John Falotico and Billy Gardella, Falotico's immediate supervisor.

Falotico interviewed Zaino again at the 60th Precinct's detective squad room on the second floor, which hampered reporters from snooping. Zaino was trying to talk a police artist through a sketching session while members of the detective squad threw questions at the youth, trying to get information they might have missed. When Falotico arrived, it became his ball game. Falotico spoke calmly to his witness, all the while keeping his eyes on the picture materializing before them.

"Hey, Tommy," began the veteran detective, "how come you didn't have your car with you?"

"Because," started Tommy, keeping his eyes glued on the drawing, "my friend Joey wanted to use it. I'd just finished this super paint job on it, and he wanted to impress his girl. And besides, his starter wasn't working too well, and . . . officer, the hair is wrong. It's too straight. . . . Anyway, you must know that the cops had to give me a push. Once you switched off the engine, there was no guarantee it would turn over again. So I let him have mine. We did that a lot. . . . No, still too straight. Say, why can't he get that guy's hair right?"

Falotico turned to the police artist and asked him to change the hair style slowly. "Don't make it too different. That'll maybe miss the real style." Little by little the drawing developed. In the six hours that followed, Falotico began to take a liking to young Zaino. The kid was somewhat of an artist himself. Falotico also fooled around with cars in his spare time, and the two had something in common.

"Tommy," asked the detective, "just what was happening in the car between you and Debbie?"

For the first time, the young man lifted his eyes from the drawing. "Mr. Falotico, I swear, nothing. Don't get me wrong. I tried, but she wouldn't go for anything. We were under the light, just where the other car was parked, but we moved. After we moved, they came and took the spot. You know how tight parking is there.

"But, anyway, when the shooting started, I looked through the rear-view mirror and saw it all. It was just like a Hollywood movie. The noise, flashes from the cannon, the glass, and then the screaming started. Like I told you before, right after that I pushed Debbie down and took off. I was trying to cut him off. Like he headed into the park, but there's only one way out, through the hole in the fence at the far side of the ball field. I knew he'd run through there, then either up the block or through the passage of the apartment houses and onto the next street. I was going to the police station, and it's in the same direction of both the ball field and the apartment houses."

Falotico asked, "But you could have gotten shot your-self."

"To tell the truth, I just didn't think of that at the time. Later I thought of it, but at the time I just reacted."

Zaino looked back to the sketch that police artist William McCormack was painstakingly working on. "Still, the hair, it just isn't right."

"Why not? Perhaps you'd like to sketch it, son," inquired McCormack, one of the three officers who comprise the crim-inal identification (artist) group. "Son, we don't know how many of the sketches we do result in arrests, maybe twenty-five percent. Perhaps we'll be lucky and get the brass ring with this one. You know, we use sketches even more than the FBI does. They have only one artist for the whole FBI. Alto-gether, the three of us prepare about six hundred sketches a year. Sometimes they work, sometimes they don't." Mc-Cormack put his pencil down and picked up a cigarette. It was time for a break, for him and Tommy Zaino. He continued talking. "In 1975, we had a Staten Island student stabbed in a subway. We had lots of good witnesses, just like you. Well, we got a sketch together on the spot, and three hours later a cop arrested the killer from the sketch he'd gotten less than ten minutes before.

"In another case, a teacher, twenty-eight-year-old RoseAnn Quinn, was raped and murdered on the West Side. That was in 1973. Well, we did a sketch there too, and in a few days a friend recognized him and told the police. So, you see, sometimes it works. By the way, the guy who was turned in was eventually convicted of the killing. So all the time we put in here just could be the key to getting the Son of Sam." Both McCormack and Falotico knew how to play their man correctly. They both hit it off with young Zaino, until finally Tommy called a halt to the drawing.

"Mr. Falotico, Mr. McCormack, this looks like him, but there's still something missing. I can't put my finger on it, but. . . ."

"Don't worry, kid. If it's close, we have a chance," said the artist. The sketch would be released to the press, and each

New York City cop would get one on his next tour of duty.
More copies would be sent to surrounding communities in
Westchester, Nassau, and New Jersey.

"THERE WAS this one guy who was what we call a bed-
bug," recalls Detective Falotico. "He began by telling us how
he was there and what happened. And he was damn close to
knowing how it went down. For a while there, we thought we
had him. We went at him, Sergeant Shea and myself, for
three-quarters of an hour. He wouldn't tell us who he was,
just how he did it.

"He told us: 'Well, I was hiding in the park and then saw
the kids. I didn't like those girls, so I followed them to the
car, and when they got in, I stepped into the street and pulled
the gun, then shot. After that I ran. Later I threw the gun into
the Bay. You guys were getting too close to me.'

"Well, it was pretty close, and we looked at each other.
After half an hour there was a knock at the interrogation
room. Shea went to the door and motioned me over. I kept
my eye on this guy. There was something strange about him.
But then, there had to be something strange about anyone
who was blowing away all these kids. Well, outside in the hall
was this uniformed cop from the 62nd. He said, 'I know this
guy. He's always in our hair. I know where he lives. I've been
to his house a couple of times, and I know his old man.' Well,
if this cop knew him, it wasn't too likely that he was our guy.
But we kept him locked up for a few hours and checked him
out with some other cops. They all knew he was a pain, but
not a killer. But, if you think he didn't bother me for a while,
you're wrong, dead wrong."

SERGEANT JAMES SHEA, who had grown up in Bensonhurst, was planning to spend Sunday, July 31, with his family
and take his children to the beach. At about 10:00 A.M. he
turned on WINS radio for a weather report. Instead he heard
a newscaster announcing that the .44-caliber killer had struck
in Brooklyn, in the 10th Homicide Zone.

"Betty," he said, turning to his wife, "it's our case. I think I'd better call in. We're down to a one-man squad. Falotico is new around here, and I bet he's going to pull this one. God, has the shit really hit the fan!"

"Look," cautioned Betty, "you put in ten-hour days and when you're off you're trying to get back in there. I knew when I married a cop I'd spend some nights alone, but the days?" It didn't matter. Even before she finished, Shea was on the phone trying to get through to his squad.

When he finally got through some ten minutes later, he spoke with Sergeant Gardella, who brought him up to date on what was happening. "Jimmy, the whole place is full of brass. Guys you'd never seen before are here. We got all chiefs, and no Indians. . . . Yeah, Falotico pulled the case and we think we'll have ourselves a homicide before the day's out. Looks like the boy's going to die . . . the girl seems to be holding her own . . . no, you don't have to come in. Get your rest; you're going to need it." The conversation was over and Jimmy Shea would return to his family. As it would turn out, he reported in the next day and spent the next ten days on the case. He'd be responsible for ordering check after check on the summonses until a detective on loan from Robbery, James Justus, would discover them in the station house. He'd also be responsible for allowing another detective, Joseph Strano, to interview one Cacilia Davis, who would provide vital information as to a person who passed by her just after the shooting and—even more important—the fact that two cops in a patrol car did, in fact, give out a ticket that night.

ON SUNDAY the men of Omega geared up for another night of patrolling the streets of the Bronx and Queens. Sergeants Conlon and Coffey weren't allowed any rest. With the Son of Sam striking in Brooklyn, the two sergeants hastily put together a plan to man all the bridges, not just the Throgs Neck and Bronx–Whitestone as before. The entire city was now prey to this mad killer.

DEPUTY INSPECTOR TIMOTHY DOWD was on the phone to Chief of Detectives John Keenan. Keenan now offered the Inspector any additional manpower he could use. The Inspector declined. His force was becoming too big. However, he gladly accepted the carte blanche offered by the Chief. Dowd's men would now have the authority to circumvent any usual channels in any borough to get access to almost any record, or any man who could help catch the killer.

There was one problem: the men of the 10th Homicide hadn't been absorbed into Omega, as had been the case in all the other attacks. This was at the insistence of Captain Borrelli, who felt that they had come up with some valuable leads. Something told Borrelli to allow these guys to run with the ball just as long as things were going well. Keenan ordered Dowd to make Borrelli his liaison with the 10th. Dowd protested but Borrelli was so assigned. It was to be a fortunate decision, for in the end Borrelli gave the men of the 10th a free hand. And with the leads they developed, these men cracked the case.

YEARS EARLIER, Detective Falotico had known a woman named Tina. She was married to a retired sanitation man and ran a restaurant in the area. Hoping Tina might know something through the grapevine, Falotico drove to the restaurant only to find that Tina was no longer there. It seemed that she now owned a laundromat down the block. "The people were very helpful when we told them we were investigating the Violante shooting," he remembers.

"When we got to the laundromat, she wasn't there either. But we went through the whole story again, and we handed the people our cards, telling them to ask Tina to get in touch with me as soon as she could. Most of them were old, and scared, but they took the cards, and I hoped the message would get to her."

17

The Final Witness

On Wednesday, August 3, 1977, Officers Pete Intervallo and Tom Chamberlain were on routine nighttime patrol in their squad car. The men were deep in conversation about the Moscowitz–Violante shooting. The subject matter drifted to the connection between the shooting of Sam Carr's dog, Harvey, and the shooting of another dog, a German shepherd on Christmas Eve, 1976, at 22 Wicker Street. The Wicker Street house was only seventy-five yards from the Carr home at 316 Warburton Avenue. Chamberlain said: "Pete, remember the two letters Sam Carr showed us in April? He said he'd gotten them just two days before the Labrador was shot. Too many coincidences all in the same area."

His partner agreed. "Yeah, I've been thinking along the same lines. Every time we cruise down Warburton, I get this feeling someone's watching us."

"So do I. We really have nothing concrete to go on, but maybe we should add the Berkowitz name to the initial report?"

His partner turned to him. "And what do we look like then? Two patrolmen trying to act like detectives? It ain't going to sit well if we do."

"But, we're sitting on something. I know it. And you can't just sit on it forever. Sooner or later that whole thing's going to explode. If we run it all down, the June tenth get-well card to that lady in New Rochelle, and then Carr telling us that this Berkowitz character lives at 35 Pine," (the officers were driving along North Broadway, passing by Glenwood Avenue) "we sure have a lot of maybes, but nothing real. I'd like to see the DA make a case against him."

After the car turned right onto Lamartine Avenue, Intervallo stopped for a moment. Both men looked toward the apartment house on Pine Street. "Tom," began Intervallo, "I think I'll go up to Warburton again, just to check how things are doing at the Carrs!" Chamberlain nodded and Intervallo drove down the hill, stopping where Lamartine intersected Warburton. They proceeded for three blocks, almost to Wicker. The hundred-year-old white shingle home of Sam Carr was directly opposite. "You have to see that house to know the kind of feeling it can give you," says Tom Chamberlain. "Something weird was drawing us near, and we didn't know what."

THE MURDER of Stacy Moskowitz was breeding panic in New York City. At 11:30 P.M., August 3, a crowd of perhaps a hundred young people gathered around a yellow VW on Kings Highway and pulled the driver out when he began cursing at a couple of girls parked in front of Sal's Pizza. Members of the crowd had heard a rumor that a yellow VW was seen fleeing the scene of the shooting. Thus, when the car's occupant began cursing at the girls, beginning with "Someone ought to get you," the entire block exploded. A police cruiser on patrol just down the block came to the rescue, but not in time to keep the hapless victim from receiving a merciless beating. Suddenly now, the potential for mob violence had become reality.

The same night, detectives from the 10th Homicide Zone arrested a young, heavyset man by the name of Mario at the intersection of McDonald Avenue and Avenue U for possession of a dangerous weapon. Again a crowd materialized. It took a call for assistance to extricate the detectives and their prisoner from two hundred angry, frightened Brooklynites. The crowd became uncontrollable. Within five minutes, eleven patrol cars reached the scene (many from surrounding precincts) and the terrified prisoner, happy to be in protective custody, was whisked away to the station house.

"Things were getting hairy," says Detective Sergeant Shea. "You could feel it building. It was a giant pressure cooker, and you didn't want an explosion."

IN YONKERS, on August 4 at 5:30 P.M., Officer Tom Chamberlain turned to his partner. "Pete, some New York City Intelligence detective is coming to headquarters about the .44 killer. The guys down in the City have a theory that he might hit north of the Bronx. They want us to be ready."

Intervallo said, "Yeah, but not here. It doesn't figure. No matter who the bastard is, this isn't his hunting ground. Think of the racial makeup in Yonkers. He shoots white people. We're loaded with blacks and Hispanics."

"So what?" Chamberlain said. He was getting excited. "Look at the crazy things that go on over at 316 Warburton. That detective ought to still be at headquarters when we get off."

"Yeah," said Pete Intervallo. "He's going to be here a couple of days. I bet Chief Polson is getting out some kind of bulletin today or tomorrow on the sketch the City has sent up." The patrol car continued toward Trevor Park, which abuts the Hudson River. Gangs of young toughs had been dismantling the park after drinking beer and smoking marijuana. Sergeant Novotny had instructed Chamberlain and Intervallo to pay particular attention to the area during their tour. It was only 6:00 P.M., yet the small park was already teeming with unemployed young people looking for a good time. But there was no real action yet. The officers decided to make a U-turn and pass the Carrs' house once again.

"Tom? What do we really know about this Berkowitz character? I mean, what do we have on him? The Cassara woman from New Rochelle called the detectives this morning and said she knew he was responsible for everything." Intervallo slowed the car and said "And she's real heavy on Berkowitz. She really believes that . . ."

Chamberlain interrupted. "So? Everyone is calling in about someone."

"Yeah, but? Just look at what we have on that dog-shooting on Wicker last Christmas." The car was approaching Wicker Street and Officer Intervallo made a left and brought the car to a stop adjacent to the rear yard of the Carr house. Across the street and to their right was the front yard of the house, where the shooting had occurred. "Just look at this. Both places, the Carrs' and Netos'. Two yards, two dogs, two shootings." Just ahead was the rear of 35 Pine Street, a six-story apartment building. "I think it's about time we did our own close check into David Berkowitz," Intervallo ended.

It was midnight when the two officers completed their tour. But instead of returning home, they stayed in the factorylike building that served as Yonkers police headquarters. There they ran the name David Berkowitz through the state computer network for a second time.

At 1:45 A.M., the computer answered their inquiry. David Berkowitz, of 35 Pine Street, Yonkers, was the owner of a yellow Ford Galaxie, license number 561-XLB. "Now at least we know he hasn't dropped the registration on his car," said Pete Intervallo. David's driver's license had been suspended due to his nonappearance on a summons issued April 16. The officers could now legally stop their man if they caught him driving. Of course they didn't actually know what he looked like other than the superficial description given by the computer (male, white, blue eyes, 5' 10", 180 pounds). But they did have the license number of his car and that was a plus.

The telephone call placed by Mrs. Cassara, picked up by a Yonkers detective we will call McHenry, included a description that closely matched the New York State Motor Vehicle Department's printout: height 5′ 10″, weight 205–210 pounds, black curly hair, Caucasian, age approximately twenty-four to twenty-six. However, neither Intervallo nor Chamberlain was privy to this information. Thus they'd have to go solely on the state description.

Suddenly Chamberlain shook his head. "Maybe . . . it's crazy, but could he really be the one?"

"What? Who?" said Intervallo.

"That guy down in the City who's been doing the killings. Could Berkowitz be the Son of Sam?"

Intervallo looked at the building just ahead. His expression showed he was deep in thought. "Anything's possible." Those two words would take on even greater meaning when they finally did see the Cassara report. On their next tour, Friday, August 5, the officers headed directly to 35 Pine Street to have a talk with the rental agent. She was cooperative.

"Here's the apartment's file. Yes, David Berkowitz is the occupant of 7E. He's been very prompt in paying his rent."

"Where does it say he works?" asked Chamberlain.

"At IBI Security, in Queens," she said. The two policemen looked at each other. Security guards usually meant guns. The state printout had no notation of any pistol registered to David Berkowitz (rifles aren't included in computer information). But New York State Police estimate there are more than two million unregistered handguns in the state, more than a million in New York City alone.

Intervallo noted the address and phone number of IBI. "We'll check it out when we get off, Tom."

An hour later, Chamberlain called IBI Security. He identified himself and said "We're doing an investigation into an employee of yours, David Berkowitz of 35 Pine Street, Yonkers. What can you tell us about him?"

The woman at the other end of the line said "Berkowitz?

Let me get his file. I don't think he's with us any longer."
After a few seconds she got back on the line. "Like I said, he
isn't with us any more. He left IBI in July of '76."

"Do you have any request from another employer about
him?" asked the policeman.

"No. Just that he was going to drive a cab somewhere in
the Bronx."

"Where?"

"It doesn't say," she answered.

"Thanks," said Chamberlain as he hung up the phone. He
turned to his partner and said, "Pete, I think we've got something here. This guy's been around guns, and he's probably
driving a cab somewhere in the city. He should know his way
around pretty good."

"Yeah, and those security guys kind of bounce around
from place to place. He could have been in the area of any
one of those shootings. That quitting in July. The first shooting was in the Bronx in July, wasn't it?"

"So, what do we do with it?" asked Intervallo. "We still
have nothing but maybes. Who the hell can we bring this to?
They'd laugh us out of headquarters." Chamberlain and
Intervallo were patrolmen, not detectives. It was their responsibility to patrol, to fill out reports, not to conduct
independent investigations, and especially homicide investigations. Police work, like everything else, grows more spe-
cialized each year. Patrolmen keep the peace in the streets,
write traffic tickets, and recover lost dogs. Investigating murders is only for detectives.

But Intervallo and Chamberlain persisted. They tried to
locate the taxi company where Berkowitz had allegedly gone
to work. They called each company listed in the Bronx Yellow Pages, two hundred eleven in all. Beyond that there were
more than a thousand taxi companies operating in Manhattan,
Queens, and Westchester. Nassau County, Long Island, had
one hundred seventeen additional, plus hundreds in New Jersey—and, of course, hundreds upon hundreds of illegal gypsy
cabs. It could have taken a second Omega Task Force to run
down the one cab company employing David Berkowitz.

Failing with the cab companies, Chamberlain and Intervallo went back to copies of the two Carr letters. They compared them to the Breslin letter that had been published in part by the *Daily News*. Certain cross-references excited them. "That Wicked King Wicker part matches where the dog was shot Christmas Eve, Wicker Street," said Intervallo.

"And his name, the Son of Sam. It's got to be Sam Carr," said Chamberlain. "Then this guy writes about John Wheaties. Well, we have John Carr and Wheat Carr. It fits."

"So what? You see it, and I see it. But who the fuck is going to believe us? So it all fits. To who? Berkowitz? We got nothing on him, nothing at all. What we got is a big fat lawsuit by him."

"But we have to tell someone, don't we?"

"Why?" asked his partner. "Why?"

"Because we're right about him. You know it and I know it."

IT WAS 5:30 P.M. when the two officers brought their latest suspicions to their supervisor, thirty-five-year-old Mike Novotny, a squad sergeant at the North Command building of the Yonkers Police Department.

The building is a three-story combination police station and firehouse. Constructed in the English Tudor style of the turn of the century, it overlooks the Hudson River from its site on Shonnard Terrace, less than half a mile north of 35 Pine Street. On the first floor, just inside the structure's entrance, is the typical high table, flanked by twin white electrified globes. Behind the polished wood sit the squad commander and his assistants.

Sergeant Novotny, slightly overweight and balding, was called aside by the two patrolmen as they were checking in after the completion of their tour.

"Sarge," said Peter Intervallo, "we think it's time we moved on this Berkowitz character. Even though there's nothing concrete beyond that traffic stuff—we have that feeling, he's into much more than we know about."

"He could be the Son of Sam or whatever," Chamberlain said.

The officers outlined their case for the sergeant. Finally Novotny nodded. "I think you guys got something good." It would be quite a coup for the Yonkers Police Department to come up with the Son of Sam when their brothers in New York City were banging their heads against the wall. "Listen," said Novotny, "that New York City detective is upstairs right now in our Intelligence Division. Why don't you two go up there and lay out what you've got?"

The two patrolmen took the rear stairs to the second floor and walked to the detective's room. Seated across from Yonkers Detective Bill Grogan, forty-four, tall, thin, with long sideburns, was New York City Detective Richard Salvesen. Grogan introduced Chamberlain and Intervallo to Salvesen—medium build, dark eyes and hair, thirty-four. The City Intelligence Division, housed at One Police Plaza, gathers information on specific persons with criminal connections or so-called organized crime, subversive groups, and suspects in major cases.

Salvesen was relaying a theory devised by a police psychiatrist. "The doc makes this Son of Sam to be a paranoid schizo," Salvesen said.

"I read that," Grogan said, "in the papers a couple of days ago."

"What you didn't read is what else the psychiatrist believes. He says that paranoid schizos subconsciously work in triangles. For some reason, which is beyond me, these crazies pattern their killings. It seems that there's something about a triangle that gets them going. I suppose this theory is as good as anything else we have.

"Now," Salvesen said, "he's killed in the Bronx and Queens. He's killed in Brooklyn. Some doctors think that he'll make his next attack at a point to close the triangle."

"And that place could be Yonkers," Grogan said.

"That's what they say."

Dr. Edward Wind of Long Island Jewish Hospital explains, "A classic paranoid schizophrene would feel persecuted. Furthermore, if he did kill, he'd probably kill in different locations not caring about being caught. As for the triangle theory, any three points would make a triangle."

It was now 6:30 P.M. Chamberlain and Intervallo repeated to Salvesen what they had told Sergeant Novotny. The two young suburban cops suddenly found themselves at the center of a hunt manned by more than three hundred experienced detectives.

"What kind of guy do you think this Berkowitz is?" asked Salvesen.

"He's a loner, for sure," answered Pete. "We've tried to spot him—actually to see him—but it's been impossible."

"And," Chamberlain said, "his neighbors don't know anything about him, either. He doesn't socialize."

"Do you guys have any idea where he works?"

"Probably in some cab company down in the city. We ran a check with the firm listed in his apartment application, a security outfit in Queens, and it turns out that he quit that job quite a few months ago. One of the people there remembered him saying he was going to be driving a cab somewhere in the Bronx. We called around the bigger licensed ones there, but came up empty."

"Yeah," Salvesen said, "and I'm sure you know there are thousands of unlicensed gypsy cabs on the streets."

"We couldn't even begin to check those," said Intervallo.

Salvesen got up and began to pace the room. "What makes you think this guy could be our man?"

"You have to look at the whole set of circumstances," Chamberlain said. "First, the Christmas Eve shooting of the German shepherd, fifty yards from the rear of the Carrs' backyard. Then the shooting of the Labrador, Harvey, owned by Sam Carr. Carr has also received a couple of nutty threatening letters. The last one was on April 19."

Officer Intervallo now picked up the ball and ran with it: "We knew there was something there, but Berkowitz hadn't come up yet. On June eleventh, the Carrs called us to their house and told us about a couple in New Rochelle who had received a get-well card from them. But the Carrs hadn't sent any get-well card. The New Rochelle couple, the Cassaras, contacted the Carrs, since Mr. Carr's name was on the return address. The two couples got together, and in their talk the name David Berkowitz popped up. He'd been a short-time tenant of the Cassaras. They remembered that he had an intense dislike for dogs.

"We saw copies of the letters, and while they weren't signed, there is no doubt in either of our minds that the same hand wrote all of them."

"It sure looks like you guys have come up with something," Salvesen said. "I wish there was more. But it's a beginning and it looks pretty damn good to me." Salvesen was impressed. "Since the Moskowitz–Violante shooting in Brooklyn," he said, "every one of our prime suspects has been cleared. You guys may have more going than the entire New York City Police Department."

"What are you going to do with what we've given you?" asked Chamberlain.

"I'll pass it along to New York Intelligence just as soon as I get back downtown. Then they make their evaluations and recommendations. Next they pass it on to the guys at the task force in Queens."

ON WEDNESDAY, AUGUST 3, three days after the death of Stacy Moskowitz, a woman the police identify simply as Tina convinced her friend Cacilia Davis, a forty-nine-year-old native of Austria, to step forward with information in her possession. Mrs. Davis had emigrated to the United States in 1955 and became a citizen in 1957. She was petite, blonde, trim, and could easily pass for a woman much younger. Growing up in the Gestapo era, Mrs. Davis mistrusted police. It took Tina and her husband, Steve, more than five hours to convince their friend to speak.

Tina convinced her that a detective she knew, John Falotico, was trustworthy. He had left his card for Tina in a local laundromat as a message. Now, at 4:30 P.M., Tina placed a call to the 10th Homicide Zone.

"I was off at the time," says Falotico. "At this point Joe Strano came into the investigation. I had my group [Falotico and Detective Ed Zigo] in the mornings, and we left at 4:00 P.M. Another group of detectives was assigned through the evenings to take phone calls."

"I came in that evening, the third," says Detective Strano, "and the phones were jumping off the hook. People were calling in information, making inquiries, trying to help. I was free for a moment, then the phone began again." The detective answered it, pencil in hand.

"I'd like to speak to Detective John Falotico," the caller said.

"Detective Falotico is off duty. Can I be of assistance?" he said. The voice at the other end was a woman's, somewhat hesitant. "I work with John. I'm Detective Strano."

"Maybe," she said. "How could someone who might have some information about that terrible shooting at the park tell what she knew without getting themselves involved? Is it possible?"

The detective had dealt with this kind of opening before. "Miss," the detective said, "where would this person have been at the time of the shooting?"

"At her home . . . at Bay 17th Street," she said.

Strano froze. Bay 17th Street is just one block from the scene. Maybe she could have seen or heard something, he thought to himself.

"Detective Strano," the woman said, "could this person . . . with the information be protected, by the police?"

By this time, Strano felt he was onto something. He convinced the woman to give him her name and address. Strano talked until she agreed to allow him to come to her home. Strano quickly spoke to his superior, Sergeant Shea, and ran down his hunch. "It's worth a try, isn't it, Jimmy?" he said.

"Why not, Joe?" said Shea. "She lives in the right spot. Take your partner and go over there."

Using his own car, a Rambler station wagon, Strano and Detective Smith drove to the address on Bay 17th Street, a garden apartment a block from Bay 16th Street Park.

Tina greeted the detectives at the door and quickly ushered them past the living room into the kitchen. As they walked through the apartment, Strano saw a woman sitting on a couch in the living room, hands folded, eyes down. The two policemen sat in the kitchen. "Can I get you some coffee?" Tina said. They accepted, trying to start a conversation.

"Nice apartment you have here," said Strano, hoping to put Tina and her husband Steve at ease. "That breakfront in the entry, my aunt has one just like it." In the back of his mind, Strano suspected Tina and Steve hadn't called the 10th because of themselves. It must be because of the woman in the living room. He had to be careful not to frighten her. "Please, Tina, I'll have another cup of coffee."

The cat-and-mouse game went on for forty-five minutes. "Tina, does that woman in there," the detective pointed to the living room, "know anything that could be helpful to us?" Tina and Steve seemed shocked. How had the detective known? It would take another five minutes to calm the couple. All the while, Cacilia Davis was listening. Finally, Strano walked to the living-room entrance. Speaking softly, he coaxed her into the kitchen. "Mrs. . . . ?" he said.

"Davis . . . Cacilia Davis," she said. The woman sat down with the two detectives, still frightened, looking at her hands. She wouldn't look up.

"Cacilia," Strano said, "I'm just a cop trying to find the person who killed a young girl and blinded a boy. Anything you know, anything you can help us with, would be appreciated. We have to find this killer before he goes out and shoots some other kids." She did not lift her eyes. "Mrs. Davis, anything you tell us will be kept in strict confidence. No one will know you've spoken to us." Her eyes came up. Tears were forming.

"But the man who shot them. If he knew about me, he'd maybe search me out and shoot me? Please, keep my name out of the papers. No reporters. I don't want the killer to find out about me.''

"You have my word," Strano said.

Mrs. Davis began in a low halting voice: "I had gotten home late that night and . . . and had parked my car down the block. My dog, Snowball, hadn't been out all day. So I put on his leash and took him downstairs.

"I went down the street, like I always do, to Shore Road, and walked along it. Snowball likes to smell around the bushes there. The street was filled with cars, probably with young people; they're always there on weekends.

"After ten or fifteen minutes I started back. But I had the feeling that someone was following me." Mrs. Davis' voice almost broke.

"I attempted to calm her," says Detective Strano. "I asked her to try and remember what the man looked like. She hesitated, but then answered."

"From a distance I couldn't tell, except he looked like he was trying to hide behind a tree. But the tree was too small, too narrow. He stood out. He kept on staring in my direction. Snowball stopped for a minute or two, and I just stood there looking at the man. Then he began walking in my direction, smiling, a peculiar smile. It wasn't anything sinister, just a friendly kind of smile, almost.

"I noticed he had something in his hand. It looked like a small radio. He kind of held it partly up his sleeve. Then I didn't know if it was a radio. I froze.

"The man walked right up to me, very slowly, yet deliberately, until he was about five feet away. He made this frowning type of look. Then he made this military type turn, and walked away in the direction of my building.

"From where I was standing, there is an opening that leads to a courtyard. On the other side of the yard is another opening that leads to the side of the park where the handball courts are."

Both detectives were familiar with the park. They knew exactly the spot Mrs. Davis was alluding to. There was a hole in the park's fence there. That hole could have provided escape for the killer when he ran into the park, as recounted by the only eyewitness to the shooting, Tommy Zaino. Strano decided to get back to the encounter. "Cacilia, let's get back to what this man was carrying."

"When he walked away from me, I realized it wasn't a radio, wasn't . . . I think it was a gun," she said. "But, he didn't hold it like it was. . . . He held it differently. The handle was in his palm. The barrel was hidden." At this point the detective took out his Smith & Wesson .38, unloaded it, and stood up. The people in the dinette watched.

"Mrs. Davis, I'm going to hold my gun the way you said he held his." The detective grabbed the butt end of the .38, allowing the stubby two-inch barrel to extend into the sleeve of his sports coat. "Now, was this what you saw?"

"Yes," she answered.

"Then what happened, Mrs. Davis?"

"I was frightened. I walked into my house and began to slip off Snowball's collar. Just then I heard pops, or something that sounded like firecrackers. They were kind of loud, but far off. I didn't think too much of the noise at the time.

"The next morning, when I took Snowball out for his morning walk, there were crowds of people at Shore Road. It was then that I learned what happened the night before. Suddenly I realized that I must have seen the killer. I panicked, and I couldn't say anything.

"But you can't keep something like that to yourself. I couldn't sleep, nothing. So it was then I went to Tina and told her what happened. She told me that she'd call the police because she knew a detective at the local precinct. She wasn't sure if you'd have to tell people what I saw . . . I hope not." Her eyes pleaded with Strano.

"Tell me, Cacilia. Would you remember him if you saw him again?"

"I would never forget his face until the day I die. I'll never forget. It was frightening." She buried her own face in her hands.

The detectives waited. Tina placed a fresh cup of coffee in front of Mrs. Davis and the woman sipped. Once again Strano spoke. "Cacilia, I'd like to bring an artist here to work with you, to try and get a likeness of him. Don't worry, though, the man is a police officer and has worked with many people before."

"All right," she answered finally, looking from face to face. There were tears in her eyes, tears of fear.

"Tina, I like this china we're drinking out of. I'd like to get it for my mother. Where did you buy it?" Strano said. Once again he turned his attention away from Cacilia Davis. It was a tactic he'd use frequently in the next few days. Midway through the next day, police artist William McCormack had finished with a sketch that pleased Mrs. Davis. Strano and Smith brought the finished product back to the 10th Homicide, where Sergeant Shea arranged to print thousands of the sketches for distribution to police throughout the city.

"From her initial statements to me, I concluded that Mrs. Davis could provide us with a real description of the killer," says Detective Strano. The drawing she approved showed a killer with black shiny hair, curly, relatively tight-knit. The nose was bent. Mrs. Davis referred to the nose as "an Indian's or Israeli's."

Within fifteen minutes after hearing from Strano, Detective Sergeant Jimmy Shea called Chief of Detectives John Keenan and Brooklyn Borough Commander William Fitzpatrick. After a conference at the top levels of command, the senior officers came to the same conclusion that Sergeant Shea had reached: Cacilia Davis had indeed seen the Son of Sam. Chief Fitzpatrick then said to Sergeant Shea, "Jimmy, let Strano keep at this woman. Let him try to get every possible detail from her. You'll never know when she comes up with that one item we need." Shea agreed.

AT THE 109th Precinct on Monday, August 1, there wasn't a place to sit. Officers had come in voluntarily on their day off. Others were pulling double shifts in an all-out effort to catch the killer. Unknown to Deputy Inspector Dowd was the fact that Detective Joe Strano of 10th Homicide had come up with the "perfect" witness. Captain Joe Borrelli, now Dowd's liaison with Brooklyn Homicide, was also in the dark. Strano hadn't had time to make a written report. Orders from the Borough Commander came in a phone conversation between Sergeant Shea and Chief Fitzpatrick. Strano was to continue with the witness unhindered. Nobody had telephoned Omega. Captain Borrelli's presence at the 10th seemed to be enough. It would take a day before the normal written reports, called DD-5s, were filed. Thus, that day of first contact between Strano and Davis was known only to a handful of police within the Brooklyn 10th and at borough headquarters.

Sometimes fate plays the major hand in the order of things. Strano had been seated in the squad room at the right time, at the right phone, to receive the call from Tina.

ALL THROUGH the final days of the investigation the police did not worry about the safety of Mrs. Davis. They did worry about Tommy Zaino's. So, added to his daily routine of investigating with Cacilia, Detective Strano was given the added chore of picking up Tommy at the Holiday Inn in Staten Island, where the police had decided to keep him each night. Strano lived in Staten Island. This added job would keep him away from the investigation for at least two hours a day.

Once Strano drove Zaino to the auto-body shop in Coney Island, he had to wait for an officer to relieve him. Then he'd drive directly to Bay 17th Street to begin the search with Mrs. Davis.

Mrs. Davis had said that the killer wore a blue, possibly denim, jacket. "He was also wearing jeans and a shirt, like a Qiana with flowers on it."

On Thursday morning, August 4, Strano said: "Cacilia, let's get back to the jacket. Can you give me a better description of it?"

"Yes. It was blue, an Eisenhower type. And when he walked away I could see the back of it. It had a yoke across it and it made him look kind of athletic. And something else. His legs were thick. Too thick for the rest of him. And he didn't walk exactly right. It isn't something I can explain, but it just wasn't right.''

Armed with his eyewitness's description, the detective decided to go on a shopping trip with her, in an effort to locate the same type of garment. "I went shopping with her for two days," he says. "We walked in and out of men's stores for hours on end. We shopped in Bensonhurst and Bay Ridge. Finally we ended up in the giant Kings Plaza shopping complex, down on Flatbush Avenue near Marine Park. We kept looking at leisure suits and denim jackets. It was funny because in all that time we never bought anything.

"I'd never been on so many shopping trips with a woman in my life. If my wife knew," he says, "she might have decided to leave me."

Strano was also hoping that he and Mrs. Davis might spot the killer in a Brooklyn store. "A long shot," he says. "A very long shot, but entirely possible." More than that, he was looking for a store that carried the kind of jacket Cacilia had seen the killer wear.

On Thursday, August 4th, Strano and Mrs. Davis found themselves in Mel's Men's Shop. "Yes," the proprietor, Mel Davis said, "I know the kind of jacket you're talking about. We had them a couple of years ago, but sold them all out."

Strano pressed. "Who was the manufacturer?"

"Tell you the truth, I don't remember. It was some small firm on Seventh Avenue, in the garment district. Not one of the big firms. It wasn't a big seller, and once I got rid of the last of them I never reordered."

Strano spent the remainder of the day searching through a list of manufacturers. He came up blank. "It was then that I knew. I was barking up the wrong tree. It wouldn't be possible to trace the killer through his jacket."

ON THURSDAY AFTERNOON, August 4, David Berkowitz decided to drive along the Hudson in Riverdale, the western

portion of the Bronx, along Warburton Avenue south until it
became Riverdale Avenue, just past Main Street in the center
of Yonkers. Less than two miles farther on, he crossed into
the Bronx, continuing due south. The city was sweltering in
the midsummer heat. The temperature hit 86 degrees. David
continued on to West 254th Street, taking a right which
brought him to the northern part of Riverdale Park. He parked
his car, placed the .44 in a bag, then under the front seat, and
climbed out.

"I spent more than three hours walking around the park.
There were lots of people having picnics and playing ball. It
was a nice day to be out with your family." (It was five
months since Berkowitz had seen his mother or half-sister.)

At 6:00 P.M. David returned to his car and resumed driving
south on Riverdale Avenue. He eventually turned east into
the central Bronx, arriving at his old apartment house on
Barnes Avenue near 10:30 P.M. The demons began to speak
to him there, and he fled. "As soon as I got there, they
started. It was terrible. I knew I'd never get away from them,
and I drove away."

By 11:00 P.M. he returned to Buhre Avenue. He drove past
Donna Lauria's apartment house and the site of his first killing. "They promised me that I'd marry her. But they lied.
They always lied to me." He never stopped. Instead, he
drove directly back to 35 Pine Street, Yonkers. David parked
the Galaxie and ran up the five flights of stairs to his small
apartment. There he thought he'd be safe.

THAT SAME Thursday afternoon, Strano began to press
Mrs. Davis hard for information. "Cacilia," he said, "what
I'm going to ask you now is very important. There are questions that have come up and only you can clear them." (Questions had indeed been asked at 10th Homicide. Strano and
Falotico found themselves at odds. Strano believed that Cacilia had indeed seen the gunman. "She had to have seen
him," says Strano. "He was in the right place, acting suspicious, and carrying what looked like a gun.")

THE FINAL WITNESS • 301

Falotico did not. ("We had Tommy Zaino's description of the killer," says Falotico. "And there was no doubt in anyone's mind that Zaino had positively seen the killer. Tommy Zaino's description of the killer and his clothing didn't match Mrs. Davis' account.") Strano was at a loss to explain why. A question arose as to whether or not Mrs. Davis had, in fact, been outside at 2:05 A.M. "She could have had the time wrong quite easily," says Falotico. "She was scared and confused."

In order to accept her description of the man she'd seen, Strano had to get some facts that tied her to the scene at the right time.

"I want you to tell me everything, Cacilia. One more time from the beginning," Strano said. "When you left your car, did you see anything you haven't told me about?"

"No. I think I told you everything, Joe," said Mrs. Davis.

"Cacilia, let's kind of walk through what you did. You went inside and got Snowball. Then you came out. Was there anyone else in the street? Maybe someone was there who saw you, or saw the man? Please, think hard."

"Well," Mrs. Davis said, "I remember a Jewish lady. I think her name was Goldberg. Her car had been double-parked. She always left it double-parked. But she moved it before I came back out."

"Well, then. We're now a little past two in the morning."

"Yes," Mrs. Davis said, "and then the police were writing tickets out."

"What?" Strano almost shouted. "Tickets?" He was dumbfounded. According to all the reports, no summonses had been served in the neighborhood that night. (Both Falotico and Sergeant Coffey's men had checked almost immediately if summonses had been issued, and nothing had turned up.) Now everything Mrs. Davis had said was in doubt.

"What do you mean the police were giving tickets?" Strano asked.

"There was a police car there. The officers were writing tickets. I thought to myself later, my God, while people were getting killed, cops are running around giving tickets, and they didn't even know what was going on a block away.''

"Cacilia, there were no summonses served. We know that because we checked it out,'' Detective Smith said.

"Don't tell me there were no summonses served—there was a summons served. I had gone out with my boyfriend [Mrs. Davis is a divorcée]. We had been to a bazaar on 75th Street that night. After the bazaar, we went for something to eat, then he drove me home. He couldn't find a place to park because there were so many other cars around. He couldn't even double-park. He would have had to park three cars out. There was a car double-parked and one at the hydrant—that's where my boyfriend usually parks while I go up and get the dog. He usually stays and watches me while I walk Snowball. He didn't even stay behind that night. He was triple-parked, and the reason he didn't stay is probably because he saw the cop car coming.

"A cop began giving summonses out. He gave one while my dog was at the hydrant, so I know they were being served. I noticed that the cop was a heavy-set man.''

"Are you sure it was a patrolman?'' insisted Strano.

"Two patrolmen. One was heavy-set. He was out of the car. The other one was sitting inside. They were laughing at something. I was kind of angry because the Jewish lady up the block, she always double-parks and locks everybody in. I was wishing she could have gotten the ticket.''

Strano returned to 10th Homicide with Cacilia's startling statement. Fearing the "I told you so" comments from his fellow detectives, he kept quiet about what she had said. A half hour later, Strano told Shea. Shea decided to follow up.

The sergeant checked the file for the names of the officers who were manning the sector car. Once more, the names of Cataneo and Logan came up. He called through to their precinct requesting a general description of the officers. Cataneo's fit. Mrs. Davis had been positive that a heavy-set officer had placed the ticket on the car's windshield. "OK, Jimmy. At least Mrs. Davis is right on that point,'' said Strano. "If she has the officer right, she damn well must be right on the summons part of her story.''

At 7:00 P.M., Sergeant Jimmy Shea called the 61st Precinct requesting to be put through to Officers Cataneo and Logan. The officers had checked out at 6:00 P.M. Any further check would have to wait until morning.

AT OMEGA headquarters in the 109th Precinct in Queens, Detective Sergeant Joe Coffey looked at police artist Bill McCormack's sketch and thought "It looks like that Bronx Congressman, Herman Badillo." It wasn't laughable.

Other detectives, more direct, described the picture as "bullshit."

"There's no way in hell he's going to look like that," commented Detective George Moscardini. "They never look like the witnesses say they do anyhow." (In fact, it was sketch No. 325, prepared on 8/4/76 with the cooperation of Jody Valenti, that came closest to a likeness of David Berkowitz.) McCormack's latest sketch was unlike the other four he had prepared.

18

Capture

These were hard times at Omega headquarters. The police had checked out a dozen leading suspects. Among them were a priest, two schoolteachers, two cops, and a doctor. All were cleared. The Omega men were frustrated and disappointed. "My own feeling," Coffey says, "was that the killer went to Brooklyn because it seemed safer after all the publicity. But we knew we shouldn't abandon the Bronx and Queens. I thought that was where he'd strike again. I knew he wouldn't stop with the last one."

On Thursday afternoon, August 4, a special conference was called in the Chief of Detectives' office on the thirteenth floor at One Police Plaza. In attendance were Police Commissioner Michael Codd, Chief of Detectives John Keenan, Inspector Charles Kelly from the Bronx, Inspector Dowd, Captain Borrelli, and Sergeant Coffey. Chairs had been drawn into a semicircle in front of Chief Keenan's desk. The Commissioner was seated behind the desk facing his officers. Behind him, on the light-blue wall, were pictures of President

Jimmy Carter and Mayor Abraham Beame. Commissioner Codd convened the meeting, asking for a full rundown of just what was happening in the field.

"We've nearly three hundred men operating out of the 109th around the clock," Deputy Inspector Dowd answered. "On Friday, Saturday, and Sunday nights, two hundred men are on patrol in prime areas. We've also checked out and cleared nearly seventeen hundred leads and are continuing to follow up additional calls into our headquarters."

"Have you come up with anything?" Codd asked. "I mean, when will there be a break?"

"I don't know, Commissioner," Dowd said.

ON MONDAY, AUGUST 22, 1977, the *Daily News* received its following week's Doonesbury comic strips from the Universal Press Syndicate. The strip, created by Garry Trudeau, was a spoof on how both the *News* and its ace reporter, Jimmy Breslin, were handling the Son of Sam affair. Trudeau began by identifying the newspaper as the *Daily News,* and continued with a take-off on the Son of Sam, disguised by the name of the "Son of Arnold and Mary Leiberman."

Upon seeing the comic strips, *News* editor Michael O'Neil chose not to run them. The censorship was noticed immediately by the opposition. "It seems that today's strip of the Pulitzer Prize winning cartoon hit a bit too close to home for the 42nd Street bunch," commented the *Post* in its page six column of August 29, running the first four frames of the strip.

When asked for a reason for not running Doonesbury, the *News* had a "NO COMMENT" reply. However, the *Post* wasn't going to allow the *News* to get off that easily. In its next edition, on August 30, the *Post* printed the second four frames of the cartoon.

In the very next issue of the *Post,* on August 31, page six reported that the *News* had "leaned on" Universal Press Syndicate not to make the strip available for any further reprints by the *Post.* Going one step further, the *News*'s attorney served a "cease and desist" letter on the *Post* to prevent that newspaper from any further publication of the comic strip.

Instead of running the original cartoon, the *News* substituted a 1971 "rerun" of another Doonesbury. The *Post,* however, ran the text that told of "Son of Arnold and Mary Leiberman" arguing with a *News* promotion assistant because he had been unable to reach Breslin on the phone. In the place of Breslin, he was offered Mr. Hamill. The offer was rejected as he thought "Hamill's pleas to Sam sort of rambled."

On September 1, 1977, page six again poked fun at the *News.* "If you want to complain to the *News,* call 949-1234," said the *Post.* "They're the people who are afraid to let you laugh along with this week's Doonesbury."

In a parting shot, the *Post* chose its words carefully. In the September 2, 1977, issue of page six, the *Post* said, "On Monday, the *News* will be running the regular Doonesbury again —as long, that is, as it doesn't offend the strange sensibilities of the folks on 42nd Street."

ON SATURDAY, AUGUST 6, Tom Chamberlain worked an early day shift. Intervallo was off, and Chamberlain rode with an officer named Eddie Wissner, thirty-seven.

Just as the two patrolmen got to their car in the parking lot, they were ordered to respond to a call. "Suspected arson —35 Pine Street." It was 7:09 A.M.

They drove the half mile to the familiar apartment house. "Back here again," thought Chamberlain as the car pulled to a stop in front of the broad white entrance. "We went directly to the sixth floor," says Chamberlain. "The air was pretty heavy with what was left of the smoke. It made my eyes tear."

The two policemen proceeded down the corridor to apartment 6E. There, waiting for them, was a tall, stocky man wearing glasses who identified himself as the occupant.

"I'm Craig Glassman," he said. "Some son of a bitch set this right in front of my door."

Glassman began kicking at the ashes. He reached into his rear pocket and took out a leather shieldholder and held it up to the two Yonkers cops. "I'm with the County's Sheriff's Department."

"Actually," Chamberlain says, "Glassman wasn't a deputy sheriff. That made him a part-time peace officer. But, because I thought him to be a cop, I allowed him to carry on a conversation, rather than questioning him. Eddie was sketching the hallway and the position of the fire."

"See," Glassman said, holding out his left fist. "The nut who did this threw in some bullets." He opened his hand, exposing ten .22-caliber long-rifle cartridges, intact.

"Could have sounded like Vietnam," Chamberlain said, "if they'd gone off."

"Yeah, could have," Glassman said. "I smelled the smoke and ran to the door. When I opened it the fire was almost out. Probably the garbage he used was wet. Then I ran back inside and got a pot of water and threw it on what was left of it. It probably never got hot enough to set the bullets off. Then I called you guys right away. . . . Oh, yeah, I ran to the stairway in between, thinking that maybe he used it to get away. I'd have arrested him if I could have caught him."

"Have any idea who could have done this?" Chamberlain asked.

"Idea? Sure I have an idea. It's someone who doesn't want me around."

"Anyone specific?" Chamberlain said.

"Not really. Somebody's been threatening me. I've gotten two crazy letters, and I've turned them over to the Sheriff's Department in White Plains. Whoever did this is the same person who's sent me those crazy letters."

Chamberlain thought of "crazy letters" that had been mailed to Sam Carr and Jack Cassara. "Do you have copies of the letters you turned over to the Sheriff's Department?"

"Sure, but why?" asked Glassman.

"I got a hunch. Let me see them and if I'm right, maybe I can help you."

Glassman opened the apartment door and stepped over the fire's remains, followed by Officer Chamberlain. Wissner remained outside, completing his work for the report to the detectives.

Glassman went directly to a bureau and took out photocopies of two letters. He handed them to Chamberlain, who started to read them. He immediately noted the similarity in handwriting of these letters and those received by Sam Carr back in April. The one that interested him most began

I KNOW CAPTAIN CARR PUT YOU UP TO THIS. . . .

"Right then," Chamberlain says, "I knew these letters had to be connected to the Carrs. I excused myself and went back out to the hallway. I walked over to Eddie and said, 'Get up to the roof and try to look down into the apartment just above this one. See if there's anything funny going on in there.' "

His partner took the fire stairs to the roof; Chamberlain returned to the Glassman studio apartment. "I decided to give Glassman the information I'd passed on to Salvesen the day before."

Chamberlain sat down on the single couch adjacent to the window that overlooked the Hudson River and Sam Carr's house on Warburton Street. "My partner and I have been suspicious of your upstairs neighbor, David Berkowitz," said the officer. "In our opinion, he could very well be the one who was writing all the letters. He's probably the guy who set this fire also."

"I've heard someone walking around up there at crazy hours," Glassman said, looking at the ceiling.

"Well, I can give you his car license-plate number if you want it," said Chamberlain.

"Sure," said Glassman.

"He's twenty-four years old, about five feet ten, maybe 205 pounds, with dark hair. He's driving a yellow 1970 Ford Galaxie. The plate number is 561-XLB. You ought to give him the once-over with your guys down in White Plains," said Chamberlain. "Maybe they can come up with something on him in their files. We really have nothing at all on him."

Somewhat confused, Glassman agreed to pass the information along to Sheriff Thomas Delaney. It seemed incongruous to Glassman that an upstairs neighbor, with whom he'd had no contact, would have reason to attack him. However, to be on the safe side, Craig would take special care to carry his automatic with him from then on. (Glassman has a New York State pistol permit.) He would also make certain that the windows opening onto the common fire escape with his upstairs neighbor, Berkowitz, were secure at all times.

Chamberlain returned to the hallway where Eddie Wissner was waiting. "Can't see anything in that apartment," Eddie reported. "Whoever's there has blankets nailed to cover all the windows. But I found some more shells in the ashes." Wissner showed Chamberlain ten additional cartridges he'd pulled from the mess, making a total of twenty .22-caliber shells. At this point, armed with the fact that the Sheriff's Department seemed to be on the case, Chamberlain thought the time had come to bring what he had to the Yonkers detectives. He still wasn't sure that Bill Grogan had really believed him.

Chamberlain called through on the interoffice phone to Detective Michael Lorenzo. "I gave everything we had to the New York detective, Salvesen," he said. "Novotny gave us permission to go up and speak to him."

"Anything come of it?" the Yonkers detective inquired.

"Don't know," said the patrolman. "He said it was good, and that he'd pass it along to their Intelligence guys, but it's probably too soon for any action."

"OK, then," said Lorenzo. "I'm going to try to get the Cassara woman and find out what the story is with her. I'll get back to you just as soon as I know something." Chamberlain was relieved. At last something was going to be done. Someone was going to follow up.

Detective Lorenzo, forty-six, five feet ten inches, heavyset and balding, walked to the file cabinet. He adjusted his glasses, then searched for the file on Cassara. The folder contained a single sheet with Nann Cassara's address and phone number. There was a notation about her call, and the name David Berkowitz, nothing else. He dialed the number. There was no answer.

Three hours later, Lorenzo placed a second call to Mrs. Cassara. This time she was home. After a brief conversation, it appears that Chamberlain and Intervallo had indeed come up with something of value. But at the moment, everything the two patrolmen had was purely circumstantial. It appears that Berkowitz was their man. As Chamberlain remembers, "It wasn't something you'd run out and make arrests on. But the elements were all there. It seemed that everyone was just on the verge of moving, but we were all waiting for that final piece of evidence to make it a cut-and-dried case. Too many suspects are arrested only to have their cases thrown out in a court due to an illegal search or the like. If this was our man, then we wanted to do everything by the book so that our case would stick."

Detective Lorenzo called Tom Chamberlain and told him about the conversation he'd had with Mrs. Cassara. Then he said, "By the way, what do you think about the stuff we've gotten from New York?"

Chamberlain responded, "It's kind of sketchy. But you get a feeling that they have a lot more than they're showing. I'd love to know what they really have from that columnist Breslin's letter. I bet they've only released a small part of everything."

"I have the same thought," said Lorenzo. "But we aren't going to pry anything from them they don't want released. It's understandable, because whenever they get him, they'll have to have something left to positively identify their guy. Like something only he'd know. There's got to be something in those letters that could help. We'll just have to wait for whatever it is."

Chamberlain understood it was standard procedure for police departments to withhold certain key facts. Yonkers did it, as did New York City. Police just didn't want vital clues floating around for the newspaper or television guys to get hold of. There wasn't any way one department could control the leaks in another. So, to avoid the problem, information stayed "in the shop."

At that very moment, a floor above Craig Glassman, David Berkowitz "was getting tired of the whole thing." He began planning one final climactic spree of mass murder.

AT HIS JOB, David kept more to himself than before. "The demons were pushing me all the time. They knew sooner or later I'd be caught. But that didn't really bother them. It had all been planned out long before they found me." David ate outside the Post Office cafeteria, in a nearby little-used hallway. It was "safer" for him. The demons seemed to be lost in this building, and they hadn't yet found his new hiding place. "It wouldn't be long until they found me. But for the time being, I could lose them there."

David also avoided contact with his newfound family.

"When I tried to question him further, he just wouldn't talk," says his half-sister, Roz. "I knew there was something terribly wrong. I could see he was troubled. But he just wouldn't talk about it. I tried to get him to seek help, psychiatric help, but he told me it couldn't help him. He'd said that before.

"After that day, we didn't see each other again. He called me a few times, and also called my mom, but the calls stopped by the end of July. All of us were concerned about David. But none of us ever thought about him being that man who was shooting those young people. It never even crossed my mind."

David's own account of his imaginings is contradictory and ominous. "Soon," he says, "it would be all over."

What would be over, David?

"The end of the reign of terror was near."

Would the reign end quietly?

"No. Word was going out through the dogs, about the final

job, my final assignment. After that one, the police would probably destroy me. The demons would replace me then. But that could take time, for them to kind of recruit someone else. They had their sights set on other people, I'm sure. But it would still take them time. So on the final assignment, I'd have to kill as many as I could, as quickly as possible. That would give the demons meat for a long spell. They'd have flesh and blood enough for a long season—to eat and drink the blood. You know, to sacrifice."

Where were you going to kill, David?

"A place where I'd been camping years before. Southampton. It was summer and there'd be lots of young people there. There'd be enough blood and flesh for them to last a while."

DAVID had set the fire outside Glassman's door on the morning of August 6, using a cardboard box and refuse he'd taken from his apartment. He piled the rubbish against the metal door and lit it. Waiting a moment, he waited for the flames to dance almost to the ceiling. Then he reached into his pocket, where he had put a handful of .22-caliber cartridges, and threw twenty of them into the fire. He turned and used the familiar fire stairs to run up the one flight to his apartment. He pressed his ear to the door jamb, waiting for the sound of the exploding shells that never came. The paper bags burned quickly. Then there was nothing else to feed the fire. By the time Glassman discovered what was going on, it was out. David felt he had been foiled.

Frustrated, the killer lay on his bed crying. Glassman had defeated him. He was truly a slave, Glassman his master. David spent five hours in his bed. His tears slowly turned into fright. "The demons would be very angry with me now. I tried to burn him out, like I did Carr, but he won."

By 4:30 P.M., David decided to take his pistol and the .45-caliber semiautomatic rifle and drive to the Hamptons. Always careful about his personal hygiene, David showered. Then he put on a freshly ironed work shirt and denim pants.

He was careful to use the same wide leather belt each time he went "hunting." It provided a secure place to tuck the .44.

He walked to the dresser and lifted the heavy Bulldog off a pile of girlie magazines, swung the heavy cylinder away from the weapon's frame, and checked the five .44-caliber Smith & Wesson shells in it. He returned the cylinder to its normal position and tucked the gun into his waistband. It was loaded and ready.

David walked to the front closet and removed the Commando Mark III .45-caliber semiautomatic rifle, serial number 23954. He picked up two of the four thirty-shot clips and checked them. They were fully loaded with hollow-point ammunition, lethal at close range. The weapon could fire all thirty rounds as quickly as he pulled the trigger—thirty rounds in less than as many seconds. If he was accurate, David could strike and kill one person for each pull on the trigger. In all, counting for some bullets to pass through the person initially struck and strike a second, Suffolk County police estimate that there could have easily been twenty dead and an equal number of seriously wounded.

Reaching back into the closet, David took out a green duffel bag, the one that had seen him through the service. The name *D. Berkowitz* was printed along its side in two-and-a-half-inch white block letters. He placed the automatic rifle in the duffel bag along with his other guns. David then slipped on his loose-fitting denim jacket. Everything was in order. He felt good at the prospect of leaving the cramped quarters for the relief of the open road. It was time to hunt.

By 6:30 the sun was falling in the western sky, its orange rays beating against the blankets that covered the windows. He wanted to wait for the coolness of night, but decided it was time to leave. He was breaking his normal routine: "I had to. I failed with the fire and the demons wanted me to get out to do their bidding."

He double-locked the door to his apartment and made his way to the fire stairs. Because of the severe slope of Pine Street, the building's lobby floor was on the second level.

David rushed down the five flights and walked through the two glass lobby doors and onto the street. He paid little heed to the bevy of youngsters who were sitting on the planters that bracketed the entranceway. He headed directly for the 1970 yellow four-door Ford Galaxie, license plates 561-XLB, some thirty feet to his right. He placed the duffel bag in the vehicle's trunk. Within minutes he was on North Broadway, headed for the familiar route that would take him over the Bronx–Whitestone Bridge. While on the steel structure, he looked west toward New York City. The sun, bright orange, hung just above the skyline. This evening he'd swing onto the Cross Island Parkway and head south for four miles until it connected with the Long Island Expressway.

It took David nearly two and a half hours to reach Southampton. During his drive, storm clouds built up, bringing early darkness to the Long Island countryside.

Southampton is a chic throwback to an earlier era; Teddy Roosevelt had expounded its merits more than sixty years before. Today, expensive stately mansions still cater to the rich and superrich. Turn-of-the-century buildings line narrow streets with such names as Huckleberry Lane, Scrimshaw Drive, and the newer Cox's Walk—a gift from the unwanted intrusion of New York City's swinging singles scene.

David cruised through the town looking for someone whose death would please the demons.

The troubled gray clouds overhead darkened. Flashes of lightning exploded. A midsummer thunderstorm tore across the sky. People ran into doorways or sought shelter in their cars as the first drops of warm rain struck the pavement. David decided to park rather than to drive about. "Maybe it was going to be over in a couple of minutes. You know how those summer storms come and go so quickly."

David attributes the rain to the demons. "They had enough force to call these clouds to stop me."

But why would they want to stop you, David? Didn't they want you to kill as many people as you could?

"Yes. But they always selected the people I'd shoot. It

wasn't up to me. I never made choices—they always did. They wanted me to kill, but there had to be a nice day for it. Since the day had turned bad, they called the whole thing off. I personally didn't call it off; I had no power to do that. If it's raining, then there is nobody on the streets. What are you going to do? They just let me go home. Next weekend was going to be the weekend. I wasn't disappointed, I was really glad that it was all over. I couldn't wait for it all to end.

"As for the demons not stopping the rain; they couldn't. They were the bad, and the forces of good were just too strong for them. So the rain was a good thing, beating out evil. Like I said, I just went home."

So either the good or the evil summoned the clouds. David contradicts himself. He remains confused.

EARLIER that afternoon of August 6, Sam Carr, acting on the Berkowitz story his daughter had heard at the Yonkers Police Department, called Task Force Omega. He told everything to a detective on the other end of the line.

But, according to Carr, "I got the feeling that they weren't paying attention. It seemed that they were just going to take down what I said and file it. I could tell that from the way the policeman reacted. He seemed bored."

Carr climbed into his Chrysler station wagon and, unknowingly, followed the same route Berkowitz had taken during his drives into Queens and Long Island. It took him less than an hour to find the 109th on Union Street. He walked inside and was directed to the stairway to the second floor, where the Omega force was located.

LESS THAN A WEEK after the capture of the Son of Sam—and in the light of statements made by Sam Carr, to *The Times, News, Post,* Associated Press, and others—reporters gathered around Field Supervisor Joseph Coffey to ask pointed questions concerning the task force's inability to act on information supplied it. "So actually, Sergeant, a man named Sam Carr did in fact walk into the 109th with the identity of the killer?" said one reporter.

The lights of the cameras weren't new to Joe Coffey. He had appeared on television before. The veteran sergeant spoke slowly, wanting to make certain he wasn't misquoted or misunderstood. "Well, it is true that someone [Carr] had come in with the name of his suspect. But it's important to understand that we were getting three hundred a day of them. Suspects I mean, either over the phone, or walk-ins. Many of them sounded good.

"To deal with this number, the supervisors devised a system where they were responsible to initially go over each report. These complaint sheets were first separated into boroughs, then into priority. We were getting so many of them that it became impossible to handle them all. The supervisors were forced to make decisions; I made them. When you're dealing with three hundred plus inquiries, you're forced to make those decisions."

"Sergeant Coffey," a newsman shouted, "if they were broken down by borough, how were the ones from Yonkers or New Jersey treated? Specifically, how was the Carr report handled?"

Coffey shifted his weight. "That was a bit more complicated," he said. "Those from outside the city were given to detectives in the boroughs closest to where the suspect might live. So, with the Carr report, eventually it would have gone to the guys concerned with the North Bronx."

"But, Sergeant," the reporter persisted. "Didn't the Carr story seem like a hot lead to anyone? After all, there were the letters, the shooting of Carr's dog, and the Yonkers cops who were on it."

"Carr hadn't actually seen Berkowitz at any time, with or without a gun," said Coffey. He claimed there was a nut shooting at two dogs [Carr's and Netos'], but he was unable to say he saw this guy commit either of the acts. There just were too many ifs involved. If we'd acted on Carr's statement and gone up to Yonkers. If David was home at the time. And then the biggest *if* of all: If when we got there and he didn't start shooting, or didn't invite us in and freely speak to us, we'd have nothing."

"But, Sergeant Coffey," said another reporter, "his story turned out to be true. Even though most of it was theory, speculation, it turned out to be true. Why didn't you act?"

"Buts aren't police work. Theory and practice are far apart. We did place his statement on the second priority file to be checked out later."

"How much later?" the reporters asked.

"Eventually. Exactly how much I couldn't say. But eventually we'd have sent someone up there to check out the story. But right at that time, we had hotter things to work on. There were guys seen with guns."

The next question was directed at Captain Joseph Borrelli, who was standing a step behind and to the right of Coffey. "Captain Borrelli," asked a reporter, "how do you see the Carr statement to the Task Force, in light of the sequence of events?"

"It's important to understand that all the information we received, and I mean all information, from whatever source, had to be evaluated. Everything was placed in a priority order," said the Captain. "As it turned out, three critical pieces of evidence were available; the intelligence from Yonkers, our personal interview with Carr, and the summons. The problem was that they existed separately. Had any two of them been received by the Task Force, we would have placed the individual in question in the High Priority classification immediately. We would have then acted on the information and dispatched detectives to Yonkers.

"Hypothetically, had the situation in Yonkers developed for the Task Force men, as it did in the original arrest situation, the results would have been the same. Had it developed differently, it would have dictated different methods requiring the gathering and comparison of forensic evidence to establish probable cause for an arrest warrant.

"But all the pieces to the puzzle just weren't in the same place. We had only Carr's statement. And it wasn't enough to move on immediately. We had hundreds upon hundreds of other similar-type statements we'd been working on in turn. Some of them seemed to us to be much stronger."

The reporters turned back to Coffey. "Sergeant Coffey," one of them said, "is that just an excuse?"

"No, not really," says Coffey. "We faced a staggering amount of paperwork. We'd have needed a thousand full-time detectives to chase down every lead. You were forced to make decisions—evaluations. Alone, the Carr statement just wasn't enough. Later when the report from the Police Intelligence Division came in [the day after the capture], we'd have been up there in a shot. But at that moment, we really had nothing." As it was, Carr had brought in the name of the killer and the police failed to act.

ON MONDAY, August 8, Officers Chamberlain and Intervallo called Detective Richie Salvesen.

"Richie," said Tom Chamberlain, "I responded to a fire at the front door of the apartment directly under Berkowitz's. It's occupied by a Westchester deputy sheriff. And this guy has also received a couple of letters.

"Richie, it's got to be the same guy who wrote to the Carrs." The Yonkers officers spoke to the detective for fifteen minutes, running down certain phrases included in the Glassman letters. Each pointed directly to someone obsessed with demons, blood, and killing. Specific references were made to "streets running red with blood at the judgment."

Chamberlain paid particular attention to one sentence. "Richie, this guy said 'You drove me into the night to do your bidding.' Now, if that doesn't ring a bell, I don't know what will. Your man's hitting at night. If it is Berkowitz, he's telling us that he's going into the night due to some command from Glassman. I don't understand why. I'm not a doctor. But, it sure looks to me that he's your guy."

"Does the letter say anything else?" asked the detective on the other end of the line twenty-five miles away at One Police Plaza.

"You want the corker? Well, listen to this—'True, I am the killer, but Craig, the killings are at your command. I shall see you standing naked at the judgment seat. . . . Upon your condemnation the world shall rise in jubilation. The terrible, wicked Craig is dead, they shall shout.' '' There was silence at the other end of the line.

"Well, Richie?'' inquired Chamberlain.

"Well . . . you sure got something. I'm getting right on it. I'm going to get this on its way immediately. We should be getting back to you in a couple of days.'' Time was running out, there were not many innings left, and New York City Intelligence had taken itself out of the ball game.

Chamberlain and Intervallo, satisfied that the New York City cops were on top of everything, went back to normal patrol work in Yonkers. A day after the capture of the Son of Sam, their information, given Salvesen, would arrive at the 109th Precinct headquarters of Omega.

SERGEANT JIM SHEA in Brooklyn's 10th Homicide had another suspect. "A man came forward,'' Shea says, "and claimed he had chased a car in Bay Ridge on the night of the Moskowitz–Violante shooting. The car was going like hell and cut him off. It might have been the killer getting away.''

The witness, Anthony Terraro, had pursued the car for two or three minutes, but when Shea questioned him, he could not positively describe the year, make, or even color.

The New York City police force maintains a so-called Auto Squad, which is mainly responsible for looking into auto thefts and exporting of stolen vehicles. The squad keeps extensive manufacturers' books containing pictures of cars: front views, rear views, and a variety of side angles. The books cover every make and model of every automobile sold in the United States or Canada for twenty-five years.

Shea brought Terraro together with a police hypnotist in the Manhattan Beach section of Brooklyn. He sat on a straight-backed chair and concentrated on the words of the hypnotist. In minutes he began to speak about what had happened in days just past and the hypnotist zeroed in with specific questions.

He was asked to recall color, scene, license-plate number. "Was the top of the car round or flat?'' asked the hypnotist.

"It looked kind of rounded, like the top of a cupcake."

"Were the lights far apart or close together?"

"Not too far, not too close. But they weren't too far off the ground."

"Good, Tony. Go to the rear window. Was it big and broad, or narrow?"

"It wasn't really either. It was a rectangle, a curved rectangle."

The hypnotist and a police expert fingered their way through the Auto Squad's books. "Was it an American car?"

"No, it looked like a foreign car. Maybe an older car."

After an hour, the hypnotist had led Tony through enough different types to be able to pinpoint the car as a yellow Volkswagen, with broad rear tires and a single exhaust; a souped-up version of the famous Bug.

"Now, Tony," said the hypnotist, "what about the license plate? It was night. Your car was right behind. Did the light from your headlights reflect off his plates?"

"Yes, they were flashing off the plates from time to time."

"Can you tell me any of the numbers or letters of that plate?"

"No . . . maybe. There could have been a Q or an 0. I can't see any others."

"One other question, Tony. Now think very hard. The color of that license plate. It's very important. Was it yellow [a New York State plate]?"

"No . . . not yellow."

"Are you certain?"

"Yes, I'm certain. It wasn't yellow. But they kept flashing back at me."

"Were they white?"

"No, not white, but almost white."

"Tony, could they be a very light yellow, a pale yellow, you say?"

"Yes, a pale yellow [New Jersey plates]."

The hypnotist had gone as far as he could.

Shea made a request that Police Officer Steve Bonansigna be assigned to him. He had used Steve on a prior homicide investigation involving a car theft ring operating in Brooklyn. Bonansigna is an expert in the field of auto identification and modification. "Steve's one of the hardest workers I've ever known," says Sergeant Shea.

Shea put Officer Bonansigna in a private office, gave him his own phone and a couple of patrolmen to assist. "He immediately requested, through the New Jersey State Police, a complete computer printout of all the Volkswagens registered in the Garden State. These would include all models, years, and colors. In a day, printouts listing more than 350,000 VWs came back in ten cartons that stacked almost to the ceiling. The officers began running through the entire printout according to a special code. They had a monumental task before them. The "code" printed beside each individual registration consisted of a series of numbers and letters that represented first the model year, then model, then body type (2 dr, 4 dr, or station wagon), and finally color.

"We simply went along eliminating all the 'can't be's,' right away," says Sergeant Shea. "Eventually the three guys came up with a list of a couple of hundred that had to be checked by the New Jersey State Police." The assignment ate up 200 man-hours, but finally all 350,000 listings were checked.

Detective Joe Strano reported for duty at Brooklyn's 10th Homicide with a mixture of hope and apprehension. In Cacilia Davis, he believed he had found the single best witness to date. She was his hope. Apprehension came from his belief that if it ever came to a face to face confrontation with the killer, he could very well be shot. It was that same sense of the unknown every police officer has when dealing with someone who is irrational.

"I live in Staten Island," Strano says, "and by this time I was getting some kidding from the neighbors. Not funny kidding, either. It was a little more like laughing through a graveyard. These people were my friends, and they were concerned. They didn't know how to approach the subject so they did it by trying to kid me about it.

"Living in the city, I felt the same fears as anyone else,

maybe more. Being a homicide detective doesn't make you immortal. Hell, you don't even get a bulletproof vest.

"A killer is loose in the streets. And you, being a homicide detective, like Kojak, become the neighborhood authority. These people were scared. Everyone was. Somehow their little jokes kind of helped them through their fears.

" 'Hey, Joe,' the neighbors would ask, 'this guy . . . I mean, is he as dangerous as the papers make him out to be? . . . Is he coming over the bridge to Staten Island? Did you hear anything, Joe? Hey, Joe, my wife is afraid to leave the house. I'm tired of doing the shopping.'

" 'Hey, Joe,' they'd almost plead. 'You got all those other guys.'

" 'Hey, Joe, do you think he'd really come here?'

" 'Hey, Strano. My wife and me, we sit in our car, afraid to get out sometimes.'

" 'Hey, Strano, I'm not kidding now,' as his voice would drop. 'What's the chance my wife and I are gonna get shot?' "

Joe's answers were reassuring and professional. He told the neighbors that the killer had made a mistake coming to Brooklyn. He told them that there were good leads and that he'd follow the leads until the Son of Sam was caught. He said these things "to make the neighbors feel secure."

But Joe was more candid with his wife, Eileen. There was a story that the killer fired only four of the five bullets in his revolver. Who was he saving that last bullet for? It was something to think about. Joe had told a neighbor that the "last one was for suicide, probably." He even forced a smile. But the Stranos wondered if the killer wasn't really saving that last bullet "to use on whoever is going to take him."

"Be careful," Eileen said when Strano drove off to work.

A little after 8:00 A.M. Strano's brown Rambler station wagon pulled up to the side entrance of the Holiday Inn. Tommy Zaino was waiting, anxious to get to his job. Strano put him in the front seat and took off for the Verrazano Narrows Bridge that links Staten Island with Brooklyn. He then swung onto the Shore Parkway, continuing onto the Coney Island Avenue exit. He took different exits each day to confuse anyone who might be following. Ten minutes later he had deposited Zaino in the body shop, then called in for a uniformed man to relieve him.

Within a half hour, a patrolman arrived. Strano drove to 10th Homicide, where Sergeant Shea told him to continue working on the clothing aspect of Cacilia's story.

Strano, using his own car, left for Mrs. Davis' apartment. It would be another day of walking in and out of men's clothing stores in a vain attempt to find that one look-alike jacket she'd described the killer to be wearing. By now the pair had worked down to the Army-Navy stores.

By five in the evening, Detective Strano dropped off an exhausted Mrs. Davis at her home. He continued onto the 10th, checking out at 5:49 P.M. He'd put in a tiring day, almost eleven hours. It would be 7:30 before he'd return to his home in Staten Island, getting caught in rush-hour traffic over the world's longest suspension bridge. That night there was no dinner for the large detective. He lay down on the bed and fell asleep.

JOHN FALOTICO had his own thoughts about who the best witness was. He was banking on Tommy Zaino. Falotico knew that the young man had seen the killer in the act of shooting into Bobby Violante's car. Zaino was the first and only witness the police could point to who they knew had, beyond doubt, seen the killer. "Maybe yes, maybe no" were Falotico's thoughts when it came to Mrs. Davis. All she claimed to have seen was a man who walked up to her. "But the description she'd given just didn't match Zaino's. And I knew Zaino had seen the killer up close. So I put everything on his story. I was certain that if we were to get a break, it would come through Zaino. On Monday, August first, at ten P.M., I drove along with Eddie Zigo to speak to Tommy Zaino at his body shop in Coney Island.

"I fool around with cars myself," says Falotico. "So Tommy and I got along pretty well. He wasn't really too happy with the sketch the police artist had come up with. He kept on talking about the hair and the guy's nose.

"Tommy was a kind of artist, and he sketched a couple of changes for me. But the basic drawing seemed pretty good, considering anything else we had to go on. We spent the remainder of the day going through the stuff I'd gotten the morning after the shooting. But the things I was told by the police in the crowd led nowhere. But that's detective work. You kind of plug at it until that one key piece falls into place."

BUT BY NOW, for all the hundreds of police, the case was primarily in the hands of eight men. In fiction, the detective who has worked the hardest triumphs on the last few pages. In the real hunt for David Berkowitz, a lot of detectives worked hard. In the Bronx, George Lemburg, Ron Marsenison, and Richard Paul were running themselves ragged following leads throughout the borough and into Westchester. In Queens, Marlin Hopkins, John O'Connell, James Gallagher, George Moscardini, and Sergeant Joe Coffey were plugging away on other assignments.

Captain Joseph Borrelli, who had run the special task force for three months before the arrival of Deputy Inspector Dowd, spent the day at 10th Homicide, sizing up what the detectives were doing. He had made the decision to keep the Brooklyn detectives separate from the Omega Task Force, just as long as they were running hot.

But, for the most part, the focus, the base of action, had moved to Brooklyn—because the Son of Sam had moved his target area—to Brooklyn.

At 1:00 P.M., Friday, August 5, Sergeant Shea ordered another check for the missing summonses. This time, Detective Eddie Zigo was assigned to run a final sequential review of all numbered summonses in the squad books. "Anyone in the area at the time of the shooting might possibly be a potential witness," says Sergeant Shea.

Zigo found no further summonses and when Detective Jimmy Justus arrived at 10th Homicide (he was on loan from

Brooklyn Robbery on a day-to-day basis) later that afternoon, Sergeant Shea ordered him to run down the single uninvestigated summons. It had been written by another patrol car from the precinct, and detectives from the 10th had been unable to locate the owner of the car.

"I played around with the computer at the 62nd Precinct," says Justus. "I determined the plate number belonged to a new registration that hadn't gotten into the state computer system yet."

But the discovery of a single summons written by a patrol car other than that of Logan and Cataneo made Shea, Strano, and Justus believe that more summonses might have been given out that night than were showing up. "It just didn't sit right with us," said Jimmy Justus. "I got back on the phone with the local precinct and was informed that all files had been gone over by the Task Force, then had been released to the 10th. 'Well,' I said, 'I don't care. I'm checking again.' I was then told that the room the summonses were kept in was locked up tight." Justus didn't like the smell of what was going down. "Hey, I want to get in there, right away."

"You can't," was the reply.

"Hell I can't. I'm going to come down with a bolt cutter and cut the goddamn door open. I want every summons that was issued that night, from everyone."

It seemed futile. The lieutenant in charge made it clear that the room was locked and would remain so.

A half hour went by. Justus decided to call the precinct once again. This time the lieutenant was more cooperative. He gave Justus a list of five more summonses. "At this point," he remembers, "I wasn't thinking that any one of the summonses would belong to the killer.

"Now I began to check through the computer once again, this time with the five additional summonses. I checked the plate numbers and all combinations of those numbers. One was eliminated as a computer error. Quick checks of the remaining four showed that two were new issues and not yet into the State Motor Vehicle computer system. One was issued to a vehicle owned by a woman in Staten Island. She loaned it to her son who was at a party that night.

"The last one stood out like lightning. It belonged to this guy Berkowitz in Yonkers."

IT SHOULD be remembered that when Officers Logan and Cataneo returned to their station house on July 31, after the shootings of Stacy and Bobby, they were interviewed by Sergeant Joseph Coffey of the Omega Task Force. They denied issuing any summonses earlier that night. On Tuesday the 2nd, Sergeant Jimmy Shea of the 10th Homicide called and asked them the same question. Once again they made a denial. When the author spoke to Officer Logan on April 12, 1980, his answer was as follows:

"I had totally no recollection of what anything was like on the night of July 31. We got tied up in this thing all of a sudden, from a quiet summer's night to pandemonium. We discussed it later on, but to both of us—it was like it never happened—the summons never being issued. In fact, a couple of days after they were found, I asked Mike, 'How did the summonses get in the box (the box that all summonses are dropped into after a tour)?' Well, he says, 'I don't know.' I asked if he handed them in, and he answered, 'I just don't remember.' "

Then, how did they get handed in?

"We don't know how they got handed in. I have no recollection of handing them in, but they did get handed in. What usually happens is that after you write them, you put them over the car's visor. At the end of the tour, usually all your paper work is up there on the visor. You pull it all at the end of the tour and turn it all in. Now, possibly it was left in the car, and the crew that took over the same car saw them and dumped them in with theirs. I don't remember handing them in, and Mike doesn't either."

Joe Coffey has his own view of why the summonses were so difficult to find. "Let me speculate," begins the sergeant. "There's a paranoia within the police department of Big

328 • SON OF SAM

Brother—of being criticized from above. The summonses in question were given very close to the time of the attack at the park. Both patrolmen knew they had written summonses and that they were very close to everything when the shootings went down. They were very close, they had to be, like Jesus . . . seconds away! So, probably they figured, 'Well, why put ourselves in a position of being close to a major crime and having missed it. Not knowing detective work, not knowing that we were going to find out anyway, they figured, 'We just better deny!' "

AT 6:00 P.M., Sergeant Shea's squad went off duty. The checking would continue on Monday, after they returned from the weekend. Strano spent his weekend, Saturday and Sunday, August 6 and 7, working around his house in Staten Island; Shea did the same at his home in Rockaway Point. Detective John Falotico had a car to repair at J&D Auto Collision on 16th Avenue in Brooklyn, and Detective Zigo spent a rare weekend relaxing with his family.

When the squad returned to duty on Monday, August 8, they devoted their time to the question of the yellow Volkswagen. Detective Justus would come in on Tuesday, instead of going to his regular assignment at Brooklyn Robbery, to continue calling potential witnesses. But for Monday, the pressing issue Shea's squad was tracing was the Volkswagen.

ON TUESDAY MORNING, AUGUST 9, David Berkowitz stayed in his room. The demons were constantly at him, hounding him to kill. He had returned empty-handed from the Hamptons. The demons, he says, refused to accept the fact that it had rained. Now they were planning his demise.

David wanted to sleep.

ON TUESDAY, AUGUST 9, Detective Sergeant Jimmy Shea made a simple statement to his wife Betty. "This case is going to end on Wednesday."

"How, Wednesday?" she asked.

"Don't ask me how I know. But, I feel it. I'm telling you, it's going to go tomorrow."

SHEA, Strano, Falotico and Justus were all on a 4 P.M. to 1 A.M. tour. When Justus arrived, Sergeant Shea assigned him to continue working on the summonses. The one that remained was issued to a white (the computer called it yellow) Ford Galaxie registered to a David Berkowitz, 35 Pine Street, Yonkers. Justus had previously tried four times to call Berkowitz. No answer. "Justus, try and get the guy on the phone," Shea said. Once again, there was no answer.

"It didn't sit right with me," said Justus. "First of all, Berkowitz was a Jewish name. And the summons was for a car in the wrong place at the wrong time. Berkowitz, from Yonkers, didn't have any reason to be down in Brooklyn at that time of the night, no damn reason. It seemed out of place that a Jewish person from Yonkers would have been down in this particular Italian area. There was nothing left but for me to check this one through the Yonkers Police Department."

Justus picked up the phone and dialed (914) 963-4900, the telephone number for Yonkers police headquarters. "I'm Detective James Justus of 10th Homicide, Brooklyn. Please put me through to the Detective Division." The call was routed through to the second floor office of Yonkers' Detectives. They weren't in.

"I'd like to leave a message for them to send a notification to the home of David Berkowitz, 35 Pine Street, to have him contact me as soon as possible. It's in relation to a case I'm working on. So, put a rush on it."

Two hours passed, and Justus checked and rechecked. It was possible that additional ones would turn up. There were none.

But, the name Berkowitz kept eating at him, and he decided to call the Criminal Identification Bureau at One Police Plaza. As it turned out, David Berkowitz, of 35 Pine Street, Yonkers, had no record in the city. At that point, Sergeant Shea walked over to Detective Justus and said, "Jimmy, I think it's time you get as much as you can on this Berkowitz. Somehow, it isn't sitting right with me."

"Sarge, I've had the same thoughts," Justus answered.

At 6:15 P.M., Detective Jimmy Justus placed a second call to the Yonkers Police Department. He got a dispatcher named Wheat Carr.

"I'm Detective James Justus of Brooklyn Homicide. I'm calling in reference to the .44 caliber case. I'd like to have a couple of your detectives do a background check on a David Berkowitz, of 35 Pine Street."

"BERKOWITZ!" she shouted into the phone. "I'll tell you about that character."

"What do you mean?" Justus said. "Do you know him?" Justus was calling for a routine background check, and the dispatcher had jumped at him.

"Sure I know him," she said. "My family has been having nothing but trouble with him. If you have a minute, I'll give you everything you need."

"What's your name?" Justus asked.

"I'm Wheat Carr, a dispatcher for the Yonkers Police Department. My father's name is Sam Carr, and he's been the brunt of some pretty weird things that have been going on here."

When the dispatcher said Sam Carr, Justus sat up. Sam Carr and the Son of Sam went together.

The woman continued. "We live directly behind 35 Pine Street. In fact, you can see his apartment house from our rear windows. My whole family and a couple of neighbors think he shot our dog, Harvey. In fact, the bullet is still in the dog.

"In the beginning of June a family called us from New Rochelle about a card they'd supposedly gotten from my dad. They came over and showed it to us. It looked just like the letters my father had been getting."

"Did you report any of this to the Yonkers police?"

"Of course we did. In fact, a couple of our patrolmen are investigating the different incidents. One of them is Tom Chamberlain. He and his partner have had Berkowitz under observation for this whole past month."

"Wheat," Justus said, "do you think it would be possible for you to have Officer Chamberlain or his partner call me here?"

"I'll call him at home if you'd like."

"Please do."

Fifteen minutes later Officer Tom Chamberlain called Detective Justus at 10th Homicide. It was now 6:30 P.M. In the next ten minutes Chamberlain and Justus went over everything the two Yonkers officers had compiled on David Berkowitz and the seemingly related occurrences in Yonkers and New Rochelle.

"You know," Chamberlain said, "if you call Sam Carr, he'll give you a better account of the shooting of his dog. They can't get the slug out of the dog because of the possibility of permanent injury. But if it's in the interest of the investigation, you can always get a court order." He paused. "By the way, everything I've just given you I already have given to a Detective Salvesen in your own Intelligence Division. He said he'd pass it on to you guys." (Chamberlain had mistakenly believed that Justus was a member of the Omega Task Force.)

"Do you have any idea just where Berkowitz comes from?" the Brooklyn detective asked.

"We did a little nosing around and found out that he was from Pelham Bay. . . ."

In the background Jimmy Justus began shouting, "Sarge, Sarge, this guy's from Pelham Bay!" The officer returned his attention to the Yonkers office, yelled a simple "Thanks!", and hung up. Pelham was the key. Justus didn't need anything else.

Back in his home, Officer Tom Chamberlain looked at a dead receiver. The case had just passed him by.

It had been speculated by high-ranking members within the Chief of Detectives' Office that the killer could have possibly been a resident of the East Bronx or lower Westchester. Unknown to Officer Chamberlain, the New York City police theorized this because all of the Son of Sam's attacks had occurred near the series of highways connecting Long Island with the Bronx, with access across possibly either the Throgs Neck or Bronx–Whitestone bridges.

Jimmy Justus remembers, "I called my wife and told her I thought I had gotten some great information, and 'I believe I have the .44-Caliber Killer.' So she said, 'What's going to happen?' I responded, 'Well, tomorrow we're going up.' I slept over in the precinct that night."

JIMMY JUSTUS and James Shea weren't the only ones to feel they had achieved a breakthrough. From the moment the Berkowitz summons came up, Detective Strano felt the excitement. "I was elated. Now we were in the right ballpark."

At 11:30 P.M., Justus called the Yonkers police again. This time he spoke to the detectives. They said that Berkowitz had burned a door, had probably shot another dog, and they added something to what Wheat Carr had said. She guessed that a large caliber bullet had been used in the shooting of her father's dog. Well, the three Brooklyn detectives looked at each other. "I can speak for myself," says Detective Strano—"I can't speak for the others—we were pretty sure what we had. We had the SON OF SAM, no question about it, none whatsoever.

"I was ready and set to go at the time. But, it was now about 2:00 A.M., and I wasn't the boss. Sergeant Shea said, 'It's late. Let's try and get more on him. We have tomorrow to get the rest. We can't talk to the detectives up in Yonkers right now. Let's get a better profile on this guy before we make our move. If, in fact, we do go up there, we'll have to have at least three or four men. So, I think we'll just wait until morning. Be in early and we'll pick up from there.'

"I went home to Staten Island," Strano says, "and woke my wife. She had been excited all week because I had come up with Cacilia Davis. It was early in the morning, after two-thirty. I told her what was happening and instructed her, 'Make sure you wake me up early, 'cause I have to be in work first thing in the morning.' "

"I decided Strano, Falotico, and I would go up to Yonkers in the morning," said Sergeant Shea. "We'd first speak to the Yonkers Police Department detectives, and from there go on to speak to Berkowitz himself. I was particularly interested in the psychological profile that was done on him, and also in ballistics evidence on the dog shooting he was suspected of doing. We'd have loved to have been able to compare that evidence to what we already had in the Moskowitz homicide and to try to cull any further information we could before we went to Berkowitz himself."

WEDNESDAY MORNING broke warm and clear for fifteen million inhabitants of the New York metropolitan area. By 8:00 A.M. the temperature had reached 73 degrees; the day would be abnormally hot. The *Post* would tell of the hardening Israeli position on yielding any territory to the Arabs. Each of New York's daily newspapers released the newest police sketch of the killer. The *Daily News* ran the Son of Sam picture full face with the word WANTED across the top of the edition in two-and-a-half-inch block letters.

The New York Times ran a smaller version of the same sketch in the lower left-hand portion of its front page.

The previous day's news of a bomb's being discovered in the Amex Building at 1270 Avenue of the Americas had been omitted. The building had been targeted by the Puerto Rican terrorist organization, FALN. Only a week before a bomb had exploded in another building, killing one man and injuring seven. But such news was merely temporary as the summer's heat turned the city's attention to baseball.

The day before, major league baseball had inducted six new members into the Hall of Fame in Cooperstown, New York. Selected for 1977 were Ernie Banks (a nineteen-year veteran of the Chicago Cubs), Al Lopez, Joe Sewell, Martin Dihigo, John Harry ("Pop") Lloyd, and Amos Russie. Lloyd and Dihigo were Negro League stars. Today Nino Espinosa would make the sports pages with his fine pitching performance against the Cards as the Mets would beat the team from St. Louis 4–2 on Reitz's homer in the last of the ninth inning.

Another story, of perhaps even greater interest to New York sports fans, was that Yankee catcher Thurman Munson had shaved off his eleven-day-old beard for the good of the team. The Yankees were at it once again; the fans loved it. Too bad the Bronx Bombers had another day off. The fans surely would have liked to see George Steinbrenner seated behind the Yankee dugout when Thurman came out to take his turn in the batting-practice cage. But tomorrow would come soon enough.

Tonight the Cosmos would open the North American Soccer League's playoff schedule with a game at Giants' Stadium in the Meadowlands against the Tampa Bay Rowdies. Yes, it was a summer to be remembered in the Big Apple.

JUST north of the city, David Berkowitz was sleeping late.

Rising at 1:00 P.M., David remained in his apartment, cleaning his guns. "Tonight they'd have me go out again. This time I'd take everything with me. I was ready, not necessarily to go back to the Hamptons, but to one of the discos in Riverdale."

David went to his car in the early afternoon and placed the duffel bag on the floor behind the front seat. Inside the bag were the automatic rifle, four clips fully loaded; an Ithaca Deerslayer 12-gauge pump-action shotgun, serial number 371494956; a Charter Arms AR-7 Explorer .22 rimfire semi-automatic rifle, serial number TN3-13-155; and a Glenfield Model 60 .22-caliber rifle, serial number 25444401, along with enough ammunition to fight an army.

He returned to his apartment and poured himself a glass of wine. "It was blackberry wine. That's one of my favorites," says David.

For the remainder of the day, David loaded and reloaded the .44 Bulldog. "Tonight was to be another night of hunting. The demons were getting restless. But it wasn't a day that anything was going to happen. I mean there'd be no killing that day, or that night. If there was going to be anything, I'd have been hyped up. But everything was cool. I was feeling good and just played around in the apartment all day."

IN THE APARTMENT below, Craig Glassman had returned from his job as a male nurse at Montefiore Hospital in the Bronx. He was tired and decided to sleep before doing his weekly apartment clean-up. Wednesday was his washday. Later in the afternoon he'd gather his week's wash and take the elevator to the building's basement where there was a bank of washing machines and dryers. "I could hear him pacing the floor upstairs," Glassman remembers.

Captain Borrelli spent the day at 10th Homicide in Brooklyn. But first he drove to the 109th to go over some paper work.

August 10 was a day off for Sergeant Joe Coffey. He spent it at his small Cape Cod-style house in Levittown, catching up on chores. The kids were home on summer vacation, and it gave the thirty-nine-year-old detective an opportunity to get to know them once again. "I had become a stranger to my own family. I was spending so much time on this case that I sometimes wondered if I'd miss my own house when I came home in the dark," he says.

Yonkers Patrolmen Chamberlain and Intervallo were both "taking days" (the police phrase for using accrued vacation time) that Wednesday. What was about to unfold at 35 Pine Street could have been half a world away. All through the day, neither officer was informed of anything. Chamberlain remembers, "After my conversation with the New York detective on the phone, it seemed that everyone forgot us. We had no idea what was happening. I don't think Pete or I thought for a moment that this was the day when it would all be over."

DEPUTY INSPECTOR DOWD shut himself up inside his office at the 109th in Queens. The press was barking at his heels, and he had nothing to tell them. The newest sketch of the killer would appear in the city's newspapers by early afternoon and he was bracing himself for the flood of calls that would tie up the Omega phones for hours. It was the same routine whenever the department released another composite. "Hundreds of people" had "just seen the killer." That meant forms had to be filled out and officers had to be assigned to check every one that had the remotest chance of being a true lead. Dowd hunched over his desk, working with the duty chart, trying to juggle the schedules of the three hundred men under his command.

AFTER THREE HOURS of restless sleep, Detective Joe Strano woke up at seven. He tiptoed to the bathroom and began to shave. In a minute, his wife was peering in, sleepy-eyed. "Okay, Joseph, why so early today?" she asked, already knowing the answer.

"Eileen, honey, today's it! I just know we'll get him today. I want to get Zaino out of the hotel and over to his body shop so I can be in on the arrest."

"And what if you're not?" she asked softly. She understood this was the most important arrest he'd ever have a chance to be part of.

The big, handsome Italian looked up at his wife in disbelief. "Are you kidding? I've broken this for them, me and Justus and Shea. They couldn't leave us out of it." He went back to his shaving, muttering under his breath. Eileen Strano hurried to the kitchen to make a pot of coffee. She'd try to catch him on the run with something hot. She knew he'd never sit down for a real breakfast.

Strano drove his 1970 brown station wagon to the Holiday Inn just this side of the giant bridge. He woke Tommy, relieved the officer who had guarded him that night, and quickly drove Zaino across the bridge.

Once inside the body shop he called Sergeant Shea. "I'm here," he said, "at Zaino's place. Now get me out. There's no one for me to leave him with." It took half an hour before Detective John Falotico arrived to relieve Strano.

Strano drove directly to the office, arriving a little after 10:00 A.M. "When I got back there, we still hadn't heard from Jimmy Justus. Poor Jimmy was stuck at the Grand Jury that day because one of his cases had finally hit the courts. No way he wanted to be stuck in court that day, not while this was coming down.

"I just knew that we were going to be sent up to Yonkers."

DETECTIVE JUSTUS kept calling back to the 10th at regular intervals. He knew he might be stuck in the Supreme Court Building in downtown Brooklyn for hours. "I told them I'd try to get out just as soon as possible and that I'd rush over to Robbery and pick up some of the guys. Then I'd run up to Yonkers. Shea told me that wouldn't be necessary, that they'd wait for me."

As soon as he completed his testimony, Justus drove back to his regular office in Brooklyn Robbery and grabbed his two partners, Detectives Irwin Vale and August Maurina, along with his supervisor, Sergeant Larry Ponsi. Then he called Shea at 10th Homicide. "Jimmy, I'm on my way."

"Don't bother. We've already sent two men to Yonkers to investigate," Shea said. "If anything develops, I'll get back to you." Justus stayed at Robbery.

He waited all day for a call that never came.

EVERYONE wanted to be in on the arrest. Shea's game plan was for him, Strano, Falotico, and whoever else he thought necessary to go up to Yonkers and put 35 Pine Street under surveillance. But at 11:00 A.M. a call came through from Borough Commander William Fitzpatrick's office to get a sample of the killer's clothing ready for the evening news. Shea protested, "I don't think it's going to be necessary, sir. It looks like things are ready to break here. If we can just have a few hours."

The voice at the other end insisted: "Break? Everyone is always saying things are ready to break. Meantime, the Chief wants that clothing."

"But the guy who's been trying to find the clothes is going to be on the stakeout," said Sergeant Shea. "I just can't pull him off to look for something that might not exist. He's spent the last couple of days searching all the fucking clothing stores in the borough, Captain Coleman."

"Well, if he can't find the stuff in Brooklyn, send him to the manufacturers in Manhattan. That's an order!" There was no room for argument. "And you stay put at the 10th, in case we have to get in touch with you. Coordinate everything from the squad room." Not only was Detective Strano taken out of the action, but now Sergeant Shea was ordered out, too.

At 12:20 P.M., Detective Eddie Zigo, fifty, walked into the office. Strano had left, and Shea was the only officer in the shop. He called Zigo over and began giving him a rundown on just what was developing. Zigo was familiar with the case, having worked with Falotico interviewing Tommy Zaino and in trying to find the mysterious summons. "Eddie, just as soon as I can get a couple of guys together, you're going up to Yonkers to see what's doing," said Shea. Zigo was working on another homicide at the time, but the 10th was short-handed.

"You want me to go there now?" Zigo asked.

"Not yet. You can't go alone. But, the very next guy who walks in the door goes up there with you."

Just at that moment, Detective John Longo, forty-nine, came through the door. He was carrying a large carton with containers of coffee and Danish for anyone who happened to be there. It was a tradition that the last guy in for the tour caught the coffee break. Longo placed the box on the center desk and looked around. "Hey, Eddie," he called to Zigo, "where the hell is everyone?"

The sound of Longo's voice brought Shea out of his office. "Listen, you guys," Shea said, taking a container of coffee out of the box and handing it to Longo. "Be like Kojak. Drink this vile stuff in the car while you're driving."

The detective looked at his sergeant, not knowing what was going on. "Hey, Sarge, I got this . . ."

"Look," interrupted Shea, "you and Eddie get your tails out of here. He'll explain what we think we have. Better take a couple of containers and the Danish. It's probably all you're going to have to eat for a while. And remember," he directed this at Zigo, "I must have the ballistic evidence if possible. If the Yonkers cops have one of the slugs from the dog [they did not], get it back to me immediately." The two officers began to leave, but Shea stopped them. "When you have everything set up, the layout and the surveillance at his place, one of you try to spot that yellow Galaxie. As soon as you have the whole picture, with the car, call in."

Carrying containers of coffee—like television detectives —plus the assorted Danish pastries to tide them through surveillance, Longo and Zigo hurried downstairs to their unmarked car.

Before driving off, they checked their guns.

JOE STRANO had cursed the order that sent him to Manhattan. He went directly to the West Side offices of Faded Glory, at 411 Broadway, and the trip from the 10th to Manhattan and back ate up more than three hours. He found a jacket that was similar to but not exactly like the one Mrs. Davis had described. He arrived back at the 10th Homicide at 3:30 P.M. "I was surprised to find Jimmy Shea still there," he said. "I thought for sure he'd be up in Yonkers by then."

A few minutes later, a young woman entered the office. She had called earlier about being chased by a car near Shore Parkway a few hours before the Moskowitz–Violante shootings. Sergeant Shea had just begun to question her when Lieutenant John McCarthy, who was substituting for the vacationing regular zone commander, appeared at the doorway and motioned for the sergeant to come outside. Sergeant Shea turned to the young woman and said, "Go along with Detective Strano. He'll get you a cup of coffee out in the hallway."

The lieutenant whispered, "Come here, Jimmy. We got to get on the phone. There's something happening."

McCarthy, forty-two, trim and well-groomed, led Shea to a bleak office barely large enough for a desk, typewriter, and file cabinet. He shut the door. Eddie Zigo was on the line from Yonkers.

The lieutenant and the sergeant each picked up a phone.

"Lieutenant," Zigo's voice was slow and professional. "We've got him."

The two officers looked at each other. Zigo had been instructed to keep the area under watch, not to take action. "What the hell do you mean, Eddie?" questioned Shea.

"Jimmy, I found the car. It's sitting just down the block from his apartment house."

"So?"

"So I went up to it and looked in. Just behind the front seat is an Army duffel bag with his name on it, and a machine gun sticking out."

"A machine gun? Are you sure?" asked the lieutenant.

"Sure I am. The rear door was open, and I went inside."

Sergeant Shea called out, "Eddie, why the hell did you do that? I told you to look for the car, not to enter it." Shea understood that evidence acquired from an illegal search of a suspect's car is inadmissible in court.

"But it was open," said Zigo again.

McCarthy took the lead. "Ed, you get yourself away from that car and don't touch anything else. Give me the number of the phone you're at and we'll call you back in a few minutes."

McCarthy dialed the number for Borough Commander William Fitzpatrick. Both he and Shea provided a complete rundown of the situation in Yonkers. Fitzpatrick said, "Get some more men up there right away. Tell Zigo not to do anything else unless his suspect decides to make a run for it. I'm going to get on the phone to Chief Keenan. I'll pass on his orders to you."

McCarthy left the room for his own office. Shea called Zigo in the phone booth in Yonkers. "Eddie, Fitzpatrick says you aren't to do anything until we get some more men up there. I'm sure there'll be some brass showing up within the hour. In the meantime, keep his car under surveillance, and see to it that he doesn't escape."

BACK in the Chief of Detectives' Office on the thirteenth floor of One Police Plaza, the phones were ringing. Borough Commander Fitzpatrick immediately told Chief Keenan "This Berkowitz character is the one that had the ticket written to him the night of the Moskowitz shooting. The squad commander at the 10th, a Sergeant Shea, sent two of his men up to Yonkers to investigate. And one of them found the guy's car. Guess what was in the back seat . . . a goddamn machine gun. I think the 10th's got him."

Chief of Detectives Keenan thought for a moment, then issued his orders to Fitzpatrick to be passed on to the 10th: "Tell whoever's in command in Brooklyn to get some more men to the scene as fast as he can. Let the Lieutenant and the Sergeant stay put at their office so I can get in touch with them if I need to. Let them get another sergeant to go along with the detectives he sends up to Yonkers.

"In the meantime, Bill, I'll take care of legal over here, then I'm going to Queens to pick up Timmy Dowd, and together we'll get up to Yonkers. You can send someone to represent you."

The orders were passed to the 10th, then in turn to Eddie Zigo, who was glued to the pay phone in the 85-degree heat and 80-plus humidity of the day. "Sarge, when the hell are we going to move in on him? He's our guy. We just can't sit on him forever."

"Eddie, it comes right from the Chief himself. Sit and wait. Don't force anything. I'm going to send up some more men. Some of the brass is bound to show up also. You'll get your orders soon enough." With that, Detective Zigo returned to his partner, Johnny Longo. He told Longo what he'd been ordered to do, and the detectives returned to their car at the head of Pine Street, where they could keep the building's entrance and their suspect's car in full view.

DETECTIVE JOHN FALOTICO had to wait until 3:30 P.M. before he was relieved at Zaino's body shop. Then Falotico got into his Chevy sedan and drove the two miles back to the 10th. "I remember leaving my sports jacket in my car, and I put my revolver into my pocket," he says. "Then I went into the precinct. All I was going to do was to run upstairs, sign out, and get home to a cool shower. But when I got upstairs, everyone was running around, hitting the phones, and tracing routes on street maps. I hadn't gotten to my desk when Sergeant Shea grabbed my arm and said, 'John, I think it's important you get in on this. Things are beginning to happen in Yonkers.'"

Sergeant William Gardella and Detective Charlie Higgins had come in early for their 4:00 P.M. tour and were briefed by Shea. "Hey," called out Billy Gardella, thirty-four, to Falotico, "get your coat and come on with us."

"If it's as good as it sounds," called back Falotico, "to hell with my coat."

"It's as good as it sounds," answered Gardella, who was getting last-minute instructions from Sergeant Shea. The three detectives, Gardella, Higgins, and Falotico, headed for the stairway. "This explains," Falotico points out, "why in photographs of Berkowitz's capture, I appear in a short-sleeved shirt, without a jacket."

It took an hour and forty-five minutes to drive to Pine Street. The three detectives were caught in a routine summer's traffic jam on Manhattan's East River Drive. "For some reason," explains Falotico, "Higgins had chosen the worst possible route, considering the time of day. But, when you look at a street map, Pine Street is right on the most western portion of Yonkers. It's right up against the Hudson River. I guess Charlie thought we'd make time through traffic with our siren and light. We didn't."

IT WAS NEARLY 6:00 P.M. when the battered blue squad car containing Gardella, Higgins, and Falotico pulled up to the head of Pine and Glenwood. Standing next to Eddie Zigo's car was Deputy Inspector Bernard McRann, fifty-eight; his assistant, Captain Harold Coleman; and Detectives Zigo and Longo of 10th Homicide. McRann and Coleman were about to drive to Yonkers Police Department headquarters to meet with Chief of Detectives Keenan and Deputy Inspector Dowd when the Brooklyn detectives piled out of their car. The group walked a dozen steps down Glenwood so that they couldn't be seen from the Pine Street entrance.

"Okay, Gardella," instructed McRann, "you're in charge. Stake out the Ford with the three detectives you've got. Zigo's coming with me. If anyone tries to use the car, place him under arrest, then call the Chief. He should be at Yonkers headquarters in the next fifteen minutes."

The veteran Inspector then turned to Detective Zigo. "Eddie, you've got to come with me to Yonkers headquarters. Join up with one of our lawyers, find a Yonkers judge, and swear out a search warrant."

Zigo objected for a moment. When and if the arrest went down, he wanted to be at the scene. But he also knew the importance of the search warrant and a direct order, so he returned to the Inspector's car and waited for McRann to finish.

The remaining six men stood in a group for a few minutes discussing the legality of simply picking up someone off the street without a warrant. "If he just walks to the car, we really can't arrest him," commented Falotico.

McRann countered, "Look, we have the right to take anyone in for questioning. Let's use that until a warrant is drawn. Let's pick him up first, then let the lawyers battle it out."

None of the New York cops knew where Yonkers police headquarters was, thus no one knew when Eddie Zigo would return. Inspector McRann was leaving the team of four detectives to stake out a big apartment house, with a wooded area to its rear and a street that ran down toward them and then curved up to the left. The escape possibilities were enormous. The force was absurdly small.

"Okay," Gardella said. "So it's four of us to do everything, and we're not even sure he's in there. Let's assume that he is, since his car is there."

Higgins tried a joke to break the tension. "Well, Sarge, if you're not sure, why don't you just walk up to his apartment and knock on the door?" The other guys didn't laugh. This was dangerous business, and it was entirely possible that someone might have to do just that. No one liked the idea.

"All right," answered Gardella, fifteen years younger than the men he was commanding, "we have to cover the building first. Charlie and John, you guys get to the roof with a walkie-talkie. But first, John, I want you to put your vehicle at the end of the street so as to cut off any means of escape if we can't get him before he pulls the car out." At that moment, a Yonkers Police Department cruiser came down Glenwood and made a left onto Pine Street. The four New York City detectives watched in disbelief as the white vehicle came to a stop directly in front of 35 Pine Street, a tall uniformed officer getting out with a shopping bag in his hand.

"What the hell is he doing there?" questioned Sergeant Gardella, echoing their combined thoughts. The officer was taking a normal meal break at a friend's apartment at 35 Pine Street.

Gardella ran back to his car and frantically called New York City Police Detective headquarters on the detective band. He requested that they relay a message to the Yonkers Police Department to "Get the cruiser out of the way."

"It was touch and go for at least ten minutes," remembers Falotico. "If Berkowitz had come out then, he'd know something was up. Suddenly the Yonkers cop came running out of the apartment house and started up the cruiser. "We could see him looking around, then he drove away."

The detectives didn't know if the Berkowitz apartment was in the front or in the rear. Had their man seen the police cruiser, or had he missed it? Was he home, or away?

AT 7:35 P.M. the group of New York City cops was spreading out. Higgins was going to move his car to where Gardella had ordered him to. After the vehicle was in place, he and his partner would move cautiously to the roof of 35 Pine. Sergeant Gardella and Detective Falotico had walked back to their car and were settling in at the head of the street from where they could scan the entire block. The late summer light was beginning to fade.

At that moment, a heavy-set white male walked out of the stone-and-glass entrance of 35 Pine Street. He went up the two concrete steps that brought him to street level, stopped, then turned north and began to walk in the direction of the officers and the Ford Galaxie.

Instantly, Gardella and Falotico slid out of their car and began to run toward the man. Falotico was in the street, having gotten out from behind the wheel; Gardella was on the sidewalk. The suspect's car was forty-five yards away and they kept to the cover of the parked vehicles as they ran. Higgins and Longo immediately drew their guns and covered their partners.

Midway down the street, Falotico drew his gun from his pocket and shielded it by holding it against his body. A muscular man with broad shoulders, he turned the trot into a sprint. Their suspect had looked into the car, then had turned away. Apparently the man was going back to the apartment house. The officers were committed. It was too late to turn back now.

"Just a minute, Dave," Falotico said. It was an old police ploy. Call a suspect by name, and if he's the one you're after, he'll turn around.

The man turned. He looked surprised.

"David, stay where you are," Falotico instructed.

"I'm not David," the man responded.

Falotico remembers feeling his heart thump. After all this, was he holding the gun on the wrong man? "If you're not Dave, show me who you are." Falotico's unmistakably Brooklynese voice rose in menace. "Slowly."

"Are you the police?"

"Yes, we're the police. Stand where you are. Don't move your hands."

"Hey, I'm one too!"

"Identify yourself."

"I'm with the Westchester Sheriff's Department. I'm a Deputy Sheriff." Craig Glassman slowly pulled a shield from his left hip pocket. He held his other hand away from his body to make it clear to the four officers that he was not reaching for a gun.

"Are you guys here about the fire? I live in the apartment right below David Berkowitz," Glassman continued. "He's home now. I heard him walking around. You can go in and get him. He's there."

"No, we don't want to yet," answered Gardella. The police were still waiting for a warrant. They took Glassman's arm and ushered him up Pine Street toward Glenwood.

"Hey, I was the one he tried to burn out," explained Glassman. "I filed a harassment complaint against him. Is that why you guys are here?" Again they didn't answer him.

"If Berkowitz had come out during that period," Falotico says, "it could have blown everything. He might have gotten panicky and begun to shoot. Who knows what would have happened?"

By this time, residents and passersby were aware that something involving police was happening on Pine Street. The cops had made a scene running down the block with their guns drawn, then walking back with Glassman. The street was taking on a carnival attitude. People were bringing out aluminum beach chairs and sitting on their porches watching. Young boys gathered at the intersection of Glenwood and Pine watching the questioning of Glassman. Word was spreading like wildfire: "The cops are going to arrest someone."

"Can I do anything for you guys?" Glassman said.

"Just go back home," Gardella said, "and go about your

normal routine." Glassman was instructed specifically not to go upstairs to the Berkowitz apartment or to do anything that might tip off the suspect that the police were there. He returned to his own apartment and decided to do his laundry. Life goes on, he thought. He took two pillow cases full of laundry to the basement and loaded two machines. An unsettling idea struck him. There were only four detectives watching the building. But the building had *seven* exits.

He removed his dirty laundry from the machines, took it back to his apartment, changed into Bermuda shorts, and walked out onto Pine Street once again. It was 9:00 P.M.

At that moment a blue van pulled into the parking spot directly behind Berkowitz's car. Detective Falotico got out of the unmarked police car and walked to the van. The driver was still inside, gathering some packages, when the detective approached. Falotico flashed his shield and said "Hey, we're working on something here. Would you mind giving us a hand?"

"Sure," the surprised man answered. "What can I do?"

"Just release the brake and roll against the car in front of you."

"That's all?"

"Yeah, thanks," said the detective.

With the van against the rear bumper of the Galaxie, and with just ten inches separating the front of Berkowitz's car from the Buick parked in front, he was locked in.

The crowd was dispersing. After an hour, there had been no action. Adults went into their homes. Young people drifted toward nearby Trevor Park on the Hudson River to seek relief from the heat. Glassman was not yet sure just why the police were there, or even that they weren't Yonkers detectives, but he certainly did not want Berkowitz to escape.

When Glassman reached Sergeant Gardella's car, only two officers remained. Higgins and Longo had entered 35 Pine and had made their way to the roof.

"Sergeant, I don't think you know it, but there are seven

exits from my building," Glassman said, leaning on the passenger-side door. "You know, there's one that leads out the back across the courtyard and onto Wicker Street."

Gardella turned to Falotico. The detectives looked at each other. Then Gardella spoke to Glassman. "Do me a favor. Watch that area from inside the building. I'm going to call for backups."

As an auxiliary deputy sheriff, Glassman needed specific authorization from the Under-Sheriff to go on duty, even in an emergency. The detectives told him to return to his apartment again, to phone White Plains for authorization. When he reentered Pine Street this time, at 9:45 P.M. he had his 9-mm automatic tucked behind his right hip, under a shirt that hung down over his Bermuda shorts.

Falotico wanted Glassman off the street, believing that Longo and Higgins could cover the rear of the apartment house from their position on the roof, and he told the auxiliary sheriff to hop into the rear seat of the police car. At that moment a message crackled over the special detective band on the second radio all New York City Detective Bureau cars have: "Shots fired, 334 East 28th Street." Glassman looked shocked. "You mean you guys aren't Yonkers cops?"

"No, we're not," replied Sergeant Gardella.

"Then why are you after . . . ?" It suddenly dawned on him. "You mean the Son of Sam is Berkowitz?"

At this moment, at precisely 10:00 P.M., a heavy, shuffling figure emerged from the entrance of 35 Pine and started toward the yellow Ford Galaxie.

"Is he Berkowitz?" Falotico snapped.

"I don't know," Glassman said.

"What the hell do you mean, you don't know?"

"Look, I've only actually seen Berkowitz once."

"When was that?"

"This morning when I was going to work. I was on High Street and drove past someone in the yellow Ford. I'm just not sure."

The three men studied the suspect. He was walking

slowly, looking at the flowers that grew on the bushes alongside the fence outside the apartment building. In his left hand he was carrying a small package, possibly a paper bag. It was folded up tight, almost into a triangular shape. That familiar shape rang a bell with Falotico. "Policemen sometimes carry their guns to work in a paper bag during the summer when it's too hot to wear a jacket. When you wrap the paper around the gun, it takes on a triangular shape.

"Hey, Billy, see the paper bag. He could have a gun in there." Gardella was thinking the same thing.

Falotico remembered Tommy Zaino's description of how the killer ran back to the park after firing into the Violante car. "He kind of shuffled his feet along. It wasn't like someone normally runs. His feet kind of never left the ground."

Glassman sat silently in the left rear passenger seat. His eyes followed the heavy figure, dressed in a denim jacket, as the suspect walked slowly toward the parked Galaxie. He walked around the front of the car, squeezing through the narrow opening between the front bumper and the car just ahead, and reached the driver's door. He groped for the car key.

"The warrant," Falotico thought, as he sat straight up. "We have the guy in front of us, but we don't have the goddamn warrant. Where the hell is Eddie?"

The suspect opened the door, threw the triangular package onto the front seat, then rolled down the driver's window.

The hell with the damn warrant.

"Let's go!" Falotico yelled.

"Stay where you are," Gardella told Glassman, who was ready to get out of the rear seat.

The officers slid out of their seats and began running down the sloping street on the sidewalk. They were shielded from Berkowitz's view by the van.

Falotico glanced at Gardella. Billy had his pistol out, holding it up against his shoulder, muzzle pointed to the sky. Falotico's revolver was in his pocket. His hand grasped it, but he didn't bring it out.

In the Ford, David's fingers stroked the paper bag containing the loaded .44 Bulldog. "It wasn't a good night for hunting," remembers the Son of Sam. "If it were, I'd have been more agitated. They never would have been able to sneak up on me if things had been right for hunting."

He started the car, never noticing the approaching men. David sat back, breathing in the night air. It was a change from the trapped humid atmosphere he had created for himself by placing the blankets over the windows in his seventh floor apartment.

As the detectives neared the car, Falotico darted into the street, approaching the driver from the rear.

"The police method of covering a car," Falotico says, "is to approach the right rear side first. That's right rear of the passenger's side. The driver can't see you in his rear-view mirror. It's his blind side."

Gardella reached the right side of the rear window and brought the barrel of his .38 to bear on the suspect's head. He rapped the muzzle against the glass and shouted "*Freeze . . . Freeze. Police.*"

Falotico took the gun out of his pants pocket, then moved about a yard away from the left side of the car. That way he couldn't get hit by the driver's door if the suspect opened it suddenly. "I had my pistol pointed at his temple."

If the suspect had moved a hand toward the bag that lay on the seat next to him, Falotico and Gardella say they would have fired. Then the suspect, like the victims, would have died in an explosion of blood and shattered glass. "My finger was pressing the trigger, but he wasn't moving," says Falotico.

"I was watching his head for any sudden movement," remembers Gardella. "That feeling of life and death is something indescribable. You'd have to be a deer hunter and a poet to put it into words, and I'm not either."

The suspect moved his head toward the direction of Gardella's voice. His eyes struck the detective, then he turned back toward Falotico. "The guy just turned around and smiled at us," says Falotico. "He had that stupid smile on his face, like it was all a kid's game."

The suspect's hands remained on the steering wheel. He continued to smile—although two guns were pointing at his head. He didn't move. Falotico remembers the sound of the engine idling, then hearing heavy footsteps. He glanced up the street and saw Glassman lumbering at him, gun in hand. "Let me take care of it," he yelled, "I'll handle it!" Falotico shoved him aside. Glassman regained his balance and backed off, his gun pointing at the detective's back.

The suspect watched the drama unfold as if he was a spectator. He never stopped smiling.

Gardella had continued to aim his gun at the suspect's head. Falotico now turned his full attention back to the car. Holding his Smith & Wesson .38 revolver with both hands, he shoved it through the open window until it was six inches from the smiling suspect's nose.

"Dave," Falotico said in a soft slow voice, "you just follow my directions and you won't get hurt."

The suspect continued to smile in a moronic manner. Hell, Falotico thought. I don't have a killer here. I have some sort of clown. This guy keeps smiling with a .38 up his nose.

"I'm going to open the car door, Dave," Falotico said. "I'm going to ask you to do everything very slowly.

"Now keep your hands on the steering wheel. Don't let them slip off. I want both your feet to slide out of the car and touch the pavement.

"Now come out of the car, hands outstretched." Falotico placed his left hand in the small of the suspect's back and turned him around. "Now, put your palms on the roof of the car." Falotico then used his foot to kick the suspect's feet back and apart. This left the suspect off balance and relatively harmless.

Sergeant Gardella came around the car. He held his gun on the suspect from one side, Falotico from the other. Falotico gave the suspect a quick patdown. He seemed to be unarmed. The .44 was still inside the Ford, wrapped in the paper bag.

Falotico reached into his rear pocket and took out his walkie-talkie. He called to Higgins and Longo, who were still on the roof, watching the rear fire escapes and yard. They were unaware of what had happened in the street below. The detective couldn't make contact with them. For some reason, the transceiver went on the blink.

Frustrated, Falotico turned his attention back to his suspect.

It was 10:08 P.M. "Now that I've got you," Falotico said to the suspect, "who have I got?"

"You know," the suspect said in what Falotico remembers as a soft, almost sweet voice.

"No, I don't. You tell me."

David turned his head and looked at the middle-aged Italian detective. His face had that same childlike smile on it. "I'm Sam."

"You're Sam? Sam who?"

"Sam. Dave Berkowitz."

"It was then that I knew. I mean I knew for sure. This guy was not a clown. He was the Son of Sam. I'd just caught the Son of Sam."

"Do you own this car?" asked Falotico. He was trying to stay calm. "Let me see your driver's license and registration."

David reached into his pants pocket and took out an old beaten leather wallet. He opened it. His license and registration were right on top. He handed the pieces of paper to the waiting detective, who had placed his pistol back in his pocket.

"I looked at the name. It said David Berkowitz. I knew at that point I had the owner of the car. My instructions from Jimmy Shea and from Inspector McRann were to take the owner of the car into custody if he attempted to leave."

Falotico nodded toward Sergeant Gardella and he said, "I think we have our guy, Billy."

Falotico took Berkowitz's wallet and placed it in his own pocket. He then reached out and took Gardella's handcuffs and snapped them onto Berkowitz's wrists, behind his back. The two detectives led their man back to the sergeant's car, followed by Craig Glassman. As they walked, Gardella read the suspect his rights. The street was empty.

It was 10:20 P.M., Wednesday, August 10, 1977. Thirteen days, twelve months, and five deaths after the murder of Donna Lauria, the police at last had their man.

The arrest warrant still hadn't arrived.

GARDELLA decided that he and Longo would stay on Pine Street "to guard the car and apartment." Falotico and Higgins would take the prisoner to Yonkers police headquarters.

"How the hell am I going to get there?" Falotico asked. "We got here by pure luck. I haven't any idea where their headquarters is." He turned to Glassman, who stood outside the huddle of detectives, "Hey, Craig, you know where Yonkers headquarters is?"

"Yeah, I'll take you there."

Falotico slipped into the rear seat of the car alongside Berkowitz. Glassman climbed into the front seat next to Detective Charlie Higgins, who would drive. The car pulled out onto Pine Street with Glassman giving directions to Higgins.

Gardella told Longo to secure the apartment, while he would look after the car. Gardella pulled the police car alongside the Galaxie and called back to City headquarters on the special detective band. "We got the suspect in custody," he said. "Two detectives are now en route to Yonkers PD. Please inform Yonkers and the Chief that they should be arriving within ten minutes."

Almost immediately, a detective at One Police Plaza picked up the phone and relayed the message to Yonkers headquarters. The detective band in Gardella's car was only tuned to New York City frequencies. Any message for Chief of Detectives Keenan would have to be made by phone.

At Yonkers police headquarters, the message was received by Chief Keenan, Deputy Inspector Dowd, and their entourage. Keenan was concerned that everyone stay calm so as not to violate the rights of the prisoner when he arrived. He was further concerned as Detectives Shilenski and Zigo still hadn't returned with the search warrant or an arrest warrant.

AS THE POLICE CAR began its two-mile drive to headquarters on St. Casimir Avenue, Craig Glassman turned around from his position in the front passenger's seat. "Do you know me?" he asked.

"Sure I do," answered the smiling prisoner. "You're Craig."

Glassman began to speak to Berkowitz. "I'm the guy whose door you set afire."

Falotico interjected himself into the conversation, "Okay, let's all of us be quiet." Before he'd allow any further conversation, Falotico was going to read his prisoner his rights for a second time.

When he finished, David indicated that he understood. "I'll tell you guys anything you want to know. I don't have anything to hide."

Glassman turned around once again. "Why me, Berkowitz? I didn't even know you."

David just kept on smiling, looking out the side window at the passing streets, and smiling. He reminded Falotico of a child on holiday. "Craig, you're one of them. I knew you were there the whole time."

"Okay, I said stop it, you two!" Falotico said in a strong voice. "Let's be quiet until we get to police headquarters. Craig, how much further?"

Glassman glanced out the windshield, then said, "Turn right at the next corner, and it's midway up the block on the left."

Detective Higgins slowed as he came to the side parking lot of Yonkers police headquarters. The lot was already filled. Officers were standing at the entrance, directing traffic through to the rear.

When the car bumped over the curb, Higgins hung his head out and shouted, "We've got him in here. Where do we go?"

It was as if an electric spark hit the air. Everyone ran forward to peer into the police car. Falotico could see a sprinkling of familiar faces in the growing crowd. Cameras were pushed forward. Strobes flashed. In less than half an hour since the arrest, the newspapers and television people sent whoever was in the office to cover the most sensational arrest in the history of New York.

A Yonkers uniformed officer motioned the car to the rear parking lot. The lot was ringed with policemen. Higgins gunned the engine and the car leapt forward. He brought the car to a halt in the center of the lot. Everyone sat still, Berkowitz included, not knowing if they should get out or remain inside the car for the ride back to the City. In a moment Falotico spotted a tall, thin man approaching the car from the building's rear entrance. "I immediately recognized him as being Deputy Inspector Timothy Dowd, Commander of Omega Force."

IT HAD BEEN Chief Keenan's plan to have Inspector Dowd approach the car alone. He believed that the Son of Sam would surely recognize the Inspector, for Dowd's picture had been in the newspapers and on television often during the past five months. Keenan chose to remain in the building so as not to confuse the suspect.

As Dowd walked the twenty yards between the car and the building entrance, the four men in the car got out. They were standing together, Falotico's hand wrapped around Berkowitz's right arm. As the Inspector approached, Falotico called: "Inspector, there's someone I'd like you to meet."

Dowd walked directly to Berkowitz.

"Hello, Inspector Dowd," Berkowitz said.

The Inspector seemed stunned by Berkowitz's greeting. He had expected something entirely different. "He wasn't afraid and didn't look the part," said Dowd. Instead, he was being greeted by someone who seemed to be enjoying everything. Dowd then asked, "You know me?," his voice almost breaking.

"Yeah," Berkowitz said. "I've seen you on television and in the papers."

Dowd turned to Falotico. "Is this the one we've been looking for?"

"I believe so, Inspector," Falotico answered.

"Well, then. Before we get inside, I want to talk to him for a couple of minutes. I'll have lots of questions to answer to the press. I have some questions of my own."

Dowd took Berkowitz to one side and began speaking to him: "Why? Why did you go to Brooklyn two weeks ago?"

Berkowitz looked at him smiling. "Because. . . ." It was an answer a kindergartener gives when he really doesn't have one. The Inspector followed up with some specific questioning on key facts of the Voskerichian killing (her clothes), the Suriani–Esau shooting (the location of the Parkway), and the Moskowitz–Violante shootings (the layout of the park). When he was finished, Dowd motioned to the detectives to come and take their man.

"It's him," Dowd said, and he turned and led them into the building. All the hate had left him in the few minutes he spent alone with Berkowitz. He had expected to confront a killer. Instead he found a small boy.

INSIDE YONKERS police headquarters, Chief Keenan took charge. An initial statement from David was taken by Dowd and Falotico, with Keenan supervising. "We made a complete rundown of each shooting incident, paying special attention to each of the five that resulted in deaths. It was amazing. He had total recall of each incident."

Dowd didn't have too much on the one in Brooklyn. Falotico knew it from beginning to end.

David knew it better.

THE MAYOR of the City of New York had gone to bed early. Deep in sleep, he heard the incessant ring of the private line next to his bed. He reached for the phone. It was the Police Department's Deputy Commissioner for Public Information, Frank McLaughlin. "Mayor," he said excitedly, "we got him!"

"Who?" questioned the half-asleep Mayor.

"Him. The Son of Sam. The detectives have him in custody."

Beame sat up, waking his wife with his left hand. "Mary, get up. They've captured the Son of Sam," he shouted.

"I thought it was tremendous news," Beame says today. "I don't think I have a recollection of anything happening during my administration, one single thing, which at the moment gave me the kind of wonderful feeling that this did. Sure, there were things which, spread over a little time cumulatively may have been very important. But this one . . . really!"

DETECTIVE MARLIN HOPKINS was dead-tired. He went to bed at 10:00 P.M., but kept the television on. By 1:00 A.M. he was still watching the late movie. His eyes began to close and he turned off the set just before a flash bulletin began running across the bottom of the screen.

"I closed my eyes and began to doze off. Within five minutes the phone began to ring. I picked it up and a voice came over the line asking if I was Detective Hopkins."

Marlin cupped the phone with his hand, trying not to wake his wife. "Yeah, I'm Hopkins."

"Report to the Chief of Detectives' Office. The Son of Sam has been captured." The line went dead.

The detective froze. "I couldn't talk. Maybe it was a crank call, or something. I had never even given his capture any real thought." Months and months had been spent looking. Capture had seemed such a remote possibility. "It just didn't register. I couldn't believe it. I was in a daze. It was like the end of a movie, and I couldn't believe it."

YONKERS PATROLMAN TOM CHAMBERLAIN got a phone call from Wheat Carr at his home at 10:00 P.M. "Tom, they've got the apartment house staked out. The arrest is probably happening right now.'' That call served to confirm what he and his partner had suspected for the past week. David Berkowitz was the Son of Sam.

"I turned on the television and sat glued to it, waiting for a flash. In the meantime, calls kept coming in to me from guys at headquarters. Everyone was telling me that our suspicions were right. But I kept waiting for the news.

"When it flashed across the screen, tears came to my eyes. Jesus. We were right all along, and it had paid off.

"It was a hell of a night."

Any tears of joy, Tom?

"No, just a sense of relief."

"I REMEMBER my first reaction," says Officer Pete Intervallo. "Tommy called and told me that Wheat had called him telling him the arrest was going down. I remember saying, 'Well, then, I guess it's over. It's got to be him, Tommy.' '' He then hung up the telephone and watched television, as did the majority of officers involved in the case.

He recalls the exact words that came over the screen: NEW YORK CITY POLICE HAVE JUST ARRESTED A SUSPECT IN THE SON OF SAM MURDERS. "I remember I looked at the screen and tears began coming to my eyes. I cried like a baby, I just cried and cried. At that point I didn't care that it wasn't me who made the arrest. It didn't matter. Tommy and I were right, and Berkowitz couldn't hurt anyone else."

AT THE MOMENT Pete Intervallo was watching the bulletin flash across the television in Westchester, Tommy Zaino and his police bodyguard saw the same bulletin in the lounge at the Holiday Inn in Staten Island. "I remember reading the words, then the glass I was holding fell out of my hands and shattered on the floor."

The detective with him pulled him out of his seat, and together they ran to the nearest phone. "I couldn't believe it until the detective told me softly 'Tommy, you can go home tonight.' ''

CAPTAIN JOSEPH BORRELLI had remained at the 10th when Strano and Shea left at 9:00 P.M. with Detective Frank Rossi. They had put in a long fruitless day and had no idea about what was happening in Yonkers. Borrelli stayed to man the phones and was the first to hear of the arrest.

"Everyone was gone," he remembers. "There was no one to tell, so I just yelled. I had to let it all out. It was a great feeling. The greatest!

"I headed to my car about 12:20 to drive into Manhattan to police headquarters. All the way my heart was pumping. I knew he'd been captured, and there was no one to talk to. It was something that kept building inside me until I felt like I was going to burst. Damn, I was so proud of those guys."

STRANO, ROSSI, AND SHEA had gone for dinner to an Italian restaurant two blocks off the water in Coney Island. It had charm and the owners treated the detectives like members of the family.

When they got there, Sergeant Shea saw a friend of his with a copy of the *Daily News* under his arm. He called out to him "Don't be too surprised if the headlines on that paper aren't changed by morning."

At midnight the little group broke up; Shea went home, Detectives Rossi and Strano returned to the precinct to get Strano's car. Strano got in and drove off; Frank Rossi went upstairs.

Rossi got the news first from the Chief's office. "I ran to the phone and called Joe and Jimmy's homes. I knew they wouldn't be home yet, but I just couldn't wait. I left messages that they had to call back just as soon as they got in."

When Jimmy Shea walked into his house, his wife Betty told him Frank Rossi had called, and that he was to call back immediately. "I knew what it was. They had made the arrest up in Yonkers. Thank God it was all over.

"I stayed up talking to my wife and my eldest, Carol Ann. We were all too excited to go to bed."

Detective Strano drove leisurely back over the Verrazano Narrows Bridge without putting on the car's radio. "I was feeling depressed because I knew it was going to be over without me being there.

"When I pulled into the driveway I found that everyone was waiting for me. My wife and cousins were on the lawn. I told them that I thought things would finally break some time tonight and went inside. As the front door closed behind me the phone began to ring. I raced for the receiver and held it to my ear. It was Frank Rossi back at the 10th.

"Get to a TV," he shouted. "They got him!"

"I shouted out to the people on the lawn, '*They got him! They got him!*' There was a moment of silence and then everyone came through the door laughing . . . and crying. The tension was over. No matter how it happened, it didn't matter. It was over. I fought back the tears."

The newspapers the next day carried banner headlines.

CAUGHT, headlined the *New York Post* in big red letters. (That day's *Post* sold 350,000 extra copies.)

SUSPECT IN 'SON OF SAM' MURDERS ARRESTED IN YONKERS: POLICE SAY .44-CALIBER WEAPON IS RECOVERED announced *The New York Times*. Berkowitz had the most powerful newspaper in the world pushing the story of the Middle East peace talks to column four.

The *Daily News* ran the story across its entire front page.

THE HUNT was over. It was safe again for young people to walk the streets, for couples to neck in cars.

"It had to come to an end. They had used me, the demons. They always used people. Now they'd have to find someone else to do those things. I was happy it was over. Believe me, I was happy," said the Son of Sam.

Yolanda Voskerichian, Virginia's mother, summed up for all the victims, for all the families, for all the city: "It was good that finally he was caught. It couldn't go on, it just couldn't go on."

SERGEANT JOSEPH COFFEY was home when the arrest was made in Yonkers. At 11:06 P.M. a call came from the Chief's office. "Joe Coffey?" asked an excited voice on the other end of the line.

"Yes, I'm Coffey."

"Joe," said the detective, "Brooklyn's got a guy up in Yonkers who looks like he could be your killer." Before he could answer, the detective at One Police Plaza hung up. That was the extent of the conversation.

Coffey kept seated for a moment, then called out to his wife. "Pat, it's over. They got him."

"Got who?" she asked.

"Him . . . the .44."

Coffey began to dress, all the while thinking to himself "I hope so. But it wasn't definite and I've had other suspects turn out to be something else. It's something you can't be certain of."

Coffey hurried out of the house and drove to police headquarters, knowing that sooner or later he'd be needed. "I was one of the few people who had the investigation from day one and knew all the facts. I knew the circumstance of each shooting, the descriptions, the sites and everything else necessary for interrogation." When he arrived at the thirteenth-floor office of the Chief of Detectives, he was ordered to interview the suspect. He stood outside the Chief's conference room trying to compose himself before entering.

"I stood there, hands together. I wanted to kill this guy on the spot. I was that much involved. Then I walked into the room."

The room was painted a sterile police-department beige. It was furnished with gray metal chairs with alternate gray, blue, and green cushions. At the far wall were a series of high, sealed windows that looked out at the Municipal Building. Coffey could see lights moving slowly on the street below. Ahead was the suspect, seated facing away from the sergeant, toward the windows. Berkowitz was handcuffed to the chair. Next to him was Detective Jimmy Fox, who was assigned to provide security for the prisoner.

Berkowitz turned around and faced Coffey. "God!" thought Coffey. "He looks just like I knew he would." The sergeant's eyes and Berkowitz's met. They stared at each other for a moment. Then Berkowitz smiled. Coffey had to calm down. He walked to the nearest window and looked out at the Federal House of Detention. He tried to pick out moving cars. Anything to get his mind off Berkowitz, off his emotions.

In a couple of minutes he calmed down, and he turned back to David. "Hello, I'm Sergeant Joseph Coffey. I've been asked to interview you."

Berkowitz continued smiling and said, "Hi, I'm Dave Berkowitz."

JUST OUTSIDE the conference room, police officers congratulated one another. Finally the Mayor entered, all smiles, and went around the room shaking everyone's hand. There were faces he knew and some he didn't, but everyone received a handshake and a "Thank you." When Beame reached the Deputy Commissioner for Public Information, Frank McLaughlin, he said, "Frank, where's the liquor?"

McLaughlin answered, "Your Honor, there's a department regulation against having any . . ."

The Mayor took out his wallet and counted off two hundred dollars, handing it to McLaughlin: "The hell with department rules. I'm the Mayor, and I say that rule is suspended for tonight. Now get someone to go out and buy . . . whatever."

SERGEANT COFFEY questioned David for more than an hour, patiently covering each of the shootings in specific detail. There was no doubt about it: Berkowitz was the one. In each attack he had acted alone. It would have been impossible for anyone other than David to have committed the crimes and recite those small details that only the killer could have known.

Throughout the interrogation, Berkowitz answered every

question coolly, without hiding anything. Finally it was over. Coffey got up to leave.

"Good night, Sergeant Coffey," David said in his quiet voice.

A chill ran down Coffey's spine. Outside the conference room, Inspector Richard Nicastro, the Queens Borough Commander, was standing next to Jimmy Breslin, the only reporter allowed up from where the press was waiting on the auditorium floor.

"What do you think, Joe?" asked Nicastro.

"Let me tell you something," Coffey said. "When I first walked into that room I was full of rage. But after talking to him. . . . You know. . . . You really want to know how I feel right now? I feel sorry for him. That man is a fucking vegetable!"

Nicastro said, "Why do you say that?"

"How could anyone sit there and talk about murdering people like we talk about changing underwear? It was like talking to a head of cabbage."

The Inspector threw his arm around Coffey's waist and lead him to the table holding the bottles of liquor the Mayor had bought. Nicastro picked up a plastic cup and poured out two inches of Scotch.

He said, "Did you calm down yet?"

"Yes."

Nicastro handed the cup to Coffey.

"Have a drink, Joe."

Epilogue

The events that followed the capture of David Berkowitz could have come from a grade-B movie script. No sooner had the police car that carried the Son of Sam left Yonkers to drive to New York City police headquarters at One Police Plaza in lower Manhattan than the district attorneys of Queens, Brooklyn, and the Bronx were being notified of his capture. They, in turn, ordered their assistants (ADAs) in charge of each homicide division to rush to the office of the Chief of Detectives and get the suspect's first statements.

Thus, no fewer than six assistant district attorneys were waiting just inside the Chief of Detectives' conference room on the thirteenth floor of One Police Plaza when news of the arrival of the Son of Sam was called upstairs from the rear garage entrance. "Everyone was waiting for that call," said Brooklyn ADA Ronald Aiello. "When it rang, we all looked at each other. God, you could cut the atmosphere with a knife."

At the back entrance of One Police Plaza, Detectives Zigo

and Falotico came out of the rear of the car, carefully holding their manacled prisoner between them. A horde of reporters and photographers suddenly surged forward from behind hastily erected barricades.

David smiled at everyone. The Son of Sam might have become an international name, but David Berkowitz was still an unknown, and the situation was about to change. The press had their "hero," and were out to make the most of the opportunity. "I never seen anything like it," says David. "The photographers were getting the cameras knocked out of their hands. They fell like dominos, you know. When they fell down they got stepped over by the police. They were only interested in taking pictures . . . of anything. They took pictures of the backs of each other's heads. I never seen anything . . . it was comical. I saw them all.

"One of them stepped out in front of a car and almost got hit. The police even had it hard. They had trouble moving me. They had to push [the photographers and reporters] out of the way. I never experienced anything like it. I guess I smiled. So right away they began saying, 'Ah, you see, he's smiling. He's happy he did it.' I guess it's what everyone thought. They saw my picture and said, 'He's smiling, so he must be happy that he killed the people.' I thought of it as a job. I never was real happy."

Captain Harold Coleman began shouting to the uniformed men: "Move them back. Make a path so we can get through!" The officers created a small opening by pushing against the massed ranks of the press. Falotico and Zigo pulled at David, and the trio began moving toward the entrance just ten feet away. Reporters shouted questions. The officers didn't answer, but quickly turned their attention to the Son of Sam as microphones were pushed in his direction. Cameras rolled as high-intensity lights went on. Electronic flashes popped like gunfire.

In the midst of the confusion, David remained calm, the childlike smile on his lips. He said nothing, but his experience was captured on film. Within ten hours, his face was featured on front pages of newspapers around the world, and millions of people sat down to breakfast to find the Son of Sam smiling at them.

Falotico and Zigo weren't happy. "It was something we didn't have control of," says John Falotico. "Like it was in the back of my mind about Oswald being shot by Jack Ruby in Texas. I couldn't watch everyone's hands. So we tried to bull our way through."

The detectives finally pulled David through the mob and into the protection of the inner corridor. It all took about a minute, but it seemed an eternity to the officers. David, the solitary haunted man who had lived most of his life without friends, wanting attention and longing to be noticed, was now the focal point of a whirlwind. The Son of Sam had suddenly taken form and substance. He was David Berkowitz.

As he disappeared into the rear entrance of One Police Plaza, the reporters and cameramen suddenly turned and ran along the street toward the main entrance of police headquarters. Rumor had it that there was going to be a news conference in the auditorium; seats would be assigned on a first-come, first-served basis. Everyone wanted to be in the front row in hopes of getting the best picture, or being close enough to be able to ask a key question.

Meanwhile, the name David Berkowitz was speeding its way through the nation's communications networks. Television broadcasts were interrupted for bulletins as far away as London, Los Angeles, Frankfurt, and Tokyo. Network news directors in New York and Burbank hurried from their homes to their offices to rearrange the daily schedules for their crews. Major blocks of time were set aside, to be filled in by reporters who had been sent to David's home address and to wherever he had worked or lived prior to his capture.

After his interrogation by Sergeant Coffey and the various assistant district attorneys, David was taken to the 84th Precinct in Brooklyn. There he was booked for the murder of Stacy Moskowitz and attempted murder of Robert Violante. Reporters weren't present, because they were awaiting the start of the news conference at police headquarters.

At ten o'clock, a police spokesman announced that the conference would be put off until 1:00 P.M. Reporters took the opportunity to get something to eat and phone their news directors. Some passed the time trying to get any new nugget of information from police officers, although there was nothing they didn't already know. At 12:10 P.M. they were told to assemble in the auditorium. When they walked in, Barbara Walters was already seated in the front row.

Mayor Beame entered the auditorium at 1:00 P.M. The conference started as the Mayor said a few words: "I'm very proud of our dedicated officers. However, Commissioner Michael Codd is better able to detail the capture of the Son of Sam."

Commissioner Codd took the podium and began to recite the events that occurred in Yonkers the preceding night. Codd revealed that there had been a minimum of 75 full-time detectives and 225 patrolmen working on the case. The Commissioner also stated that the suspect had been a New York City auxiliary police officer for three years. Detective Edward Zigo, the officer who had obtained the search warrant to the Berkowitz car and apartment one hour after David's arrest, held the famous .44 Charter Arms Bulldog aloft. At that moment, but far from the spotlight, the actual arresting officer, Detective John Falotico, was busy booking his suspect at the 84th Precinct. At 2:35 P.M., the conference was over and the Mayor and Commissioner went back upstairs to the Chief of Detectives' Office. Bone-tired reporters rushed to telephones to call in their stories.

The next morning David Berkowitz was to be arraigned in Brooklyn's Criminal Court. However, the question as to who would legally represent David had not as yet been resolved. At 6:30 A.M., Thursday, August 11, attorneys Ira J. Jultak and Leon Stern received a call from a member of David's family who asked that they be counsel for David. David's adoptive father, Nat, was on his way to New York from Florida. Because only Nat could hire counsel for David, Jultak telephoned ADA Ron Aiello, Chief of the Brooklyn DA's Homicide Bureau. "Ron, we have a problem, as you can imagine. I'd like you to put off the arraignment until David's father arrives. He'll be in before noon," said Jultak.

"Impossible," was Aiello's answer. "Berkowitz's case will have to come up in the regular rotation."

"Ron, I can't believe this case will come up in ordinary rotation."

Aiello wouldn't relent. At 11:30 A.M., the arraignment was held before Judge Richard A. Brown. David Berkowitz was represented by attorneys Leon Stern, Ira Jultak, and one Philip Peltz, who appeared in court claiming he was David's lawyer. All three lawyers were appointed for the arraignment only. The hearing ended in ten minutes with Berkowitz being remanded to Kings County Hospital. There he would undergo psychiatric observation.

After the hearing, Nat Berkowitz formally retained attorneys Stern and Jultak. On August 14, 1977, United States Attorney Robert B. Fiske, Jr., called for an immediate Bar Association investigation of Attorney Philip Peltz. This request came on the heels of an announcement that Peltz had offered the *News* and the *Post* more than ninety minutes of taped interviews between him and the Son of Sam for newspaper serialization and book rights. The offering price was $100,000. Noting that Mr. Peltz had previously been convicted of security and conspiracy violations and sent to prison, Fiske said, "How is this man still practicing law?" On August 15, Peltz asked to be allowed to leave the case. On August 17, he was replaced by still another lawyer, Mark Heller, who claimed that he had been retained by David's half-sister, Roslyn, on Sunday night, August 14. On September 15, Heller also withdrew from the case.

DAVID had been placed in block G of the Kings County Hospital complex, where a team of psychiatrists began the lengthy process of evaluating his sanity. Their determination would ultimately decide whether or not the Son of Sam would stand trial. Dr. Daniel W. Schwartz, director of forensic psychiatric services at Kings County and associate professor of psychiatry at Downstate Medical Center in Brooklyn, was in charge. Judge Brown had stated that it would be up to Dr. Schwartz and his staff "to determine if Mr. Berkowitz is suffering from any mental disease or defect that would preclude a trial."

What then would the psychiatrists attempt to determine? First, "does Berkowitz fully understand that he is being charged with murder [the nature of the offense], namely the murder of Stacy Moskowitz. Second, is the defendant able to assist his attorneys in their preparation of a defense? These were the only relevant issues." Yet there was to be a third, possibly more important issue that would be significant if a trial was to be held. Was David insane? Did he know what he was doing when he attacked Robert Violante and Stacy Moskowitz? If he did not, he could be remanded to a state mental institution as being not guilty by reason of insanity, and he would stay there for a period of time, ending only when state-appointed psychiatrists deemed he was no longer a menace to society.

David thus could be incarcerated for life, or for a period as short as one year.

Says attorney Jultak, "I believed that the situation was one with potentially politically disastrous overtones. Elections were forthcoming. I was sure that a finding of incompetency was something that no one wanted, because community outrage was such that David just had to stand trial."

Certainly the press was fanning the flames. At the same time David was arraigned in Brooklyn's Criminal Court, four newsmen were arrested for breaking into David's apartment and charged with criminal trespass, a Class A misdemeanor. Taken into custody were David Berliner and Robert Klafus, who stated they were working on the story for the *Washington Post;* Ted Cowell, a freelance photographer for *Time* magazine; and Lenny Dietrick, a staff photographer for the *Daily News.*

It was not immediately determined how the four had gained entrance to the apartment, but Officer Tom Chamberlain said, "Police had to use their keys on the three locks they had placed on the outside of the Berkowitz door to stop just such an incident."

Craig Glassman, Mr. Berkowitz's downstairs neighbor, said, "I heard footsteps above me and knew that the apartment had been sealed shut. So I got on the phone to the Yonkers Police Department, and they responded immediately."

Yes, David had become news . . . big news. The Son of Sam was selling papers, lots of papers.

The *Post* recorded the capture of the Son of Sam in a striking red headline, CAUGHT. Normal sales for the *Post* were 607,000 copies. That first afternoon, the paper sold a whopping record 1,000,000 newspapers. The *Daily News* upped its daily total to 2,200,000, an increase of nearly 350,000. Presses rolled each day until the last possible moment when a new edition had to be replated to get out the Late City final.

Blessed by the sudden boost in circulation, the *News* and *Post* now made every effort to keep the figures high. *The New York Times* reported on August 22, 1977, that both publications (the *News* and the *Post*) had gone beyond reporting by "transforming a killer into a celebrity." It seemed that neither journal was content to allow the capture of David Berkowitz to be the end of their front-page headlines. They followed each arraignment, each hearing, each letter or incident in detail. Editors sent scores of reporters to hunt out anyone who might provide a juicy tidbit for publication. Relatives, friends, acquaintances, police, and attorneys were all fair game in the press's relentless search for a scoop. And every day that they ran a story about Son of Sam, their circulation increased.

Both newspapers were asked by the *Times* to comment on the story that they paid Iris Gerhardt, a one-time girlfriend of David's, for the use of various personal letters he had written to her while in the Army. Robert Spitzler, managing editor of the *Post,* refused to comment. However, Michael J. O'Neil, the editor of the *Daily News,* said, "I don't see anything fundamentally wrong with buying material. Newspapers purchase exclusive photographs on a freelance basis, thus the purchase of these letters can be compared to buying freelance material. I don't believe in this instance it was an abuse of checkbook journalism."

But neither paper stopped with the purchase of these letters. Both the *News* and the *Post* ran stories saying that Berkowitz might have had an accomplice. The police investigated immediately. "We found no truth in any of those allegations," Keenan said. "And we closed our investigation."

On December 5, 1977, the saga of the Son of Sam was picked up again by the New York *Post.* Beneath the front page headline, SAM SLEEPS, David Berkowitz was shown sleeping in his cell at Kings County Hospital. This photograph was "one of a series obtained exclusively by the *Post,*" the newspaper boasted. On page 32 of the same edition was a letter attributed to Berkowitz, plus three more photographs depicting David writing letters in the hospital's day room, sitting on the edge of his bed, and sleeping. The caption of the last photograph read: "Another day of writing is over . . . and Berkowitz sleeps." The paper gave no photographic credits for the pictures.

It later came to light that a camera had been smuggled into Kings County Hospital. An investigation was begun by the Department of Corrections. A Corrections officer was dismissed, and the reporter involved was charged with attempted bribery, brought to trial, and acquitted. However, a member of the jury was quoted in *The New York Times* as saying, "The owners of the newspaper should have been on trial, not the reporter."

Following closely on the heels of the *Post*'s December 5th "exclusive," the Garber Publishing Company ran off a parody of the paper calling it *Not the New York Post* and the front page showed a doctored photo of the Son of Sam sleeping with his arms around a Teddy Bear.

While these bits of journalism were going on, the Carr

family was experiencing its own tragic woes. On February 16, 1978, after returning from a trip to his father's Yonkers home, John Carr (Sam Carr's eldest son) committed suicide while staying at a friend's apartment on the Minot Air Force Base in North Dakota.

At this point in time, at least three societies that specialize in the occult used this to tie the Son of Sam to the Carrs' misfortunes. Rumors circulated that John Carr had been a friend of David's and in some way had been involved in David's assaults.

Next, the Gannett Westchester newspapers, using free-lance reporters, ran a series of articles saying there was a possibility that David had not acted alone. On October 12, 1979, they broke a story with the headline, SON OF SAM PROBE REOPENED BY NYC POLICE. The articles were based upon statements made by Sheriff Leon Schwan of Ward County, North Dakota, who said, "We and the city of Minot [N.D.] police are assisting the investigation New York has begun. There are some things out here they're very interested in." But the New York City Police Department had never authorized any reopening of the investigation. What had happened was that a single NYPD detective, acting on his own, went to North Dakota. Once there, he introduced himself to the Sheriff, identified a companion as also being a detective, and stated that he was working on an active investigation of the Son of Sam case.

One month later, the detective refused to answer his commander's questions about the sources of his information, or to the identity of the second man he had introduced as a police officer. The detective was then brought up on departmental charges.

Next, in January 1980, Michael Carr, the youngest son of Sam Carr, was killed in an automobile accident while driving at high speed and intoxicated on New York City's decaying and treacherous West Side Highway. It was as if the Son of Sam had jinxed the Carr family and, once again, the papers ran stories that boosted their circulation.

ON AUGUST 23, 1977, in a makeshift courtroom in the G-Wing at Kings County Hospital, the Court arraigned David Berkowitz for the murders of Christine Freund, Virginia Voskerichian, and the attempted murders of Donna DeMasi, Joanne Lomino, Carl Denaro, Judy Placido, and Salvatore Lupo. The next day, the court arraigned David Berkowitz for the murders of Valentina Suriani, Alexander Esau and Donna Lauria. The indictment also charged David Berkowitz with the attempted murder of Jody Valenti.

At this arraignment, Justice Alexander Chananau of the Supreme Court of Bronx County asked the defendant, "Are you David Berkowitz?"

"No!" was his answer.

The court was silent. Reporters looked at each other. Everyone was stunned. Defense Attorney Mark Heller stepped forward. He said, "Your Honor, if it would please the Court, I request that all further questions be directed to Counsel, as it is obvious that the defendant will not cooperate."

Ira Jultak says, "It didn't surprise me. It was just the first time that David's psychosis surfaced in public. If the judge had asked him who he was, he probably would have said he was someone else. After all, he always believed that he was acting on Sam's orders."

What remained was the return of the psychiatric report to Justice Gerald Held of Brooklyn. Copies of the "secret" document were given to the Justice, district attorneys, and defense counsel. Before the report was unsealed by the Court, New York's WPIX-TV (owned by the *Daily News*) carried an exclusive story that Berkowitz had been found competent to stand trial.

In the summation of their report returned to Justice Held on Monday, August 29, Drs. Schwartz and Weidenbacher took a firm position: "It is the opinion of each of us that the defendant is an incapacitated person, as a result of mental disease or defect, lacks capacity to understand the proceeding against him or to assist in his own defense.

"1. diagnosis: paranoia

"2. prognosis: guarded

"3. Nature and extent of examination: the patient was examined psychiatrically on August 12, 13, 14 (Dr. Schwartz), August 17 (Dr. Weidenbacher), and August 18 and 22 (by both MDs) for a total of approximately 11 hours."

Kings County District Attorney Eugene Gold immediately served the defense attorneys with papers moving to controvert the psychiatric reports saying that David was incompetent. "It was an unusual move," says Jultak. "A motion to controvert the report's findings and to have the state's own psychiatrists asked to reexamine the prisoner is rarely made. The state just doesn't challenge its own psychiatrists." Then District Attorney Gold made another motion. He asked the court to appoint a specific psychiatrist, one who would act for the prosecution.

The court granted the motion, and Dr. David Abrahamsen was retained by DA Gold and approved by the court. He was to conduct an independent examination. As a result of that examination, Dr. Abrahamsen found David competent to stand trial and to aid in his own defense. However, the doctor's report also said: "David feels that his distorted beliefs are of such importance that all other topics should be relegated to the sidelines. Thus, the defendant's main excuse for committing the crimes is his delusions.

"It is also noteworthy that the delusions the defendant states he has, seem to be more transitory and situational, rather than constant. They may, in fact, be exaggerated by him."

In conclusion, Dr. Abrahamsen stated, "While the defendant shows paranoid traits, they do not interfere with his fitness to stand trial."

Justice John R. Starkey now judged David competent to stand trial. Shortly thereafter Judge Starkey was removed from the case and replaced by Judge Joseph Corso. Defense counsel then asked for a new competency hearing and requested that Dr. Martin Lubin, the former chief of forensic psychiatry at Bellevue Hospital, be allowed to examine David for the defense. Once again, Dr. Abrahamsen would examine for DA Gold.

As a result of the reexamination, Dr. Weidenbacher found David competent, because David was now a Christian and was espousing *bona-fide* Baptist doctrines. Dr. Schwartz said he was now unable to make a determination, and Dr. Lubin found David incompetent. Dr. Abrahamsen testified: "Your Honor, the defendant is as normal as anyone else. Maybe a little neurotic."

Based on Abrahamsen's testimony, the court set a date for trial, at which time David entered his plea.

JUDGE CORSO: Clerk, please take his plea.

THE CLERK: What is your name?

DEFENDANT: David Berkowitz.

THE CLERK: Are Mr. Leon Stern and Mr. Ira Jultak, who stand beside you now, your attorneys?

DEFENDANT: Yes.

THE CLERK: Do you wish to withdraw your plea of not guilty heretofore entered to indictment 2673 of 1977, and plead guilty to the crimes of murder in the second degree and attempted murder in the second degree and assault in the first degree and criminal possession of a weapon in the second degree?

DEFENDANT: Yes.

THE CLERK: Be seated.

It was over.

David had pleaded guilty.

There would never be a trial, just a sentence for each charge, and they could be consecutive—totaling 365 years in jail. David would permit no appeal. But, as Ira Jultak points out: "Consecutive sentences have been consistently held by the New York Court of Appeals, to be improper. Yet, they were made. Perhaps they were in answer to the furor of the moment?'' In reality, David could be pardoned in twenty-two years.

Today, three and a half years after sentencing, David Berkowitz, prisoner 78-A-1976, is in Attica Correctional Facility, Attica, New York.

The fact that there was no trial made the questions of both his arrest without an arrest warrant, and the search of his car without a search warrant, moot. There remains the question of what would have happened had he pled not guilty, or if his defense had been not guilty by reason of insanity. Could he have been convicted?

Off the record, one State Supreme Court judge says: "Without a warrant, Berkowitz would still have been convicted. There would have been a ruling along these lines: Berkowitz represented a clear and present danger to society. That danger was so great that it would have been the dominant issue. Warrant or no warrant, he would have gone to jail." And, the justice added, "His lawyers could have appealed to Burger's court, and would have lost."

A second justice comments: "Berkowitz would have been convicted and sent away by any court. There was no chance he wouldn't. No judge, no administration would have survived if it were responsible for setting him free."

WHAT HAVE WE LEARNED from David Berkowitz? The police point out that no group of citizens can ever consider themselves safe from a psychotic killer who operates alone and in a random pattern of assaults. As Detective Ron Marsenison aptly put it in describing the near panic that existed in New York City during the fourteen months that David Berkowitz stalked young victims: "People who had moved into white, seemingly 'safe' neighborhoods suddenly found their dreams were threatened. Their security was less than what they had bargained for."

Another perceptive analysis comes from defense counsel Ira Jultak, a former student of philosophy. "Our society cannot cope with anything so repulsive as a mass murderer," he says. "Society wants simple answers to complex questions that are unanswerable. That is why we blithely say that David shot girls because he was unsuccessful with women. When David came before the courts, society wanted vengeance and got it. We have to rethink our system of criminal justice, perhaps institute a bifurcated system in which we first determine if a man is guilty and then decide the issue of insanity.

"David made us all afraid. He threatened the citizens of an entire metropolis, the safety of twelve million people. He threatened our institutions, indeed the very fabric and the safeguards of our society. Unless we carefully psychoanalyze David we will never understand what makes him tick, or what makes any psychotic killer tick. David's case simply doesn't make sense as it has been resolved to date. Could society have seen the danger in the pattern of David's earlier life— when his stepmother died, or when he was in school, or when he was in the Army? I cannot help but wonder where the guilt really lies?"

THE SURVIVING VICTIMS have tried to put their lives together as best they can. Joanne Lomino and Robert Violante are respectively crippled and blind. Others carry physical and emotional scars. Some of the police officers have new assignments; others have gone on to retirement. David's mother and half-sister still live where they did before David walked back into their lives. And the parents of the young people David killed still dream about their children, making dinner and setting the table for daughters who will never return.

Appendix

Diaries, Notes, and Letters Written by David Berkowitz after His Capture

11/8/7?

People feel a certain eeriness about me — something cold, inhuman, monsterous. This is the power and personality of the demons.

This is the spell used by "Them" to turn people away from me and create a situation of isolation, lonliness, and personal frustration, as part of their Master Plan.

There is no doubt in my mind that a demon has been living in me since birth. All my life I've been wild, violent, temporal, mean, cruel, sadistic, an acting with irrational anger and destructive.

When I was a child I often had very real and quite

11/8/77

severe nightmares. In fact,
they were so bad I often had
to sleep with a light on,
or, with my father in the
room, or I had to sleep
with my parents.

I saw monsters often and
I heard them, which often caused
me to go screaming hysterically
into my parents room. I
would say that they, (~~monsters~~)
the bad dreams, were very
severe.

Now, I know, that they
were real—just like now.
I've been tormented all my
life by them—never having
peace or quite.

In fact, last week I went
"beserk" (?) because they
slapped me in the head
and made terrible noises.

Going back to 10/28/77
~~and made terrible noises~~.

When I look at all the
prisoners in kings county Hospital I cannot help but feel
sorry for them. Their like
lost souls; many in and out
of institutions for all of their
lives; little hope., no family,
no friends.

I think people only want
peace and comfort in life
but apparently few know how
to find it. It seems like
the only saviour these
patients have is thorazine
but they really need Jesus.

I never thought my life
would turn out like this—
what a mess.

If it wasn't for my
family and their love, and

10/28/77

my lawyers and their support-
ive help I don't believe I
would survive this ordeal.
Some, I guess, are more fortunate than others. Love
and companionship and a
closeness to God are all that
is necessary to challenge the
adversary, Satan (Sam).
    Yes, the demons are real.
I saw them, felt their presence,
and I heard them.

11/28/77

    I only wish they would
let me read the newspapers
here. Especially when its about
me. I feel I just have to
know what people are saying
about me.
    The judge (Mr. Starkie)
hates me I'm certain. He

must think I'm some type of woman hater. But I thought the newspapers had done away with that theory when I was apprehended.

If a girl had recently jilted me as the judge suspects then I would like to know who she was myself. Who could this mystery woman be?

I am a gladitor against the forces of darkness! I am come into these circumstances so that I might save many lives. I am willing to die to be at peace, to obtain it. I am willing to go to jail so I might be free. My life must be dedicated to the people of earth. Might it be possible to convince the world about the dark spirit forces that live on earth? I will die for this cause! Oh, death, you are victory.

After reading the book Hostage to the Devil by Malachi Martin I now have no doubt that I am a person who has been visited by an alien force or being.

The evidence is overwhelming. Especially since my life fits in so well with the pattern of a person possessed on by an intelligent force.

The best evidence is a letter to my father dated long before the shootings began. This letter stated a devine mission that I felt was intended for me — one of importance although now that I look back at it the whole mission makes no sense. Page 523 of H. to the D. the last paragraph — "It always alienated them from their surroundings and from those nearest to them. The

general feeling was that great
things could happen to them".

There were even times after
my arrest in which I doubted
the reality of the demons,
thinking of myself to be a person
hallucinating or living a delusion
but now, after reading Mr. Martins
work, I am convinced beyond
my own self doubt about demons.

Now I must go about to
correct the wrongs of Son of Sam
although they were good works
when you look at them from
distorted "alien" eyes and from
an "evil" intelligence point of view.
I need to have more personal
freedoms such as keeping a
pen in my cell, being able to
go out, under guard and mail
letters, go to the post office,

and have a hotline telephone in my cell that leads directly to Chief of Detectives Heenan's office. I know that if the police set up ~~a task~~ a "Demon Task Force" then a tremendous step would be taken. It would be a monumental step in the annals of justice and historical law.

Also, society needs to erect a "Demon Hospital" in which suspected cases of demon possession could be treated and alleviated. There is no telling how many crimes may ~~be~~ have been committed by the possessed or how desperately they too need help.

The demons have an amazing way of leaving you feeling

like an empty vacum — leaving your life void of many things. However, the unclean spirits will fill the very same void which they so subtly created with evil light (darkness) and evil knowledge. "The void has been filled" I told Mr. Breslin; however, it was replaced with a dark foul substance that resulted in death and destruction. It is this distorted view that makes everything good look bad and everything evil appear right. So I gave up my personal freedom thinking it had, only to obtain a type of freedom equivalent equivalent to that of a

dog on a long chain.
I can work but I can't
have freedom. I can be
loved but I cannot love.
I could feel and admire good
yet, have no good in me.

There is, no doubt, a deep
hidden array of forces behind
the Son of Sam killings. This
is not a trial simply to
be put into black and white.
This trial has far greater
significance and far greater
depth then one could
imagine.
The S.O.S. shootings probe
hidden motives and expose
spirits and forces that never before
surfaced in an open courtroom.
Good and Evil, God and Lucifer,
yet, while every seat in the

courtroom is taken, likewise, every corner space at the ceiling will be taken by ~~sp~~ those of the spirit world. There is no doubt in my mind that the outcome of this trial would affect all of God's angels and all of Satan's demons.

I believe the depth of this trial and the complexity of it was felt by Judge Starkie who eventually ~~paniked~~ paniced and sought ~~escc~~ escape. He apparently realized what this trial entails and he either realized that he couldn't handle it and/or God had chosen a different judge for his purpose. I also believe Judge Starkie felt an alien presence in his head and he felt himself losing control yet he continued to play into His (the spirits) hands.

Coincidently, one of the demons, disguised in a human body was present at the trial and was also sitting in the p last row in the courtroom. I have no doubt that mental telepathy was used here to control Starkies mind.

I have a fear now that I to will become a demon or, I may be a demon right now.

Sometimes the need to kill becomes so overwhelming that I fear myself. However, I know that this is not me. I'm certain there is someone inside me, an alien presence whose need to obtain blood and kill is in relation to his rebellion to God.

This belief of an alien presence is not an escape of responsibility because I am looking forward to a jail cell as opposed to having an apartment filled with demons. Furthermore, I David Berkowitz, do not wish to kill anymore but live my life in peace and with a positive purpose.

I wrestle with the evil one daily and silently. I know that if I were home alone I would be busting up my household possessions or punching myself in the head and arguing with the demons who ran amok in my apartment.

Mr. Williams is one of the demons who has made his way into my apartment and into my life. He was constantly tormenting me; making loud, constant noises and wierd deafing sounds.

One day, about 5:30 am, I had not slept all night and I was tense. Mr williams had been hidden behind the wall making the noises,

when out of anger I charged
up to the wall of my
apartment and leaped into
the air to deliver a flying
kick sending my foot
through the wall and
almost into my neighbors
apartment. However, it was
all foolishness because I
couldn't stop Mr. Williams
and the torment, and I wound
up destroying my own property.

My apartment is what I
called it even though I
always felt that I didn't
own it! I mean I paid
the rent but I hated that
apartment so much because
of the demons that dwelled
in it — I was even thinking
of setting fire to it.

I paid the rent; I signed the lease, I moved in it seeking ~~out~~ quiet and rest only to find noise and terror. No, this isn't my apartment. It was reserved for me in the hopes of trapping me, leaving me near broke and unable to escape from the final foe — "Sam Cari" who is but isn't. Sam, who is dead but alive and who torments the earth.

This whole thing with my apartment was a set up. It was no doubt planned long ago.

I know demons control me because when Dr. Schwartz and doctor Abramsen tried to question me about the church group I found myself unable and unwilling to speak. I have no doubt that they make me say things so bad and stupid, yet, they do it so subtly as to leave themselves complotly hidden.

What can I do? How can I make people understand?

I am married and with good reason that I may, one day, evolve into a humanoid or demon in a more complete state. I fear that with the lose of my humaness I will become like a zombie. As a matter of note,

some people thought I was
void of emotions when they
examined me. This is
exactly what happens to
those possessed. I want
my soul back! I want
what was taken from me!
I have a right to be
human.
     Who can understand
the mysteries of the forces
of darkness?
     I also feel that I am
losing my mind, it all seems
so unreal, so crazy.
I just wonder how many
servants of the demonic
army either die or rot
in institutions?

     I am Abaddon the
Destroyer. I take the

lives of those unwilling
to give them up. I
obtain their blood ~~from~~
for Sam and the demons.

Yes, it is hopless, useless
and outright foolish to
convince a lost world
of the existense of its own
ruler - Satan. He is the
god of this world.

There were so many things
that I wanted to do, so many
places I wanted to visit.
However, I couldn't. I had
no rights as a person.
I just couldn't enjoy myself
when I had time off -
my mission was all I lived
for and I hated it. I
hated my life as SON OF SAM.

But what could I do?
Even when I went to Florida
I couldn't even stop to
sightsee - I had no peace
or rest. You could tell
by the way I drove
down there non-stop, then
to texas non-stop, that I
did, in fact, have a supernatural power and a
special satanic mission.

I am the demon from the
bottomless pit here on
earth to create havoc and
terror. I am War, I am
death. I am destruction!

I know who has whored
and pimped. I know who has
committed grievous sins and
who has spit on their mother
and father! Where is the
great one who can cast me
away into darkness? Where is
his coming? I suppose that
he likes me at my temporary
place — in Daned the shit
the filth

I am the filth and the come,
I am the wretch th filth the
vomit! I on be the Son of Sam
who fears nothing I destroy!
I kill and stomp to pieces
the people of earth in the name

of that wretched.

I am King I am hell I am
death. Nysa the whore the
harlot shall not escape Gods
curse her children shall die
all three for she whored her
baby and sold her flesh for a
mere penonce. Who is like
the great whore the harlot of
cum who sells herself. Who
is like the Son of Sam, me,
a fallen angel who has come
to kill and to establish
the kingdom of terror and
misery - me Son of Sam
the killer who fears neither
death nor hell.

Who is as Stacy who sells
her soul for a penis?
Let us make war with
civilisation and destroy and
cause terror.

let the loud noises and the cries of the demons continue forever. Let the gates of hell colapse and let the lost escape to torment the living

i am the Son of Sam and where if live is nobodys business. Don't listen to David the fool for i am the accurate king. i am the schmut of the sewer i am all powerful me and my father Abaddon!

As peace comes to earth throyh the guns of kings.

Who is sly and cunning? Who can outwit the president? Son of Sam and legion of us who destroy and vomit uncontrollably.

Son of Sam

The hours pass by so slowly its hard to make them pass. I guess I have to take the 9 hours piece by piece and not take the day on a whole. Next to the demons, the worse thing is boredom.

The only things I have in my cell are toilet paper, a couple of books and miscellaneou reading materials (mainly religious), however, I cannot keep a pen or pencil in my cell. Nor, am I allowed to read newspapers.

My pass times are reading, sleeping, pacing my cell and daydreaming.

What is death that a person should fear it? Perhaps one really fears having to lose ones possessions, loved one's or maybe the person fears having to meet God and be shown all of their sins.

Demons certainly have their hands in death for their purpose is to destroy and cause suffering.

Am I really a creature or an animal or is this what the demons are causing the people to think of me as?

I miss the freedom of travel – New Paltz, Bear Mountain, Ferry Point Park. It was a glorious experience to just get in ~~your~~ my car and travel. But in the end, the last few years, the freedom of travel has been denied to me as part of the "Master Plan" that would leave me near broke and trapped in an apartment without the ability to escape.

Someone, a woman named Helen had sent me a beautiful sweater and another man from Alabama sent me a Bible that must of cost $30.00. I just don't understand the kindness of people. Its hard to believe that people like me.

I am tormented
I cry in my cell
I miss my Daddy
I hate myself
I am very uptight
I hear demons
I see demons
I need to talk to someone
I cannot be left alone
I will have a breakdown
I cannot be understood
I am truthful
I am doomed

I know that I am
not well hearing inner
voices, having dogs talk
to me and being controlled
by demons yet, I want
to get better.

If I ever get to a
mental hospital I
want to cooperate with
the doctors completely.

I dont want to
stay behind the walls
forever.

I owe my father a
chance to receive hope.

I owe society a
chance to make myself
good and repay them

for all the troubles I caused as a result of my illness.

Someday, people will see a new David Berkowitz and the end of Son of Sam.

Son of Sam can be dead forever if the courts, doctors, and me are willing to work together. I am.

I owe my freedom to Jesus Christ the Son of God. "I and the father are one," says Jesus.

11/26/77

I have made myself a promise not to remain locked up behind bars forever. I have a debut to pay to society and one day I will be free to repay it.

I must repay society and now that I am a Christian I will work to help other people find true freedom and eternal life.

In this hospital I found Jesus Christ and it is Him who I am obligated to. I must tell society about the truth and hope.

11/28/77

I have given up the hope of warning the world about demons.

There is no use in telling people of something that isn't there.

I guess its me who isnt well - delusions. However, I see that there are certain people who are out to destroy me. Right now, all thats needed is help for me because I dont want to wrestle with demons all my life.

Therefore, I need to

go to a hospital.

I cannot figure out what made me kill those poor people but I am sorry because its my fault. If I had not been so stubborn I could of been in a hospital getting help.

I called out for help for so long but nobody either someone didnt here me or I didnt here them.

What will happen to me? If I go to prison I would be doomed because nobody would help me.

I am determined not
to perish but to
survive this ordeal
and come through
okay and well.

I need someone to
talk to and sit
with or I need to
go upstate and rest.

Dear Dad,

Please dad I need you now. I've reached an agreement with the doctors that I am not well. I'm sure that you must realize that I'm no cold blooded killer. Rather, there is a problem with my mind.

I know now that you were right. I should of listened to you and Hal about getting psfyci-atric help long before.

"I only wished that I would of listened to you so this never would of happened to these poor people.

My mind is slipping into absolute maddness I know. I feel like I am on the verge of a complete mental collapse. Who can help me.

I am often in my cell crying like a ~~baby~~ baby.

Yes, I am possessed and the demons are causing me deep depression. I cannot relax or rest. I pace my cell constantly.

I am never happy

Rather I am sad.

very often I cry
when alone in my cell

I am very nervous

I can never rest
or relax

help I am going to have
a nervous breakdown

— I am possessed!

😐 I sleep restlessly

😀 I feel like screaming

😑 I must be put to death

😈 demons torment me.

✝ I am not going to make it.

Index

SON OF SAM
BY LAWRENCE D. KLAUSNER

This is the incredible story of how a single man terrorized the twelve million citizens of the metropolis of New York.

It is also the story of the greatest manhunt in the history of the New York Police Department—the intimate narrative of the men assigned to tracking down a lone killer who prowled supposedly safe. neighborhoods and, at random, shot pretty young girls with a .44-caliber revolver. The police task force investigated 3,167 suspects (some of them cops) before they arrested the killer. Politicians watched a city writhe in panic. Newspapers played upon the fears of their readers. And the criminal justice system showed itself incapable of coping with the man who committed such horrendous crimes.

It all began with a young boy setting fires. Then David Berkowitz committed his first act of wanton violence on Christmas Eve, 1975, when he stabbed two women with a hunting knife. He next bought a gun and became Son of Sam, the demon-haunted .44-caliber killer. Within the next two years he fired his weapon thirty-two times, killing six victims and wounding seven in eight known attacks. Most of the victims were women, young and pretty, good students, and from loving

(continued from front flap)

families. There were other crimes, too.

The book is based on more than 300 tape recordings of David Berkowitz's conversations with psychiatrists, police, district attorneys, defense counsel, plus his never-before-revealed handwritten notes and diaries. It is the story of a psychotic killer. It tells the public what it has never known, the facts that would have been exposed if Son of Sam had ever stood trial. It tells of David Berkowitz's boyhood, his hopes, his fears, his deepening despair, the demons that demanded he kill for them, his initial sense of disgust, his increasing sense of infallibility.

Beyond that, the author has interviewed everyone intimately connected with the case and has woven their previously untold stories into the book. There are the accounts of the surviving victims and their families, the families of young women and men who were killed, politicians and police, detectives and their families, district attorneys, psychiatrists, and defense counsel—all the people who were touched by the horror of Son of Sam.

BALLISTICS

B.S. ✲ 9871 7 /29 / 76 45th PRECINCT	DECEASED LAURIA, DONNA INJURED VALENTE, JODY 61 ✲ 6960
B.S. ✲ 14087 10 / 23 / 76 109th PRECINCT	INJURED DE NARO, CARL 61 ✲ 16822
B.S. ✲ 15815 11 / 27 / 76 105th PRECINCT	INJURED LOMINO, JOANE INJURED DE MASI, DONNA 61 # 15288
B.S. ✲ 1422 1 / 30 /77 112th PRECINCT	DECEASED : FREUND, CHRISTINA 61 # 1360
B.S. # 3255 3 / 8 / 77 112th PRECINCT	DECEASED VASKERITCHIN, VIRGINIA 61 # 3705
B.S. # 5285 4 / 17 / 77 45th PRECINCT	DECEASED SURIANI, VALENTINE DECEASED ESAU, ALEX 61 ✲ 2791
B.S. # 8456 6/ 26 / 77 111 th PRECINCT	INJURED PLACIDO, JUDITH INJURED LUPO, SAL 61 # 6773
B.S. ✲ 10020 7 / 31 / 77 62nd PRECINCT	DECEASED MOSKOWITZ , STACY INJURED VIOLANTE,ROBERT 61 ✲ 11129

* CONSISTENT WITH CHARTER ARMS RIFLING